Alexander
Hamilton

AND THE PERSISTENCE OF MYTH

AMERICAN POLITICAL THOUGHT

Edited by

Wilson Carey McWilliams and Lance Banning

Alexander
Hamilton

AND THE PERSISTENCE OF MYTH

Stephen F. Knott

UNIVERSITY PRESS OF KANSAS

Published by the University Press of Kansas (Lawrence, Kansas 66049), which was
organized by the Kansas Board of Regents and is operated and funded by Emporia
State University, Fort Hays State University, Kansas State University, Pittsburg State
University, the University of Kansas, and Wichita State University

Library of Congress Cataloging-in-Publication Data

Knott, Stephen F.
    Alexander Hamilton and the persistence of myth / Stephen F. Knott.
       p. cm. — (American political thought)
    Includes bibliographical references and index.
    ISBN 0-7006-1157-6 (alk. paper)
    1. Hamilton, Alexander, 1757–1804—Influence.   2. Hamilton, Alexander,
1757–1804—Public opinion.   3. Public opinion—United States.   4. United
States—Politics and government—Philosophy.   5. National characteristics,
American.   6. Statesmen—United States—Biography.   I. Title.   II. Series.
E302.6.H2 .K66 2002
973.4'092—dc21   2001004660

British Library Cataloguing in Publication Data is available.

Printed in the United States of America

10 9 8 7 6 5 4 3 2 1

The paper used in this publication meets the minimum requirements of the
American National Standard for Permanence of Paper for Printed Library Materials
z39.48–1984.

Let me not to the marriage of true
   minds
Admit impediments. Love is not love
Which alters when it alteration finds,
Or bends with the remover to remove:
O, no! it is an ever-fixed mark,
That looks on tempests and is never
   shaken . . .
Love's not Time's fool, though rosy lips
   and cheeks
Within his bending sickle's compass
   come;
Love alters not with his brief hours and
   weeks,
But bears it out even to the edge of
   doom.
If this be error, and upon me prov'd,
I never writ, nor no man ever lov'd.
Shakespeare, Sonnet 116

CONTENTS

The personalities, principles, and practices of the American founders continue to fascinate serious Americans well over two hundred years after the birth of the nation. As a young boy I was captivated by the reminders of America's revolutionary past in my native New England, but my interest in the founding era truly blossomed under the inspired teaching of Robert Scigliano of Boston College, to whom this book is dedicated.

While Professor Scigliano emphasized the study of the founders as revealed in their writings, I was also intrigued by the way their progeny invoked their memory in the ongoing debate over the meaning of America. After reading Merrill Peterson's *The Jefferson Image in the American Mind* and *Lincoln in American Memory*, I began to contemplate Alexander Hamilton's fragile standing among his fellow citizens. Although I differ with Peterson's account of Hamilton and his great Virginian rival, and to some extent have chosen a different approach in recounting the vagaries of Hamilton's reputation, I am grateful for the inspiration.

My first step down the path of examining all things Hamilton began with a paper I presented at the annual meeting of the American Political Science Association in August 1997. In it I focused on the interpretation of Hamilton by twentieth-century academics, politicians, and journalists. Convinced that I was onto something interesting, I decided to broaden my scope, beginning with the moment Aaron Burr's fatal bullet found its target. As I waded through the mass of material written about Hamilton since his untimely death in July 1804, it quickly became evident that he ranks as one of the more divisive figures in American history. Even though we have become a Hamiltonian nation, in many ways we remain uncomfortable with him. In this book I seek to explain this quandary.

Like any project of this sort, my book would not have been possible without the generous assistance of so many others. I am grateful for the help of Fred Woodward, Melinda Wirkus, and Susan Schott of the University Press of Kansas, Lance Banning, Wilson

Carey McWilliams, Forrest McDonald, Robert Scigliano, Peter McNamara, Karl Walling, Ken Masugi, Richard K. Matthews, Hal Bidlack, Paul Carrese, Delane Clark, Jeff Morrison, Pamela K. Jensen, John Elliot, and Fred Baumann. The Library and Information Services staff at Kenyon College was especially helpful in tracking down Hamiltonia; I would like to thank Dan Temple, Joan Pomajevich, Joan Nielson, and Cindy Wallace for their labors.

I am particularly indebted to my wife, Lorna, who took time out from her study of Jean-Jacques Rousseau to edit large portions of this book. Her suggestions significantly improved the final product. Though Hamilton probably would have dismissed Rousseau as a theorist of questionable worth, he can rest assured that one of Rousseau's students did him justice.

Alexander
Hamilton
AND THE PERSISTENCE OF MYTH

In an early instance of what would become an American ritual, Alexander Hamilton and Vice President Aaron Burr left New York City on Wednesday morning, 11 July 1804, and crossed into New Jersey for purposes of killing. At the very least, Burr was intent on killing. Hamilton's admirers tend to accept the view first put forward by his second, Nathaniel Pendleton, that Hamilton intentionally fired his shot into the air. Burr, possessed either of little conscience or better aim, fired a bullet through Hamilton's liver that lodged near his spine. He died thirty-six hours later.[1] Actually, dueling was not a test of killing but a test of bravery, as it was not uncommon for duelers to fire past one another to gauge the courage of the other gentleman. Hamilton was no admirer of the practice, having lost his nineteen-year-old son Philip in a duel in 1801. Yet in accepting Burr's challenge and losing his life, Hamilton committed his last patriotic act, for he ensured that Aaron Burr (1756–1836) would never again be a viable player in the politics of the early Republic.

The news of Hamilton's death unnerved his fellow citizens in New York City and Federalists around the nation. The staff of the *New York Evening Post,* which Hamilton helped found in November 1801, was particularly shaken by the news. While Hamilton was still clinging to life on Thursday 12 July, the *Post* wrote that "universal anxiety" was agitating "all classes of people in this city" and noted that there was little hope for the general's recovery. The paper warned that "but a few hours more must close the scene forever." In the midst of a notice of the arrival of a ship carrying mail from England, the paper announced, "We stop the press to announce the melancholy tidings that GENERAL HAMILTON IS DEAD!" On Friday 13 July (the printer, perhaps rattled by the fast-breaking story, dated the masthead 13 June), the paper published a letter by Benjamin Moore, the Episcopal bishop of New York and president of Columbia College, detailing Hamilton's last hours and describing the planning for the funeral that was to take place the next day. It proved to be one of the grandest processions ever witnessed by the city's inhabitants.[2]

On Hamilton's twenty-five dollar mahogany coffin lay his hat and sword.[3] His four young sons, Alexander, James Alexander, John Church, and William Stephen, walked behind the general's gray horse. Two black servants dressed in white with matching turbans attended the horse, the boots and spurs reversed. A death march performed by the Sixth Regiment of militia echoed through the streets as the members of the Society of the Cincinnati, clergy of all denominations, "Mr. Gouverneur Morris in his carriage," the president, professors, and students of Columbia College, and others made the two-hour procession through Beekman, Pearl, and Whitehall Streets, up Broadway and to the church. Bringing up the rear of the procession, in good Federalist fashion, were "the Citizens in general." The streets were so crowded with spectators that many observers climbed trees or stood on the rooftops of houses, and the windows were filled with people. It was an immensely solemn occasion: as one reporter observed, "Not a smile was visible, and hardly a whisper was to be heard, but tears were seen rolling down the cheeks of the affected multitude."

Arriving at the church, Hamilton's casket was placed on a bier directly in front of the portico where a stage had been erected for Gouverneur Morris (1752–1816) to deliver the eulogy.[4] Following the service, Hamilton was buried in the Trinity Church graveyard on Wall Street, of all places. The pageantry of the occasion would no doubt have impressed Hamilton, particularly when French and British warships anchored in the harbor fired a salute. The reporter for the *New York Evening Post* who witnessed the burial observed that the solemnities ended with "three vollies over the grave" and concluded his account of the funeral by remarking, "We have no observations to add. This scene was enough to melt a monument of marble."

The momentous and moving affair celebrated the life and actions of one of the most significant of the American founding fathers; and to those present, at least, there was little doubt that Hamilton's accomplishments would secure his place in history. As Morris observed in his eulogy, Hamilton's orphan sons would inherit little from their father — except fame. The marble monument that eventually adorned his grave read in part, "The Statesman of consummate Wisdom whose Talents and Virtues will be admired . . . long after this Marble shall have mouldered into Dust."[5] Curiously, however, this has not been the case: in the future, both the man and his principles proved to be a suitable foil for generations of prominent Americans intent on validating their devotion to the common man.

Alexander Hamilton was born on the Caribbean island of Nevis, into what today would be described as a dysfunctional family. Little is known of his youth, including the exact date of his birth, with some scholars believing it to be 1755 and others 1757. He appears to have been a precocious, hardworking child, mature beyond his age. Before reaching his teenage years he worked as an "all-purpose flunky," as historian Forrest McDonald put it, at an import-export firm and quickly emerged as the de facto manager of the operation.[6] His earliest surviving letter reveals much about his determination to improve his lot, though not at the expense of his honor. Writing to his friend Edward Stevens in 1769, Hamilton confessed that "my Ambition is [so] prevalent that I contemn the grov'ling and condition of a Clerk or the like, to which my Fortune &c. condemns me and would willingly risk my life tho' not my Character to exalt my Station." He concluded his letter by noting, "I wish there was a War."[7]

Thanks to the generosity of a benefactor, Hamilton arrived in the United States in 1772 and enrolled in Elizabethtown (N.J.) Academy to prepare for Princeton. His request to set his own pace toward graduation from Princeton was rebuffed, and he then enrolled in King's College, now Columbia University. He was quickly caught up in the revolutionary fervor gripping New York City and by 1774 was delivering patriotic speeches to crowds of New Yorkers. That same year he began work on two political pamphlets defending the American cause, *A Full Vindication of the Measures of the Congress* and *The Farmer Refuted*.[8]

The outbreak of the American Revolution saw Hamilton abandon his studies at King's College to become an artillery officer. He joined General Washington's staff in February 1777 and soon found himself at the center of the great events of the war. Eager to distinguish himself in combat, he secured Washington's approval to lead an attack at the Battle of Yorktown in 1781, which spurred British General Cornwallis's surrender. Although often frustrated with the drudgery associated with staff work, Hamilton's firsthand experience witnessing endless congressional delays in providing supplies for the army, along with repeated leaks of secret information, unstable finances, and excessive dependence on the states for men and material, had an indelible impact on his views on government.

Hamilton's postwar experiences only heightened his sense of disillusionment with the American Confederation. He served for a time in the Congress under the Articles of Confederation and tried in vain to strengthen the paltry powers of the central government. He was particularly concerned with the new government's ability to pay its debts and acquire dependable sources of revenue. Devoted to the idea that his countrymen needed to "think continentally," Hamilton was instrumental in the movement to call a convention to revise the Articles of Confederation, and he attended the Annapolis Convention of 1786 that issued the call for the states to send representatives to Philadelphia in May 1787 to address the Confederation's inadequacies. As the lone nationalist delegate from New York to the Constitutional Convention, Hamilton was somewhat ineffectual, in part due to his hard-core nationalism but also because of the opposition he met within his own state delegation. However, he may have assisted the cause of the nationalists by staking out extreme positions that made more moderate centralizing proposals politically palatable.[9] Hamilton's greatest achievement during this critical period was organizing the publication of a series of eighty-five essays that became known as *The Federalist*. He wrote the majority of the essays and enlisted James Madison and John Jay in the endeavor, with Madison's contributions being of particular significance. Hamilton also played a critical role in the ratification of the Constitution in New York, defeating the efforts of some of the most powerful political figures in the state who had rallied to the antifederalist banner.

As the new American government prepared to assemble in New York City in 1789, Hamilton was asked by President George Washington to become the nation's first secretary of the treasury. While serving in this capacity, Hamilton became embroiled in controversies that followed him to his grave. These disputes will be discussed throughout this book, but three of the most significant are worthy of mention here. His proposals for a national bank and his suggestions for eliminating the debt accumulated by the states and the Confederation presented the first major political crisis for the new regime. Much to the distress of President Washington (who generally sided with Hamilton over Jefferson), Hamilton's proposals prompted the formation of two rival political factions, one led by Secretary of State Thomas Jefferson and the other by Hamilton. Jefferson and James Madison viewed Hamilton's economic plans, particularly his desire to see the United States emerge as a manufacturing power, as a threat to Southern agrarian interests, an underhanded attempt to benefit wealthy urban speculators at the expense of rural yeoman farmers. More important, however, they saw Hamilton's proposals as a threat to liberty itself. The two Virginians were concerned about the impact of manufacturing and financial speculation on the character of a republican citizenry and believed that only those individuals capable of economic self-sufficiency could remain truly free. Jefferson and Hamilton also clashed hotly over the appropriate American response to the revolutionary government in France. Hamilton believed the French Revolution exemplified the worst excesses of mob rule, but Jefferson saw it as a continuation of the struggle for liberty and self-government begun by the American people. Finally, the two cabinet officers were deeply divided over the power of the federal judiciary and the extent to which the president possessed implied powers under the Constitution: in general, Hamilton favored a broad interpretation of executive and judicial power in contrast to Jefferson and Madison, who leaned toward a strict interpretation of these powers.

The division between Hamilton and Jefferson caused by these and other issues was no mere fissure. Over time, Jefferson became convinced that Hamilton possessed an undue affection for all things British and wished to establish an American aristocracy, if not a hereditary monarchy. Jefferson, and Madison of course, knew of Hamilton's proposal at the Constitutional Convention that the president and the Senate hold their offices for life (during good behavior), a suggestion that raised concern about Hamilton's commitment to popular government. Jefferson believed that Hamilton admired strong men and cited as evidence a comment he allegedly had made at a dinner party praising Julius Caesar as the greatest man who ever lived. This evidence, coupled with Hamilton's financial proposals and his expansive views of the power of the national government, led Jefferson and his supporters to view him as a budding autocrat who sought to suffocate the infant American regime in its cradle. Jefferson's Hamilton was hungry for power and literally and figuratively wedded to monied interests (Hamilton had married Elizabeth Schuyler, a member of a wealthy New York family, in 1780). Most Jeffersonians sincerely believed that Hamilton lay in wait for the crisis that would pave the way for a betrayal of the principles of 1776. Hamilton's role in suppressing the Whiskey Rebellion in 1794, an agrarian antitax uprising in western Pennsylvania, struck Jefferson and Madison as typical of his disdain for the populace, revealing his preference for relying on the sword to solve problems (and aggrandize himself). And the Federalist party confirmed the worst fears of its Jeffersonian critics when it adopted the Alien and Sedition Acts in 1798, an overreaction to the formation of republican societies in the United States sympathetic to the revolutionary government of France.

But Jefferson's animus, however consistent, was not in itself sufficient to undo Hamilton's prospects; he assisted in his own political destruction in several cases. By the time of Jefferson's election to the presidency in 1800, Hamilton was politically spent, in part due to revelations of an extramarital affair and payments to a cuckolded husband. More important, his party had lost the struggle for the hearts and minds of an increasing democratic franchise: though Jefferson may have overstated the case at times, it is clear that Hamilton's view of what America should be was not shared by most Americans at the time. Hamilton's final political wound, self-inflicted, was the publication of a letter attacking John Adams in the 1800 presidential campaign, which helped ensure the election of Thomas Jefferson.[10] It is interesting to speculate on what thoughts Hamilton may have had as he lingered near death in the aftermath of his encounter with Aaron Burr at Weehawken, New Jersey, not far from the site where his eldest son had been killed in a duel. He may well have wondered if the journey that began in Nevis had been worthwhile, and how, or if, his countrymen would remember him in the ages to come.

The division between Jefferson and Hamilton has permeated the consciousness and self-understanding of Americans in many ways. As recently as 1987, President Ronald Reagan, speaking at a bicentennial celebration, could capture and express perfectly the prevailing national sentiment with the simple affirmation that "we're still Jefferson's children." But Reagan might well have added these comments from his friend George Will: "There is an elegant memorial in Washington to Jefferson, but none to Hamilton. However, if you seek Hamilton's monument, look around. You are living in it. We honor Jefferson, but live in Hamilton's country."[11] Although George Washington, Thomas Jefferson, James Madison, and Abraham Lincoln have eclipsed him in the American mind, it is my belief that Alexander Hamilton made the twentieth century the American century. Clearly, the more immediate sources of American power in that century were traceable to the actions of Lincoln, in preserving the nation, and to the two Roosevelts, Woodrow Wilson, and many of the cold war presidents. But the foundation of America's superpower status was laid in the early days of the Republic when Alexander Hamilton, who had a vision of American greatness, battled with forces fearful of the concentrated political, economic, and military power necessary to achieve that greatness. All his endeavors were directed toward establishing the United States as a formidable nation, efforts that have ultimately come to fruition. The Hamiltonian blueprint for America, which lay in consider-able tension with Jefferson's hopes for the new nation, consisted in the cre-ation of an integrated economy eventually capable of surpassing that of the European powers in manufactures; a federal judiciary with adequate powers to protect property and liberties from democratic excess; the establishment of a professional army and navy; and an energetic chief executive with commander-in-chief powers that would enable him to repel foreign attacks and suppress domestic insurrections.

Though much of Hamilton's vision has come to pass, he has never won the affection of many of his countrymen, in part because of his tendency to insult our democratic sensibilities with alleged impolitic comments about the character of the people. Ironically, despite years of scathing criticism directed against his hated rival, President Jefferson was in many ways a distinctly Hamiltonian executive — but his charge that Hamilton was un-American echoes to this day.[12] Hamilton's reputation has no doubt also been hurt in that he was less of a Renaissance man than Jefferson. To borrow from the latter's biographer Gilbert Chinard, Hamilton had no interest in playing the violin, dancing the minuet, or designing farm implements. Our neglect of Hamilton can also be attributed to the fact that he made us what we are; Jefferson's malleable legacy appeals to visionaries seeking a new and better world. Jefferson's dream of an America constantly remaking itself and shed-ding the shackles of the past captures the American imagination, for dreams are frequently more appealing than reality, and it is often easier to celebrate what might be than to defend what is. Jefferson was the poet of the Ameri-can founding; Hamilton was the nation builder who infused the essential elements of permanence and stability into the American system. It is not unusual for poets to portray themselves as somehow above the fray, disdain-ing or at best taking for granted the petty practical matters that make civil society possible, such as a sturdy framework of laws backed by viable govern-ment institutions. But Hamilton's public life was dedicated to erecting such a structure, and the question remains whether the credit given the poet should exceed that given the practitioner. In this book I seek to explain the evolu-tion of Hamilton's controversial image in the American mind.

1

"And Night Returning Brings Me No Relief"
Hamilton and the Founding Generation

The battle over interpreting Hamilton's role in the founding of the nation began within days after he was buried. President Thomas Jefferson and his supporters reacted with silence in public and, in some cases, in private concern that the emotional reaction to Hamilton's death might impair their party's political prospects in the 1804 elections. Hearing the news of the duel, the Sage of Monticello was his usual sphinxlike self, offering little comment other than noting in a letter to his daughter, "I presume Mr. Randolph's newspapers will inform him of the death of Colo. Hamilton, which took place on the 12th." The next day he sent his friend Philip Mazzei a letter mentioning various "remarkable deaths lately," including Samuel Adams, who had died months earlier, Jefferson's own daughter, Maria, and Alexander Hamilton. There may have been some repressed feelings of relief that this colossus had finally been done in, and, of all things, by the vice president of the United States.[1] A nineteenth-century Oliver Stone would have reveled in this scenario, vulnerable as it was to a conspiratorial interpretation, for in one act, two of Jefferson's political rivals were no longer threats to his power.

At the time of Hamilton's death the conflict between the two men had receded, as Hamilton and his party were overwhelmed by a popular and successful Jefferson presidency. Hamilton's premature demise and Jefferson's longevity (1743–1826) provided the latter with twenty-two years in which to portray their differences in a most favorable light without fear of rebuttal. Jefferson attributed to Hamilton an affinity for Caesar that was probably untrue and sought to undermine his Americanism by labeling him as something akin to a British agent. Their confrontation began during the period when Jefferson was secretary of state (March 1790–December 1793) and Hamilton was secretary of the treasury. Questions over commerce and banking, constitutional interpretation, federalism, and American policy toward Great Britain and France drove the two men apart.

Jefferson often dealt with unpleasant situations like his relationship with Hamilton in an indirect manner, usually through the use of surrogates. He shied from direct confrontation, unlike Hamilton, who often clumsily chose a frontal assault when a flanking maneuver would have sufficed. Hamilton's sense of honor inclined him toward open encounters; Jefferson's aversion to coercion, as well as his shyness, led him to seek circuitous routes to achieve his ends. James Madison and James Monroe were Jefferson's point men in his struggles with Hamilton, and anonymous leaks to journalists or to congressional allies often served as their preferred method of attack. Though Hamilton also engaged in such tactics, Jefferson habitually resorted to these devices both out of character and necessity, given his covert role as the opposition leader of the administration to which he belonged.

Only in private letters or in later works such as the *Anas* did Jefferson candidly reveal his thoughts on Hamilton. The *Anas* was a loose collection of anecdotes based on notes jotted down during his years in power and was designed to counter John Marshall's *Life of Washington,* that "five volume libel" that portrayed Jefferson and his adherents in a less than flattering light. Jefferson wrote a preface to the *Anas* on 4 February 1818 and withheld publication of the collection until after his death.[2] Though he cleansed the record to remove the more embarrassing entries, expressions of contempt for Hamilton and his policies remained intact. His financial system was a "machine for the corruption of the legislature," for he "was not only a monarchist, but for a monarchy bottomed on corruption." This "singular character" possessed some virtues, among which was his acute understanding and his "disinterested, honest, and honorable [conduct] in all private transactions." However, Hamilton's corrupt machinations were the result of his being "bewitched and perverted by the British example." Jefferson cited a report in the *Anas* describing a toast to King George III at a New York City dinner party in which "Hamilton started up on his feet, and insisted on a bumper and three cheers." Much of the *Anas* contains unsubstantiated gossip from sources such as John

Beckley's passing on reports of Hamilton's efforts on behalf of "the paper and stock-jobbing interest." (Beckley played a key role in the effort to destroy Hamilton in 1797 by leaking information to the press on the Reynolds affair.) Convinced that Hamilton had aided and abetted corruption as treasury secretary, Jefferson, in one of his first acts as president, ordered his secretary of the treasury, Albert Gallatin (1761–1849), to search the department's files for incriminating evidence. When none was found, Jefferson saw this not as an exoneration of Hamilton but as further evidence of his skill at deceit.[3]

Jefferson's attitude toward Hamilton was partly the result of his preference for men who would defer to him. He preferred associates who saw themselves as part of his extended family, a family that did not quarrel but that reached consensus through the benign, oblique guidance of the Sage himself. (He regarded his slaves, for instance, as part of his family at Monticello.) The younger Hamilton (by fourteen years) did not defer; moreover, his exemplary military record was a constant reminder to the revolutionary Virginian that only one of them had ever directly faced hostile fire from British soldiers. When the yellow fever epidemic ravaged Philadelphia in 1793, Jefferson mocked Hamilton's fear of the disease and questioned his bravery. He wrote Madison, "A man as timid as he is on the water, as timid on horseback, as timid in sickness, would be a phaenomenon if the courage of which he has the reputation in military occasions were genuine."[4]

At bottom, Jefferson could not countenance the fact that an immigrant upstart without the appropriate pedigree had dared challenge him. In a letter to President Washington, Jefferson stated that he would not let his reputation be "clouded by the slanders of a man whose history, from the moment at which history can stoop to notice him, is a tissue of machinations against the liberty of the country which has not only recieved [sic] and given him bread, but heaped it's [sic] honors on his head." Gilbert Chinard (1881–1972), a sympathetic biographer of Jefferson, said of this letter to Washington, "In one sentence [Jefferson] had expressed not only condemnation of Hamilton's policies but all the scorn of a Virginian, of the old stock, for the immigrant of doubtful birth, who was almost an alien. He knew full well the weight such a consideration might have on the mind of Washington; it was a subtle but potent appeal to the solidarity of the old Americans against the newcomer."[5] It was the first of many attacks questioning Hamilton's Americanism.

Jefferson's animus toward Hamilton persisted until his death in 1826. The future president Martin Van Buren related an account of a visit he made to Monticello twenty years after Hamilton's death: "In all my conversations with [Jefferson] in 1824, when he spoke of the course pursued by the Federal party, [he] invariably personified it by saying 'Hamilton' did or insisted thus; and, on the other hand, 'the Republicans' held or claimed so and so; and that upon my calling his attention to the peculiarity of his expression, he smiled and attributed his habit to the universal conviction of the Republicans that Hamilton directed every thing."[6] This is classic Jefferson, reluctant to portray himself wielding power. The Republican family worked as a collegial body, but the more hierarchical Federalists had their strong man issuing directives from above.

Although Hamilton had collaborated with James Madison (1751–1836) in writing *The Federalist,* the two men had drifted apart during the Washington administration over the same issues that divided Hamilton from Jefferson. This break must have been far more painful to Hamilton than his rift with Jefferson, to whom he was never particularly close. Allied with Jefferson, Madison became the de facto leader of the opposition to Hamilton's initiatives in the House of Representatives. Later in his life Madison was quoted as saying, "I deserted Colonel Hamilton, or rather Colonel H. deserted me; in a word, the divergence between us took place — from his wishing to *adminis-tration,* or rather to administer the government . . . into what he thought it ought to be; while, on my part, I endeavored to make it conform to the Constitution as understood by the Convention that produced and recommended it, and particularly by the State conventions that *adopted* it." Jefferson and Madison were convinced that through administrative sleight of hand Hamilton was "monarchising" the Constitution with the ultimate goal, as Jefferson wrote, of "worm[ing] out the elective principle."[7]

Madison and Jefferson were joined in their suspicion of Hamilton by James Monroe (1758–1831), who believed that the "enterprizes" advocated by Hamilton while he was treasury secretary were "calculated to elevate the government above the people." Monroe was a key figure in Jefferson and Madison's effort to curb Hamilton's power in the 1790s. That effort almost succeeded in 1792, when Monroe thought he had evidence that Hamilton had engaged in improprieties related to his public duties as treasury secretary. Monroe had instead stumbled upon the so-called Reynolds affair, Hamilton's extramarital affair with Maria Reynolds. In 1797 the Reynolds affair became a public matter when James Callender published *The History of the United States for 1796*, accusing Hamilton of financial improprieties with Maria Reynolds's husband James. Hamilton publicly admitted the affair with James's wife but denied any official misconduct, explaining in his defense that "my real crime is an amorous connection with his wife." Callender charged that Hamilton confessed to an affair with Maria Reynolds in order to conceal more serious accusations, as Hamilton put it, of "improper pecuniary speculation." Hamilton believed that Monroe had prompted Callender to publish the Reynolds allegations, and the animosity between the two men had been so great that it almost led to a duel.[8]

Concern that Hamilton's reputation may have been unduly inflated by his untimely death was widespread among his opponents. When Madison heard of the Burr-Hamilton adventure, as he put it, he wrote Monroe, observing that "the newspapers which you receive will give you the adventure between Burr and Hamilton. You will easily understand the different uses to which the event is turned." Madison's letter echoed the concerns expressed by Hamilton's successor at the Treasury Department, Albert Gallatin, that "much real sympathy and sincere regret have naturally been excited by that catastrophe. But unquenchable hatred of Burr and federal policy have combined in producing an artificial sensation much beyond what might have been expected; and a majority of both parties seem disposed at this moment to deify Hamilton."[9] This assessment was shared by Senator John Armstrong Jr. (1758–1843), who later witnessed the burning of Washington as Madison's secretary of war. He wrote Madison that "the public sympathy is a good deal excited for Hamilton and his family, whether this is spontaneous or artificial I do not know, but it probably partakes of both characters." Armstrong noted with disdain that "the English interest" hoped to build a statue to Hamilton.[10] Noah Webster (1758–1843), who had once referred to Hamilton as an evil genius, wrote to Madison on 20 August complaining that Hamilton's eulogists were praising him for achievements that Webster believed belonged to Madison, for instance, credit for the calling of the Constitutional Convention of 1787. Madison told Webster that "I had observed, as you have done, that a great number of loose assertions have at different times been made with respect to the origin of the reform in our system of federal government, and that this has particularly happened on the late occasion which so strongly excited the effusions of party and personal zeal for the fame of Gen. Hamilton." Although Madison conceded that "the discernment of Gen. Hamilton must have rendered him an early patron of the idea," he contended that the push for constitutional change was the result not of "a single agent" but of many forces and individuals.[11]

Beyond the inner circle of Jeffersonians, the reaction to Hamilton's death varied by region. In the South, the response was often favorable to Aaron Burr. John Randolph of Roanoke (1773–1833), a relative of Jefferson's and at one time something of a de facto Republican majority leader in the House, declared after reading the preduel correspondence between Burr and Hamilton that the former had demonstrated "an unshaken adherence to his object and an undeviating pursuit of it, not to be eluded or baffled. It reminded me of a sinking fox pressed by a vigorous old hound, where no shift is permitted to avail him." He added, "I feel for Hamilton's immediate connections real concern; for himself, nothing."[12] Andrew Jackson (1767–1845) was informed of Hamilton's death in a letter mailed from Philadelphia on 15 July 1804 from a linguistically challenged acquaintance: "You will have heard of the dueal between Burr & Hamilton at N. York Genl. H. died on Friday & was Burred Yesterday. This unfortunate affair has created much anxiety even in this place, & in New York much more." A year and a half later, another acquaintance attempted to persuade Jackson against a duel, noting that in the case of "Colo Burr . . . I sepose if dueling could be justifiable, it must have bin in his case, and it is beleaved he has not had ease in mind sinc the fatal hour he killed Hambleton."[13] Jackson eventually provided refuge for Aaron Burr in Nashville as he meandered west in search of an empire. Whether their mutual interest in dueling was discussed at the dinner table is uncertain.[14] While the duel shocked most of the nation and led to the usual expressions of outrage over this barbaric tradition, the practice remained firmly entrenched, particularly in the South. Although Jefferson decried dueling as "the most barbarous of appeals," Andrew Jackson, along with Thomas Hart Benton, Henry Clay, John Randolph, Jefferson Davis, Alexander Stephens, Judah Benjamin, and Sam Houston, engaged in duels and often on more than one occasion. Governor James Hamilton of South Carolina reportedly fought in fourteen duels and was standing at the end of each, although the same could not be said for his opponents.[15]

An exception to the general Southern indifference toward Hamilton's death could be found in Charleston, South Carolina. The Federalist newspaper, the *Charleston Courier*, editorialized emphatically that "perhaps no illustrious personage, ancient or modern, has ever had a more glorious monument heaped upon his ashes, than General Hamilton. . . . His friends and fellow citizens are inconsolable. . . . What did Hamilton want of the essential constituents of a great man? Who is there in the ancient or modern world that . . . has surpassed him? . . . We believe none. . . . Yes, Hamilton is gone, for ever gone!" The most prominent Southern Federalist, Charles Cotesworth Pinckney (1746–1825) of South Carolina, a signer of the Constitution and a political ally of Hamilton, urged the members of the Society of the Cincinnati, a fraternal organization of Revolutionary War officers, to condemn dueling. Pinckney observed that Hamilton's death "has been sensibly felt and lamented in this part of the union, even by those who . . . did not coincide with him in politics." He urged that an appropriate "tribute of respect to the sentiments and memory of our late illustrious chief" would be "to declare their abhorrence of this practice. . . . Dueling is no criterion of bravery." Pinckney's friend, the minister Richard Furman, held a public memorial for Hamilton in the Baptist Church in Charleston on 15 August 1804 entitled "Death's Dominion Over Man Considered: A Sermon Occasioned by the Death of the Honorable Major General Alexander Hamilton." In general, Hamilton and Hamiltonianism remained unpopular in the South, but among the small cadre of Southern Federalists, mostly South Carolinians, Burr was considered a murderer, and hatred of him persisted for years. As the *Charleston Courier* put it, Burr might say, "'Why now my golden dream is out.' . . . But, so far unlike Richard, he has lost the bright reward of daring minds . . . FOR EVER."[16]

Mourning for Hamilton was at its strongest in New England and in the Middle Atlantic states. Perhaps the most notable orations delivered in the wake of his death came from two New England Federalists, Harrison Gray Otis (1765–1848) and Fisher Ames (1758–1808). Otis delivered his eulogy at King's Chapel in Boston on 26 July 1804 and used the occasion to praise Hamilton for his opposition to the French Revolution: "At this dangerous and dazzling crisis, there were but few men entirely exempt from the general delirium. Among that few was Hamilton. . . . He was assured that every people which should espouse the cause of France would pass under her yoke, and that the people of France, like every nation which surrenders its reason to the mercy of demagogues, would be driven by the storms of anarchy upon the shores of despotism." Perhaps not surprisingly, estimations of the oration differed widely according to political party. It was a disappointment to Federalists, who found it to be an incomplete picture of Hamilton, but at least one Republican praised Otis as "the least objectionable of these eulogists, because the least false and fulsome."[17]

Ames, perhaps after Hamilton the most brilliant of the Federalists, was no lover of democracy and what he viewed as Jeffersonian Jacobinism. He once referred to revolutionary France as "that open Hell" and was concerned that the United States might suffer the same fate. Hamilton's death had "sorely wounded" Ames; in response he delivered an address that was read to a small group of friends and then published in the *Boston Repertory* in July 1804. It is the most powerful of the testimonials to Hamilton, for Ames was convinced that Hamilton was a great statesman and observed that "with really great men as with great literary works, the excellence of both is best tested by the extent and durableness of their impression. . . . In this case, it is safe and correct to judge by effects; we sometimes calculate the height of a mountain, by measuring the length of its shadow." The public, Ames held, would render a verdict more just to Hamilton than the verdict from "persons of conspicuous merit," for "the body of the people . . . cannot feel a spirit of rivalship towards those whom they see elevated by nature and education so far above their heads." Ames believed that "party rancor, eager to maim the living, scorns to strip the slain," and with the passage of time and the dispersion of information, an "equitable" public would prove to be intelligent judges of Hamilton's greatness. The "uncommonly profound public sorrow" occasioned by Hamilton's death was an indication that his reputation would be secure, for the American people were weeping "as the Romans did over the ashes of Germanicus." Hamilton's high standing was even more impressive, Ames argued, because he attained this reputation without flattering the people, and "he had not made himself dear to the passions of the multitude by condescending, in defiance of his honor and conscience, to become their instrument." It was by his "bold and inflexible adherence to the truth" that he rose to prominence, and "the true popularity, the homage that is paid to virtue, followed him."[18] Unfortunately, if this ever were the case, it has not endured. Generations of American leaders have concluded that flattering the people is a necessary component of statesmanship, and the American public has demonstrated a certain tentativeness, at best, in acknowledging, never mind celebrating, those "elevated . . . above their heads."

Other Federalist contemporaries of Hamilton were deeply distressed by his death. One of his closest friends, Rufus King (1755–1827), had tried to talk Hamilton out of the duel and was appalled when he confided to him that he was not going to fire at Burr. King argued that Hamilton "owed it to his family and the rights of self-defence" to shoot his opponent but realizing that his friend would not listen, resigned himself to the inevitable. "With a mind most capacious and discriminating that I ever knew," Hamilton followed "certain rules upon the subject of Duels. . . . With these guides . . . he could not have avoided a meeting with Col. Burr, had he even declined the first challenge." King was devastated by his friend's death, inscribing in a notebook under the name Hamilton:

> In every virtuous act, and glorious strife,
> He shone the first and best —
> Homer — il.2 208
>
> Each rising sun beholds my ceaseless grief
> And night returning brings me no relief.[19]

Chief Justice John Marshall (1755–1835) was also distraught when he heard of Hamilton's death. Just weeks after the duel, on 6 August 1804, Marshall received a poignant letter from Philip Schuyler, Hamilton's father-in-law, describing the emotional reaction of his daughter to seeing friends whom "her Hamilton loved" and then eulogizing "my Hamilton." Marshall lamented "the loss of the great man" but hoped that the result of the duel "may have some tendency to cast odium on a practice which deserves every censure." After Hamilton's death, Marshall was surprised to learn that (Webster's lament notwithstanding) Hamilton had been primarily responsible for the calling of the Constitutional Convention. Marshall was also impressed to discover that Hamilton had refused "the emoluments his military service gave him a right to claim." According to Timothy Pickering, Marshall told him in February 1811 that "his reading of all the papers of Genl. Washington, had enabled him to form an opinion of General Hamilton and he then pronounced him the greatest man (or one of the greatest men) that had ever appeared in the United States."[20] Writing to the eminent jurist Joseph Story (1779–1845) in the 1820s, Marshall recalled the bitter controversy surrounding the visit from Citizen Genet and Washington's issuance of the Neutrality Proclamation. Marshall was the target of the "resentments of the great political party which led Vir-

ginia," and had been for some time, but the issuance of the Neutrality Proclamation and Marshall's active support for it subjected him to attacks of "great
virulence in the papers." He was, however, notwithstanding these attacks, "so
far honoured in Virginia as to be associated with Alexander Hamilton, as least
so far as to be termed his instrument."[21] Marshall deeply admired Hamilton's
mastery of jurisprudence, and years later, Justice Story remembered, "I have
heard . . . John Marshall, and Chancellor Livingston say that Hamilton's reach
of thought was so far beyond theirs that by his side they were schoolboys."
Story himself observed of Hamilton in 1835 that he was "the greatest and wisest man of this country. He saw fifty years ahead, and what he saw then, is
fact now."[22]

Though the reaction among Federalists or former Federalists to Hamilton's
death was often quite emotional, the news from Weehawken did not particularly disturb the family of former president John Adams (1735–1826). Hamilton
had helped derail Adams's campaign for reelection in 1800 when he wrote a
derogatory account of the latter's presidency, which was sent to key Federalists and ultimately became public.[23] Abigail Adams (1744–1818) confided to a
friend that "altho I do not wear crape I rejoice not in the face [fate] of a man
who possest talents and was capable of rendering himself highly serviceable
to the country — he had merited their praise and their gratitude. . . . If there
was much to praise — there was much to pardon and forgive. Why then idolize a man, who showd on many occasions that he was a frail, weak man subdued by his passions. . . . He was a vain ambitious man aspiring to govern
when it was his duty to submit."[24]

Senator John Quincy Adams (1767–1848) shared his mother's belief that
Hamilton lacked "sufficient control over his own passions" as well as a "sufficient elevation over the prejudices of the world." Yet Adams was surprisingly
shaken by the news of Hamilton's death, writing his wife that "conversation
now can scarcely turn upon any other subject than the late horrible duel at
New York. . . . I cannot conceive any possible circumstances which can justify the conduct of Mr. Burr." John Quincy's wife, Louisa, urged him to attend a memorial service for Hamilton in Boston, but he rejected her advice:
"Neither the manner of his death nor his base treatment of more than one
of my connections, would permit me to join in any outward demonstra-
tion of regret which I could not feel at heart. . . . I had no respect for the
man."[25]

The senior Adams, retired in Quincy, despised Hamilton. In October 1802, Adams had begun writing his autobiography in an attempt to vindicate his public career. While he abandoned the project in midsentence in 1807, in the interim he managed to record some particularly venomous comments about Hamilton. Early in their relationship there appeared to be some cordiality between them, as when Adams's son Charles was placed in Hamilton's law office in 1789. Yet Adams wrote in his autobiography that he believed Hamilton had resented him since 1776, when Adams had spoken in favor of General Horatio Gates over Hamilton's father-in-law Philip Schuyler for promotion to major general in the Continental army. This opposition to Schuyler, he judged, "had been rankling in Hamilton's heart from 1776 till he wrote his Libel against me in 1799." Adams apparently firmly believed this — even though Hamilton did not marry Elizabeth Schuyler until 1780. In 1796, when told that Rhode Island wanted Alexander Hamilton for vice president, Adams drolly noted, "I was wholly silent." Writing in his autobiography, Adams ingenuously stated that he had "forgiven this Arch Ennemy"; however, "Vice, Folly, and Villany are not to be forgotten, because the guilty Wretch repented, in his dying Moments." Adams could not be stopped: "Nor am I obliged by any Principles of Morality or Religion to suffer my Character to lie under infamous Calumnies, because the Author of them, with a Pistol Bullet through his Spinal Marrow, died a Penitent." Commenting on Hamilton's immigrant status, he concluded, "Born on a Speck more obscure than Corsica, from an Original not only contemptible but infamous, with infinitely less courage and Capacity than Bonaparte ... he would have involved [the United States] in all the bloodshed and distractions of foreign and civil War at once." At one point Adams recalled when Hamilton first came to his attention and observed, "The World has heard enough of him since." His most famous comment revealed again his contempt for the self-made upstart immigrant, whom he described as this "bastard brat of a Scotch pedlar" who had lived his life in a "delirium of Ambition." Like Jefferson and his Republican allies, Adams was disturbed at what he viewed as an attempt by Hamilton's followers to capitalize on his death. As he noted bitterly in a letter to Jefferson in 1816, Hamilton's most determined enemies did not "like to get rid of him, in that Way," and yet "His Party seized the moment ... and Why? Merely to disgrace the old Whiggs, and keep the Funds and Banks in Countenance."[26]

The reaction to Hamilton's demise from the founding generation occasionally defied predictability. Benjamin Rush (1746–1813), a signer of the Declaration of Independence and the man later responsible for the rapprochement between Jefferson and John Adams, noted the widespread mourning for Hamilton in his Commonplace Book. Although Rush had reason to dislike Hamilton for blocking his selection as a professor at Columbia College Medical School, he nonetheless found him to be "learned, ingenious, and eloquent" but also "the object of universal admiration and attachment of one party, and of hatred of the other party which then constituted the American people. He was greatly and universally lamented." Even Noah Webster, whose initial reaction to Hamilton's death was to complain about excessive eulogizing, later paid some grudging respect to his adherence to principle. He wrote Rufus King three years after the duel that "between the unbending firmness of an H[amilton]n, the obsequiousness of a J[efferso]n, there is a way to preserve the confidence of the populace, without a sacrifice of integrity."[27]

One utterly predictable response to the tragedy of Hamilton's death came from the author of *Common Sense*, Thomas Paine (1737–1809). No one held Hamilton in more contempt than Paine, with the possible exception of John Adams. Paine was disgusted with Gouverneur Morris's funeral oration, viewing it as grammatically and historically incorrect. Paine attacked both Hamilton and Morris for their support of an energetic government but took solace in the fact that their day had passed: with the election of Jefferson as president, "the representative system" corrected this wrong and "preserve[d] rights." Paine was satisfied with what he viewed as the appropriately modest number of newspaper accounts regarding Hamilton's death, although one editorial in the *New York Gazette* prompted from him a particularly dismissive response: this "nonsense from New York" about "his extraordinary worth . . . happens not to be the case." Paine dismissed the eulogy written by the Reverend John M. Mason as authored by someone of comparable madness to George III, suggesting that Mason had a "crack in the brain . . . a touch of what they now call in England the 'King's Evil.'" Paine accused Mason and Bishop Benjamin Moore, who had administered last rites to him, of reducing "General Hamilton's character to that of a feeble-minded man, who in going out of the world wanted a passport from a priest." Shortly after the duel, while traveling on a stagecoach from New Rochelle, New York, to New York City, a passenger goaded Paine by loudly boasting of Hamilton's attributes.

"Rank nonsense," replied Paine, who had to endure the taunts of a coach full of Federalists. The assault probably came as no surprise to a man whose reputation among Federalists had been damaged long ago by his denunciation of George Washington, a denunciation occasioned in part by Paine's belief that Alexander Hamilton was "President over him."[28]

Hamilton's death was particularly painful to a Federalist newspaper editor, Harry Croswell (1778–1858), who was charged and eventually convicted of seditiously libeling President Jefferson by New York's Jeffersonian attorney general, Ambrose Spencer. Spencer shared his party leader's belief that regulation of the press was an appropriate action for state governments. In a letter to the governor of Pennsylvania, President Jefferson had encouraged "a few prosecutions" that "would have a wholesome effect in restoring the integrity of the presses."[29] In one of his last legal cases before his death, Hamilton handled Croswell's appeal of his conviction before the New York Supreme Court in 1804. Hamilton's argument failed to overturn Croswell's conviction, but it was instrumental in convincing the New York state legislature, and many others, to allow for the truthfulness of an allegation to be admitted in evidence in a criminal libel suit. While frequently portrayed in our time and in the early years of the Republic as an enemy of a free press, Hamilton's role in the Croswell case belied his critics' stereotype. Hearing of Hamilton's death, Croswell wrote, "To me he once rendered unequalled service . . . in my defence, and in defence of the American press. . . . For this service, voluntarily rendered, I owed him a debt of gratitude which never could be cancelled."[30]

The first book to appear in the aftermath of Hamilton's death was published on 20 August 1804, at the request of Hamilton's widow, Elizabeth (Betsey) Hamilton (1757–1854). William Coleman (1766–1829), the editor of the *New York Evening Post,* assembled the collection of editorials, sermons, poems, and resolutions from various civic groups. Coleman had been selected by Hamilton to edit the *Evening Post* in 1801, and Hamilton often dictated editorials to him, as well as occasionally contributing anonymous articles. Coleman's tribute to Hamilton was entitled *A Collection of the Facts and Documents Relative to the Death of Major General Alexander Hamilton; With Comments: Together with the various Orations, Sermons, and Eulogies, that Have Been Published or Written on His Life and Character.* The quality of the entries ranged from the maudlin to the moving and included the tributes from Charles Pinckney and Fisher Ames. Though it is not certain how many copies of the book were printed, Coleman hoped *A Collection of the Facts* would provide "a satisfactory account of the shocking catastrophe which has deprived America of her most valuable citizen, and our age of the greatest man." Coleman remained as the editor of the *Evening Post* long after Hamilton's death, defending Federalist principles to the end of his life in 1829, when the party and all that it stood for had been overwhelmed by Jeffersonian and Jacksonian Democracy.[31]

Betsey Hamilton, who survived her husband by fifty years, was determined that his memory not be lost to history, enlisting the aid of her sons in gathering her husband's papers and seeking comments from his friends and associates. However, her efforts to commission something of an authorized biography were frustrated by her inability to find someone with the youth and perseverance necessary to complete the task. A succession of candidates were queried for the job: the Reverend John M. Mason, Joseph Hopkinson, and William Coleman were either considered or commissioned, but none finished the work. Finally, in 1829, it appeared that the aging Federalist Timothy Pickering would write the biography. The Hamilton family gave him all the papers in their possession and paid him a five hundred dollar advance for the project. Pickering saw the biography as an opportunity to refute the many myths that had tarnished Hamilton's reputation, but at eighty-two his health soon failed and the work was never completed. Betsey Hamilton then requested that her minister, Francis Bayles, write Hamilton's life history, but this too failed. Eventually her son John Church Hamilton published in 1834 one of the first biographies of his father, covering his life until 1788.[32]

Hamilton's children doggedly sought to preserve his memory, with John Church (1792–1882) in particular becoming the chief defender of his father's reputation. Though none of Alexander Hamilton's children matched his accomplishments, some of his sons went on to distinguished careers in public service. James Alexander (1788–1878) was appointed acting secretary of state by President Andrew Jackson, an alliance that most likely would have distressed the elder Hamilton. Another son, Alexander (1786–1875), revealed a streak akin to his father's love of military adventure when in 1811 he fought under the Duke of Wellington in Portugal. William Stephen (1797–1850) attended the U.S. Military Academy but left before graduating and served as U.S. surveyor of public lands in Illinois and as a scout during the Black Hawk War.[33] Some biographers believe that Hamilton's eldest son Philip (1782–1801) inherited his father's talents, but he was killed in a duel a few months shy of his twentieth birthday. A second son, also named Philip (1802–1884), married the daughter of Andrew Jackson's secretary of state and secretary of the treasury, Louis McLane, and served as an assistant district attorney in New York City. Hamilton had two daughters, Angelica and Eliza. Angelica appeared to have responded to Philip's death with an emotional breakdown, and Eliza took care of her mother until the latter's death in November 1854 at the age of ninety-seven. Hamilton's widow had lived most of her last years in Washington, D.C., where she befriended Dolley Madison and with whom she helped raise money to build the Washington Monument. She was buried next to her husband in the Trinity churchyard in New York City.[34]

The contest between Hamilton and Jefferson for the soul of the nation was one of the most divisive in the country's history, and for over two hundred years Americans have revisited this dispute, hoping to clarify their understanding of both the past and the present. Each man appreciated fully the impact of his actions on the future course of the nation; and with so much at stake, it was perhaps inevitable that the record would be subject to partisan distortion. Moderation and reason have not always prevailed when Americans describe those events, either then or now.

Fortunately, followers of both camps no longer resort to violence as they did in the 1790s and early 1800s. William Coleman engaged in a duel with the Jeffersonian harbormaster of New York City and killed him; at another time Coleman was walking in the city and was seriously wounded by a Jeffersonian physician who used a stiletto to perform a surgical operation on the unsuspecting Coleman. In Salem, Massachusetts, the future Supreme Court justice Joseph Story engaged in "fisty cuffs" with a Federalist who differed with him over politics. In Albany two men in their seventies pummeled one another with their canes while arguing over politics and were seriously injured. Several New England town meetings erupted when Federalists and Jeffersonians crossed the aisle from their respective camps and attempted to beat the opposition. A Boston Federalist, Thomas Selfridge, killed a Republican newspaper editor; the editor's son later attempted to kill Selfridge but was shot down by him. A person entering a tavern dominated by the opposing party's clientele was often subject to a verbal beating — or worse. This violence occasionally reached the floor of Congress and polarized America to a point seldom equaled in the nation's history.[35]

In his exhaustive treatment of press coverage during the Federalist period, Donald H. Stewart has observed that both parties appealed to "fear or hate rather than reason. If the labels newspapers applied to opponents and their policies gained currency, the labels would produce, without supporting evidence, unthinking popular rejection of the groups and ideas under attack." Nowhere was this technique more successful than in the Republican tactic of accusing the Federalists of plotting to establish a monarchy. As Stewart noted, during the twelve years of Federalist governance, "aristocrat" or "monarchist" was the epithet of choice hurled by the Republican opposition, despite any evidence of a Federalist scheme to establish a monarchy. Jeffersonians were reluctant publicly to accuse George Washington of seeking such a result but did not hesitate to accuse Hamilton of being a closet Caesar. Although Federalist newspapers were often as vicious in their attacks on Jefferson and Madison, the Federalists lost the propaganda war, in part because Hamilton and his supporters were not as deft at polemics as the Jeffersonians.

One of the more successful purveyors of misinformation regarding Hamilton was Philip Freneau. Handpicked by Jefferson and Madison to edit the *National Gazette* in 1791, Freneau initially praised Hamilton's financial measures but quickly shifted his position on cue from the Virginians. The shift occurred in the wake of three essays written by Madison warning of the evils of the British system. From that point, Freneau was unrelenting in describing every proposal of Hamilton's as a covert attempt, as Stewart put it, to "fasten a crown upon America." It was class politics at its worst, for Hamilton was accused of selling the Union to foreign and domestic speculators at the expense of "the industrious mechanic, the laborious farmer, and generally the poorer class of people." Jefferson was satisfied with Freneau for having "saved our Constitution which was galloping fast into monarchy";[36] and the image of Hamilton as monocrat, Anglophile, and enemy of liberty, first promulgated by Freneau at Jefferson's behest, remains the predominant impression of Hamilton in the American mind.

Hamilton's adversaries often referred to his 18 June 1787 speech at the Constitutional Convention to bolster their case that he was un-American. The notion that he was an Englishman at heart was a caricature derived from Hamilton's statement that British government was "the best in the world," and, despite its defects, provided a suitable model in some respects for the new American Constitution. Critics also seized upon his advocacy of the election of a president for life (assuming good behavior) and his preference for an elected Senate with lifetime tenure. What is often ignored in accounts portraying Hamilton as hostile to popular rule was his proposal for a House of Representatives elected by universal male suffrage, a proposal more democratic than that which ultimately emerged under the new government. It is true that Hamilton sought a stable national government capable of "vigorous execution" and "good administration," and while he believed that the institutions of government should be rooted in popular consent, he also thought they must be able to resist popular whims.[37] It requires a leap of the imagination to find monarchical inclinations in his comments or actions, but curiously, it is a leap that many Americans are still inclined to take.

Thomas Jefferson's campaign against Alexander Hamilton persisted long after Hamilton's death. The memory of a dead Hamilton was seen as a threat to Jeffersonianism, perhaps even more of a threat than a living Hamilton, whose tactical political skills were somewhat wanting. Jefferson and his lieutenants succeeded in burying Hamilton and Federalism in what has to be considered one of the most effective and resilient campaigns in the history of American politics. Jefferson succeeded partly because both he and Madison outlived Hamilton by decades and were better able to influence the historical record. Jefferson attempted to gloss over and explain some of his more outlandish statements regarding the French Revolution, for instance, but Hamilton's record was presented to the world without the influence of any sober second thoughts. His alleged comment, reported by Jefferson twenty years after the fact, that the greatest man in the history of the world was Julius Caesar is but one instance of Jefferson's effort to spin history. Hamilton, of course, was long dead when Jefferson reported this tale. Even Jefferson's and Madison's deaths brought no respite to Hamilton. As the American constitutional Republic began to segue into a democracy, Jefferson's ideological heirs, Andrew Jackson, Martin Van Buren, and James K. Polk, continued to question Hamilton's Americanism. Although surely motivated partly by differences of principle, these men also understood well that Hamilton-bashing reaped handsome political rewards for the Democratic party.

Jefferson won the battle for the hearts and minds of most Americans, although he briefly lost the struggle within the scholarly community during the latter half of the nineteenth century. In the twentieth century, Jeffersonians wrote the histories, and outside of a small cadre of Republican politicians and conservative academics and a few American businessmen, Hamiltonianism was commonly perceived as not quite American. The image of Hamilton fashioned by Jefferson and his allies has endured and flourished, and the Hamilton of American memory is a Hamilton who championed privilege and who was a foe of liberty. Never has such a resilient description of a political figure, based on so little evidence, been circulated and accepted by so many.

2

Hamilton and the Jacksonian Era
The Monster Bank and the Coming of War

As the founding generation passed on, a second generation of American political leaders emerged to carry on the struggle begun by Jefferson and Hamilton.[1] Although the Federalist party was dead, remnants of Hamiltonian thought could be found in such statesmen as Daniel Webster, Henry Clay, John Marshall, and ironically John Quincy Adams, all of whom would be subjected to many of the same allegations of elitist designs that confronted Hamilton. The popular image of Hamilton as an un-American monarchist was solidified during the Jacksonian era in part because American politics, at least presidential politics, was dominated by men (Andrew Jackson, Martin Van Buren, John Tyler, James Polk) who were inclined, in most instances, to champion the Jeffersonian platform of states' rights, agrarianism, expansion of suffrage, and strict constitutional interpretation and to oppose internal improvements and government intervention in the economy. Although they certainly shared and perhaps even expanded on Hamilton's notion of an energetic executive, at least in the cases of Jackson (1767–1845) and Polk (1795–1849), they remained faithful to Jeffersonian principles. Hamilton's name was frequently invoked by these men and their followers, for as Marvin Meyers has observed, "For most of the country the Federalist conservatism of Hamilton or John Adams was stone dead: its ghost walked only in the speeches of Jacksonians trying to frighten honest citizens out of their opposition."[2]

Andrew Jackson's hostility toward and disdain for Hamilton were evident when he provided a warm reception for Hamilton's killer in

May 1805. Aaron Burr stayed with Jackson for several days, and his arrival in Nashville produced an outpouring of support, with cannons firing salutes and dinners given in his honor. As Jackson's biographer Robert Remini has observed, killing Hamilton "restored Burr's standing in the Republican party as far as westerners were concerned." Jackson's contempt for Hamilton and Federalism stemmed from his "political creed," which was formed, as he put it, "in the old republican school" committed to states' rights. Jacksonianism was by definition a refutation of the principles of Federalism, as Jackson clearly stated in his first presidential address to Congress. The foremost principle of the American experiment, he contended, was that "the majority is to govern"; and in fundamental disagreement with Hamilton's arguments for the beneficial filtering effects of representation, he maintained that "as few impediments as possible should exist to the free operation of the public will." He once wrote his private secretary, "The people are the government, administering it by their agents; they are the Government, the sovereign power."[3] Though Hamilton would not have disagreed with this statement, he did believe that the people could err and that statesmanship involved more than simply implementing the popular will.

During his brief tenure as a member of the House of Representatives (1796–1797), Jackson opposed an effort to issue a farewell address praising outgoing President George Washington, in part due to his disdain for Hamilton's financial policies. Referring to Washington, he once observed that the "Executive of the Union . . . [had] been Grasping after power, and in many instances, Exercised powers, that he was not Constitutionally invested with." The type of strong central government favored by Hamilton was "calculated to raise around the administration a moneyed aristocracy dangerous to the liberties of the country." When John Quincy Adams and Henry Clay took the presidency away from him in 1824 with their "corrupt bargain," the event was seen by Jacksonians as an attempt, as Remini characterized it, to "steal the government in order to reassert Hamiltonian doctrines."

Jackson was determined to avenge this injustice in the election of 1828. The party's de facto strategist, Martin Van Buren, couched that election as a showdown between the Hamiltonianism of Adams and Clay and the Jeffersonian Republicanism of Jackson and John C. Calhoun,[4] and it is fair to say that the movement begun by Jefferson in the Revolution of 1800 reached its climax with Andrew Jackson's election in 1828. Whatever misgivings Jefferson had about Jackson, and he had some, there was no denying that Jackson was a natural outgrowth of Jefferson's efforts to champion the common man and to move the American polity in a more populist direction.[5]

During the age of Jackson, Hamilton served as a useful foil for Democrats committed to tarring their opponents, particularly Whigs, as elitists corruptly allied with the second Bank of the United States (BUS). Criticism of, and opposition to, the BUS formed an ideological center for those critical of Hamilton and his political aims. The BUS was an insult to Jacksonian first principles, an elitist East Coast institution that corruptly benefited its friends and ignored the interests of the people. It was frequently referred to as a monster by Jacksonians, for it "carried the bad seed of Hamilton's first monster, matured all the old evils, and created some new ones," including "constitutional impiety, consolidated national power, aristocratic privilege, and plutocratic corruption."[6] Jackson believed that the Bank had promoted "aristocratical tendencies" and that it was his solemn duty to "restrain the sinister aspirations of wealth, and to check the growth of an authority so unfriendly to . . . the just rights of the people." The threat to the "mass of the people" emanated from "combinations of the wealthy and professional classes — from an aristocracy which thro' the influence of riches and talents, insidiously employed, sometimes succeeds . . . in establishing the most odious and oppressive Government under the form of a free institution."[7]

Jackson's campaign against the BUS was a continuation of the kind of politics that had been so effective against Hamilton and the Federalists. (Ironically, one of Hamilton's sons, James, was an ally of Jackson's in the Bank war and helped to draft a message to Congress urging that the Bank's charter not be renewed.[8]) It was, as Daniel Webster put it, an attempt by the president to "influence the poor against the rich. It wantonly attacks whole classes of the people, for the purpose of turning against them the prejudices and resentments of other classes."[9]

The intersection of the Bank, Hamilton, and the Jacksonians is most intriguing when one examines the role of Martin Van Buren (1782–1862), Jackson's secretary of state and vice president. A lifelong New Yorker, Van Buren was well acquainted with Hamilton's record and attempted to undo much of his legacy. As a young man, he witnessed a speech Hamilton delivered in Albany designed to dissuade New York Federalists from supporting Aaron Burr for governor. The audience was composed mostly of "gray heads" who had come together to hear "the most eloquent man of his day. . . . My seat was so near to Hamilton that I could hear distinctly every word he said." Hamilton's "imposing manner and stirring eloquence" impressed Van Buren.[10]

Nevertheless, the young Van Buren allied himself with Hamilton's opponents. One of Van Buren's mentors in New York was William P. Van Ness, who served as Burr's second at the duel in Weehawken, and Burr too was quite fond of the young lawyer from Kinderhook. Van Ness had helped Van Buren launch his legal career and drew the young attorney into Republican state politics, and when Van Ness was indicted as an accessory to murder for Hamilton's death, it was Martin Van Buren who lobbied the governor of New York on his behalf and successfully represented the defendant in court.[11]

Van Buren bluntly stated his opinion of Hamilton in his *Inquiry into the Origin and Course of Political Parties in the United States* (1867), a somewhat rambling account of the efforts of Jefferson and Madison to counter Hamiltonianism. Van Buren frequently invoked Hamilton's name as the champion of monarchy and the founder of a party whose main characteristic, under whatever label it chose, was contempt for the wisdom of the people. Van Buren's Hamilton (often seen through the eyes of Jefferson, whom he consulted) "held [the people] incapable of judging such questions" of great importance to their own happiness and welfare. Van Buren repeatedly praised Hamilton as a "remarkable man," but at the same time he found himself "dissenting more thoroughly than ever from his principles." And although he rejected Charles Francis Adams's suggestion that Hamilton fostered an atmosphere of crisis during the Quasi-War with France in order to seize power through a coup, Van Buren had no doubt that Hamilton was "in principle a monarchist." Conceding that Washington placed Hamilton "virtually at the head of his administration" and that his opinions guided the policies of both the Washington and Adams administrations, Van Buren nonetheless rejected the allegation that Hamilton controlled "the mind of Washington." He struggled in his *Inquiry* to avoid giving Hamiltonianism Washington's imprimatur and consistently sought to demonstrate the latter's fidelity to republicanism. He contended also that Washington exerted a moderating influence on Hamilton, suggesting that one possible explanation for the discrepancy between Hamilton's principles and his actions, for his apparent reluctance to pursue his monarchical schemes, was his knowledge that

Washington would never consent to such a plot.[12] Nonetheless, Van Buren maintained to the end of his life that Hamilton sought the "introduction of monarchical institutions" into the United States.[13]

Not surprisingly, Van Buren's antipathy toward Hamiltonianism was also demonstrated in his enduring animosity toward the Bank of the United States. James A. Hamilton later recorded a conversation with Van Buren in which he denied he was opposed to the BUS on constitutional grounds, and one of his leading biographers noted the absence of evidence linking him to the war on the Bank or to Jackson's famous veto.[14] Yet it is also true that Van Buren never wavered in his opposition to the Bank or what he referred to as the "money power." Whether he was motivated by principle or partisanship is uncertain, but it is certain that he spoke out strongly against the bank in a speech delivered at a convention of New York Republicans when he was twenty-nine and remained committed to this position throughout his political career.[15] Late in his life he wrote that advocates for the Bank were wealthy Americans whose strongest passion was to be "allied to power, permanently, if possible. . . . [Wealth] maintains a constant struggle for the establishment of a moneyed oligarchy, the most selfish and monopolizing of all depositories of political power."[16]

For those in fundamental disagreement with the existence of the BUS, one of the chief villains in the drama surrounding the Bank war was Nicholas Biddle (1786–1844), the Bank's president. Van Buren maintained that Biddle took steps designed to cause "public and private distress" and to "force the people" to accept a monopoly they did not want; but regardless of whether "the weakness or wickedness of the attempt is the most striking," Biddle's "Reign of Terror" was, he predicted, doomed to fail. This vision of Biddle as a corrupt manipulator permeated Jacksonian rhetoric; Jackson himself described one of Biddle's actions as a desperate attempt to preserve the Bank by purposely loaning out millions to avoid paying the national debt and to "gain power . . . and force the government . . . to grant it a new charter." Ironically, Biddle viewed himself as a follower of Hamiltonian principles, but his father had been one of the many friends of Aaron Burr who provided shelter for him after he fled New York. Despite the senior Biddle's Federalist affiliations, he vowed that if any attempt had been made to seize Burr, "he would not have been easily taken." All of this was long forgotten a quarter century later when Nicholas Biddle was demonized by Democrats as the new

Hamilton. In the end, the Democrats triumphed: Biddle and his Bank were destroyed by Jackson's veto of a bill rechartering it. John Quincy Adams observed, three years before Biddle's death, that the former president of the Bank "broods with smiling face and stifled groans over the wreck of splendid blasted expectations and ruined hopes."[17]

A colorful figure in the Jacksonian quest to dilute Hamiltonianism was Senator Thomas Hart Benton (1782–1858) of Missouri. Although in 1813 Jackson and Benton had tried to kill each other in a duel, by 1823 the two had overcome their animosity and were political allies.[18] It was Benton's belief that the Bank, an "anti-republican monopoly," had tended "to aggravate the inequality of fortunes; to make the rich richer, and the poor poorer; to multiply nabobs and paupers." Following his defeat for reelection to the Senate, Benton began writing *Thirty Years' View*, his attempt to salvage the reputation of the Democratic party in the face of what he observed as a pro-Federalist slant in the writings of Alexis de Tocqueville. According to Benton, Hamilton had persuaded Washington to establish the First Bank of the United States on the grounds of "expediency [and] necessity" in the face of an Indian War in the Northwest Territories, which threatened to tax the resources of the new government. "General Hamilton," Benton observed, "argued that with the aid of a national bank, the war would be better and more successfully conducted. . . . That war terminated well; and the bank having been established in the mean time, got the credit of having furnished its 'sinews.'" Continuing his overview, Benton explained that the poor American performance in the War of 1812 was blamed in part on the absence of a national bank and led to many of its "old, most able, and conscientious opponents giving in to it, Mr. Madison at their head." After the Bank was destroyed by Jackson and the panic of 1837 ensued, Benton placed the blame for this disaster squarely on Hamilton, arguing that it was "the natural fruit" of Hamilton's deviation from the intentions of his founding colleagues, in particular his modeling the BUS after the "corrupt" Bank of England. Benton was convinced that President Polk's successful conduct of the Mexican War without the aid of a national bank successfully refuted Hamilton's wartime necessity argument. A national bank was "shown to be 'unnecessary,' and therefore unconstitutional."[19]

Other Jacksonians were as zealous as their leader in condemning Hamilton and his principles. As candidates in their home states of Tennessee and New

Hampshire, James K. Polk and Franklin Pierce (1804–1869) discovered that conjuring up the ghost of Hamilton was an effective vote-gathering technique. Polk viewed the political struggles of his day as well as those of the founding as a battle, as one of his biographers put it, between "simple morality and a conspiracy of wealth and power." Polk served in Congress from 1825 to 1839, and during his election campaigns against Whig candidates his standard stump speech began with attacks on the monarchical and centralizing tendencies of Alexander Hamilton.[20] As chairman of the House Ways and Means committee during the Jackson years, and later as Speaker of the House, he became de facto spokesman for the Jacksonians in Congress and was a key figure in the destruction of the Bank. In his view the Whigs were the political descendants of the Federalists, and both had betrayed the nation's founding principles. He dismissed the Whigs in a diary entry for 4 January 1847 with his ultimate term of opprobrium — they were Federalists. Franklin Pierce, (Young Hickory), also accused his Whig rivals of being Federalists and devotees of Hamilton, a tactic designed to brand them as champions of wealth and privilege.[21]

During the Jacksonian era Hamilton also became the occasional subject of writings by prominent American literary figures. Franklin Pierce's friend and campaign biographer Nathaniel Hawthorne (1804–1864), a lifelong admirer of Andrew Jackson, wrote an essay on Hamilton in 1836, when Hawthorne was serving as editor of the *American Magazine of Useful and Entertaining Knowledge*. Although praising Hamilton for a number of accomplishments, Hawthorne took exception to his zeal for an energetic government that "went to an extent, which, by the light of subsequent experience, we are now wise enough to shun." Hamilton was further reproached because he "had not sufficient faith in the capacity of the people for self government," and his "nominal republic would have been very like a monarchy in its institutions." Later in his life, Hawthorne's stance toward Hamilton seemed to veer in a more hostile direction; in *A Book of Autographs* (1844) he noted that despite many admirable qualities that made him a hero to Federalists, Hamilton shared all of their "distrust of the people, which so inevitably and so righteously brought about their ruin."[22]

Hawthorne's literary colleague James Fenimore Cooper (1789–1851) was raised in a Federalist family by a father who was a member of Congress and a friend of Washington, Jay, and Hamilton. Hamilton acted as the elder

Cooper's lawyer during the months when he was writing *The Federalist,* and James Fenimore Cooper carefully read these same essays later in his life. Cooper apparently belonged to the Democratic party during the Jackson years and once noted that the children of Federalist stalwarts should be "almost always decided democrats." During an extended sojourn in Europe from 1826 to 1833, his devotion to American constitutionalism deepened, and he spent considerable time devouring the writings of the founding era.[23] He once wrote an acquaintance in England that the British aristocracy had much to learn from the American experience, and he probably had the Federalists in mind when he explained that "our gentry put themselves in opposition to the mass, after the revolution, simply because . . . they fancied there were irreconcilable interests to separate the rich man from the poor man. . . . They consequently supported theories adverse to the amalgamation, and as a matter of course, the instinct of the multitude warned them against trusting men opposed to their rights."[24] Cooper's attitude toward Hamilton and the Federalists seemed to harden the longer he stayed in Europe. Writing in 1836, he argued that Hamilton and other Federalists sought to destroy the Republic: "You know I was educated in the particular opinions of this political sect; that I had every opportunity of ascertaining their real sentiments; and I cannot but know, that, while the great majority of them dreamed of no more than arresting what they believed to be the dangerous inroads of democracy, some of their leaders aimed at a return, in principle, to the old system."[25] He was most likely referring to Hamilton, about whom he had once observed, "I have no doubt that Hamilton was, at heart, a monarchist. This is no imputation on his talents, for all the theories of the day had that tendency." Cooper attributed Hamilton's admiration for monarchy to the fact that he had observed the institution only from afar: "Had Hamilton been sent to Europe . . . his sagacity would at once have enabled him to separate the ore from the dross, and to have found how little there is of the former. But as a theory, his creative mind only aided in lending it plausibility and force; whereas, had he been able to correct his premises by actual observation, the deductions would have been very different."[26]

Cooper's admiration for Andrew Jackson and the Democratic party was far from unqualified; he was disturbed, for instance, by the excessive leveling inclinations found in some strands of Jacksonian thought and was increasingly distressed by the tyranny of public opinion and the ensuing mediocrity that permeated American life. But he shared the fears of many Americans of his day that the manners and morals of the Republic were being undermined by the mindless pursuit of wealth. He was, as Marvin Meyers believed, "a variety of Tory Democrat who gave his qualified allegiance to the party engaged in resisting the conspicuous agents of social and economic subversion." For Cooper, the monster Bank was the most prominent symbol of a new generation of "speculative promoters of paper towns and enterprises" and Jackson something of a latter-day George Washington, personifying the virtues of the early Republic with his "manly and marked features" and his decision, courage, and patriotism.[27]

Cooper's fellow New Yorker, Washington Irving (1783–1859), aspired to an evenhandedness that resulted in a somewhat schizophrenic sympathy for both Aaron Burr and Alexander Hamilton. The author of "Rip Van Winkle" and the *Life of George Washington* was one of the most popular writers of the new nation and intimately connected with the notable personalities of nineteenth-century New York. While traveling in Europe at the time of the famous duel, Irving wrote his brother that his blood "boil[ed]" when he read that Burr and his associates were being "persecuted." Although he was, "at first, [an] admirer [of] Gen. Hamilton [and] a partizan [*sic*]," he nonetheless also felt "a high sense of the merits of B(urr) and an indignation at seeing him persecuted." Irving viewed Burr's postduel prosecution as "melancholy proof to what a rancorous height political animosities are attaining in our country."[28] Reporting on Burr's treason trial in Richmond in 1807, he confessed that "I consider him as a man so fallen, so shorn of power to do national injury, that I feel no sensation remaining but compassion for him."[29]

But Irving took his children to visit the Hamilton monument in Weehawken in 1810[30] and admired his "high intellectual qualities" and the fact that he was "the associate of Washington and one of the founders of our Constitution."[31] In his *Life of George Washington,* Irving observed that Hamilton left the "impress of his genius on the institutions of the country," and his "energy, skill and intelligence" and "quick discernment and precocious judgment" were appreciated by Washington.[32] Irving downplayed Hamilton's alleged monarchical tendencies and offered a more subtle interpretation of his thought by suggesting that he was "sincerely disposed to support the republican form, with regard to our country" yet preferred "theoretically [a] monarchical form." Somewhat uniquely, Irving emphasized the considerable difference between theory and practice, suggesting that many of Hamilton's supporters may have uttered similar opinions "pretty freely at dinner-tables" but maintaining that these were "probably merely speculative opinions" with no sinister intent "by men who had no thought of paving the way for a monarchy."

The possibility of war increased throughout the 1850s as the notable congressional statesmen of the Jacksonian era, Daniel Webster (1782–1852), John C. Calhoun (1782–1850), and Henry Clay (1777–1852), faded from the scene. Whatever differences the three men had with one another, they all acknowledged Hamilton's importance as a founding father. Clay generally if sometimes covertly admired Hamilton, but Calhoun, particularly in his later years, came to regard him as the source of the South's discontent. In public remarks, Calhoun tended to praise Hamilton's patriotism, though in private correspondence he was less complimentary. Of the three, Daniel Webster had the strongest admiration for him.

Webster's legendary oratorical skills were first demonstrated during a Fourth of July speech in 1800 to the citizens of Hanover, New Hampshire, when he was eighteen years old. A devout Federalist, Webster was a junior at Dartmouth when he declared in his speech that the Federalist party had in its ranks "two thirds of the talent, the character, and the property of the nation."[33] In the prime of his political career he did not hesitate to praise Hamilton, although he was unimpressed by his behavior during the election of 1800 when he attacked the public conduct and character of John Adams: "Two things I can't say I like," he wrote a friend after the election, "Jefferson's election to the Presidency, and Hamilton's letter. Of the two, I prefer the former. There is some consistency in the Jacobins raising Thomas to the Executive Chair; it is in conformity to their avowed principles. But Hamilton's letter is void of congruity."[34]

Webster was an apprentice in a Boston law firm when he heard the news of Hamilton's death in 1804, quite possibly from William Coleman's New York Herald, the nationally circulated edition of the New York Evening Post that Webster subscribed to from 1802 to August 1804. Apparently moved by the tragedy, he wanted to obtain copies of the tributes paid to Hamilton, and unaware of the forthcoming collection compiled by Coleman, he wrote, "I do not learn that anybody is publishing in a volume the Eulogies on Hamilton. I have spoken to a book-binder to bind for me several of the best in a decent, respectable volume." Webster was most impressed with a eulogy delivered by Eliphalet Nott (1773–1860), an Albany clergyman and president of Union College. Webster pronounced it a masterpiece and was frustrated to discover that there was not "a copy to be had in this Town" and that he was reduced to reading a newspaper report that contained a "scanty portion of its excellencies."[35]

Webster invoked Hamilton's legacy to great effect while presenting oral arguments before the Supreme Court on behalf of the Second Bank of the United States in *McCulloch v. Maryland* (1819). This landmark case dealt with the implied constitutional powers of the national government and had significant implications for the American system of federalism. Webster drew extensively from Hamilton's opinion to President Washington regarding the constitutionality of the First Bank of the United States. Hamilton argued in 1791 that the necessary and proper clause found in Article 1, section 8, of the Constitution granted certain implied powers to the national government — "if the end be clearly comprehended within any of the specified powers" and "if the measure have an obvious relation to that end, and is not forbidden by any particular provision of the constitution — it may safely be deemed to come within the compass of national authority." Webster echoed Hamilton's position in his oral argument before the Court, and John Marshall eventually transformed the argument into law with his opinion in the *McCulloch* case.[36]

In 1824, the same year he helped elect John Quincy Adams as president over Andrew Jackson, Webster attempted to publish a history of the Federalist party. He hoped that it would track the party's rise and fall from its origins through the Madison administration, although many viewed this as an attempt by the renowned orator to burnish his reputation and thus assist in a future quest for the White House. Webster hired an author to write the text, but the book appears to have been abandoned after controversy arose over the intended portrayal of Hamilton and Timothy Pickering. Perhaps Webster hoped to preserve his political viability in an increasingly populist nation by denigrating "high Federalists" such as Hamilton. He denied any such intent, writing one of the project's benefactors that "certainly it never entered into my imagination that any thing should be written to disparage the well earned fame of Col Pickering or Genl Hamilton. Any expression of my regard for them would be wholly superfluous."[37]

Throughout his life, Webster believed that the Jacobins had been grossly unfair in their attacks on Hamilton. In 1837, while a U.S. senator from Massachusetts, he was moved by an address written by James Kent (1763–1847), a noted New York judge and legal scholar. Kent observed that "among his brethren Hamilton was indisputably preeminent. This was universally conceded. He rose at once to the loftiest heights of professional eminence, by his profound penetration, his power of analysis, the comprehensive grasp and strength of his understanding, and the firmness, frankness, and integrity of his character." Kent also proclaimed, somewhat astonishingly, that if Hamilton had lived twenty years longer "he would have rivaled Socrates or Bacon." Webster wrote Kent, "How glorious it is to dwell among the recollections of the great Dead! Your account of Hamilton — I say *your* account of Hamilton — amply compensates for all the loads of obloquy, that Jacobinism ever heaped upon him." Webster requested that Kent send a copy to his son Daniel Fletcher Webster, who has "good principles [and] cannot think wrong."[38]

Webster was no stranger to delivering warm tributes to Hamilton. In an address in March 1831 before an audience of distinguished gentlemen of New York, Webster observed that the "great object" of Hamilton's desire was "some closer bond of union for the States." He praised Hamilton for his role in the Annapolis convention that led to the calling of the Constitutional Convention. Stretching the truth, he remarked that Hamilton was "an active and efficient member" of the Philadelphia convention. Hamilton reached the pinnacle of glory with his efforts to achieve ratification of the Constitution in New York, for "the whole question was likely to depend on the decision of New York." His coauthorship of *The Federalist* during the ratification campaign in New York generated essays that were "important commentaries on the text [of the Constitution], and accurate expositions, in general, of its objects and purposes." Washington's "discerning eye" led him to call upon Hamilton to take responsibility for "the most important [post] in the administration of the new system." Reaching one of his famous rhetorical climaxes, Webster argued that the whole world admired Hamilton, for "he smote the rock of the national resources, and abundant streams of revenue gushed forth. He touched the dead corpse of the Public Credit, and it sprung upon its feet. The fabled birth of Minerva, from the brain of Jove, was hardly more sudden or more perfect than the financial system of the United States, as it burst forth from the conceptions of Alexander Hamilton."[39]

Daniel Webster was a true heir of Hamilton, a strong advocate for union whose impact on nineteenth-century American politics cannot be overstated. His famous replies on the floor of the Senate to John C. Calhoun and Robert Y. Hayne (1791–1839) of South Carolina became instant classics. Webster and his principles appeared increasingly anachronistic in the America of the 1850s, more so than his two great contemporaries, Clay and Calhoun. He confessed that he loved "to linger around these original fountains, and to drink deep of their waters" in his study of the founding, and his admiration for the founders and the Federalists in particular prompted him to remark that he belonged with "generations that had gone by."[40]

John C. Calhoun was the least enthusiastic of the great triumvirate in his regard for Hamilton but nonetheless possessed something of a grudging respect for his achievements. His admiration for Hamilton was at its most intense early in his career, when he helped lead the war hawks in support of the War of 1812 and during his subsequent tenure as James Monroe's secretary of war. Calhoun also turned to Hamilton in the aftermath of the War of 1812, when Speaker Henry Clay selected him to chair a House committee to review the chaotic state of the postwar currency and to respond to President Madison's appeal to restore American finances, using Hamilton's 1791 bank proposal as an outline for the committee's 1816 proposal that Madison signed into law.[41] Calhoun again borrowed Hamilton's ideas when he served as secretary of war, advocating the establishment of an expandable army with a large core of permanent professional officers who could quickly take command of a demobilized peacetime military and convert it to a war footing as rapidly as possible.[42]

Calhoun's early nationalism was eclipsed later in his life, however, by his fear of the growing power of the federal government and its attendant corruption; and concomitant with his fear, not surprisingly, was a lessening of his admiration for Hamilton. Calhoun believed that the American Republic had begun to degenerate almost immediately after the founding, when Hamilton engineered the "unholy alliance" between the banks and the federal government that bound together "the great and powerful classes of society." He wrote in 1840 that if Hamilton's financial policies had not been enacted, including the creation of a Bank of the United States, "the whole course of our politicks [sic] under our system would have been entirely different." Calhoun believed the way to reverse these dangerous trends, which could ultimately lead to a federal government controlled by abolitionists, was "no less than to turn back the Government to where it commenced operations in 1789 . . . to take a fresh start, a new departure, on the State Rights Republican tack."[43]

Despite Hamilton's disastrous financial policies, however, Calhoun originally saw in the founder a model of sorts for the increased power of the states over and against the national government. He held that Daniel Webster was guilty of distorting Hamilton's legacy by linking it with the doctrine of "consolidation." Calhoun contended in 1833 that his own views of the Constitution were often portrayed as "novel," but he believed this perception was mistaken, for "the novelty is not on my side, but on that of the senator from Massachusetts. The doctrine of consolidation which he maintains is of recent growth. It is not the doctrine of Hamilton, Ames, or any of the distinguished federalists of that period, all of whom strenuously maintained the federative character of the Constitution." Calhoun's aim was "fixed," as he put it, to "restore the Constitution to its primitive purity." The difficulty, he suggested, was that advocates of consolidation had concealed their intentions in the rhetoric of states' rights and republicanism, despite harboring principles far more extreme than "Hamilton and Ames ever conceived."[44] But by 1838, Calhoun had changed his opinion. Replying once again to Webster, he made clear that he no longer believed that the New Englander had distorted Hamilton's views but indeed saw him as a legitimate heir of the founder of consolidation. Webster belonged "to another and opposite school, which, to designate by its most distinguished leader, may be called the school of Hamilton; a man distinguished for his great abilities, perfect frankness, and ardent patriotism, but who was decidedly inferior to Mr. Jefferson in genius, the power of original thinking, and the clearness and depth of his conception of the true nature and character of our Government." The Federal or National party, he contended, had consistently supported the alliance between the government and the banks, forming a most powerful force for consolidation. The "great original leader" of that party, Alexander Hamilton, never displayed "profounder sagacity, or greater boldness, than in consummating this unholy alliance, on his own responsibility, in direct defiance of law; by his treasury order of '89. It has done more to consolidate the Government, and destroy the federative character of our political system, than all other measures put together."

In Calhoun's assessment, "Jefferson had more genius" and Hamilton had "more abilities" — but leaned more to "power" than to "liberty." By the late 1830s both men had "impressed themselves deeply on the movements of the Government, but as yet Hamilton far more so than Jefferson," although Calhoun believed that in the long run the Jefferson "impression" would "prove the more durable of the two." This was due in part to Hamilton's "great and leading error" of viewing the British system of government as analogous to the American system, when in both "spirit and genius" never "were two free Governments so perfectly dissimilar."[45] Calhoun repeatedly argued that Hamilton imposed a system of government at odds with the intentions of the framers of the Constitution and alien to the American spirit. Though he may have failed to achieve his goals in the Constitutional Convention, Hamilton nonetheless succeeded in enlarging government power "through a liberal and broad construction," which led to the funding system, "the union of the government and the banks," and an "oppressive protective system." As a result of Hamilton's machinations, "The government thus received its first and powerful impulse in a direction unsuited to its genius and character, and from which, it has never yet fully recovered." By the early 1840s Calhoun believed that the Whig party was dominated by disciples of Hamilton: the party's goal was to "rebuild the old plunder system of Gen Hamilton," and it was the duty of Calhoun and his adherents to thwart this design.[46]

Between 1845 and 1850 Calhoun labored to complete two works summarizing his understanding of the purposes of government, particularly in the American context. *A Disquisition on Government* and *A Discourse on the Constitution and Government of the United States* were published shortly after his death in 1850. In his unfinished *Discourse* he reiterated his argument that much of what ailed America stemmed from Hamilton's defiance of the spirit and intentions of the framers. Celebrating the principles enunciated by Madison and Jefferson in the Virginia and Kentucky Resolutions, Calhoun saw in their strict interpretation of the national government's powers a conclusive refutation of "the position, taken by Gen. Hamilton, that it belongs to the discretion of the national legislature to pronounce upon objects, which concern the general welfare." President Jefferson's efforts to reverse the effects of Hamiltonian consolidation, while well intentioned and somewhat successful, for the most part failed to "arrest many great and radical evils . . . nothing towards reversing the order of Gen. Hamilton which united the government with the banks." Jefferson's failure, however, was understandable, partly because "Gen. Hamilton had laid the foundation of his policy so deep, and with so much skill, that it was difficult, if not impossible, to reverse it."[47]

Calhoun saw ominous similarities between Hamilton and one of his own great contemporaries, Henry Clay. Clay was known as the Father of the American System, a series of proposals envisioning a national bank, internal improvements, and a protective tariff as the hallmarks of an integrated national economy. Calhoun and others attacked Clay's proposals as a threat to the Republic, in part due to their similarity to Hamilton's consolidationist policies. Indeed, Hamilton himself had referred in *The Federalist* to a potential economy of "one great American system, superior to the controul of all transatlantic force or influence, and able to dictate the terms of connection between the old and the new world!"

Despite his later philosophical affinity with Hamiltonianism, Clay had defended Hamilton's killer against treasonable conspiracy charges in 1806. When the Federalist U.S. attorney for Kentucky had indicted Aaron Burr for his empire-building schemes in the West, Clay served as his chief counsel and was successful in persuading a jury to dismiss the indictment. Later in his career, and despite his pursuit of a nationalist agenda derived in many respects from Hamiltonian principles, Clay seldom expressed any admiration for Hamilton. Having begun his career as a devout Jeffersonian in Republican Kentucky, paying tribute to Hamilton would not have been politically prudent: suspicion of Clay was formidable enough without the added curse of his publicly acknowledging a debt to Hamilton.[48]

Clay originally had the support of Republicans. One account of a speech he delivered at the time of the Alien and Sedition Acts of 1798 noted that he "poured forth such an impassioned torrent of denunciation" that when Federalist orators attempted to speak they were shouted down by the enraged crowd.[49] Another report described Clay and his allies deifying Jefferson and viewing Hamilton as "an unprincipled West Indian Creole who aspired to be an American Caesar." Even toasts by Republicans to George Washington were qualified: "George Washington: down to the year 1787 but no farther."

However, as a young member of the Kentucky Assembly, Clay broke with Republican ranks and supported internal improvements and a state-sponsored bank. In December 1807 he was elected speaker of the house in Kentucky, despite criticism from doctrinaire Jeffersonians that his high-toned speeches could well have been written by Alexander Hamilton.[50] And these criticisms perhaps hit their mark. Although perhaps willing to accept state-sponsored institutions, Clay continued to balk at the idea of a national bank. While serving in the U.S. Senate in 1811 he spoke in opposition to a bill re-chartering the Bank of the United States, sardonically referring to Hamilton as "the sagacious Secretary of the Treasury" and observing that his argument for a national bank cunningly took "shelter behind general, high sounding, and imposing terms." Clay also criticized Hamilton's implied powers doctrine, arguing that "the power to charter companies is not specified in the grant, and I contend is of a nature not transferable by mere implication."

But by 1816 Speaker of the House Henry Clay reversed his position yet again and secured the passage of a bank bill that would have made Hamilton proud. Evidence that Hamilton influenced Clay's economic thought can be found in his famous tariff speech of 30–31 March 1824. Clay borrowed from Hamilton the idea that manufacturing and agriculture both had their place in the American economy and noted the importance of economic activity in the formation of the character of the citizenry. He argued that "the best security against the demoralization of society, is the constant and profitable employment of its members. The greatest danger to public liberty is from idleness and vice." Clay maintained a lifelong interest in the promotion of manufacturing and pursued this object, even when his official responsibilities were focused elsewhere: while serving as John Quincy Adams's secretary of state, he helped revitalize the Pennsylvania Society for the Promotion of Manufactures and the Mechanic Arts, originally founded by Alexander Hamilton, and actively promoted tariffs for the protection of American industry.[51]

Henry Clay clearly understood the political costs associated with defying public opinion and praising the high-toned Federalist Alexander Hamilton in the age of Jackson. Yet evidence of his surreptitious admiration for Hamilton can be found in his private correspondence. Writing to an acquaintance in 1823, he confessed that in reading some of John Adams's letters he was struck by the "bloated egotism" and "extravagant vanity" he encountered, and he quarreled with Adams's observations on Hamilton: "He treats poor Hamilton and Pickering without mercy. He does not even allow Hamilton talents! and represents him the most profligate and licentious of men."[52] Writing to Alexander Hamilton Jr. in 1840 Clay further observed that "whilst our country remains, [Alexander Hamilton] will be remembered as among its most distinguished Statesmen. Of his ability and his patriotism none ought to doubt. He entertained some opinions which, if he had lived to this time, he would have modified or corrected; and those, who disagreed with him, on other points, have found that he was not as far from the mark as they were."[53] Another of Hamilton's sons, John Church, attempted to console Clay in the wake of one of his many presidential campaign defeats, his loss to James K. Polk in 1844. John Church expressed views that the senior Hamilton probably would have endorsed: "Democracy, if it has shewn great levity, is not the less stern in its decrees. In your person it has assailed the most powerful opponent of its excesses, & may now trample & riot in its usurpations. . . . The general standard of our National morals will sink more & more — year after year amid frequent & sudden changes which prevent the formation of established character."[54]

Like Alexander Hamilton, Clay was an imperfect man whose principal goal was the preservation and enhancement of the Union. Unlike Hamilton, he rose to power on the fickle platform of appeals to the vanity of the common man. In the end, however, both Clay and Hamilton were portrayed as enemies of the people (and to a great extent rejected by them), due to the successful efforts of demagogues preying on their fear of economic complexity and change. Those Americans inclined to seek simple explanations in conspiratorial theories — blaming foreign intrigue, eastern bankers, or evil businessmen intent on harnessing the power of government for all that was wrong with America — spurned both men.

Although Clay never captured the White House, the Whig victory in the election of 1840 briefly rekindled hope among some conservative Whigs that a revival of Federalist or at least neofederalist principles and practices might occur. A victory address in Wilkes-Barre, Pennsylvania, in December 1840 even saw one Whig leader praise Hamilton and the Federalists. However, most members of both the Whig and Democratic parties continued to distance themselves from the Tory Federalists. Philip Hone, a Whig party leader in New York City, noted in a diary entry from June 1840 that the term Federalist "continue[s] to be a term of reproach and the means of exciting the bad feelings and prejudices of the people," even though the Federalist party "as it was originally constituted, embraced nearly all the great and glorious spirits of the Revolution, and all the real friends of the people. It numbered its Washington and Greene in the field of battle . . . and its Hamilton and

Marshall at the forum." Hone commented bitterly that William Henry Harrison (1773–1841) went out of his way in 1840 to denounce "indignantly" accusations that he once was a Federalist, even though he had in fact been acquainted with Hamilton, who had thought highly of the future president. Harrison was a smart enough politician to realize that this aspect of his past be best left unmentioned, and he was not alone in spurning connections with earlier Federalists: by 1844, one would have been hard-pressed to discern any Federalist influence at the Whig party convention. The Whig flight from Federalist principles was perfectly exemplified when John C. Hamilton reported to the convention that the tariff policies of his party were designed to "equalize the condition of men," a position unlikely to have pleased his father.[55]

The declining reputations of the Federalists came at a time of increasing regard for more radical American founders such as Thomas Paine. Paine had died in 1809 in relative neglect and poverty, but by the 1820s and 1830s workingmen launched something of a Paine revival. His birthday on 29 January was marked by celebrations of laborers in cities such as Boston, New York, Philadelphia, and Cincinnati. A large birthday ball was held in New York in 1834, and *The Age of Reason* was hailed as a volume "containing more truth than any volume under the sun" at Paine birthday dinners.[56]

Paine's fundamentalist populism influenced generations of American radicals, including some followers of Jefferson and Jackson. He most likely would have been pleased with the triumph of Jeffersonian and Jacksonian thought that was near complete by the mid-nineteenth century. One disturbing consequence of this triumph was the intolerance directed toward those who dared question the prevailing leveling ideology. One somewhat troubled observer of this situation was John Quincy Adams. In April 1837 he read for the first time portions of the papers of James Madison, who had died the previous year, including Madison's report of the June 1787 speech Hamilton delivered at the Constitutional Convention outlining his plan of government. Adams wrote in his diary,

The speech occupied a whole day, and was of great ability. The plan was theoretically better than that which was adopted, but energetic, and approaching the British Constitution far closer, and such as the public opinions of the day never would have tolerated. Still less would it be endured by the democratic spirit of the present age — far more democratic than that; for, after half a century of inex-

tinguishable wars between the democracy of the European race and its monarchy and aristocracy, the democracy is yet in the ascendant. . . . If Hamilton were
now living, he would not dare, in an assembly of Americans, even with closed
doors, to avow the opinions of this speech, or to present such a plan even as a
speculation.[57]

On the eve of the Civil War, Jefferson's party remained true to much of its
founder's principles. In general, these principles can be characterized as a
commitment to states' rights, westward expansion and Indian removal, agrarianism, the protection of the institution of slavery, an aversion to economic
complexity, and a certain leveling spirit. Though Jefferson's defenders might
describe this characterization as overstated, and Jefferson himself may not
have actively pursued all these policies, he unleashed and often supported
those forces or individuals who did. Few of these principles can be attributed
to Hamilton or the Federalists, with the possible exception of westward expansion, although on this point the Federalists were often more cautious than
is generally acknowledged. Alexander Hamilton had envisioned a United
States composed of a free workforce engaged in diverse economic activity,
regulated by an energetic national government capable of emerging as a world
power. Although by the 1850s this vision had been under constant attack from
a party dominated by slave interests and fearful of change, for most Americans it was Alexander Hamilton and his political descendants who were the
alleged enemies of liberty and opportunity.

3

Hamilton Rises Again
Civil War and His Vindication

The Civil War ushered in an era that saw Alexander Hamilton eclipse Thomas Jefferson as a revered figure in the minds of most Americans, at least in the North. Jefferson's reputation suffered on the two major issues at stake: defenders of the Union condemned his authorship of the secessionist Kentucky Resolutions of 1798, and his notoriety as one of the largest slaveholders in Virginia repelled those people who saw the war as a struggle for abolition. For many observers, at least in the North, America's bloodiest war vindicated Hamilton: the advocate of a strong national government that eclipsed in importance the particular states seemed to many to have advanced ideas that, had they been heeded, could have avoided the turmoil and bloodshed that had pulled the nation apart. The fate of a work of statuary captured the spirit of the new era: in 1847, President James Polk had ordered that a statue of Thomas Jefferson in the Capitol rotunda be relocated to the White House and prominently displayed on the lawn of the executive mansion; but by 1875, with General Ulysses S. Grant ensconced in the White House, it was on its way back up Pennsylvania Avenue to the Capitol. This change in the tide of public opinion was captured nicely by George W. Curtis (1824–1892), an editor at *Harper's Weekly* and a member of the editorial staff of the *New York Tribune,* one of many observers who saw the Civil War as a vindication of Hamilton. According to Curtis, Hamilton "was one of our truly great men, as Jefferson was the least of the truly great."[1]

These sentiments were shared by the general and future president James A. Garfield (1831–1881) of Ohio, who began to study Hamilton's writings in 1861. By the end of the war Garfield was claiming that "the fame of Jefferson is waning, and the fame of Hamilton is waxing, in the estimation of the American people" and that the United States was "gravitating towards a stronger government." Garfield spent two weeks before delivering a Fourth of July oration in 1861 revisiting his history books on the Constitution, including reading *The Federalist* and portions of Tocqueville, study that "confirmed [me] in my love for Hamilton and weakened my regard for Jefferson." He judged the reversal of fortunes of the two founders, effected by the Civil War, to be permanent and predicted that "the next half century will see the fame of those two men change places in the popular estimation." In his opinion, Jeffersonianism had been "fully tested and . . . [was] a failure": Jefferson's role in the Kentucky and Virginia Resolutions "contained the germ of nullification and secession, and we are today reaping the fruits," but "Hamilton was right in his main propositions . . . all my readings confirm this."[2]

Garfield's somewhat notorious colleague in the officer corps of the Union army, General Benjamin (the Beast) Butler (1818–1893), also found in the brutality of the Civil War a vindication of the central tenets of Hamilton's views on the country. Butler's controversial role as military governor of New Orleans had brought him international notoriety, and after the war he served as one of the House floor managers for the impeachment of President Andrew Johnson. Raised in a Jeffersonian family and taught to "abhor federalism, of which Hamilton was the exponent," Butler nonetheless concluded after a lifetime of reflection that Hamilton had the "sagacity" to foresee that the national government must prevail over the states, a principle that he now endorsed. Although he still embraced the "philosophical lubrications" of Thomas Jefferson concerning the "rights and privileges of the citizen," he found himself highly impressed by Hamilton's "great genius and clear reasoning," which shaped the American government and led him to declare in his autobiography, "as to the powers and duties of the government of the United States, I am a Hamiltonian Federalist."[3]

During the Civil War era, Hamilton's reputation among the Ivy League–educated elite of New England soared to unparalleled heights.[4] To them, the tragic events associated with the disintegration of the Union only affirmed his genius. Connected to one another by marriage, education, or some distant historical bond, they were something of a walking archive — sources of institutional memory for a nation coming apart. Charles Francis Adams (1807–1886), the noted orator Edward Everett (1794–1865), Rufus Choate (1799–1859), and Richard Henry Dana Jr. (1815–1882) saw much to admire in Hamilton, though with some reservations.

Charles Francis Adams was the grandson and son of a president and Abraham Lincoln's wartime ambassador to Great Britain. Adams viewed his father, John Quincy, as "the only picture of a full grown statesman that the history of the United States has yet produced." He confessed, however, that some American statesmen "when directed to a special object have given indications of more positive power," with Jefferson, Hamilton, Webster, and perhaps John Marshall rising to this level. Hamilton's deficiency vis-à-vis John Quincy Adams was thus explained: "Read the writings of Hamilton. You see ability, sagacity and penetration, but you will find it hard to keep awake." In an 1841 review of James Madison's notes taken at the Constitutional Convention, Adams's description of Hamilton was more evenhanded than that of his illustrious forebears. Though Hamilton did not possess "those finer and more delicate feelings of lofty morality," he did have the gift of a "singularly comprehensive mind." Among the men of the Revolution, Adams knew of "no one, who, for the attributes which usually mark genius, was more distinguished," but despite (or, perhaps, because of) his tremendous achievements, "there was not, probably, an instant of his life in which he enjoyed the perfect sympathy of the mass of the people," and when he died, he left "no popular regrets behind." Adams acknowledged, further, that Hamilton's inability to secure popular approval was not solely due to his being out of sync with most Americans, observing that he had often been subjected to attacks by Jefferson and Madison, who "have not spared efforts to throw . . . much public odium upon his character."[5]

Charles Francis Adams's brother-in-law Edward Everett was president of Harvard College, secretary of state, a U.S. senator, and an overshadowed orator at Gettysburg. Everett admiringly characterized Hamilton as the "young New York lawyer" who, at Lafayette's side at Yorktown, led the charge that broke the British. The "gallant and lamented Hamilton" possessed "one of the most persuasive voices that ever spoke through the lips of man," and it was the "illustrious Hamilton," the "first great champion of American manufactures," who started New York on the way to becoming "the throne of the western commercial world."[6] Everett's friend and congressional colleague

Rufus Choate, a senator from Massachusetts, shared in this admiration. Greatly impressed by Hamilton's courage, he explained that Hamilton was "pursued as all central figures in great triumphal processions are pursued . . . by calumny." Choate marveled at Hamilton's ability to treat a subject with depth and a complete devotion to the truth: he discovered in his works "clear processes of intellect" and judged that in the Croswell case Hamilton made "the greatest argument ever uttered in this country."[7] For all Hamilton's brilliance, however, Choate found him flawed in one crucial respect: he told his friend Richard Henry Dana in 1853 that "he was engaged in an ex[amination] of Hamilton, & was at a loss to discover that poetry, for which all his contemporaries gave him credit." Dana maintained that Hamilton "was heroic & chivalrous" but agreed with Choate's assessment. Choate's judgment, however, was not shared by all. He recounted a tale that had been told to him by an acquaintance who escorted Aaron Burr on a visit to the Boston Athenaeum. The escort attempted to divert Burr away from a bust of Hamilton that was on display, thinking it would offend, but to his surprise, Burr approached the bust and said "in a very loud tone, 'Ah! Here is Hamilton.' And, passing his finger along certain lines of his face, said, 'There was the poetry.'"[8]

The editors of the *New York Times* frequently turned to Hamilton for guidance during the darkest days of the Civil War era. On 31 January 1861, the *Times* condemned the "studious perversion" of the Constitution by "South Carolina politicians" who claimed that it was a "mere league or confederacy of sovereign states." In *The Federalist,* Hamilton, "one of the wisest and ablest statesmen which America or the world ever produced," refuted these very arguments by arguing that the powers of the federal Constitution extended to the citizens of each state, not just to the states themselves. Just weeks after the rout of Union forces at Chancellorsville in May 1863, the *Times* took issue with the fierce antiwar sentiment expressed by Tammany Hall Democrats, some of whom openly advocated secession for New York City from the tyranny of the state government in Albany. The *Times* suggested that the "tendency to . . . disintegration," though very much a part of human nature, was intended to be counteracted by a Constitution designed to check the actions of purely selfish politicians. Were Hamilton and other founders alive in 1863 they would be "struck by the extraordinary tenacity . . . of the errors which they combated." The country seemed to be awash, the *Times* believed, with "hundreds of orators and newspapers" repeating the very fallacies "which the

Federalist was written to refute and of which the very adoption of the Constitution was a solemn national repudiation." The desire of politicians from Jefferson Davis to New York mayor Fernando Wood was to "preserve their own field of ambition secure from competition from the outside," and Hamilton well understood the manifest tendency of such "ambitious and designing men" to play upon the fears of concentrated power. The issue in 1789, as in 1863, was "not that we shall unite too closely, but that we shall go to pieces."[9]

Ironically, Fernando Wood, who proposed in January 1861 that New York City secede and become a "free city," had once delivered an address on the genius of Alexander Hamilton in Richmond, Virginia. Wood's speech in 1856 was part of a fund-raising effort to purchase and preserve George Washington's home at Mount Vernon. He delivered an effusive tribute to "one of the master-spirits of the revolution" and dismissed as "superficial" the idea that Hamilton was a "monarchist in principle" and "hostile to Republican Institutions." True to his Tammany Hall roots, however, Wood did issue something of a disclaimer, noting, "I do not wish to be understood as endorsing every public act he performed or every opinion he may have advanced. He held opinions in regard to a National bank, the tenure of office, and other measures of governmental policy to which I can never subscribe."[10]

Despite the widespread admiration for Hamilton's arguments for a strong central government, however, the fact that he, along with the other founders, had created a Constitution that allowed for the continuation of slavery within the country was sufficient cause to condemn him. Yet the issue was not a touchstone by which one could easily predict either pro-Hamilton or anti-Hamilton sentiments. Some abolitionists such as William Lloyd Garrison (1805–1879) held all the founders, including Hamilton and the other antislavery framers, as guilty as their Southern brethren for failing to abolish the peculiar institution. Garrison damned the Constitution as an "agreement with Hell" and burned a copy of it on the Fourth of July, 1854.[11] Garrison had not always held the founders in such contempt. In his youth, he had admired the Federalists as the party of "the immortal Washington," whose principles were "sanctioned by Jay and Hamilton, and Ames, with a host of other distinguished patriots." He mourned the passing of that first generation of statesmen, including Hamilton, whose "magic eloquence and pen . . . are mute in the grave." As late as 1834, when Garrison's position on abolition began to harden, he yearned for "the thundering, majestic, prevailing eloquence of a Hamilton . . . that all understandings might be enlightened, and all hearts subdued."[12] But his admiration for Hamilton's eloquence could not undo what, to Garrison, was his cardinal sin: possessed even of such rhetorical skills, Hamilton was complicit in allowing slavery to exist within the new nation.

Ironically, Garrison's later view of the founders and slavery coincided with those of Chief Justice Roger Taney (1777–1864). Early in his life Taney had been a Federalist, but over time he began to identify with the Jeffersonians and became an ardent supporter of Andrew Jackson, who appointed him to the Supreme Court. Taney agreed with Garrison that the Constitution was a document intended to protect slavery, written by slaveholders or those sympathetic or indifferent to its existence. Taney noted in the *Dred Scott* decision that when the Declaration and Constitution were written, African Americans were "so far inferior, that they had no rights which the white man was bound to respect." In discussing Taney's conversion to Jeffersonianism, one of his biographers noted, "It is significant that the works of Jefferson, and not those of John Adams, or Alexander Hamilton, or other leading Federalists, were left on his shelves at the time of his death."[13]

Yet the former slave and eloquent spokesman for abolition Frederick Douglass (1817–1895) differed with Garrison and Taney's interpretation of the Constitution as a proslavery document. Douglass argued that "from the Declaration downward" Justice Taney and William Lloyd Garrison had misrepresented the intentions of the founders. He occasionally cited Hamilton's record as evidence that the framers foresaw the inclusion of African Americans in the American experiment and indeed vindicated all the major founders on this issue — including Jefferson: "Washington and Jefferson, and Adams, and Jay, and Franklin, and Rush, and Hamilton . . . held no such degrading views on the subject as are imputed by Judge Taney to the Fathers of the Republic." Douglass believed that these men looked toward the "gradual but certain" abolition of slavery. When the Civil War finally came, he was repulsed by the use of the terms "rebel" and "traitor" to describe secessionists, for "Washington, Jefferson, John Jay, John Adams, Benjamin Franklin, Alexander Hamilton, and many other brave and good men, have worn these appellations, and I hate to see them now worn by wretches who, instead of being rebels against slavery, are actually rebelling against the principles of human liberty."[14]

The abolitionist Senator Charles Sumner (1811–1874) predictably admired Hamilton for his assertive nationalism and his apparent hostility to states' rights. In an address at the Cooper Institute in November 1867, in the midst of his efforts to force President Andrew Johnson to implement a radical Reconstruction policy on the defeated South, Sumner addressed the question, "Are We a Nation?" The Massachusetts senator wistfully spoke of the "National Convention" of 1787, this "august body" presided over by Washington: "Who would not be glad to look upon Franklin, Hamilton, and Madison, standing in their places while Washington passed?" Sumner lauded Hamilton and those nationalist founders as "the best men" who "in their longing for national unity, all concurred in the necessity of immediate action to save the country. Foremost in time, as in genius, was Alexander Hamilton."[15]

Sumner's friend and frequent adviser was the German-born Francis Lieber (1798–1872), a professor of politics, history, and the law. A veteran of the Battle of Waterloo, Lieber immigrated to the United States in 1827 and became the first editor of *Encyclopedia Americana*. He befriended Alexis de Tocqueville during his tour of the United States in 1831 and 1832 and eventually joined the faculty of Hamilton's alma mater, Columbia College. A protégé of the great German historian Barthold Niebuhr, Lieber observed that his mentor "repeatedly said to me that he considered Hamilton far the greatest genius and profoundest statesman America had produced." Lieber was a champion of American nationalism, his hero Alexander Hamilton, and he coupled this admiration with disdain for Hamilton's great foe. On Independence Day, 1870, he wrote to future president James Garfield, "Jefferson, the founder of the Union! He was the very underminer of the Union — a most mischievous ferret." Understandably, Lieber disdained the parochial, nativist sentiments that dogged them both, plaintively asking, "Did Hamilton [provide] less service than any statesman or general born within the limits of this country?" Lieber's nationalism was put to the test in the Civil War; three sons served in the Union army, and one, Hamilton Lieber, was seriously wounded at the Battle of Fort Donelson.[16]

Paradoxically, perhaps, the figure who ascended into the American pantheon for preserving the Union and abolishing slavery appeared to celebrate most highly the slave-owning author of the Kentucky and Virginia Resolutions. In a letter written in 1859, Abraham Lincoln (1809–1865) had observed that "the principles of Jefferson are the definitions and axioms of free society" and offered this salute: "All honor to Jefferson." Yet Lincoln's colleague and biographer William H. Herndon wrote, "Mr. Lincoln hated Thomas Jefferson as a man" and as "a politician."[17] If Herndon's account is accurate, perhaps an explanation for this apparent contradiction can be found in Lincoln's determination to place slavery on the road to extinction — and to do so with the very means provided by Jefferson's Declaration of Independence, in which he found a potent weapon with which to shame Stephen Douglas and the Democrats. Lincoln held that the self-evident truths of the Declaration were universal truths, transcending state or national boundaries, applicable to all men at all times in all places and, by this reading, found in the document a formidable obstacle to the institution of slavery.

Lincoln also believed the Declaration promoted "the critical Whig demand for economic expansion," as Allen C. Guelzo has put it. Lincoln envisioned an America where no obstacles deterred "the paths of laudable pursuit for all" and held that the betterment of one's economic condition lay at the foundation of equality: "It was that which gave promise that in due time the weights should be lifted from the shoulders of all men, and that all should have an equal chance. This is the sentiment embodied in that Declaration of Independence."[18] In finding such policy within the Declaration, Lincoln adopted and endorsed Hamilton's vision of a dynamic, economically mobile society: oddly, however, and even though it stood in stark contrast to the static, agrarian nation envisioned by Jefferson, he attributed this vision to Jefferson.

Lincoln's policies were rooted in Hamilton and Clay's American System, and his Hamiltonianism was evident in his support for internal improvements such as railroad and canal expansion and land-grant colleges. Most important, his celebration of the wage laborer as against the slave in an increasingly industrial America was decidedly Hamiltonian. Yet Lincoln was relatively silent about Hamilton. In the index to Lincoln's *Collected Works* there are seven references to Alexander Hamilton and well over forty to Thomas Jefferson, many focusing on the Declaration of Independence.[19] The first reference to Hamilton is a letter to an editor from a witness, apparently hostile, to a speech Lincoln delivered in March 1844 while he campaigned for Whig candidates for Congress and the presidency. Lincoln defended tariffs as beneficial to farmers, and at some portion in the middle of his speech he was handed "some extracts from the papers of Alex. Hamilton; then he rolled his eyes and shook his head, as if he had seen an Irishman." As a member of Congress, Lincoln adhered to the Whig view of limited presidential power, particularly in regard to the veto and the desirability of executive deference to the legislature. While promoting the candidacy of Zachary Taylor in the election of 1848, Lincoln likened Taylor's restrained view of the veto to Jefferson's and noted, apparently disapprovingly, Hamilton's more expansive view of that power.[20]

Only in his famous address at the Cooper Union in February 1860 did Lincoln invoke Hamilton's name in praise. His address was an effort to respond to Senator Stephen Douglas's argument that the Constitution as written by the framers forbade the federal government from controlling slavery in federal territories. Lincoln argued that despite their silence on the question, "several of the most noted anti-slavery men of those times — as Dr. Franklin, Alexander Hamilton and Gouverneur Morris" — would probably have affirmed the power of the federal government to regulate the spread of slavery into the territories. He arrived at this conclusion by "looking into their acts and declarations on those other phases, as the foreign slave trade, and the morality and policy of slavery generally."[21]

Lincoln's unorthodox reading of the Declaration, his adoption of Hamiltonian policies, and reluctance to attribute those policies to Hamilton — or even his willful misattribution of them — may reveal his political genius. His political lineage was Southern Whig, in the tradition of Henry Clay (Lincoln's "beau ideal of a statesman"), and as such he may have possessed the same reluctance as Clay in proclaiming any affection for a dead Federalist, despite Hamilton's increased respectability.[22] More intriguing, however, is the possibility that Lincoln's apparent preference for Jefferson over Hamilton was a tactic designed to use the South's most revered founder against them: by introducing Hamilton's ideas behind the éminence grise of Jefferson, Lincoln placed some of his Southern foes in a position of having either publicly to repudiate Jefferson's importance or to concede to some extent his alleged views. At the same time, Lincoln's design gave to those in the South less ideologically committed a patina of Southern respectability, in the form of Jefferson's heritage, for any deviation from the hard-line views. If this is a plausible account, Lincoln appears to have recognized that the effectiveness of this tack was limited to the time before hostilities hardened each side's positions and before differences became irreconcilable. Allen Guelzo notes that prior to 1854 Lincoln publicly referred only twice to the Declaration but alluded to it more frequently after this date, and the Civil War scholar Phillip S. Paludan has observed that Lincoln eventually stopped mentioning Jefferson in his remarks during the war years. After 3 December 1861, Lincoln referred to Jefferson only once during the remainder of his presidency, and that was in response to a serenade that included a reference to the Declaration.[23]

Though evidence of Lincoln's esteem for Hamilton is difficult to detect, many members of his administration were Hamiltonians. The president's young assistant, John Hay, was an admirer of Hamilton and once wrote Henry Adams that Hamilton deserved "a fairer show for his money. I know you do not rate him so highly as some of us do." Lincoln's secretary of state William Seward viewed Hamilton as "the wisest statesman and the greatest public benefactor that in all her history the State of New York has produced" and "one of the greatest and most celebrated men of America." Secretary of the Treasury Salmon P. Chase saw Hamilton's spirit animating "our Constitution, our institutions, and our history."[24]

The question of classifying Lincoln as a Jeffersonian or Hamiltonian has been a subject of dispute among Lincoln scholars for decades. One Lincoln biographer, Stephen B. Oates, has argued that Lincoln paid particular attention in his reading as a young man to "the Revolution and the Federalist era" and applauded "the nationalist programs of Alexander Hamilton."[25] Another biographer, J. G. Randall, has observed that "Jefferson offered more of a cue for interpreting Lincoln than Hamilton." Randall noted Lincoln's fundamental agreement with Hamilton on the need for a national bank, internal improvements, and a protective tariff. Beyond these matters, however, "the similarity to Hamilton ends," for "in the bedrock of his beliefs . . . Lincoln was like Jefferson." Randall believed that Lincoln's trust in the people's judgment placed him squarely in the Jeffersonian tradition: Randall's Lincoln "owed little to Hamilton who wanted a government to please the moneyed interests. . . . Human rights meant more to him than profits."[26]

One biographer who strongly objected to classifying Lincoln as a Jeffersonian was the poet Edgar Lee Masters (1869–1950), who rose to literary prominence as a result of his *Spoon River Anthology* (1915). Masters's *Lincoln the Man* was dedicated to the memory of Thomas Jefferson, "the preeminent philosopher-statesman of the United States, and their greatest president." Masters believed that Lincoln "crushed the principles of free government" by abandoning his Jeffersonian and Jacksonian roots and becoming a "worshipper of Henry Clay . . . the beloved son of Alexander Hamilton with his corrupt funding schemes" and his principles of "plunder." Masters contended that Lincoln's Hamiltonian expansion of executive authority and his consolidation of federal power ultimately destroyed Jefferson's republic. His policies culminated in a Reconstruction of the South that was a form of "despotism," for "every drop of blood drawn with the lash was made to be repaid by a thousand drawn by the sword, and sucked forth by the tax-gatherer, the parasite and the thief." In the early years of the twentieth century, Masters found America to be an imperial nation dominated by a Republican party controlled by banks and monopolies, all the result of Lincoln's "filling in the outlines of implied powers, which [he] did more than even Hamilton and Webster to vitalize."[27]

Abraham Lincoln's Confederate counterpart, Jefferson Davis (1808–1889), frequently alluded to Hamilton's pronouncements on slavery, secession, and states' rights, references designed to prove that even this most nationalist of founders rejected extreme centralization and supported the right of states to determine the status of slavery within their borders. Davis seems to have believed that Northern admirers of Hamilton had inflated his nationalism, a belief similar to that held by John C. Calhoun in the early stages of his career. Davis's Hamilton would never have condoned the federal government's using force to compel a state to act in accordance with its edicts. Interestingly, Davis had a cordial relationship with one of Hamilton's sons, Alexander Hamilton Jr., and the two men corresponded on occasion with each other. In February 1848, fresh from his national acclaim as a hero of the Mexican War, Davis tried to help the younger Hamilton locate some of his father's correspondence: "I have not been able to find the letters of <y>our distinguished countryman, your Father, written to Genl. Washington."[28] During his tenure as Franklin Pierce's secretary of war, Davis became involved in a bitter conflict over a chain of command issue with General Winfield Scott, the general in chief of the U.S. Army. In their correspondence, both men sought to enlist Hamilton's arguments from *The Federalist*, with Davis accusing Scott of distorting Hamilton's views. The exchanges between the two men were remarkably rancorous; in one instance Scott contrasted Davis to Hamilton, whom he saw as personifying a "nobler bearing among public men," which prevailed "in the earlier and better days of our republic."[29]

Although the younger Davis was somewhat of a nationalist and an expansionist, the increasing tensions between North and South over the issue of the extension of slavery into the territories led him to adopt a more sectionalist stance. In July 1851, speaking in Fayette, Mississippi, Senator Davis condemned those who spoke of coercing states through force, observing that "others of the famous legislators of the country had always manifested a horror of warring with a State, and even Mr. Hamilton had opposed all coercive measures." Throughout the 1850s Davis bemoaned the increasing power of the federal government and the threatened erosion of state authority, claiming it had gone beyond anything anticipated by even the staunchest advocates of nationalism among the founders: "Centralization claimed a power beyond any thing which Hamilton ever dreamed of when it assumed to prescribe to the states the rule by which the right of suffrage should be measured." On the eve of Lincoln's election in 1860, Davis repeated his assertion that the Constitution did not authorize the federal government to use force against a state and claimed that even Hamilton and Madison, who often disagreed, concurred that this authority did not exist. Davis often invoked Hamilton as an example of a Northerner from the early Republic who had the ability to compromise with the South, citing in particular Hamilton's cooperation with Madison on a fugitive slave issue as an example of men whose "loftiness [and] genius . . . put to shame the puny efforts now made to disturb that which lies at the very foundation of the Government under which we live."[30] And as the South inched toward secession, Davis had nothing but praise for the leading advocate of Union, Alexander Hamilton: "Mr. Hamilton, who, if I were to express a judgment by way of comparison, I would say was the master intellect of the age in which he lived; whose mind seemed to penetrate profoundly every question with which he grappled, and who seldom failed to exhaust the subject which he treated."[31] In a heated debate in January 1860, Davis attacked his abolitionist senatorial colleagues who appealed to Hamilton's legacy. When Senator Henry Wilson of Massachusetts argued that Hamilton was an abolitionist, Davis responded that "Hamilton was not an abolitionist in the offensive sense which belongs to the term at this day" and added, "Hamilton never had any policy to interfere with the institution except in the State of which he was a citizen."[32]

Two days before he took office as president of the Confederacy, Davis received a letter from Alexander Hamilton Jr., who congratulated him on his selection and told him that he was confident Davis had the ability either to reunite the Union or to establish a "potent" new government. The younger Hamilton wished for a peaceful separation and hoped that the Southern states would show no hostility to the North. He also enclosed a facsimile of a plan of government proposed by his father, with popularly elected senators and a president elected for seven or ten years.[33] Throughout the course of his presidency, some Southern politicians criticized Davis for being a closet Hamiltonian, particularly when he pressed for a system of military conscription. One Confederate senator feared that Davis might be toying with the idea of forming a federal party and pointedly referred to Alexander Hamilton as an example of the dangers associated with such a development.[34]

In defeat, Jefferson Davis became a vilified figure in both the North and the South. In 1881 he published *The Rise and Fall of the Confederate Government*, a spirited defense of the South's actions that included lengthy discussions of state sovereignty and the powers of the federal government. Hamilton was again cited frequently throughout the work, particularly with passages from *The Federalist* that bolstered the case for states' rights. At one point Davis cited Hamilton's statement in the New York ratifying convention that "to coerce the states is one of the maddest projects that was ever devised . . . here is a nation at war with itself . . . the thing is a dream — it is impossible."[35]

Although they differed over many issues confronting the Confederacy, Davis's vice president, Alexander Hamilton Stephens (1812–1883), shared his admiration for Hamilton. While one biographer went so far as to describe Stephens's attitude toward his namesake as one of "extravagant admiration," another observed the irony of a man named Alexander Hamilton Stephens emerging as a major figure in the Confederate government. It was doubly ironic since this former Whig and champion of the Union was "up to the final parting . . . as belligerent an advocate of Union as the founder of the Federalist party himself."[36] Stephens's postwar defense of the Confederacy, *A Constitutional View of the Late War Between the States*, referred at one point to a passage in *The Federalist* defending the Constitution's view of slaves "in the mixed character of persons and of property. This is in fact their true character." Stephens categorically attributed this statement to Hamilton, although the weight of the evidence leans to Madison's authorship of that essay.[37]

Despite this admiration for Hamilton at the top of the Confederate hierarchy, albeit based on a somewhat tortured interpretation of his principles, in general the South persisted as a stronghold of support for the principles of Jefferson and Jackson. And though Jefferson Davis treated Hamilton somewhat kindly, even enlisting him in the Cause, many other supporters of the Lost Cause were far less indulgent. These firebrands saw Hamilton as something of a coconspirator with Abraham Lincoln. In 1879 Davis received a letter from John L. O'Sullivan, a Northern Democratic newspaper editor and champion of states' rights who is credited with coining the term "manifest destiny." A friend of Nathaniel Hawthorne who had served as Franklin Pierce's ambassador to Portugal, O'Sullivan wrote Davis that "the germ of the Civil War was in the Constitution of 1787. And it was Alexander Hamilton who, more than any other man, planted it there."[38] Even committed Southern Unionists such as Andrew Johnson (1808–1875) abhorred Hamilton. In his first inaugural address as governor of Tennessee, Johnson affirmed his allegiance to the principles of the Democratic party. Remarking upon the divisions that marked the politics of the early Republic, Johnson observed that in the Constitutional Convention, "there were two parties — one of them headed by Mr. Alexander Hamilton, who contended for that form of government which was strongest and farthest removed from the mass of the people, and based upon the old monarchical, or kingly notion, that man was made for government, he not being capable of governing himself." In a July 1856 speech in Nashville, Johnson defended the presidential candidate James Buchanan as an heir to the tradition opposed to an American aristocracy. American aristocrats, "or those who assume to be the rich and the wellborn . . . contend that the . . . masses should be ruled by the few," a doctrine that "had its origin with Mr. Hamilton . . . and has been transmitted on down, under different party names, to the present period of time; and there are hundreds, not to say thousands, as rank federalists in the country now as Alexander Hamilton was in his palmiest days." Buchanan, Johnson believed, was continuing the fight that had been ongoing "since the days of Alexander Hamilton" to protect the "people's power" against an encroaching federal government. Further, Johnson viewed the Know-Nothing party and its doctrines as having its roots in the federalism of John Adams and Alexander Hamilton with their Alien and Sedition Acts.[39]

Evidence of Southern distaste for Alexander Hamilton can also be found in *The Diary of Edmund Ruffin*. Ruffin (1794–1865) was a champion of secession and is said to have fired the first shot at Fort Sumter in April 1861. In a diary entry for 6 April 1863, he noted "a remarkable resemblance" between Hamilton and Aaron Burr and claimed that Hamilton shared Burr's ambition to conquer Spanish-held territory in the Americas. His fellow countrymen, Ruffin believed, had been unjust in their treatment of Burr — for "Hamilton did not suffer in reputation & position" for plotting the same undertakings that caused Burr to be "denounced . . . as a lawless offender" and "persecuted as a traitor." Jeremiah Clemens (1814–1865), a senator from Alabama and the author of *The Rivals: A Tale of the Times of Aaron Burr, and Alexander Hamilton,* also contended that Burr was mistreated. Clemens found Burr to be "pure, upright, and untarnished as a statesman," but Hamilton was "shrewd, artful, and unscrupulous, [and] there were no means he would not employ to accomplish his ends." Clemens "entertained strong prejudices" against Hamilton from boyhood, claiming that he was "loose in his own morals, even to licentiousness" and that "slander was his favorite weapon." He added that the world had never witnessed such a combination of "greatness and meanness, of daring courage and of vile malignity" as it had in Alexander Hamilton.[40]

For most Northern Unionists, on the other hand, Hamilton remained a revered figure. Signs of the renewed interest in him in and around the war years could be seen in the number of biographies and collections of his writings that were published. Hamilton's son John Church had managed to publish his two-volume *Life of Alexander Hamilton,* the first volume appearing in 1834 and the second in 1840. At the height of the Jackson presidency he decided to write the account himself to "prevent the promulgation of new errors" concerning his father. In 1850 he began to publish *The Works of Alexander Hamilton,* a seven-volume collection that included samples of Hamilton's correspondence, cabinet papers, and reports to Congress.[41]

Two histories of the United States released as the nation lurched toward civil war painted Hamilton in a glowing light. Richard Hildreth (1807–1865), a Harvard-educated author and an early proponent of abolition, published a generally flattering account of Hamilton in his six-volume *History of the United States of America* (1849–1852). Hildreth's work influenced generations of historians from Henry Adams to Frederick Jackson Turner. He portrayed Jefferson as an unscrupulous ideologue while judging that Hamilton was "a very sagacious observer of mankind, and possessed of practical talents of the highest order . . . acting under an exalted sense of personal honor and patriotic duty." Hildreth expressed some reservations about Hamilton's effort to attach the wealthy to the new Constitution and argued that he "ascribe(d) to motives of pecuniary and personal interest a somewhat greater influence over the course of events than they actually possess." Nonetheless, he argued that with Hamilton's death, "the country experienced a loss second only to that of Washington." In what became a common theme in the writings of historians during the Civil War era, Hildreth credited Hamilton with discerning "what subsequent experience has abundantly confirmed, that the Union had rather to dread resistance of the states to federal power than executive usurpation."[42]

George Ticknor Curtis's *History of the Origin, Formation, and Adoption of the Constitution of the United States* defended Hamilton against the unjust charge that he desired a monarchical government for the United States. Hamilton possessed nothing other than "a sincere desire for the establishment and success of republican government . . . [and] republican freedom which is founded on a perfect equality of rights among citizens, exclusive of hereditary distinctions." Curtis (1812–1894) insisted on the "importance to all America, through all time, of Hamilton's public character and conduct. . . . From his first entrance, in boyhood, into public life, his patriotism had comprehended nothing less than the whole of the United States." Hamilton's nationalism impressed Curtis, and as secession loomed, he observed that Hamilton "saw that no partial confederacy of the States could be of any permanent value." When the war came, Curtis described it as a "vindication" of Hamilton's understanding.[43]

Samuel Schmucker's *Life and Times of Alexander Hamilton* appeared in 1857 and attempted to defend Hamilton against the "baseless and absurd slanders" cast by "the envious, the malicious, and the vile." If George Washington was first in the hearts of his countrymen, "Hamilton, beyond all question, deserves to be regarded as the second." Burr's marksmanship deprived the nation of the likely prospect that Hamilton would have occupied the "presidential chair" and led the nation to victory in the War of 1812. Schmucker (1823–1863) described Hamilton's premature death as a national calamity, for he was "the first of American statesmen."[44] His assessment was shared, predictably, by John Church Hamilton, who began in 1857 to publish his seven-volume *History of the Republic of the United States of America as Traced in the Writings of Alexander Hamilton and of his Contemporaries.* In his final volume, published in 1864, as the Civil War reached new heights of ferocity, John

Church observed that "stern realities are now uttering themselves aloud, and one voice is heard — 'had Hamilton's views prevailed the crisis could not have taken place.'"

That same bloody year Christopher Riethmuller's *Alexander Hamilton and His Contemporaries, or The Rise of the American Commonwealth* was published in London. Riethmuller depicted Hamilton as the high-minded opponent of the Jacobin Jefferson. A review of Riethmuller's book in *Littell's Living Age* described Jefferson as the originator of slave-owning, secessionist principles while Hamilton was the voice "to the thinkers of the North" of the "sober respect for law, that preference for legal freedom to popular license," which defined Abraham Lincoln.[45] One of the more controversial passages in Riethmuller's book speculated as to Hamilton's response to Southern secession: he conjectured that Hamilton "would have bowed to the force of circumstances, and have preferred two confederacies to one despotism." In an 1865 essay in the *Atlantic Monthly* C. C. Hazewell rejected Riethmuller's suggestion, claiming that Hamilton would have been "the firmest supporter of the war, had he lived to see it" and that "his principles would have led him to be for extreme measures." In fact, according to Hazewell, who considered him "the greatest name in American history," had Hamilton "been allowed to shape our national polity," the calamity of civil war would have been avoided altogether.[46]

This interpretation of Hamilton was not shared by one of the leading American literary figures of the era, Walt Whitman (1819–1892). Whitman's father was an acquaintance of Thomas Paine, and this undoubtedly contributed to what his son referred to as his "democratic and heretical" heritage. The senior Whitman, a confirmed Democrat, revealed his allegiance by naming Walt's brothers Thomas Jefferson Whitman and Andrew Jackson Whitman. In his youth, Walt Whitman worked as an errand boy in New York City and occasionally came into contact with Aaron Burr, whom he remembered as a kind and considerate man who often gave him some fruit as a reward for his endeavors. Whitman also recalled seeing Hamilton's widow at numerous charitable events throughout the city. He retained something of an affection for Burr late into his life, noting in 1889 that Americans "take to such characters" who are "not pure silver or gold — quite mixed, even questionable," like Burr. Whitman's political heroes were George Washington, Thomas Jefferson, and Andrew Jackson, with the "truly sublime" Jackson his ideal statesman.[47]

Whitman's political views were influenced by the writings of William Leggett (1802–1839), an editor at the *New York Evening Post* who frequently attacked the Bank of the United States and the doctrines of John Marshall and Alexander Hamilton. Leggett viewed Hamilton's scheme to create a national bank as one of the key factors in the division of American political parties: one composed of laborers, farmers, and mechanics, the other of "the rich, the proud, the privileged."[48] Some of Whitman's earliest political commentary appeared in the *Long Island Democrat*, a newspaper noted for its praise of Jefferson and Jackson and its consistent condemnations of Hamilton and Henry Clay. Whitman served as the editor of the *Brooklyn Daily Eagle* from March 1846 until January 1848 and once observed that Jefferson was "the Columbus of our political faith" and that the Democratic party was "the party of the sainted Jefferson and Jackson." While Whitman editorialized in favor of a proposal allowing the government to acquire Hamilton's papers, he had limited regard for the man himself. Whitman believed he "sowed the seeds of some good and much evil" and observed, toward the end of his life, that "Hamilton has come down to us almost deified: but was he exempt from criticism? Hamilton was an intellectualist: cold, dispassionate, calculating: yet he was truly a patriot — performed no inconsiderable part in the consummation of the American revolt: but Hamilton was a monarchist: there was nothing in him to appeal to our Democratic instincts — to the ideals we hold so dear today."[49]

Ralph Waldo Emerson (1803–1882), having been raised in the milieu of federalism and as something of an admirer of Hamilton, differed with Whitman's reading of him. Emerson once described himself in a letter to his brother as "an indifferent Whig," although it appears that the more he focused on politics (which he viewed as a great distraction), the more he recoiled from the "thin and watery blood of Whiggism."[50] Nonetheless, when he was thirty years old he listed the *Life of Alexander Hamilton* (probably anticipating the publication of John Church Hamilton's book in 1834) as one of many books he should read and later lamented the mediocrity of the principal figures of the Jackson administration when he compared them to Hamilton and Washington. Emerson caustically observed that Jackson's secretary of the treasury Levi Woodbury "occupies the <same> position once filled by Alexander Hamilton; Jackson that of Washington . . . but does any one imagine that this equal nominal standing makes the standing of these men identical? It is perfectly well known . . . to Washington & to Jackson the gulf that is between them; and likewise to Hamilton & to Woodbury." In the midst of criticizing Daniel Webster, Emerson noted in his journal in 1851 that "heretofore, great men have led [the American People], have been better than they, as Washington, Hamilton, & Madison." He took issue in his journal with the claim that the only great men of the American past were Benjamin Franklin and Jonathan Edwards, arguing that "the prophetic authors of the Federalist, Madison & Hamilton" deserved this accolade as well.[51]

As the 1860s came to a close, the New York Times once again paid homage to Hamilton's greatness. It observed that his stature among foreign observers of the United States was impressive and cited Talleyrand's belief that he had known "three great men in my life — Napoleon, Hamilton and Fox." The Times also cited Barthold Niebuhr, who contended that "Hamilton seemed to him a true political genius, and far the greatest of the time on the other side of the sea." The editorial referred its readers to a "German work of great merit," Charles Frederick Neumann's three-volume study, The History of the United States of America, published in 1865. Neumann described Hamilton as "a creative and organizing mind — the most so of his contemporaries, and probably one of the very greatest legislators and statesmen of any time." The Times asserted that there were three kinds of public men: those prominent in their day but upon their death "no more remains of them than a man who dies of self-combustion"; those who stand high and remain high, though "their line of reputation is generally an undulating one"; and those whose "name steadily grows higher and wider for centuries after their death, and such is Hamilton's."[52]

This laudatory image of Hamilton carried over into the Gilded Age, but it would never surpass the popular levels it attained during and immediately after the Civil War. Reverence for Hamilton in scholarly circles and Republican precincts in the North persisted into the early years of the twentieth century, yet among Southern leaders of opinion, disdain for him was exceeded only by the contempt felt toward Radical Republicans. The imprimatur Hamilton received from Northern intellectuals and the region's emerging industrial leaders was duly noted by Southerners and Westerners who burned with resentment at their perceived second-class status.

And the ink at Appomattox Courthouse was barely dry before Northern Democrats joined their Southern brethren in reaffirming their opposition to

Hamiltonianism and wrapping themselves in Thomas Jefferson's mantle. These Democrats were anxious to demonstrate their fidelity to the founding fathers, which many Americans had questioned during the Civil War. Adulation for Jefferson became the vehicle by which Northern Democrats could reaffirm their Americanism and also assist the cause of healing the nation's wounds by embracing a Southern founder. Moreover, they understood that their party's return to national prominence depended in good measure on the support of the solid South.

The economic disparities of the Gilded Age presented an opportunity to restore the powerful old Van Buren–Jackson coalition of Northern mechanics and Southern farmers. As huge amounts of wealth were amassed by the robber barons, Hamilton-bashing resumed with renewed vigor. This tactic proved yet again to be an effective weapon for populists of all political persuasions. Jefferson was packaged once more as the champion of the common man while Hamilton and his plutocratic Republican heirs were exploiters of the masses. There was nothing new in this; Hamilton had been tagged as the patron saint of privilege since the earliest days of the Republic. But now a far more insidious libel was added to the indictment against him. He was depicted as the founder of a powerful national government bent on racial amalgamation. As horror stories of the Federal Reconstruction effort were widely circulated in hopes of rehabilitating Jefferson's states' rights doctrine, the possibility, always remote, that Hamilton and Jefferson might be allowed to share the same pedestal became one more irreparable casualty of the Civil War.

4

Hamilton's Gilded Age
His Renaissance

As the nation celebrated its centennial in 1876, Northerners hailed Alexander Hamilton as an indispensable figure, eclipsed only by Washington as the father of the Union. The year marked the beginning of the golden age of Hamiltonian scholarship, coinciding perhaps not surprisingly with an era frequently referred to as the Gilded Age. The nation had survived the Civil War and was experiencing unprecedented economic growth; at the same time, this wealth was being concentrated in fewer hands, and the gap between rich and poor was growing. The main political issues of the time, particularly in the South and West, were concerns that the many poor were being left behind and that America's yeoman farmers were increasingly at the mercy of powerful eastern corporate interests. A growing number of populist political figures battled with Northern Republicans over these issues. These confrontations, not surprisingly, were often couched in appeals to the founding fathers. The issues that divided the country were issues that had indeed divided the founders themselves. Nonetheless, it was a heady time for admirers of Hamilton and a low point for those few scholars who sought to promote the legacy of Thomas Jefferson. The American critic and essayist John Jay Chapman (1862–1933) captured this national mood perfectly, writing in 1882, "I should be ashamed to be connected with Jefferson. . . . Hamilton was the greatest statesman of this country, head and shoulders."[1]

A succession of Gilded Age Republicans greatly admired Hamilton, with James Garfield perhaps his foremost promoter. During his campaign for president in 1880 he delivered an address at Republican headquarters in New York City, praising the accomplishments of Hamilton. Rutherford B. Hayes (1822–1893), James G. Blaine (1830–1893), Benjamin Harrison (1833–1901), and even the Democrat Grover Cleveland (1837–1908) had, if not admiration for Hamilton, a deep interest in his life and works. Harrison judged Hamilton a "conspicuous statesman" whose "great work in the Treasury Department" ensured that "the liberties wrested by arms from the British crown were made secure." Blaine, who served as Garfield's and Harrison's secretary of state and was a repeated candidate for president, described "all Mr. Hamilton's work" as having "a remarkable value and a singular application in the developments of subsequent years," particularly his "mastery of finance which gave Mr. Hamilton his enduring fame."[2]

In general, however, Hamilton was less admired by prominent Democrats, especially those in rural areas who saw Gilded Age industrialization as a threat to their way of life. Hamilton was seen as the inspiration for America's banking and corporate elite — and it was this elite that was held responsible for unfair practices against the nation's farmers. Samuel Tilden (1814–1886), Hayes's opponent in the presidential election of 1876, saw Hamilton as the leader of a faction in the Constitutional Convention that "endeavored to give our Government an aristocratic bias"; having failed there, he went on to establish a "mammoth bank . . . to concentrate and consolidate the money power." After his party lost the presidency and both houses of Congress to the Republicans in 1880, the Democratic senator William A. Wallace (1827–1896) of Pennsylvania contended that his party would rise again, given its belief "in the rights of the masses." A source of its strength was its historic rejection of Hamiltonianism. As Wallace wrote in 1881, "Care for and perfect the government, and it will protect the liberties of the people, was the thought of Hamilton. Give intelligence and information to the people, teach them that it is their government, and their interest to preserve law and order, was the thought of Jefferson. . . . The former gave the republic alien and sedition laws, direct taxation, federal marshals, and centralized rule in 1799. The latter swept these out of existence in 1800. . . . We must choose between these two now." Wallace believed that "he who looks to paternal government, to centralization . . . looks to despotism." One of his indicators that the journey to despotism was well under way was the advent of "universal negro suffrage."[3]

Throughout the centennial year of 1876 the *New York Times* featured a number of stories and editorials recalling Hamilton's contributions to the founding. In February it cited an essay published in *Harper's Magazine* claiming that Hamilton was, next to Benjamin Franklin, "the most consummate statesman among the band of eminent men who had been active in the Revolution" and that "in intellect he was probably the most creative of our early statesmen, as in sentiment Jefferson was the most widely influential." In April the *Times* printed the text of an address by Dr. John Lord on the genius of Alexander Hamilton. Lord, a history lecturer at Dartmouth College, believed that Hamilton distinguished himself from Jefferson because he "listened to no dreams, speculation, and theory. He was a practical man." Jefferson was of another class of patriots who "were in love with the ideas of Rousseau" and other "infidels." Lord reiterated a theme popular among American historians of his day, that if Hamilton's views had completely prevailed, they "might have prevented even that trouble and agitation which led to our last war." The *Times* endorsed this view in one of its own editorials in November 1876, arguing that it was "palpably apparent to the most casual student of history that had we followed Hamilton's teachings more, and Jefferson's less, the nation would not have lost a million lives, and eleven billions of treasure in a civil war. The statesmanship of the father of Democracy and the author of the resolutions of '98 [the Kentucky and Virginia Resolutions], may be very wise, but it is too costly for a new country."

There were also some lighter discussions in the pages of the *Times* during the centennial year. In April a letter to the editor raised the specter of hundreds of lost tourists wandering through the streets of Weehawken seeking the site of the nation's most famous duel. Writing under the name Historicus, a concerned citizen asked whether nothing could be done to mark the spot where Hamilton was killed. Historicus had attempted to find the spot himself "and could only learn, 'It was somewhere down near that third telegraph pole.'" Four days later, "Weehawken" reprimanded Historicus, arguing that he should have asked the owners of the property for directions. The owners, Weehawken explained, would have been more than happy to show him the fatal spot, for "it is hardly to be expected that the laborers upon the coal docks nearby should take much interest in, or know much about the matter."[4]

While scholars and Republican politicians acclaimed Hamilton during the Gilded Age, his standing among the citizenry was sometimes difficult to gauge.

Then and now, as Weehawken had implied, it is safe to assume a fairly high level of indifference from most citizens. The *Times* believed that even his hometown denied him the respect due from the public. The newspaper viewed the absence of a statue in New York City to be particularly galling, proclaiming that if "the citizens of this Metropolis do not erect a monumental statue worthy [of] the name and fame of this great man it will be because they do not read aright their own history." On another occasion the *Times* noted ironically that few citizens who walked along Broadway were aware that Hamilton was buried in Trinity churchyard — despite the appraisal, engraved on his tomb, that he would be remembered "long after this marble shall have mouldered into dust." The paper recounted an incident involving a journalist who visited the gravesite and was asked by a passerby, "Whose grave is that?" The journalist replied, "Alexander Hamilton," and the passerby asked, "Who's Hamilton?" When the journalist wondered, "Don't you know who Alexander Hamilton was?" he was told, "Oh, yes, to be sure. He was one of those Tammany thieves."[5]

In 1880 the *Times* once again observed dejectedly that a "certain element of popular appreciation has always been lacking in the estimate of... [Hamilton's] character and services." It was with great relief that the paper could report the unveiling of a statue to him in November 1880, making the ceremony its lead story for the day, including excerpts from many of the ceremonial speeches and remarking on the presence of notable dignitaries, including John C. Hamilton, New York's mayor Edward Cooper, former president Ulysses Grant, and former Massachusetts governor Alexander Bullock.[6]

The centennial year witnessed the release of one of the most laudatory books ever published about Hamilton. John Torrey Morse's *Life of Alexander Hamilton* was harshly critical of Jefferson, but its portrayal of Hamilton approached hagiography. Morse's *Life* was generally well received and became something of a standard text on its subject, though some critics, such as the *Nation*, viewed it as a "frank panegyric" marked by an indecorous manner.[7] Morse (1840–1937) viewed Jefferson as the inspiration for the secessionist doctrines of John C. Calhoun and Jefferson Davis; Hamilton championed Union and sound foreign and economic policies. According to Morse, the mourning produced by Hamilton's death was comparable to that of Lincoln's, and he cited favorably Chancellor James Kent's claim that if Hamilton had lived, "he would have rivaled Socrates or Bacon." Morse contended that

Hamilton, though partly responsible for the rift between himself and Jefferson, was the victim of a broad-based assault on his character. Jefferson behaved "most unhandsomely by Hamilton in the way of gratuitous calumny." The preferred technique of this "untrustworthy moralist" was the "subtle *letter poison*," designed to "inculcate a strong prejudice and to create a sort of flavor of dishonesty." According to Morse's account, even Hamilton's affair with Mrs. Reynolds was in some way her fault, as Hamilton was unfortunate enough "to be led into an intrigue" with a woman of "some personal attractions" but little education and "no generous traits to be set off against her want of chastity." The Harvard-educated Morse had little regard for Jeffersonian and Jacksonian politicians and clearly envisioned his writings as part of a political campaign for the hearts and minds of his countrymen: in a letter to his cousin, Henry Cabot Lodge (1850–1924), Morse abandoned any pretense of objectivity, writing in 1881, "Let the Jeffersonians and the Jacksonians beware! I will poison the popular mind!!"[8]

As the editor of the popular and influential *American Statesmen* series, published from 1882 to 1900, Morse had a penchant for selecting Ivy League–educated New Englanders to write for him. In February 1881, he invited his cousin to contribute, and Lodge responded with *Alexander Hamilton* (1882). Lodge had been a student of Henry Adams at Harvard, and later, at the *North American Review,* he served as an assistant editor to his former teacher. While at the *Review* Lodge wrote an essay on Hamilton and joined with Adams in publishing a lengthy article on the German historian Hermann Von Holst. The essay on Hamilton published in the *Review* was actually a review of Morse's biography, which Lodge criticized for its tendency "to consider Hamilton as always in the right" and for its "fatal tone of the lawyer pleading for the criminal" when dealing with indefensible aspects of Hamilton's career.[9]

Despite Lodge's continual association with members of the Adams family who were hostile to Hamilton (Henry's brother Brooks once told Lodge he was studying Hamilton's financial policies "for the pleasure of finding fault with it"), his admiration for the founder was "profound and growing."[10] The tone of Lodge's *Alexander Hamilton* was set in Morse's preface, when he claimed that "Hamilton's fame indicates the unformulated but full appreciation of the unquestionable historic fact that he was the real maker of the government of the United States." Although Lodge argued that the democratic principles of Jefferson and the nationalist principles of Hamilton had together dominated the history of the United States, he judged nonetheless that "the great Federalist has the advantage. The democratic system of Jefferson is administered in the form and on the principles of Hamilton; and while the former went with the current and fell in with the dominant forces of the time, Hamilton established his now accepted principles, and carried his program to completion in the face of relentless opposition, and against the mistaken wishes of a large part of the people."[11] Lodge's assessment was significantly more balanced than Morse's rapturous treatment of Hamilton. He treated Jefferson far more gently than had Morse and was willing to acknowledge certain character defects in Hamilton, including the "strength of his passions, which sometimes overmastered his reason" and his inability to manage men, "wherein his great rival Jefferson stood supreme." Rejecting wholly Morse's account of Hamilton's affair, Lodge declared simply that it was Hamilton's "uncurbed passion" that led him into a "low intrigue with a worthless woman." And Lodge further questioned Chancellor Kent's claim that had Hamilton lived longer he would have rivaled Socrates or Bacon, observing that "his work was done" at the time of the duel. Nevertheless, he argued that Hamilton was that rare statesman who represented "great ideas," and embodied the principle of "nationality," which was "the very breath of his public life." At a time when "American nationality meant nothing, he grasped the great conception in all its fullness, and gave all he had of will and intellect to make its realization possible. He and Washington alone perceived the destiny which was in store for the republic."[12]

Lodge's interest in Hamilton did not end with the publication of *Alexander Hamilton;* he went on to edit nine volumes of *The Works of Alexander Hamilton,* published in 1885 and 1886 and reissued in 1904.[13] In his preface to *The Works,* he reiterated the Gilded Age theme that Hamilton championed nationalism while Jefferson promoted the idea that the Union "was a confederacy" and that the conflict between those "opposing forces . . . culminated in the Civil War." By 1907 Senator Lodge boasted that his *Alexander Hamilton* had sold thirty-five thousand copies, and it continued to sell for fifty years after it was published. Throughout his life, his devotion to Hamilton never wavered. Shortly before his death he wrote that Hamilton was "the greatest constructive mind in all our history and I should come pretty near saying . . . in the history of modern statesmen in any country."[14]

Lodge's high regard for Hamilton probably did not please his mentor Henry Adams (1838–1918), who had written him in 1876 that "you do not of course expect me to acquiesce entirely in your view of A.H. . . . I dislike Hamilton because I always feel the adventurer in him. The very cause of your admiration is the cause of my distrust; he was equally ready to support a system he utterly disbelieved in as one that he liked. From the first to the last words he wrote, I read always the same Napoleonic kind of adventuredom. . . . Future political crises all through Hamilton's life were always in his mind about to make him commander-in-chief."[15] One of the more influential authors of the Gilded Age, Henry Adams had inherited his family's long-standing animus toward the immigrant upstart from Nevis. The writings of this great-grandson and grandson of a president influenced dramatically twentieth-century American perceptions of Hamilton. When Lodge's *Alexander Hamilton* was published, Adams wrote the author, "Much as I want to read your Hamilton, the subject repels me more than my regard for you attracts." When John Hay, President Lincoln's former assistant, urged Adams to mute his anti-Hamilton bias in his writings, Adams agreed but explained that "to me the man is noxious . . . because he combined all the elements of a Scottish prig in a nasty form." Adams did praise Hamilton in *The Life of Albert Gallatin* for the "vigor and capacity" of his mind and for his "stupendous" legislative and administrative accomplishments during the Washington presidency. But he also argued that the philosophical differences between Hamilton and Jefferson could not be easily reconciled: "The two brilliant men who led the two great divisions of national thought . . . were in deadly earnest, and no compromise between them ever was or ever will be possible. Mr. Jefferson meant that the American system should be a democracy. . . . Mr. Hamilton considered democracy a fatal curse, and meant to stop its progress."[16] The fundamental incompatibility between Jefferson's and Hamilton's visions for America, and Adams's perception of a deeply anti-democratic streak in the latter, was at bottom the root of his dislike of Hamilton. He once distinguished himself from Henry Cabot Lodge by claiming that his principles, contrary to Lodge's, gravitated toward "democracy and radicalism."[17]

It was his zeal to demonstrate Hamilton's alleged hostility to the common man that led Adams to engage in an act of academic dishonesty that has reverberated through scholarly circles to this day. In his classic *History of the*

United States of America During the First Administration of Thomas Jefferson
(1889), Adams cited a quote from Hamilton that has taken on a life of its own
but that should never have been included in a serious work of scholarship.
According to Adams, Hamilton was attending a dinner in New York and
in response to some expressions of support for democracy struck his hand
sharply on the table and exclaimed, "Your people, sir, — your people is a great
beast!" Adams again referred to the quote when he discussed the defection
of the Livingston family in New York from the Federalist ranks to "the mob
of free-thinking democrats, the 'great beast' of Alexander Hamilton."

As William Ander Smith has noted, Adams apparently found the quote in
the *Memoir of Theophilus Parsons* (1859), written by Theophilus Parsons Jr.
forty-six years after his father's death. The senior Parsons was a prominent
Massachusetts Federalist who was appointed U.S. attorney general by John
Adams and served as the chief justice of the Massachusetts Supreme Court.
The junior Parsons had crossed paths with Henry Adams at Harvard on many
occasions, and at one point they were colleagues on the faculty. It is possible
that this is where Adams first encountered the tale of the great beast. Nonetheless, the manner in which the story was brought to Adams's attention is
irrelevant. What is of importance is that the story was told to Parsons senior
by "a friend, to whom it was related by one who was a guest at the table." As
Smith observes, "A attended the dinner, told B, who reported the incident to
the elder Parsons. More than sixty years later the younger Parsons put the
story in print. . . . The fourth hand source is obviously shaky." Perhaps conscious of his scholarly sleight of hand, in neither instance where he mentioned
the great beast quote did Adams provide a reference for it; nonetheless, this
quote has been cited countless times by politicians, scholars, and journalists
who consider Hamilton an anomalous founder of limited significance, or at
worst, an un-American reactionary.[18]

Though Henry Adams was correct to observe that Hamilton was not a
proponent of direct democracy, it should be noted that most of the founders
had similar misgivings about the wisdom and stability of the masses. A striking example of this attitude can be found in Thomas Jefferson's description
of the people at the time of the French Revolution, whom he referred to as "a
machine not quite so blind as balls and bombs, but blind to a certain degree."
Jefferson also proposed an educational system for Virginia that would single
out the best students for advancement through a process of elimination while

the "residue" were "dismissed." In a harshly worded statement that exceeded anything ever uttered by Hamilton, Jefferson explained that "by this means twenty of the best geniusses [sic] will be raked from the rubbish annually."[19] Nonetheless, the charge that Hamilton personified and promulgated to a greater extent than any other founder an aristocratic contempt for the common man fundamentally incompatible with a democratic republic was one that, for years, stood unchallenged in the American mind. And it was around this alleged view that Hamilton's opponents and detractors gathered most consistently, both then and now.

And Henry Adams was not alone in the late nineteenth century in questioning Hamilton's fidelity to democracy. Other Gilded Age dissenters who harbored certain misgivings about his commitment to the common man included the popular historian John Fiske (1842–1901), William Graham Sumner (1840–1910), George Bancroft (1800–1891), and James Schouler (1839–1920). While they praised certain aspects of Hamilton's character and career, they were nonetheless uniform in their disapproval of his alleged antipathy toward the people. Fiske expressed concern over Hamilton's lack of "faith in democratic government" in *The Critical Period of American History, 1783–1789*. It was this failing that rendered Jefferson superior to Hamilton, he contended, for the latter did not possess the former's "serene and patient faith in the slow progressiveness of average humanity." Nonetheless, Fiske found Hamilton to be a "convincing orator and brilliant writer" and "the most precocious" young man of his day, with the possible exception of William Pitt. Hamilton's greatness lay in the fact that he vigorously supported the Constitution, despite his reservations, and became "its most brilliant advocate." He accomplished this because "he was supremely endowed with the faculty of imagining, with all the circumstantial minuteness of concrete reality, political situations different from those directly before him." Fiske believed that, despite his death at a young age, Hamilton's rare genius left a deep mark on American history.[20]

Sumner held the first chair in political and social science created at Yale and authored, among many other texts, *Alexander Hamilton*. Hamilton became "one of the leading heroes" of the founding by restoring order and financial stability in America in the wake of the turbulence set loose by the Revolution. Sumner claimed, however, that Hamilton was primarily responsible for the bitter opposition he encountered from his Virginia rivals, for he was "aggressive and arrogant; and it may well be believed that his manner to a man like Jefferson must have been very offensive to the latter." Conceding that the Jeffersonians had indeed abused Hamilton, Sumner cautioned that a biographer needed to guard against overreacting to this, for Hamilton's methods intentionally polarized the nation and were in fact calculated "to raise against himself very bitter opposition. He forced every issue in its most direct form." Nor did he inspire confidence among the people; instead, he aroused a "vague sense of alienation and distrust." Sumner concluded that Andrew Jackson was instinctively superior to Hamilton as a political philosopher for America because of his belief in limited government, and the trust in the people presupposed by such a view.[21]

George Bancroft was a rarity for a Harvard-educated Brahmin in that he was active in Democratic party politics. He served as James K. Polk's secretary of the navy and ambassador to Great Britain and as Andrew Johnson's ambassador to Prussia. A friend of Martin Van Buren, he shared some of the latter's disdain for the Bank of the United States and for Alexander Hamilton. In contrast to Henry Adams, however, Bancroft sought to soften Hamilton's image, to portray him as a centrist and to demonstrate that the good Jefferson/ bad Hamilton distinction did not necessarily hold true. Despite his partisan loyalties (one historian dismissed his work because "every volume voted for Andrew Jackson"), Bancroft described Hamilton as a "gifted young man," whose "integrity of conduct, diligence, and study" helped him influence the course of American history.[22] Bancroft tended to resort to Fourth of July sermonizing in his writing, as his description of Hamilton and Madison's collaboration on *The Federalist* reveals. These men cherished their "intimate and affectionate relations," and though "differing in temperament" they were "one in purpose and in action. To the day of their death they both were loyally devoted to the cause of union." In general, Bancroft attempted to minimize differences among the founders and to portray them in a positive light. He was not, however, without reservations about Hamilton. In 1883 he coauthored an account of Hamilton's relationship with Washington that was very critical of the former's temperament, in which he suggested that his "petulant humor" often led him to pass "beyond the bounds of the respect" that was due to the commander in chief. And Bancroft observed that Hamilton had a tendency to lean toward "authority" and had "something of a mean opinion of his fellow-men" that "cut him off from the sympathy of the masses."[23]

Harvard-educated James Schouler admired the "venerable" Bancroft's work and shared some of his concern about Hamilton's undemocratic beliefs. In his seven-volume *History of the United States of America*, and in *Alexander Hamilton*, Schouler praised him for his substantial role in launching the nation, particularly for "freeing our public credit from its prison-house and teaching it to soar." But Schouler also believed that Hamilton advocated a hereditary monarchy and viewed mankind as "vicious, except for a few choice spirits." There was something "alien" and "tropical" about Hamilton that conveyed the impression "by no means mistaken, that he was half-Briton still, divided in allegiance." His affinity for all things military began as a boy and the "fatalism of armed dictator and arbiter pervaded his vision to the end of life." More than simply a closet aristocrat, Hamilton chose as friends those "of the better sort," and over time he began more and more to disdain "the populace." Unlike the other founding fathers, Schouler contended, Hamilton's aversion to democracy was "radical and inveterate."[24]

Despite these discordant notes, for many Gilded Age scholars Hamilton remained a venerated figure. The publication of John Bach McMaster's *History of the People of the United States, From the Revolution to the Civil War* typified the historical writing of the era. McMaster (1852–1932) saw Hamilton as "by far the most brilliant and versatile" of the founders, a man who "was at once a skilful officer, a brilliant pamphleteer, an active political leader, an impressive debater, a wise statesman, an able financier, a political economist of rare sagacity. . . . Since the time of William of Orange the world had rarely seen an instance of so mature a mind in so young a lad."[25]

McMaster's praise of Hamilton was echoed by the historian Hermann Von Holst (1841–1904), a German born in Russia who later became chairman of the History Department at the University of Chicago. In *The Constitutional and Political History of the United States*, Von Holst described Hamilton as a "statesman of the first rank" and a "genius." Inverting the usual allegations, Von Holst believed of Jefferson that "ambition was the sovereign trait of his character. He was always ready to sacrifice much of his favorite theories to his feverish thirst for power and distinction." A fervent nationalist, Von Holst portrayed Hamilton as the guiding hand in the campaign to create a strong Union. Hamilton's statesmanship was favorably contrasted with those advocates of states' rights, or "particularists," whose "excited imaginations" conjured up images of a despotic national government.[26]

Von Holst was to some extent another foreign admirer of Hamilton. John Franklin Jameson (1859–1937), one of the founding fathers of the American historical profession, argued that there were "special reason[s]" why foreigners, particularly European statesmen, admired Hamilton more than his own countrymen. As he explained, "Hamilton was in fact essentially a European statesman" who belonged to a school of thought that would have a nation "ruled by the person of the weightiest brain." Jameson's observations on Hamilton were made in a review of the English author James Bryce's *American Commonwealth*. Bryce (1838–1922) described Hamilton as "this brilliant figure . . . the most interesting in the earlier history of the Republic . . . he stands in the front rank of a generation never surpassed in history" but whose countrymen "seem to have never, either in his lifetime or afterwards, duly recognized his splendid gifts." Bryce's judgment was strikingly similar to that of the noted British author and editor of the *Economist* Walter Bagehot (1826–1877), who stated in 1861 that Hamilton was "the greatest political philosopher" among American statesman.[27] Jameson's reaction to Bryce, and to the prevailing European admiration for Hamilton, echoed the old Jefferson-Jackson nativist critique of him and demonstrated that even at the peak of his popularity in the American mind the old slur that Hamilton and Hamiltonianism were un-American was alive and well.

Hamilton's Americanism was never an issue in solid Republican strongholds in the northeastern United States, however. In these financial and industrial centers, thriving Hamilton clubs were symbols of the Hamiltonian renaissance that characterized the Gilded Age. Organized to keep his memory alive, the clubs sponsored addresses from prominent speakers discussing such issues as the latest theories in the new science of business management. The New York and Chicago clubs were the most active, holding annual events, including commemorations of his birth; and the Chicago club sponsored debates for college students on the relative merits of Jefferson versus Hamilton or on other topics related to the founding. The club members' affection for Republican politicians was transparent: the Chicago club celebrated the Republican capture of Congress in the off-year elections of 1894 by presenting Thomas B. Reed (1839–1902), newly reinstalled as the Speaker of the House, with a gavel gilded with bands of gold and silver in gratitude for his efforts on behalf of sound money. Governor Theodore Roosevelt of New York addressed the Chicago club in a speech, "The Strenuous Life," in April 1899, and when he became president, he considered the club to be of such importance that he strongly urged Vice President Charles Fairbanks to speak to the organization in 1906 in order to "strik[e] the key for the Republican cause in Illinois and around the Mississippi Valley generally." Roosevelt remained a lifelong friend of the Chicago chapter, and when he addressed the club in 1910 he thanked its members for being "practically the first organization to be so unwise as to formulate a desire to have me made President."[28]

The Brooklyn, New York, chapter was also quite a force in its community. Founded in 1882, it was as an offshoot of the Hamilton Literary Society created in 1830 to support libraries and the arts. The president of Hamilton College, Melancthon Woolsey Stryker, addressed the organization on 11 January 1895, the 138th anniversary (perhaps) of Hamilton's birth, and garnered one of his best applause lines of the evening when he proclaimed, "I, too, am a Federalist." Stryker could not resist taking a swipe at Hamilton's main adversary, contending that if "that tortuous and temporizing reactionary" had not been in Paris during the Constitutional Convention he might have turned the country "away from nationality." Booker T. Washington (1856–1915) and Woodrow Wilson (1856–1924) addressed the club at the next birthday celebration in 1896. Washington appears to have been rather a favorite speaker on the Hamilton club circuit, addressing the Chicago chapter at another point in his life. Wilson spent part of his last day campaigning for president in 1912 at a dinner in his honor at the Hamilton club in Paterson, New Jersey, the city Hamilton hoped would serve as a manufacturing showplace of the future.[29]

The Chicago and Brooklyn clubs threw their active support behind an effort to build a national memorial to Hamilton in Washington, D.C. Supreme Court Justice John M. Harlan (1833–1911) was selected as president of the Alexander Hamilton Memorial Association, and its proposal for a one hundred thousand dollar monument was endorsed by President Theodore Roosevelt. The association had an odd ally, Senator William E. Borah of Idaho (1865–1940), a maverick Republican and an unabashed isolationist who was somewhat inclined toward populism and who was described by one of his biographers as "a latter day Jeffersonian." Borah spoke to the association in 1910 and urged that Hamilton's "wide range and singular brilliancy" of intellect and his "complete mastery of the great problems of that extraordinary era" entitled him to a monument. Hamilton's rise from the status of an "orphan boy" to a secure place "among a race of intellectual giants" was so impressive that he "in some ways divides the admiration of mankind with the Father of Our Country." Borah was at a loss to explain why no such monument existed "in this statue-crowded city, nor in the lonesome corridors of yonder Capitol." Perhaps Hamilton's reluctance to flatter the people was partly responsible, or, as Borah implied, his failure to honor his marital vows might have contributed to this neglect. Whatever the reason, Borah's generation needed to rectify this disgrace.[30] Some element of redress was finally attained in May 1923 when a Hamilton statue was erected outside the Treasury building. The days were numbered, however, for the Hamilton clubs: the Brooklyn club expired at the height of the New Deal in 1936, when the South Brooklyn Savings Bank completed foreclosure proceedings against the moribund organization's headquarters; and the Chicago club went bankrupt during the Great Depression. As of this writing the clubs are no longer in existence.[31]

While revered in the North, Hamilton remained a controversial figure in the South and in the West (William Borah excepted), as could be seen in the rhetoric of leaders of the Populist party. This agrarian-based party arose in 1892 to do battle with what were seen as Gilded Age excesses inspired by wealthy owners of banks and large corporations. As one of their leaders, Mary Elizabeth Lease (1853–1933) of Kansas put it, "Wall Street owns the country. . . . It is no longer a government of the people, by the people and for the people, but a government of Wall Street, by Wall Street, and for Wall Street. The great common people of this country are slaves."[32] Some Populists, such as James (Cyclone) Davis (1853–1940), argued that the source for this dismal state of affairs could be traced — not surprisingly — to the principles and practices of Alexander Hamilton. A congressman from Texas, Davis railed against Hamilton as he quoted from *The Works of Jefferson*. The issues at stake in the 1890s were the same as those that had confronted Jefferson a century earlier, the Cyclone argued, for Hamilton held that "the people were unsafe . . . they should have as little to do with government as possible. . . . The wealthy classes should rule the masses . . . an aristocracy should hold the offices and rule the people."[33]

The Populist leader in Georgia, Tom Watson (1856–1922), published a brief account of American history in 1892 that was used as a campaign document during that election year. Watson believed Hamilton and the Federalists supported a "strong centralized Govt." as a tool for "a moneyed aristocracy sup-

ported by special privilege." He referred to this unholy alliance as the System
and spoke glowingly of the attempts by Jefferson and Jackson to oppose it: of
Jackson he had once lamented, "Oh, for an hour of that stern old warrior
before whose . . . fiery wrath the combined money-kings bit the dust!"[34] In
Watson's eyes, the Republican party of 1892 was the party of "Boodlers,
Monopolists, Gamblers, Gigantic Corporations, Bondholders, Bankers,"
which — according to him — was perfectly in keeping with a party openly identified with Alexander Hamilton. In a speech delivered in 1904 at New York
City's Cooper Union, Watson struck at Hamilton in his hometown, lambast-
ing a man who was "devoted . . . to the English model" and had "no confidence in the people, no love for the people, no sympathy with the people."
Hamilton's government would enlist the wealthy as partners and give to them
alone both the "control of its laws" and the "command of its policies."[35]
Watson authored *The Life and Times of Thomas Jefferson* (warmly dedicated
to William Randolph Hearst for his "fearless and consistent interest in the
cause of the oppressed") to combat the profederalist, pro–New England slant
he detected in the historical writing of his era. These historians and their fellow travelers in the political world were merely "modern outcroppings of the
old Federalist vein." Watson's Hamilton "had no faith in the people, was in
no sense a man of the people," and sought to "run the government" in favor
of the rich. Watson further opined that "the gist of the thing was to create
the privileged class . . . create a national bank, whereby a few capitalists should
enjoy the enormous sovereign power of controlling the currency of the nation. Let these things be done, and out of these germs would grow a modern
feudalism. . . . 'The people! Why, the people is a great beast!' cried Hamilton,
meaning, of course, all of the human race who had not risen above the common herd. Greater scorn for the common herd few mortals have had than
Alexander Hamilton."[36] It is hard to imagine Henry Adams and Tom Watson
holding similar opinions on any subject, but in their distrust of Alexander
Hamilton the two men found common ground.

In the election of 1892 the Populist presidential candidate received over
1 million votes, and their candidates won many governorships and elected
several congressmen and state legislators. Four years later, the Populists rallied around William Jennings Bryan (1860–1925), the Democratic party's
nominee for president, as their presidential nominee as well. Bryan and the
Populists directed their ire against protective tariffs they believed inordinately

burdened the South and the West for the benefit of the industrialized North. But it was the issue of gold versus silver that particularly ignited Populist and Democratic party support for Bryan. He captured the nomination of both parties in 1896 by attacking the policies of President Grover Cleveland and the conservative Democrats, who defended the hard money gold standard (with Republican support) against Southern and Western demands for free silver to combat depressed farm prices, unemployment, and depression.[37] As one might expect, William Jennings Bryan revered Hamilton's great adversary from Virginia. He once explained that Thomas Jefferson was "the greatest constructive statesman democracy has produced during all the world's history." Bryan declared that — next to the Bible — he was most influenced by Jefferson's principles and found, in particular, Jefferson's states' rights doctrine to be "the surest bulwark against anti-republican tendencies" harbored by those who "distrust the people." The problem with Hamilton was that he "doubted the capacity of the people for self government, and his distrust of the masses lured him to the fatal field where he died at the hand of Aaron Burr." Certain Americans were hostile to the people even in Bryan's own time, including "many prominent men who regard Hamilton as the greatest of the political thinkers." But while the modern Republican party was Hamiltonian, this had not always been the case, he maintained: its platform in 1856 distanced itself from Hamilton by appealing to those in favor of restoring the government to the principles of Washington and Jefferson.

In an essay written for the *North American Review* in June 1899, Bryan expressed relief that the Gilded Age love affair with Hamilton appeared to be drawing to an end and proclaimed that "the renaissance of Jeffersonian principles is at hand." Later in his career, he clung to the belief that "the trend is toward democracy and away from the aristocratic ideas of Alexander Hamilton"[38] and expressed his great hope that history would judge him to be a man who "did what he could to make the government what Jefferson desired it to be."[39]

Politicians of all persuasions invoked Hamilton's name throughout the political struggles of the 1880s and 1890s. His imprimatur was sought by advocates with differing positions on trade, tariffs, the gold standard, and sundry other causes. The progressive senator Robert M. La Follette (1855–1925) noted the influence of Hamilton's thought on the Republicans during the great tariff debates of the era, particularly his impact on stand-pat Republicans like Henry Cabot Lodge, who believed it "more important to keep up the profits of the combined manufacturers." Representative Lodge was criticized on the floor of the House in 1888 for praising Hamilton's position on protective tariffs in his biography and then appearing to advocate a contrary position as a member of Congress. The Prominent Republican senator George F. Hoar (1826–1904) of Massachusetts prepared for his role in one of the gold versus free silver debates by studying Hamilton's works and came to the conclusion that he was "the ablest practical financier and economist that ever lived, certainly without a rival in this country." Hoar urged his fellow Republicans to adhere to the principles found in "the powerful authority of Hamilton," and Senator James G. Blaine quoted him repeatedly to justify his position that bimetallism was the path to follow.[40] The Democratic congressman Samuel S. Cox (1824–1889) criticized the Republicans and James G. Blaine, their presidential nominee in 1884, arguing that "Hamilton is the framework of that [party's] platform." The Democrats opposed the "fostering of one branch of industry to the detriment of another," and their platform of "hostility to monopoly" was "inherited from the days of Jefferson." Hamilton's system had failed miserably: and, wondered Cox, could Hamilton only have seen its effects in the 1880s, "would he not abandon his worship of the old Federal fetich [sic]?" Even Hamilton's involvement in personal scandal was recalled when the Republican senator Carl Schurz (1829–1906) of Missouri criticized the scandal-tarred James G. Blaine for not following Hamilton's practice of confessing to private indiscretions in order to prove the "stainlessness of his official character."[41]

During the Gilded Age no one championed Hamilton's legacy more assertively than two prominent New York political figures, William Maxwell Evarts (1818–1901) and Chauncey Depew (1834–1928). Grandson of the founder Roger Sherman, Evarts served as the attorney general of the United States, secretary of state, and senator from New York and played a key role in winning an acquittal for President Andrew Johnson during his impeachment trial in 1868. Evarts contended that Hamilton was a statesman who lent his "mastery of great affairs" and political genius to the "formation and adoption of the Constitution" and carried the new government "over the breakers of public debt and public poverty into security and prosperity." His efforts in this "mighty task" were "indispensable."[42]

Chauncey Depew was the former president of the New York Central Railroad and a lobbyist and lawyer for the Vanderbilts. Depew's devotion to the

Constitution was equaled only by his esteem for Hamilton. He viewed with horror the demands for reform coming from progressive elements in the American polity, in particular the campaign for an amendment to the Constitution allowing for direct election of U.S. senators; his efforts in the Senate delayed for ten years the passage of what became the Seventeenth Amendment.[43] Depew believed he was following Hamilton's lead: Hamilton believed "in providing every safeguard against hasty action by the people," and on this basis rejected direct election of senators. Though Depew admired Hamilton for his nationalism, perhaps even more important, he revered him for his willingness to ignore public pressure. Hamilton marshaled his "exhaustless resources to consolidate a nation" and had a clear vision of its becoming a great empire that would "command the respect of the world."[44] But just as significantly, "Popular passion never swayed his judgement; personal ambition or the applause of the hour never moved or deterred him." As a young man he demonstrated his disdain for popular excess when he dissuaded an angry mob from attacking the Tory president of King's College, the first of many instances, according to Depew, when Hamilton rallied to the "defense of property and the majesty of the law."

Depew's celebration of political leadership resistant to popular pressure appeared to many people, however, as merely a quaint holdover from bygone days and unworthy of the democratized politics of primaries and pollsters that came to dominate twentieth-century American politics. Increasing numbers of Americans were inclined to interpret both their past and their present as a struggle for power between rich and poor, and they found little to admire in Depew's fidelity to founding principles. Depew and his Federalist hero were seen as agents of the upper class who manipulated the Constitution for purposes of protecting their privileged status. Although the Hamiltonian glow from the Gilded Age survived for a brief period into the twentieth century, the concerns raised by Henry Adams and the Populists were embraced by progressive historians and political scientists whose writings influenced the new century's political leadership. Charles Beard, Vernon Parrington, Claude Bowers, and William E. Dodd absorbed the undercurrents circulating in the 1890s and incorporated these themes into their later works. They were members of a faith that, as William Ander Smith observed, "attacked trusts, plutocracy, and elitism with heroes and villains from the past."[45] This offensive did not bode well for Hamilton's reputation in the twentieth century.

The Twilight of Hamiltonianism
1901–1928

5

At the beginning of the new century, influential Americans in government, industry, and academia tended to embrace Hamiltonian principles and practices. Inclined to view industrialization and the Republican party as divinely inspired, they continued to celebrate Hamilton. This climate soon changed, however, as the progressive critique of the system and those who created it emerged as the dominant strain in American political thought. But for the time being, in those early years of the twentieth century, Hamilton could do no wrong.

There were even indications that a certain admiration for Hamilton — or, perhaps, a titillation with historical gossip — had trickled down to the great beast, if one considered the popular success of Gertrude Atherton's *The Conqueror, Being the True and Romantic Story of Alexander Hamilton*. Atherton's book sold hundreds of thousands of copies and was in print for decades, and its influence was so great that the U.S. ambassador to the Court of St. James's claimed in 1904 that it had been partly responsible for a "rehabilitation of [Hamilton's] fame," both in Britain and the United States. A prolific if not necessarily great writer, Atherton (1857–1948) published her fictionalized biography of Hamilton in part because her grandfather admired him "more than any man in American history" and "planted the long germinating seed of *The Conqueror*." Her goal was "to write a life that would stand a chance of being read . . . to give Hamilton back to the American people." Atherton traveled to St. Kitts and Nevis and conducted important research on Hamilton's mysterious Caribbean roots, becoming "almost ill" when informed that he was "colored." She was later greatly relieved to discover, however, that he descended from "people of consequence." She allowed her flair for the dramatic to get the best of her when she later hinted that George Washington may have been Hamilton's father — the consequence of a visit the young Virginian made to Barbados in the 1750s.[1]

Not surprisingly, perhaps, Atherton was merciless in her assessment of Thomas Jefferson, finding fault not only with his politics but even with his grooming: his disheveled appearance, she was certain, "set [George] Washington's teeth on edge." Atherton revealed that Jefferson soon came to despise the young upstart Hamilton for repeatedly trumping him in their contest for the president's ear, producing in Jefferson a "hat[red] of the most remorseless quality." But as he lacked the mettle to confront Hamilton openly, he did so covertly through surrogates such as Philip Freneau. Jefferson, along with James Madison and James Monroe, was part of the "Virginian junta" that "harangued and intrigued against Hamilton for years" — but who nevertheless went on to govern as Hamiltonian presidents. The fissure between the two men reached its nadir in the debate over America's response to the French Revolution, which saw Jefferson "hot with rank Democracy." In addition to his devotion to egalitarianism, part of the explanation for his affection for the French Revolution was attributable to the "plebeianism" of his father, revealed in the son's "ungainly shell, in the indifference to personal cleanliness, and in the mongrel spirit which drove him to acts of physical cowardice for which his apologists blush." Atherton's quirky obsession with appearance and lineage permeates the book, alongside her ringing endorsement of Hamilton as the father of American imperialism, a positive attribute in the eyes of someone convinced of the superiority of Anglo-American civilization.[2]

Even though Atherton dedicated her book to Allan McLane Hamilton (1848–1919), Alexander Hamilton's grandson, he made no mention of it in his *Intimate Life of Alexander Hamilton*. Allan's father was Philip Hamilton, the founder's youngest son (named after an older brother killed in a duel), and his mother was the daughter of a member of Andrew Jackson's cabinet. Allan Hamilton was a prominent turn-of-the-century neurologist who testified in over one hundred trials where the sanity of a defendant was at issue. Although *The Intimate Life* was an attempt to portray "the familiar side of [Hamilton's] life," some of the book was devoted to defending his grandfather's public record from accusations that he was an aristocrat. The accusation was credible, he maintained, only to the extent that Hamilton had contempt for the "low or coarse" and was determined to defy mob rule — though he did respect "good blood and its belongings." His grandfather's despair toward the end of his life that the Constitution was a "frail and worthless fabric" was prompted by the "disorderly reign of Jefferson and his followers." But Hamilton's prophetic hope that Americans would renew their devotion to the document was realized as a result of the Civil War. The Constitution was Hamilton's "best monument," and he deserved "most of the credit for its preparation and adoption." Jefferson and Philip Freneau were, properly, long gone and forgotten, as competent historians were finally "according [Hamilton] the tardy acknowledgement of what he has done for the United States and for the World."[3]

One prominent American who would not have objected to this appraisal was Theodore Roosevelt (1858–1919), probably the most zealous admirer of Alexander Hamilton ever to inhabit the White House. TR believed that he was "the most brilliant American statesman who ever lived, possessing the loftiest and keenest intellect of his time." Hamilton was a man of "singularly noble and lofty character" and "brilliant audacity and genius," which equipped him for the "giant tasks of constructive statesmanship with which he successfully grappled." Roosevelt's discussion of Hamilton and his opponents in his book New York probably reflected his view of the political divisions in his own time between urban eastern Republicans and rural Democrats. Roosevelt claimed that Hamilton's effort to ratify the Constitution in New York State was truly heroic, for he faced a popular governor, George Clinton, who knew how to capitalize on the "cold, suspicious temper of small country freeholders" with their "narrow" jealousies. Hamilton had the advantage of being supported by "townsmen" who were "quicker witted, and politically more far-sighted and less narrow-minded than the average country folk of that day."[4]

When TR became a member of the New York legislature in 1882, an Upstate Republican, William O'Neill, became a close friend and political ally, partly because, as Roosevelt later observed, O'Neill had "admired Alexander Hamilton as much as I did." In debates during TR's Albany years, the names of Hamilton and Jefferson were occasionally mentioned. One Tammany Hall politician, James Haggerty, attacked reformers such as Roosevelt as aristocratic Hamiltonians who distrusted the people. Roosevelt later condemned Haggerty for recurring to Jefferson for advice on dealing with contemporary issues, reminding him in no uncertain terms that the Virginian was "the strongest opponent of the adoption of the Constitution. . . . We got our Constitution, not because of, but in spite of Jefferson and his followers."[5]

On the recommendation of his friend Henry Cabot Lodge, Roosevelt wrote two volumes for John Morse's *American Statesmen* series. In 1887 he completed *Governeur Morris* and later told Morris's great-grandson that Morris and Hamilton "embodied what was best in the Federalist Party. . . . They both of them had in them the touch of the heroic, the touch of the purple, the touch of the gallant." Both Roosevelt and Lodge adored Hamilton, and on a trip to London in 1886 Roosevelt could not wait to inform Lodge that James Bryce was "especially complimentary about your Hamilton." Years later, President Roosevelt wrote to his old friend Senator Lodge from the White House, "The more I study Jefferson the more profoundly I distrust him and his influence, taken as a whole." In another letter to Lodge in 1906 TR stated that he was looking for a Supreme Court appointee who would be a "follower of Hamilton and Marshall and not a follower of Jefferson and Calhoun."[6] The problem with Jefferson, according to TR, was that he led a party that sought to "restrict the powers of the central government even to the point of impotence." Along with Madison, Jefferson was guilty of "criminal folly" in neglecting the American military in the years leading up to the War of 1812 and was "perhaps the most incapable executive that ever filled the presidential chair." While serving as one of Jefferson's successors, Roosevelt wrote to Frederick Scott Oliver, the author of a 1906 biography on Hamilton, "I have never hesitated to criticize Jefferson; he was infinitely below Hamilton. I think the worship of Jefferson a discredit to my country. . . . I think Jefferson on the whole did harm in public life."[7]

TR did praise Jefferson for teaching his "one great truth," that an American statesman should trust the people — a lesson unfortunately lost on Hamilton and the Federalists. "I have not much sympathy with Hamilton's distrust of the democracy," TR observed, and he judged Lincoln to be "superior to Hamilton just because he was a politician and was a genuine democrat." Hamilton was also unsuccessful as a party leader, TR claimed, because he was "too impatient and dictatorial, too heedless of the small arts and unwearied, intelligent industry of the party manager."[8] This trait became most apparent when Hamilton sought to keep New York City from supporting Aaron Burr in the 1800 election, when his inability to devote himself to the "mastery of the petty political detail" saw the "statesman" lose to the "skilful ward politician." Though guilty of the "unforgivable fault of distrusting the people," Hamilton and other Federalists from New York City were nevertheless the best political leaders it had produced: "She has never stood so high politically, either absolutely, or relatively to the rest of the country." TR's admiration for Hamilton was so great that at times it appeared that he believed the latter single-handedly founded the nation. Hamilton was the "chief champion in securing the adoption of the Constitution" while *The Federalist* — the creation of Hamilton, who had been helped by Madison and Jay — was "one of the greatest — I hardly know whether I would not be right to say that it is on the whole the greatest book" dealing with applied politics.[9]

A number of factors contributed to Roosevelt's reverence for Hamilton. Growing up in New York City in a family with ancestral links to him probably sparked his youthful curiosity, as did his war record. The influence of his friend Henry Cabot Lodge and his education at Harvard, acquired during the apogee of New England's reverence for Hamilton, completed the process. TR's curiosity about him never waned, even during his busy years in the White House. He read the English author Frederick Scott Oliver's *Alexander Hamilton, An Essay on American Union* and pronounced it "the best life of Alexander Hamilton that has ever been written." He strongly recommended the book to Secretary of State Elihu Root, Senator Lodge, and the U.S. ambassador to Great Britain, Whitelaw Reid.[10]

It is not surprising that Theodore Roosevelt deeply admired Oliver's book, for he believed that Hamilton's greatness to some extent exceeded that of Washington and Lincoln, as it "touches the interest of the whole world in a wider circle." Oliver argued that Hamilton's nation-building skills made him a figure with universal appeal. Roosevelt also took solace from Oliver's interpretation of Hamilton and the implied powers of the Constitution. "If nothing could be done that was not expressly named in the articles of union, these articles could never fit the uses of a great and developing state. The constitution under so strict an interpretation would be but a lifeless legal document and nothing more; a bone for dogs to quarrel over and not a rod to govern with. This constitution, Hamilton contended, was, and was meant to be, merely an outline." This was a position endorsed by TR himself in a speech delivered during the congressional elections of 1906 when he stated that certain inherent powers of the federal government existed "outside of the enumerated powers conferred upon it by the Constitution." Hamilton had acted according to this principle, TR claimed, and so must modern Americans, for a strict interpretation of the Constitution put the government "at a great disadvantage in the battle for industrial order."[11]

Roosevelt was not alone in celebrating Oliver's book. The president of Princeton University, Woodrow Wilson, described it as "one of the most interesting books of recent years," and President Nicholas Murray Butler of Columbia University claimed it was an unrivalled interpretation of Hamilton. Walter Lippmann declared that Oliver had written "one of the noblest biographies in our language." An obscure newspaper editor, Arthur H. Vandenberg, asserted that it was "the most sympathetic and discerning study of Hamilton's influence upon his time and upon posterity." Gertrude Atherton declared that it stood a chance of becoming a classic and bemoaned the fact that it had not appeared during the Civil War era. If it had, Hamilton would have been seen "as vivid a beacon-light for coherence as Jefferson has been for disintegration" and sectionalism.[12]

Theodore Roosevelt's political views lurched further to the left after his departure from the White House. Though his reverence for Hamilton continued, TR's criticism of his lack of faith in the people became more strident. In fact, throughout most of his political career Roosevelt kept his admiration for him confined to private communications, a probable political concession to the fact that he remained something of a controversial figure. TR was able to merge elements of Hamiltonian and Jeffersonian (or as he would have preferred to call it, Lincolnian) thought in his Bull Moose effort to recapture the White House. He did so by embracing the principles espoused by Herbert Croly (1869–1930) in *The Promise of American Life*. Judge Learned Hand urged Roosevelt to read the book (Henry Cabot Lodge had sent him a copy as well) and noted that it addressed a "set of political ideas which can fairly be described as neo-Hamiltonian, and whose promise is due more to you, as I believe, than to anyone else." Hand acted, as Croly put it, as "the instrument that forged the bond" between TR and himself. Roosevelt read the book and agreed with its recommendations, though it would be a mistake to overstate Croly's influence on Roosevelt, as the latter had already independently arrived at many of the same conclusions. Croly himself acknowledged this when he wrote to Judge Hand in 1910, "He [TR] is the original and supreme Hamiltonian revivalist." Nonetheless, according to Walter Lippmann, Croly "made articulate for Roosevelt his aspiration to combine the social and political reforms initiated by Bryan and La Follette with a Hamiltonian affection for a strong national government." Roosevelt described *The Promise of American Life* as "the most powerful and illuminating study of our national conditions which has appeared for many years."[13]

The gist of Croly's argument was that "neither the Jeffersonian nor the Hamiltonian doctrine was entirely adequate" to "our contemporary national problems." On the whole, Croly preferred Hamilton over Jefferson, for "he was the sound thinker, the constructive statesman, the candid and honorable, if erring, gentleman." The existence of the Union was due only to the herculean efforts of a few Federalists, "of whom Hamilton and Washington were the most important." An efficient government appeared to be Croly's Holy Grail, and the Jeffersonians in their distaste for the national government were primarily responsible for restraining its power. Hamilton was also partly to blame for this restraint, however: by distrusting the people he in turn made the people distrust his new creation. Instead of seeking a "sufficiently broad, popular basis" for his ideas, he relied on "the interested motives of a minority of well-to-do citizens" and thereby confirmed in the people's view that the rich were "the peculiar beneficiaries of the American Federal organization." Jefferson's one saving grace, according to Croly, was his boundless faith in the American people. Unfortunately, this was tainted by his "meager, narrow, and self-contradictory" conception of democracy, which generated far more serious damage for the long-term interests of the United States than any of Hamilton's acts. Jeffersonian policy was the policy of "drift"; Hamilton's was "one of energetic and intelligent assertion of the national good." Nonetheless, Jefferson's creed profoundly influenced Americans because of his "ability to formulate popular opinions, prejudices, and interests," and it led to a situation where any independent leadership was suspect. Jefferson's powerful legacy mandated that future generations of American leaders would have to "flatter and obey" the people.

Croly was somewhat optimistic that the days of drift and inefficiency were coming to an end. The promise of salvation appeared in the form of Teddy Roosevelt, who had revived the "Hamiltonian ideal of constructive national legislation" without the undemocratic trappings of Hamilton. Running in 1912 on a platform with the tag line the New Nationalism, TR proposed a far more interventionist federal government along the lines Croly had suggested. In essence, both Croly and TR's progressivism sought to "give a democratic meaning and purpose to the Hamiltonian tradition and method," since both men possessed, as Croly put it, "a frank and full confidence in an efficient national organization as the necessary agent of the national interest and purpose."[14]

But Roosevelt's campaign failed; and the progressives' qualified endorsement of Hamiltonianism did not last long, as the so-called muckrakers and forces on the left persisted in seeing Hamilton as the mentor of J. P. Morgan and Cornelius Vanderbilt. Hamilton was not alone in being portrayed as a reactionary, for many early twentieth-century observers viewed the entire founding generation with suspicion. Only in traditional Republican circles did Hamilton's reputation resist the onslaught of revisionism. Nicholas Murray Butler (1862–1947), Elihu Root (1845–1937), Joseph Hodges Choate (1832–1917), and Whitelaw Reid (1837–1912) continued the ritual of Hamilton veneration so common among northeastern families with prominent ancestors and impeccable Republican credentials. Though it is tempting to dismiss them as quaintly old-fashioned, these were people who took the Constitution seriously, studied it with great care, and buttressed their opinions with arguments drawn from an education steeped in the Western classics. And there was a striking public spiritedness about these men, whose devotion to their country and its founding principles permeated their public and private writing. Nicholas Murray Butler was a case in point. A recipient of the Nobel Peace Prize, and president of Columbia University from 1901 to 1945, he was also an active participant in Republican party politics for decades. Butler wrote that when he was a student at Columbia, he "found a philosophical basis for my Republicanism in the political doctrines of Alexander Hamilton." At the unveiling of a Hamilton statue at the city hall in Paterson, New Jersey, in 1907, Butler caused a bit of a stir when he delivered a speech excluding Jefferson from his list of Americans entitled to the highest accolade of nation builders. The select few admitted to Butler's American pantheon were Washington, Hamilton, Marshall, Webster, and Lincoln. Hamilton's inclusion was the result of his "constructive statesmanship, the tireless energy, and the persuasive eloquence" that "laid the foundations and pointed the way" to the building of a nation. Jefferson appeared to be part of what Butler described as "the selfish particularists," but Hamilton, in the face of "every sort and kind of obloquy" countered Jefferson's infatuation with the "maxims of the French Revolution" with "hard, clear thinking on the fundamental principles of politics." Butler never wavered in his devotion to Hamilton, proclaiming in 1934 that he was "our master statesman."[15]

That same year, the Nobel Prize winner and former senator Elihu Root declared that Hamilton's writings were "lucid and powerful expositions of controlling principles," which serve as the "guide by which our nation has become great and respected." Root served as William McKinley's secretary of war and TR's secretary of state and could rightly claim, "I am a convinced and uncompromising nationalist of the school of Alexander Hamilton." TR paid Root his highest compliment, describing him as the "great[est] cabinet officer as we ever had, save Alexander Hamilton alone." A graduate of Hamilton College, Root spent the last decades of his life as chairman of the board of trustees of his alma mater from 1909 until his death in 1937.[16]

Root's friend Joseph Hodges Choate (Rufus Choate's nephew) undertook numerous diplomatic missions for McKinley and TR, including the ambassadorship to Great Britain. Speaking in Scotland in 1904, Choate told his audience that Hamilton was foremost among the founding statesmen for his "intellectual brilliancy, individual force, constructive capacity, and personal influence. . . . As the Republic . . . expands and grows, his fame grows with it, and will last as long as the nation endures." Whitelaw Reid, who succeeded Choate as ambassador to Great Britain, delivered a highly critical and controversial speech attacking Jefferson while serving as the U.S. envoy. He took particular umbrage at Jefferson's "vindictive warfare" against Hamilton's fiscal policies, which he alleged included the use of blackmailers. Hamilton was a young man "with far less than Mr. Jefferson's advantages, and [only excepting the Declaration] with fully equal achievement." Reid disparaged the Virginian's war record by contrasting Hamilton's soldiering at eighteen with Jefferson, who "never entered the army at all."[17]

But Reid, Butler, Root, and Choate underestimated the strength of the emerging assortment of progressive politicians and scholars who soon nullified Choate's prediction of Hamilton's growing fame. One such scholar was Walter E. Weyl (1873–1919), a colleague of Herbert Croly's who had far less affection for Hamilton. Along with Croly and Walter Lippmann, Weyl helped to launch the *New Republic* in 1914 and was the author of *The New Democracy*, which, along with Croly's *Promise of American Life*, became something of a campaign bible for Bull Moose activists. Weyl claimed in *The New De-mocracy* that modern Americans were bewildered and "profoundly disen-chanted" and were beginning to believe that the nation "'conceived in liberty' has not borne its expected fruits." The problem was an antiquated Constitu-tion, Weyl contended, "a rigid hard-changing Constitution," a "reactionary document" that represented no one but "dead America." There was no mys-tery as to how the United States reached the point where millions of Ameri-cans were disaffected, for the Constitution was "conceived in a violent distrust of common people" and was designed to protect "'the minority of the opu-lent.'" He argued that "some of the men who drew up the instrument frankly preferred a king" and were led by "the chief spirit of them all, the brilliant Alexander Hamilton." He was appalled that "such an abhorrent ideal should have been for a moment entertained" but found this indicative of the "un-limited contempt in which the greatest political leaders of the day held the raw and vociferous American democracy."[18]

Walter Lippmann (1889–1974) admired Hamilton more than his colleague Weyl but perhaps less so than Herbert Croly. A former assistant to Lincoln Steffens, described by nearly everyone as brilliant, Lippmann developed his opinions on the founders and the founding over the course of a long career as a journalist and an author. Despite his work with Steffens, the young Lippmann embraced many Hamiltonian principles, including the need for an energetic executive presiding over a powerful national government. At the same time, however, he shared the progressives' belief in an organic and evolv-ing Constitution and held that many of the framers had a "machine concep-tion of politics," which led them to craft a Constitution that was far too cumbersome and static. Particularly galling was the tendency of the modern judiciary to ignore the drastic changes that had occurred in American soci-ety since 1787, which probably caused Lippmann to recoil from Hamilton's emphasis on the judiciary's responsibility to protect property and to act as an anchor of stability and permanence in government. He criticized some of the founders for their "naïve faith" in the "'symmetry' of executive, legisla-tive, and judiciary" and for their "fantastic attempts to circumvent human folly by balancing it with vetoes and checks." Hamilton, however, was ex-empted from Lippmann's criticism on this count. His "stupendous success" in crafting a Union was due to his understanding that an enduring Constitu-tion could not be built on "parchment barriers" or on fragile appeals to principles but only on appeals to interest. In a 1916 *New Republic* essay, he wrote, "Had Hamilton failed to attach such power [financial and commercial interests] to the Union, it is hardly conceivable that a strong central government could have been established. The greatness of his mind is not that he designed a balanced Constitution, but that he never neglected to use the interests which were alone capable of realizing it."[19] Lippmann was generous in his praise for Hamilton's nationalism, describing him as "the most imaginative of these [unionist] men" and noting that "in the crystallizing of a common will, there is always an Alexander Hamilton at work." He acknowledged that Hamilton's "consuming passion for union" led him to enlist the aid of the privileged classes, but he disputed the popular notion that Hamilton sought a strong Union in order to protect wealth: rather, he "used class privileges to make the Union." He dismissed the idea that "Hamilton turned toward the plutocracy" out of selfish motives, explaining that he did it "because he knew it was then the strongest possible foundation on which to construct an independent and stable government. He used the rich for a purpose that was greater than their riches." As a result, Hamilton became one of the "great state-builders." Lippmann also admired Hamilton's conviction that the best should govern. The Democrats seemed to promote the idea that "leadership was dangerous, excellence somewhat un-American," but the opposition from "Hamilton's time on have always professed belief that ability mattered, and that no system of government could succeed in which the best men were not preeminent."[20]

Notwithstanding his approbation of Hamilton's nation-building skills and his emphasis on efficient administration by the best and the brightest, one senses in Lippmann certain simmering doubts about this controversial founder. Similar misgivings bedeviled most progressives when they assessed Hamilton. Despite his defense of Hamilton's policy of enlisting the wealthy to support the Union, there were occasions when Lippmann recoiled from Hamilton's relationship, as he put it, with "the lucky few." Further, the more the conservative Republicans tended to idolize Hamilton, the more the young Lippmann recoiled. He once accused one of Hamilton's champions, Senator Henry Cabot Lodge, of spending too much time "gazing at bad statues of dead statesmen" and acting as a typical conservative slave to the "most incidental and trivial part of his forefathers' glory." By the 1920s, when Hamilton had been elevated to sainthood by Harding and Coolidge, and worst of all by

Treasury Secretary Andrew Mellon, Lippmann wrote: "Alexander Hamilton, for good or for evil, worked out for the United States a fiscal system that facilitated the rapid accumulation of individual fortunes by the lucky few. Hamilton frankly championed the cause of the business classes as against the farmer and laborer. The relatively high standard of wages which prevailed in Hamilton's time seemed to him an evil which could, however, be cured by exploiting the possibilities of women's and children's labor. . . . Nevertheless, as a spokesman of an economic class Hamilton was great."[21]

Lippmann, Croly, and Weyl, along with most progressives, had backed TR in the 1912 election and had observed the rise of Woodrow Wilson with some trepidation, for they initially saw him as far too enamored with Jeffersonian individualism and feeble government. The race quickly became a contest between TR and Wilson, with President William H. Taft running a distant third, though he served as a useful foil by being portrayed as a champion of privilege.[22] The victor's academic interests had repeatedly drawn him back to the American founding, where he discerned an Alexander Hamilton that both repelled and attracted him.

Wilson's friend and brother-in-law Stockton Axson said that early in his life Wilson "believed in a considerable degree of centralization, called himself a federalist, paid his devoir to Alexander Hamilton. It was long before he rightly appreciated Thomas Jefferson." Wilson read his future nemesis Henry Cabot Lodge's *Alexander Hamilton* in 1882 and noted in the margins of the book that Hamilton's effort to enlist the support of propertied interests was similar to the Republican party's effort in the 1880 election to portray themselves as the party of financial stability and the Democrats as dangerous "innovators and experimenters." He lamented the absence of American statesmen in the 1880s, arguing that "not since the revolution has there gone by an age so poor as this in such fine talents as those which crowned the head of Hamilton." In *Congressional Government: A Study in American Politics* (1885), Wilson observed that Hamilton "had inherited warm blood and a bold sagacity, while in the other [Jefferson] a negative philosophy ran suitably through cool veins."[23]

Wilson expressed his greatest regard for Hamilton in an essay he wrote in 1893, but even here one could detect his discomfort with Hamilton's un-Americanism. Some Americans "born among us were simply great Englishmen," Wilson exclaimed, "like Hamilton and Madison." These great Englishmen, however, were essential to the nation's development — and none more so than Hamilton.

Certainly one of the greatest figures in our history is the figure of Alexander Hamilton. American historians, though compelled always to admire him, often in spite of themselves, have been inclined, like the mass of men in his own day, to look at him askance. They hint, when they do not plainly say, that he was not "American." He rejected, if he did not despise, democratic principles; advocated a government as strong, almost, as a monarchy. . . . He believed in authority, and he had no faith in the aggregate wisdom of the masses. . . . His ideas of government stuck fast in the old-world polities, and his statesmanship was of Europe rather than of America. And yet the genius and the steadfast spirit of this man were absolutely indispensable to us. . . . A pliant, popular, optimistic man would have failed utterly in the task. . . . only a great conservative genius could have succeeded.

As a professor at Princeton, Wilson accepted the prevailing view at the turn of the century that Hamilton's principles had triumphed over Jefferson's. Speaking in 1901 he claimed that "the form of the Union itself is altered, to the model that was in Hamilton's thought rather than to that which Jefferson once held before us." But he continued to suggest that Hamilton was somehow un-American. A news report from 1904 quoted him as saying that Benjamin Franklin was the typical American, and by typical Wilson meant the kind of man who could live and flourish on the frontier. Hamilton, "much as I admire him, was a transplanted European in his way of thinking. He was not such a man as could have formed a vigilance committee, but Franklin was the man for the frontier."[24]

As he began to emerge as a political figure in New Jersey and around the nation, Wilson appeared determined to disassociate himself further from Hamiltonianism. In 1909, as his candidacy for governor of New Jersey loomed, he stated that "some of us are Jeffersonians, not Hamiltonians, in political creed and principle," though he still referred to Hamilton as a "great statesman." In a speech to Philadelphia Democrats in 1911 he acknowledged that Hamilton was "one of the greatest statesman that this country has ever had" but added that he was nonetheless a statesman "with whose fundamental tenets of government we must most of us dissent." He reiterated this position in remarks made in spring 1911, when he proclaimed, "I am a Democrat because I dissent from the Hamiltonian theory." After he emerged as the

Democrats' nominee for president in 1912, his rhetoric grew harsher. He proclaimed that the directors of the Standard Oil Company "control[led] the Government of the United States," a situation endorsed by the Republican party, which had wholly accepted "the theory of Hamilton" that "the only safe guides in public policies are those persons who have the largest material stake in the prosperity of the country." It was Wilson's belief that the Republicans were adhering to Hamiltonian principles in their defense of privilege. More than once in the 1912 election he stated that Taft's party "linked the government of the United States up with men who control the big finances of the United States. . . . The first man, the first great man, who avowed that theory in the United States was Alexander Hamilton."[25]

Wilson won the White House and later told his aide Colonel Edward M. House (who wrote a novel in 1912 predicting that industrial and financial troubles in the United States would lead to civil war in 1920) that Alexander Hamilton was the ablest of the founders. But publicly he continued to state that Hamilton's notion of enlisting the creditor interests of society in his scheme of government made him uncomfortable. In his bid for reelection in 1916, it all came together in remarks he made to the noted muckraker Ida M. Tarbell (1857–1944): "Hamilton was never an American. He never believed there was such a thing as the wisdom of the masses. He was a great conservative genius, and we needed that at the moment."[26] In his campaign for a second term Wilson sought to win the progressive vote, and despite running against the reform-minded Republican candidate Charles Evans Hughes, he succeeded to some extent in tarring him with the brush of privilege. For the bulk of his presidency, he continued the practice begun by TR of implementing the Croly thesis, that Hamiltonian means be used for Jeffersonian ends. In so doing, he alleviated Croly's initial concerns to the point where one commentator observed that the *New Republic* "became virtually the house organ for the Wilson administration."[27]

During his long career, Woodrow Wilson expressed misgivings about Hamilton's Americanism and his alleged efforts to protect the interests of the wealthy, even as he applauded elements of his principles and practices. In contrast, his young assistant secretary of the Navy and his Democratic successor in the Oval Office came to see Hamilton as something comparable to a cancer on the founding. Wilson understood that labeling Republicans as Hamiltonian defenders of privilege was an effective tactic, but Franklin

Roosevelt used this technique with greater frequency and far more success. Perhaps FDR's Harvard education and New York patrician background lent more credibility to the attacks in the minds of Northerners. And many of Wilson's Democratic contemporaries saw none of the greatness in Hamilton that Wilson occasionally acknowledged. Hamilton remained to them the pawn of the prosperous and the slanderer of the little man. Wilson's friend and political ally John Sharp Williams (1854–1932) was one such Democrat. Williams attended the University of Virginia Law School (as had Wilson) and considered himself to be a student of the founding and a devotee of Jefferson. He went on to become the Democratic minority leader in the House of Representatives and later a senator from Mississippi. Theodore Roosevelt dismissed him as a "true old style Jeffersonian of the barbaric blatherskite variety." Williams invoked Jefferson's name in numerous congressional debates and argued that the Democratic party would be invincible if it religiously followed the principles found in Jefferson's first inaugural.[28] He courageously delivered a series of lectures in 1912 on Jefferson in the very heartland of Hamiltonianism, Columbia University. Echoing his hero, Williams charged that Hamilton was not a worthy figure of reverence for true Americans. Hamilton "attempted to construct a constitution, peculiarly un-American, and alien, then and now, to all the habits and thoughts of Americans." Hamilton was a "reactionary," a "counter-revolutionary" who "habitually distrusted the masses" and had exclaimed at a dinner, "Your people, sir, is a great beast!" Hamilton's success in linking the interests of the wealthy to the new government made him the "idol of the monied class," and undoing this alliance had been the goal of defenders of the people since Jefferson. Williams claimed that had the Quasi-War with France evolved into a full conflagration it would have halted "the work of democratization . . . perhaps for all time" and made Hamilton a virtual "political dictator."[29]

While early twentieth-century American politicians jockeyed to wrap themselves in Jefferson's or Hamilton's mantle, in scholarly and journalistic circles there was a growing consensus that perhaps neither man, nor any founder for that matter, was worthy of emulation. J. Allen Smith (1860–1926), a political science professor at the University of Washington, expressed some of these sentiments in *The Spirit of American Government, A Study of the Constitution* (1907). He concluded that the Constitution was "framed and secured" by a conspiracy of "the property-owning class." This counterrevolutionary document was designed to frustrate popular will and to foil what should be the true end of government, "the unhampered expression and prompt enforcement of public opinion." The Supreme Court, that "small oligarchy of nine irremovable judges" who repeatedly struck down economic regulations designed to benefit the public, especially perturbed Smith. Much of the blame for this could be traced, not surprisingly, to Alexander Hamilton, whose claim that the Constitution was the ultimate expression of the public will was "a mere demagogic attempt to conceal his real motive": the protection of the nation's plutocracy from popular control. Hamilton's "conservative legalistic" writings, Smith reiterated later in his life, "perverted" the doctrine that "public officials are agents of the people."[30]

Smith's book was reviewed in *Political Science Quarterly* in 1908 by a young professor at Hamilton's alma mater, Charles A. Beard (1874–1948). Beard later incorporated elements of Smith's thesis in a controversial book that earned him a national reputation. Born and raised in a die-hard Republican family in Indiana, Beard seemed at first an unlikely figure to question the framers' motives. He left the Republican party in 1900 over the issue of imperialism, receiving his Ph.D. in political science from Columbia University in 1904, where he remained as a member of the faculty until he resigned in 1917.[31]

Beard initially intended to write a book examining the ideas of Alexander Hamilton, but that project evolved into what became known as *An Economic Interpretation of the Constitution of the United States*. He maintained that the American Constitution was "an economic document drawn with superb skill by men whose property interests were immediately at stake." As for Hamilton, Beard described him as a "colossal genius of the new system," who attempted to enlist the support for the new government of creditors and financiers, merchants and manufacturers, land speculators and promoters. He explored at length the accusations that Hamilton benefited from the financial system he implemented and generally acquitted him of any official misconduct. He concluded that while Hamilton's policies appeared not to be the result of "any of the personal interests so often ascribed to him . . . nevertheless it is apparent . . . that it was no mere abstract political science which dominated his principles of government. He knew at first hand the stuff of which government is made."[32]

An Economic Interpretation generated passionate reactions, with progressives praising it and conservatives generally outraged. The *New York Times* hailed it for its "laborious researches and luminous exposition" and observed that "the Constitution placed the dollar above the man, and now man is being placed above the dollar. Social morality is sounder in our times than in the times of the Fathers." Walter Lippmann wrote that the book marked a "turning point in the interpretation of American history," but Nicholas Murray Butler argued that Beard was a proponent of a notion connected with "the crude, unmoral and unhistorical teaching of Karl Marx." Former president Taft publicly condemned the book and suggested that Beard would have been happier if "dead beats, out-at-the-elbows demagogues, and cranks who never had any money" had written the Constitution. Future president Warren G. Harding's newspaper, the Marion (OHIO) Star, ran the headline: "SCAVENGERS, HYENA-LIKE, DESECRATE THE GRAVES OF THE DEAD PATRIOTS WE REVERE."[33]

Beard's book was an essential corrective to the American tendency to deify the founders and a reminder of the importance that interest plays in the calculations of political actors.[34] But An Economic Interpretation, though clearly a serious effort at history, was also part of an attempt to lower the reputation of the framers of the Constitution in order to pave the way for a more adaptable (i.e., progressive) form of government. In an introduction written to a later edition, he denied having any partisan motive: "I had in mind no thought of forwarding the interests of the Progressive party." Though perhaps not intending to advance the Progressive party, he clearly supported the progressive agenda of the day. He backed the initiative, referendum, and recall proposals being debated at the time and lamented the "lack of correspondence between the political system and the economic system": in particular, he objected to the Supreme Court's tendency to strike down governmental acts regulating economic activity. Much of the blame for this could be laid at the feet of the framers, who were determined "above everything else to safeguard the rights of private property against any leveling tendencies on the part of the propertyless masses." Later in his life Beard made a nationwide radio address in support of Franklin Roosevelt's Court-packing plan in order to bring "the Court back within the Constitution."[35]

In 1915 Beard joined the Committee on the Federal Constitution and drafted their proposal to ease the process of amending the document. The Jeffersonian overtones of his proposal were evident in its call for a constitutional convention to be held every twenty years if the electorate so desired. As Beard saw it, the existing Constitution weakened the ability of social movements to implement change. These movements were "built on unstable foundations" due to a Constitution that "determines and limits the efforts at social and political readjustment." The obvious solution was to bring the Constitution "under the control of the people," and Beard viewed opponents of constitutional reform with disdain. In a 1915 *New Republic* essay he described bitterly the unwarranted and hysterical reaction to Herbert Croly's eminently reasonable proposals for reforming state constitutions: "They [Croly and the progressives] were attempting to lay profane hands on the Ark of the Covenant. They were met with shrill cries about the gods, the sacred oracles . . . the fathers and the separation of powers."[36]

It should be noted that Beard was often critical of Thomas Jefferson and rejected the good Jefferson/bad Hamilton dichotomy. In a *New Republic* essay written in 1914, he observed that "to-day nearly half of us belong to the 'mobs of the great cities' — sores on the body politic," and he wondered, "what message has the sage of Monticello for us?" In a later work that discussed the party conflict between Jefferson and Hamilton, he repeated Henry Adams's great beast tale but qualified it by noting that Hamilton was supposed to have made the comment. And while he observed that "it has been the fashion to ascribe to the Federalists a political philosophy born of innate ill-will for the people," he was unwilling to dismiss this interpretation as completely unfounded: "Now this imputation is not entirely just. No doubt some of the emotions to which Federalists gave free vent were the feelings common to persons of large property — feelings of superiority and virtue. But there were practical grounds for distrusting 'the people.' Throughout the revolution 'the lower orders' had given trouble to the right wing of patriotism." In a 1929 book review where he waxed poetic about the prospects for fascism in Italy, Beard implied that the founders were to a certain extent equivalent to Benito Mussolini. When it came to condemning democracy, "the fathers of the American Republic, notably Hamilton, Madison, and John Adams, were as voluminous and vehement as any Fascist could desire."[37]

Beard inspired generations of activists and students of politics to focus on the connection between "interest[s] and idea[s]" and to recognize that the two are "inseparably united." Needing little inspiration from Beard but commending his book nonetheless, the socialist author Allan L. Benson (1871–1940) wrote *Our Dishonest Constitution*, which argued that if the founders were still "living and doing business as they did 125 years ago we should call many of them grafters." Fellow-socialist Eugene V. Debs (1855–1926) viewed both Hamilton and Theodore Roosevelt as "rank individualist[s]" who held "the common run in . . . contempt."[38] Muckrakers such as Lincoln Steffens (1866–1936) had anticipated much of Beard's thesis but presented it in a more polemical manner. Steffens shared Beard's view that principles provide camouflage for interest. As a college student he had observed that throughout British history, ideas were "merely coverings and excuses for the self-assertion of class interest. The higher the class, of course, the more aggressive it is." In the United States, Steffens believed that a government of the people was being replaced by the system, which served merely to please business. This was because Alexander Hamilton's theories still prevailed, Steffens wrote in 1904, and thus representative democracy was endangered. Hamilton attempted to launch a manufacturing experiment in Paterson, New Jersey, because there were "charters and grabs" available there that were impossible to obtain in New York. Generations of financiers viewed Hamilton as their great leader and followed his example by migrating to New Jersey for purposes of exploitation. In Steffens's view, Hamiltonians were "the very corrupters of government."[39]

Despite the growing consensus on the left that he was an unworthy exemplar for the movement, some progressives nonetheless maintained their affection for Hamilton. One such maverick was the senator and historian Albert J. Beveridge (1862–1927) of Indiana. Though he agreed with Beard's view that economic interests contributed to the formation of American political parties, he placed far more emphasis on the struggle between nationalism and localism as the underlying source of party conflict. In his Pulitzer Prize–winning biography *The Life of John Marshall,* Beveridge wrote that "Madison was equaled only by Hamilton in sheer intellectuality, but he was inferior to that colossus in courage and constructive genius." The "financial statesmanship" of Hamilton and the Federalists provided cannon fodder for the "artificer" from Virginia, who emerged to lead the opposition and create a political party "into which the people might pour all their discontent, all their fears, all their woes and all their hopes." Though Hamilton demonstrated poor judgment in writing his "fatal tirade" against John Adams in the 1800 election and in his "lifelong and increasingly venomous" pursuit of Aaron Burr, he was nonetheless "a man so transcendently great . . . easily the foremost creative mind in American statesmanship." In 1918 Teddy Roosevelt wrote Beveridge that his *Life of John Marshall* was "one of the big works done by the men of this generation" and exclaimed that Beveridge's nationalism was "the keynote of your attitude and of mine — just exactly as it was of Marshall's and of Hamilton's."[40]

The events of the 1920s damaged Hamilton's reputation and laid the groundwork for the assault on his legacy that lingers to this day. Both Warren G. Harding (1865–1923) and Calvin Coolidge (1872–1933) viewed him as one of the greatest, if not the greatest, founder. This primarily Republican celebration of Hamilton by two presidents who repulse most academics, and the tendency, rightly or wrongly, to associate their economic policies with his principles, caused Hamilton's reputation to plummet to a point from which it has not yet recovered.

The 1920s began, however, on an auspicious note for Hamilton's reputation. A Michigan newspaper editor, Arthur H. Vandenberg (1884–1951), published *The Greatest American, Alexander Hamilton* in 1921. This volume alone placed Vandenberg on a par with Gertrude Atherton or John Torrey Morse as one of Hamilton's greatest promoters, yet he followed it with a second book, *If Hamilton Were Here Today,* an equally adoring look at its subject. Both books earned the copious praise of Hamiltonphiles such as Henry Cabot Lodge, Albert Beveridge, and President Warren G. Harding. "No man's life ever gave me greater inspiration than Hamilton's," Harding wrote to Vandenberg, "and no man's life ever made greater contribution [*sic*] to the founding and the functioning of constitutional America." Charles A. Beard was not impressed, caustically observing that Vandenberg's writings had "helped to rank him among 'the leading statesmen and thinkers of Michigan.'" On becoming a U.S. senator in 1928, Vandenberg confided that his greatest ambition was to build a Hamilton monument in the capital larger than the Lincoln Memorial and the Washington Monument.[41]

In *The Greatest American,* Vandenberg paid homage to prior works that influenced his study of Hamilton, including Gertrude Atherton's *The Conqueror,* which he dubbed the great American novel. A portion of his book was devoted to the results of a poll of 108 prominent Americans, in which he asked, "What man, all things considered, in the whole history of our country down to date, is best entitled to be called 'The Greatest American?'" Vandenberg's candidate, Alexander Hamilton, did not receive a single vote. The future senator proceeded to make a case for "the Master Builder of indissoluble Union, the Gladiator who saved the Constitution . . . the Most Brilliant Author, the most Fascinating Orator and the Most Formidable Legal Luminary of his time." America of the 1920s needed, according to Vandenberg, "as rarely before, the living spirit of Alexander Hamilton."[42] He spent considerable time in *If Hamilton Were Here Today* countering the arguments of Senator Robert M. La Follette and other spurious progressives who sought to weaken the Supreme Court's power of judicial review over economic regulation. These "intemperate doctrinaire[s]" dismissed Hamilton as a reactionary, when in fact he was the "greatest Progressive of his time," for "was it not 'progressive' to achieve the Constitution, the most forward-looking event in history since the birth of Jesus Christ? . . . Was it not 'progressive' — the most progressive single act in American history — to evolve the Constitutional doctrine of liberal construction and implied powers, so that the Great Charter, though holding fast to fundamentals, did not become a strait-jacket and a garrote?" Vandenberg's contempt for those who would not hold "fast to fundamentals" infused much of his writing, and while he believed Hamilton to be something of a progressive, it was his devotion to order and stability, and to "evolution not revolution," that most impressed him.[43]

President Warren G. Harding was as zealous as Arthur Vandenberg in his admiration for Alexander Hamilton, seeing him as the intellectual godfather of the Republican party. As a young man his heroes were Napoleon and Hamilton and, like Vandenberg, he was moved by Atherton's *The Conqueror;* according to one biographer, *The Conqueror* became something of his "lay Bible." Harding used the book as the source for his favorite stock speech, "Alexander Hamilton — Prophet of American Destiny," which he delivered during many summers on the Chautauqua circuit, starting in 1904. In this speech, he claimed that "when it was most needed, there arose the greatest genius of the Republic, Alexander Hamilton. Without Hamilton there would be no American Republic today, to astonish the world with its resources and its progress." Hamilton founded "what is now the Republican party" and was a champion of nationalism while Jefferson was the founder of the Democratic party and a proponent of a loose confederacy. Harding believed that the Civil War settled these conflicting perspectives, with Hamilton's vision triumphant. He was "the commanding figure that riveted the Union, laid the broad foundations which underlie our Federal government today, and laid the plans for the future development which his prophetic vision enabled him to see."[44]

Elected to the Senate from Ohio in 1914, Harding supported the broad grant of emergency wartime measures given to President Wilson during World War I. Hamilton's Constitution had the flexibility required to respond to such crises, Harding argued, and President Washington had agreed that the delegation of power to the executive in a time of national emergency was appropriate. "In his matchless vision Hamilton saw the necessity of such provision, and his influence in the drafting of the Constitution, exerted through Washington, was such that every avenue was opened for casting to one man in a crisis all the power." Harding then observed that George Washington "pacified" Jefferson but gave "silent and effective favor to Hamilton."[45]

As a compromise choice for the Republican presidential nomination in 1920, Harding campaigned against fellow Ohioan James M. Cox (1870–1957) and his running mate Franklin D. Roosevelt. It was a classic contest between Hamiltonian and Jeffersonian candidates. Cox viewed Jefferson as the greatest American, part of a select group of American statesmen who "broadened the base of democracy and espoused the cause of the oppressed." Jefferson and Jackson, like all tribunes of the forgotten man, were "slandered" and "persecuted," for when "special privilege battles for its existence it fights with tooth and claw."[46] When the votes were counted in 1920, privilege had defeated populism.

On 17 May 1923, President Harding dedicated a statue to Hamilton on the grounds of the Treasury Department, before a crowd of almost five thousand people. He was joined on stage at the unveiling by descendants of Alexander Hamilton and assorted dignitaries, including Senator Henry Cabot Lodge. Secretary of the Treasury Andrew Mellon served as the master of ceremonies and described Hamilton as the greatest man who ever controlled the finances of the American government. The president used the occasion to deliver an attack on what he saw as the growing threat of factions in the United States, in particular those who "challenge civil and religious liberty," the latter reference seen as a criticism of the burgeoning Ku Klux Klan. Harding claimed that if more political leaders were like Hamilton, then "hope and resolution" would replace the "hatred and resentment" that were hindering postwar recovery in Europe and elsewhere. He argued that Hamilton was the "prophet of American destiny" and was foremost among those who made a "constructive contribution to the making of America." Although Washington, Jefferson, and Franklin were significant founders, "Hamilton had the conception of a Federal Government, upon which plan the American people have builded [sic] to their own satisfaction and to no small degree of world astonishment. When his plan was adopted, he became the master builder, and the integrity of the nation's financial honor is his monument for the ages." Harding dealt also with the age-old criticism leveled by Democrats that Hamilton was a monarchist, observing that "many proclaimed him a monarchist and the foe of liberty. Others thought him an imperialist and the enemy of democracy, but he was none of these. It was from Hamilton's lips that came the finest utterance ever made concerning human liberty, 'The sacred rights of mankind are written as with a sunbeam, by the hand of Divinity itself, never to be erased or obscured by mortal power.'" Harding expressed wonder that "this outstanding leader and conspicuous contributor should be so relatively inconspicuous in the historical recitals of our country," although he also observed that Hamilton had come "into full appraisal and to lofty eminence in this generation." Hamilton's unwillingness to court public favor accounted for this lack of recognition and appreciation during certain periods of American history. "He cared little for temporary popular favor," Harding accurately observed, "and put his devotion to the Republic's welfare before popular approval or personal fortune." This was perhaps Hamilton's most important legacy for contemporary Americans to ponder, Harding claimed, and he coupled it with a plea to "throttle the false cry of class where none need exist in the beckoning of American opportunity."[47] The plea was to no avail, for the progressive claim that Hamiltonian institutions sheltered the forces of wealth and privilege had been firmly embraced by Harding's opponents.

The editors at the New York Times hailed Harding's speech for its celebration of "the cardinal intellect in our history." Though it may be an overstatement to claim, as Harding did, that Hamilton was the "creative genius in the making of the Constitution," in a certain sense his assertion was true. The Times argued that Hamilton understood early the "necessity of a strong central government." Much of what he foresaw had come to pass in America, except for the expansion of "suffrage and popular control" and the modern idea that wealth was "an enemy rather than a support and element of American policy." The editorial argued that 1920s Jeffersonians were Hamiltonians "without knowing it," presumably a reference to Democratic party pleas for government regulation of the free market. The *Times* concluded, "Like it or lump it, the Federal Government of today was created by Alexander Hamilton."[48]

The master of ceremonies for the day, Treasury Secretary Andrew Mellon (1855–1937), was a Hamilton admirer who served as a favorite target of progressives throughout the Harding, Coolidge, and Hoover administrations. The Pittsburgh millionaire was a champion of tax reduction and became a hero to conservatives around the nation, who habitually referred to him as "the greatest Secretary of the Treasury since Alexander Hamilton." President Coolidge claimed that Mellon had managed the nation's finances with "a genius and success unmatched" since Hamilton. One admirer, Senator Reed Smoot (1862–1941) of Utah, who later gained notoriety as the cosponsor of crippling tariff legislation, claimed that Mellon had even surpassed Hamilton as the greatest secretary of the treasury. The *Saturday Evening Post* sympathized with Smoot's assessment: while "admitting the genius of Hamilton and the value of his constructive work on the rudimentary governmental financial system at the birth of the Republic," the magazine maintained nonetheless that no secretary "was so completely the master of finance as Mellon, nor any . . . had problems one-tenth the size and complexity of his problems since 1921."[49]

Mellon was the guest of honor at a dinner hosted by Columbia College alumni in December 1924 celebrating the 150th anniversary of Hamilton's matriculation at King's College. The dinner was something of a last hurrah for Hamiltonphiles and was presided over by the ageless Dr. Nicholas Murray Butler, who was introduced as the "all-American champion Hamilton fan." The evening's oratory was replete with tributes comparing Mellon to Hamilton. Secretary Mellon praised Hamilton for handing down "the principles which still guide us through the climaxes of this great nation," although he brushed aside comparisons of his tenure with that of Hamilton's, claiming that "each successive Secretary of the Treasury at some time during his incumbency of the office enjoys the distinction of being 'the greatest since Hamilton.' However, he goes out of office and his glory has departed." Hamilton was different, for "the genius of Hamilton radiated an effulgence which will never die."[50]

Despite Mellon's disclaimer, conservatives continued to suggest that the two men were the greatest financial minds the nation had produced. They were also, by implication, ideological brethren. All this was too much for progressive observers. The editors of the *Nation* rejected the idea that Mellon was equal or superior to Hamilton, sarcastically describing Hamilton as "the greatest Secretary of the Treasury before Andrew W. Mellon . . . as he will doubtless come to be known." Walter Lippmann argued that Hamilton used the rich for a higher purpose while Mellon sought assistance for the plutocracy as an end in itself. Senator George Norris (1861–1944), a progressive Republican who later backed the New Deal and ultimately was forced to leave his party, could not contain his scorn for Mellon. When Mellon was replaced by President Herbert Hoover and exiled to Great Britain as the American ambassador, Norris remarked that "poor old Andy" was being given a job that a Senate page could perform "equally as well as the greatest Secretary of the Treasury since Alexander Hamilton."[51] The repeated linkage of Hamilton's name with that of Mellon's served to tarnish the former's reputation for years to come: when the crash came, Hamilton was held almost as culpable as Mellon, Coolidge, and Hoover.

But for a brief time the accolades continued under Calvin Coolidge, who, the critic William Allen White (1868–1944) acidly observed, "cherish[ed] the works of the great prophet of the gods of prosperity, Alexander Hamilton." Coolidge later noted in his *Autobiography* that during his first two years as a student at Amherst College he found "very absorbing" a course taught by Anson D. Morse, a professor of history and political economy. As he recalled, Morse focused on "the era when our institutions had their beginning. Washington was treated with the greatest reverence, and a high estimate was placed on the statesmanlike qualities and financial capacity of Hamilton, but Jefferson was not neglected. In spite of his many vagaries it was shown that in saving the nation from the danger of falling under the domination of an oligarchy, and in establishing a firm rule of the people which was forever to remain, he vindicated the soundness of our political institutions."[52] While serving as Harding's vice president, Coolidge addressed the Hamilton club in Chicago in 1922 on the 165th anniversary of his birth. Speaking of Hamilton, Coolidge proclaimed that "when America ceases to remember his greatness, America will no longer be great." He hailed the historic partnership of Hamilton and Washington, observing that "along with Washington goes Hamilton, neither none the less great because their talents mutually increased the success and greatness of each other." Without Hamilton's exertions at the time of the founding, "it appears probable that . . . the American nation would not have come into being." The younger Coolidge spoke favorably of Jefferson's democratic inclinations, but the older Coolidge seemed a bit more jaded, noting dryly that Hamilton "did not make his appeal to the more ordinary and common motives of human action, which characterized the appeal of Jefferson." In fact, Jefferson seems to have been exiled from the older Coolidge's American pantheon: "When great tests have come, when supreme choices have been made, the American people have always stood with Washington, with Hamilton, and with Marshall." The Republican party was applying Hamilton's philosophy to the problems of the 1920s, Coolidge claimed. One such Hamiltonian principle was that "the government have and use the power necessary for the economic welfare of the country." This use was qualified, of course, in a statement guaranteed to agitate progressives and populists of all stripes. The purpose of regulating business, Coolidge argued, was to ensure "not that business may be hampered but that it may be free, not that it may be restricted but that it may expand."[53]

The intelligentsia of the 1920s viewed Coolidge, Harding, and Mellon as mediocrities who promoted policies favorable to the interests of the upper class. It was a good time to be a skeptic and to prove to one's fellow intellectuals that one was not enticed by the materialism of the 1920s. The English professor Vernon L. Parrington (1871–1929) saw disturbing parallels between Hamilton and contemporary Republican proponents of plutocracy, an assessment shared by the historian William E. Dodd (1869–1940). And the writer W. E. Woodward (1874–1950) built on Charles Beard's economic determinist model with his popular debunking work on George Washington, whom he portrayed in equal measure as the father of his country and as a greedy land speculator.

A colleague of J. Allen Smith's at the University of Washington, Parrington was greatly influenced by his friend's progressive interpretation of the American founding. Parrington admired Smith's "Jeffersonian ideals" and his courageous criticism of "our triumphant plutocracy." Parrington's belief in the good Jefferson/bad Hamilton view of American history could be seen throughout his three-volume Pulitzer Prize–winning *Main Currents in American Thought*, which he dedicated to J. Allen Smith. Hamilton was a formidable figure in the shaping of America, Parrington argued, but "something hard, almost brutal lurks in his thought — a note of intellectual arrogance, of cynical contempt. He was . . . without a shred of idealism." According to Parrington, Hamilton viewed men as beasts and thus argued for the rule of the "economic masters of society" to keep the common people from ruin. His vision was realized with the rise of the modern corporation and American imperialism, and though he deserved the accolade of being the father of industrialism, "our democratic liberalism" received nothing from him.[54]

Chair of the History Department at the University of Chicago and an economic determinist to the core, William E. Dodd believed that only two Americans had earned the privileged title of national sage: Thomas Jefferson and Andrew Jackson. Dodd's graduate students included Henry Steele Commager, Frank L. Owsley, and James G. Randall, who absorbed his aversion to Hamilton. A dedicated Jeffersonian and defender of the South, Dodd was later appointed the American ambassador to Germany under Franklin Roosevelt. His account of Jefferson in *Statesmen of the Old South* influenced the work of his friend Claude Bowers, along with Vernon Parrington. Dodd once stated that he was "more nearly a follower of Rousseau and Jefferson than of Burke and Alexander Hamilton." In 1908, at a dinner with Theodore Roosevelt and Lord Bryce at the White House, the president and Bryce passionately praised Hamilton "as the greatest of our statesmen," a description Dodd told a friend he refused to endorse. "The man who believes in and admires Alexander Hamilton is not democratic . . . does not believe in democracy, but good government administered from above." Dodd saw Hamilton as a member of the "extreme conservatives," whose advocacy of "commercial ventures" influenced George Washington. The latter was a reactionary conservative, as evidenced in his cooperation with Hamilton and "the bankers of Philadelphia" to subvert the Revolution. Washington's policies were designed to protect his class from the people's will, Dodd contended. On retiring, Washington retreated to Mt. Vernon, where oak forests screened him "from the gaze of the vulgar, and a hundred slaves . . . doff[ed] their hats to master." In contrast, Dodd's idealized Jefferson was "a semi-populist back country leader" who fought the "oligarchy" in Virginia and beyond.[55]

The novelist W. E. Woodward was captivated by the economic determinism rampant in the nation's scholarly circles and incorporated this slant in his popular histories, where he sought to debunk the nation's most sacred founder and his greedy Caribbean-born sidekick. Aroused by his discussions with Charles and Mary Beard to write *George Washington: The Image and the Man*, Woodward modified Beard's economic determinism by adding a racial component to the theory that captured the popular imagination through the

1930s. He was taken with the notion of some Jewish strain in Hamilton's lineage. His "philandering" mother was married to a "rich middle-aged Jew," and while it was said that she was "not a Jewess . . . her name was Rachel, a Jewish name, and her husband was a Jew." Were he alive in the 1920s, Hamilton would no doubt have attended one of the snobbiest universities, joined an exclusive fraternity, befriended wealthy students, graduated with merit, married the sister of a wealthy classmate, and become a vice president at his father-in-law's bank and eventually a partner in a Wall Street firm. Modifying Henry Adams's quote, Woodward claimed that Hamilton "called the common people 'a great brute.'" In 1936 Woodward characterized Hamilton's lifework as an effort "to create a philosophy of rich versus poor. He showed the wealthy how to acquire legislative and economic domination of the United States, and how to hold it, in one way or another." He claimed further that Hamilton was a fascist, giving birth to an idea that later flourished during the New Deal years. And sadly for America, Hamilton's ideas influenced the "slow moving mind of Washington," even though Hamilton was himself "as undemocratic as Mussolini."[56]

Throughout the 1920s and 1930s anti-Semitic tales concerning Hamilton's lineage were very much in vogue. One biography, published in 1932, raised the possibility that his father was Jewish and that this "might have contributed a racial aptitude for finance and organization." Father Charles Coughlin (1891–1979), whose radio broadcasts attracted millions of listeners, echoed suggestions that Hamilton may have been Jewish. In one of his anti-Semitic tirades delivered during the depression, Coughlin claimed that Hamilton was a Jew "who had established the nation's banking system in the interests of the rich and well born." His "nefarious plan" for the Bank of the United States was designed to "grant the right and privilege of coining money to certain of Mr. Hamilton's wealthy associates." On other occasions when Coughlin mentioned Hamilton's name he added that his "original name was Alexander Levine."[57]

Those in search of scapegoats responsible for the shattered American economy fell on Hamilton. Although Coughlin's anti-Semitic critique came from the fringes of American society, the Radio Priest had tapped into a sentiment that resonated in many sections of the nation: Alexander Hamilton was somehow not one of us. In the years to follow, under the weight of a cruel and seemingly unrelenting depression, he was exiled from the American experience.

6

Slouching Toward Oblivion
Hamilton as the New Deal's Great Beast

When the great crash came, Alexander Hamilton might as well have been the chairman of the Republican National Committee.[1] Admiration for him plummeted along with the stock market, partly out of the disgust that many Americans felt toward Warren Harding, Calvin Coolidge, and Andrew Mellon, all devotees of Hamilton.

The New Deal coalition of Southern Jeffersonians and Northern progressives brought to fruition the dream of Herbert Croly and others to pursue Jeffersonian ends with Hamiltonian means. World War I had sidetracked Woodrow Wilson's reform efforts, but Franklin Roosevelt, assisted by the trauma of the Great Depression, completed the task of building a powerful progressive coalition. It was no easy chore, and it was a testament to FDR's political genius that he succeeded. That this member of the Hudson River gentry appealed to the likes of William E. Dodd, W. E. Woodward, John Sharp Williams, and countless other populists was proof of Roosevelt's political acumen. These men had given voice to a widespread animus among Southerners toward Northern Hamiltonian plutocrats. One spectator at a rally for a Southern gubernatorial candidate in the early 1920s witnessed this enmity. The candidate's speech "could be digested into one sentence: a horrible gang of bandits, led by a man named Alexander Hamilton, is now gathering and probably arming in a place called Wall Street, preparatory to coming down and plundering the poor farmers unless I am elected." The observer added, "He was elected."[2] Though some Northern New Dealers originally admired Hamilton for his advocacy of a well-administered national government, as time wore on the rhetoric and the honors paid to Jefferson were akin to those emanating from their Southern brethren.

One of the more significant players in this drama was Claude G. Bowers (1878–1958). An influential partisan historian and journalist, in his prime he helped to shape the opinions of countless Americans, perhaps including Franklin D. Roosevelt. Born in Hamilton County, Indiana, Bowers initially admired Hamilton but after wading through his papers decided that "my instincts were opposed to the philosophy of my hero." Unsuccessful in a race for Congress in 1904, he then turned to journalism, eventually becoming an editorial writer for the *New York World* and the *New York Journal.* He viewed the American experience as a perpetual struggle between the forces of light and darkness. The dark side consisted of defenders of plutocracy, who often acted on the basis of principle but were nonetheless contemptuous of their fellow citizens, particularly farmers. The plutocrats originated with Hamilton and the Federalists and included such fellow travelers as Henry Clay, Daniel Webster, and the Radical Republicans of the Reconstruction era. The forces of light were led by Thomas Jefferson ("the greatest of all Americans"), Andrew Jackson, Andrew Johnson, Franklin D. Roosevelt, and Harry S. Truman. Bowers was the favorite historian of the New Deal and had no reservations about mixing his journalistic and scholarly endeavors with his role as a Democratic party activist and propagandist. As one of his biographers observed, Bowers never met a Democrat he didn't like.[3]

George Washington was not on Bowers's list of heroes. He contended that W. E. Woodward's debunking biography of Washington was a brilliant portrait, for it exposed the "development of the economic basis of the Revolution," partly through its accurate portrayal of him as "a business man — a materialist." Bowers believed that Washington had a "hatred of democracy" and an "indifference to the masses" and was more interested in "property than in human rights, which explain[ed] his alignment in the Hamilton-Jefferson controversy."[4]

Bowers loathed the fact that the chroniclers of American history tended to be New Englanders with a proclivity for Federalists or Republicans. He hailed the (1931) publication of Edgar Lee Masters's *Lincoln the Man,* to put it mildly, as a revisionist look at the sixteenth president. It disturbed him that the book was ignored or "savagely assailed" by many mainstream scholars.

There are a few American leaders who are supposed to be sacred from frank analysis. It is a bit curious and amusing to note that all of these belong to one school of political thought. Until quite recently even Charles Sumner was sacrosanct. If a writer is moved to "belittle" he should by all means select Jefferson or Jackson for his subject, as so many are doing all the time. It would require a volume as fat as Mr. Masters's merely to enumerate the malicious fabrications against Jefferson to be found in "histories" and yet I do not recall that any "patriots" rise in protest. . . . It is agreed among the guardians of the temple that he and others of his school of thought are fair game, and one must not be shocked if the plebeians, unfamiliar with the rule, occasionally take liberties with others.[5]

Bowers counted among his large circle of friends Eugene V. Debs, the great American socialist. He turned to him for advice on his book *Jefferson and Hamilton: The Struggle for Democracy in America,* hoping that Debs could enlighten him on the status of labor in the early Republic. Bowers told Debs that he was "working on my Jefferson-Hamilton book which will be the first honest story of that struggle which was to determine whether this should be a democratic or an aristocratic republic." He noted that fairness dictated that he would probably have to criticize Jefferson for not thinking about the needs of the "mechanics," but of course "Hamilton had a profound contempt for everyone but merchants and bankers."[6]

In *Jefferson and Hamilton* Bowers found Hamilton to be a genius, a man of integrity, and possessed of great moral courage; but he also found him "dictatorial," contended that he used Christianity to further his ends, and "thought of himself of the race of military masters." The confrontation between Jefferson and Hamilton was clearly the latter's fault, for Jefferson "long sought to get along with Hamilton." Hamilton viewed himself as the prime minister of Washington's administration, and Jefferson resented the "dictatorial airs" of his younger cabinet colleague. Making matters worse was the corruption that was starting to seep into the social life of the Federalist-dominated capital, a social scene that was "idolatrous of money and distinctions" and where few were "capable of discriminating between anarchy and democracy." In this hostile atmosphere, Jefferson would fight for the masses, a fight that "still stalks the ways of men."[7]

A number of scholars and journalists recoiled from Bowers's simplistic tale of good versus evil, but many did not. Dumas Malone (1892–1986), who eventually displaced Bowers as Jefferson's foremost twentieth-century promoter, wrote an enthusiastic review of *Jefferson and Hamilton.* Bowers's book inspired Malone to undertake his own Jefferson biography. The historian Samuel Flagg Bemis argued that *Jefferson and Hamilton* was "most interesting" and though the author "must be a Democrat," the pro-Jefferson bias that appeared in the book served as a "good antidote to the several recent studies extolling the marvels of Federalism and glorifying too exclusively the genius of Hamilton." The political scientist Arthur N. Holcombe disliked the fact that George Washington appeared as a minor character in Bowers's account but believed that the general reader would welcome a "delightfully fresh and stimulating" story that would counter the "one-sided productions of Hamiltonian hero-worshippers." William E. Dodd described *Jefferson and Hamilton* as "a marvel of interest, a portrait gallery unsurpassed," and the *Nation* selected it along with only four other books for its honor roll of 1926.[8]

Bowers was a dramatic storyteller and an effective public speaker, and his book and public appearances were warmly received, leading to his selection as the keynote speaker at the 1928 Democratic National Convention. His speech captured the prevailing sentiment of American liberalism in the 1920s. For Bowers, the ability of the Republican party to claim both Abraham Lincoln and Alexander Hamilton was an abomination. In his address, he lashed out at the Republicans, who recently had honored Hamilton at their convention:

You cannot believe with Lincoln in democracy and with Hamilton against it. You cannot believe with Lincoln that "God loved the common people or he would not have made so many of them" and with Hamilton that the people are "a great beast." You cannot believe with Lincoln that "the principles of Jefferson are the axioms and the definitions of a free society" and with Hamilton that they are the definitions of anarchy. You cannot believe with Lincoln in a government "of the people, by the people and for the people" and with Hamilton in a government of the wealthy, by the powerful and for the privileged.

He continued: "Hamilton believed that governments are created for the domination of the masses. . . . There is not a major evil of which the American people are complaining now that is not due to the triumph of the Hamiltonian conception of the state." His invocation of Lincoln's memory was odd, considering he viewed his presidency as the death knell of Jefferson's Republic. Bowers believed that Lincoln had been "aligned, unconsciously perhaps," with the same forces at work since Hamilton's time that sought to destroy Jeffersonian democracy. Lincoln's war had "shunted aside" Jefferson's ideals, and "the foundation had been laid for a plutocratic oligarchy."[9]

In the aftermath of Bowers's address, Republicans attempted to capitalize on what some saw as an unwarranted assault on Hamilton's reputation. During Constitution Week in September 1928 a delegation from two national Republican clubs laid wreaths at Hamilton's grave to "answer the keynote speech attack on Hamilton's memory made at the Democratic National Convention." Republicans attempted but failed in the 1920s to make the observance of Hamilton's birthday an annual party event, with ceremonies at his gravesite and a dinner comparable to the annual Jefferson–Jackson Day feast sponsored by the Democrats. The editorial page of the *New York Times* lamented that at a 1928 graveside ceremony held on Hamilton's birthday, "only a few were present." Fate had been unkind to Hamilton, who "has never enjoyed the popularity to which his great achievements in his adopted country's behalf entitle him. . . . Unlike his great rival Jefferson, Hamilton has never been made the subject of yearly eulogies by a political party."[10]

Though Republicans won in a landslide in the 1928 election, it was the last hurrah for the old order. Events were about to turn in favor of the Democrats, and the siren call from Claude Bowers, warning of greedy plutocrats, soon appeared quite prophetic. One associate of Franklin Roosevelt later compared Bowers's attraction to Democrats with Harriet Beecher Stowe's appeal to the early abolitionists. FDR thought it would be particularly useful if Bowers's *Tragic Era,* a racist portrayal of the Radical Republicans and Reconstruction, was widely read throughout the South; he hoped the book would lure Southerners back to the Democratic fold. Many of these traditional Democrats had abandoned their party in the 1928 election because the presidential candidate, Alfred E. Smith, was Catholic. *The Tragic Era* contained such passages as "then came the scum of Northern society . . . inflaming the negroes' egotism, and soon the lustful assaults began. Rape is the foul daughter of Reconstruction. . . . It was not until the original Klan began to ride that white women felt some sense of security. . . . The negroes . . . for a time grew humble, industrious, law abiding. . . . In the South, the Klan was organized for the protection of women, property, civilization itself." Sadly, death threats from the Ku Klux Klan forced Al Smith in 1926 to cancel a Fourth of July address at Jefferson's Monticello.[11]

Franklin Roosevelt agreed with much of Bowers's assessment of Reconstruction, writing him that "the period from 1865 to 1876 should be known as America's Dark Ages." As a reward for Bowers's yeoman service to the Democratic party, Roosevelt appointed him ambassador to Spain. FDR's aide Raymond Moley told Bowers that he was doing "the greatest kind of work for liberalism and democracy through your books." He was later appointed ambassador to Chile and served there into the Truman years. He retained the deepest affection for Roosevelt, who was "the greatest human being I had ever known, and one of the greatest in all our time."[12]

Throughout his adult life Claude Bowers never doubted that Hamilton was the font of all that ailed America. In an essay written for the *Atlantic Monthly* during the Red Scare of the 1950s, Bowers recalled Jefferson's heroic resistance to the Alien and Sedition Acts. When the nefarious Federalists began plotting to extinguish democracy, Jefferson was at Monticello "tend[ing] his flowers" and was unprepared for the ferocity of the Federalist Terror. Yet once again his nation called him into service, for around Jefferson alone "could the people be rallied." He "distrusted Hamilton's obsession on an army"; and along with other leading Federalists, the ruthless Hamilton presided over a party of warmongers, who viewed "small merchants and artisans . . . as dirt." At the height of the Quasi-War with France, the Federalists felt the "time seemed ripe to wipe out the 'heresy of democracy,'" and thus began the Terror.[13]

To the day he died Bowers was profoundly moved by the fact that the only book review ever written by Franklin Roosevelt was of his *Jefferson and Hamilton*. He wrote to FDR after the review appeared, "I wish I could tell you how delighted I am at the revelations of yourself that appear in the review. . . . I wrote the book really to recall the party of Jefferson to the real meaning of Jeffersonian Democracy, and you have brought it out." The review appeared in the *New York Evening World* on 3 December 1925 and was written by a Franklin Roosevelt (1882–1945) eager to return to political life. It probably occurred to him that a glowing review of a book written by an editorial writer for the *World* might be of some assistance in his race for governor in 1928. The review, "Is There a Jefferson on the Horizon?" served as a first-rate rallying cry for a Democratic politician eager to return to the fray; as an analysis of the founding, it was somewhat simplistic. Roosevelt began by noting that he "felt like saying 'At Last' as I read Mr. Claude G. Bowers' thrilling 'Jefferson and Hamilton,'" and exclaimed, "I have longed to write this very book." He stated that he was "fed up" with the "romantic cult" surrounding Hamilton that began with the publication of Gertrude Atherton's *Conqueror*. Though Roosevelt found Hamilton a fascinating figure and acknowledged his financial prowess, his fondness for chambers of commerce and his "contempt for the opinion of the masses" meant that if the Federalists had triumphed over Jefferson, darkness would have descended on America. "I have a breathless feeling as I lay down this book — a picture of escape after escape which this Nation passed through in those first ten years; a picture of what might have been if the Republic had been finally organized as Alexander Hamilton sought." These same forces of darkness were present in the 1920s, and the question was whether there was a Jefferson on the horizon to fend them off.[14]

Franklin Roosevelt had not always viewed Hamilton or the Federalists negatively. He had written an essay as a Harvard undergraduate that one biographer characterized as "full of hero worship." Roosevelt believed that it was "because of [Hamilton's] insistence" that the Constitutional Convention convened in 1787 and that his success in winning the ratification of the Constitution in New York was "the greatest moment in the life of Alexander Hamilton, now thirty one years old. And yet there were other moments." George Washington appointed him to "the greatest of the Cabinet offices," where Hamilton "ordered the finances of the country" and "removed for all time the risk of disintegration of the States." In 1921, when asked by Arthur Vandenberg to name the greatest American, FDR named Hamilton's fellow Federalist George Washington. FDR's conversion to Jeffersonianism appears to have occurred sometime in the mid-1920s. Perhaps he was influenced by Claude Bowers's book, although he had written to Democratic leaders in December 1924 suggesting that Jeffersonian principles were applicable to contemporary America, months before its release. In a private letter written shortly after publication of his book review, FDR argued that America in the mid-1920s was approaching "a period similar to that from 1790–1800 when Alexander Hamilton ran the federal government for the primary good of the chambers of commerce, the speculators and the inside ring of the national government. He was a fundamental believer in an aristocracy of wealth and power — Jefferson brought the government back to the hands of the average voter, through insistence on fundamental principles and the education of the average voter. We need a similar campaign of education today, and perhaps we shall find another Jefferson."[15] It is unclear whether FDR experienced a genuine conversion to Jeffersonianism based on principle or came to realize that political expediency required it. Nonetheless, his transformation was complete by the time of his presidency.

In his campaign for the White House in 1932, Roosevelt attacked Herbert Hoover and his administration for their Hamiltonian disdain for the interests of the common man. The Republican administration was more concerned with dispelling the depression-era fears of the strong, i.e., big business, than of the weak. This concern was, Roosevelt contended, "spoken in the true Hamiltonian tradition . . . the allaying of [fear] must proceed from the strong to the weak." One of FDR's more notable addresses was delivered at the Commonwealth Club in San Francisco in September of that year. He described Hamilton and the Federalists as believing that "popular Government was essentially dangerous and essentially unworkable." Hamilton was "the most brilliant, honest and able exponent of this point of view," who "believed that the safety of the Republic lay in the autocratic strength of its Government" and that the "destiny of individuals was to serve that government." The theme of Jefferson and Jackson combating the forces of privilege permeated FDR's speeches, particularly those delivered at gatherings of the party faithful. At one event in 1938 Roosevelt compared his own struggle to that of his Democratic predecessors Jefferson and Jackson. Jefferson contested Federalists who were "in favor of control by the few," and Jackson struggled against the Bank of the United States. Jackson opposed the "same evil Jefferson fought — the control of government by a small minority instead of by a popular opinion duly heeded by the Congress, the Courts and the President." In a 1940 address at the University of Pennsylvania, he claimed that Hamilton's desire for a government by "a small group of public-spirited and usually wealthy citizens" would have developed over time "into Government by selfishness or Government for personal gain or Government by class."[16]

At times FDR's quest to connect himself with Jefferson's legacy bordered on the absurd. The president asked the Library of Congress to discover if there was any link between his revolutionary forebears and Jefferson, apparently dissatisfied with the fact that his great-grandfather was an ally of Hamilton. The closest connection the researchers could discover was that Jefferson bought some feather fans from someone named Roosevelt in New York City. FDR also ordered his advisers to gather as many Jefferson quotations as possible for use in his rhetorical defense of the New Deal. Stretching credulity, he referred in one speech to Jefferson, and in a sense to himself, as "a great gentleman [and] a great commoner. The two are not incompatible."[17]

One of Roosevelt's goals was to elevate Jefferson above the partisan fray to the status of a national hero on a par with Washington and Lincoln, a rank the Virginian had not been accorded prior to the New Deal. The erection of a permanent memorial in the nation's capital to Thomas Jefferson would go far toward achieving this goal. Roosevelt first became involved in efforts of this sort when he actively participated in the campaign to preserve Jefferson's estate at Monticello, becoming a member of the Board of Governors of the Thomas Jefferson Memorial Foundation in 1930. As the nation's chief executive, he was the driving force behind the creation of the impressive Jefferson Memorial on the Tidal Basin in Washington. After years of fits and starts Roosevelt declared in November 1938 that "when the Democratic Administration came back in 1933, we all decided to have a memorial to Thomas Jefferson," and he would not allow "the worst case of flim flamming this dear old capital of ours has been subject to" to stand in the way. In his speech laying the cornerstone for the memorial, he argued that the nation was "adding the name of Thomas Jefferson to the names of George Washington and Abraham Lincoln." While not intended to honor "the founder of a party," FDR couldn't resist noting that Jefferson "lived, as we live, in the midst of a struggle between rule by the self-chosen individual or the self-appointed few and rule by the franchise and approval of the many." He dedicated Jefferson's shrine on 13 April 1943, the two hundredth anniversary of his birth. The new memorial signified, in the words of Dumas Malone, Jefferson's "recognition as a member of our Trinity of immortals."[18]

New Dealers often expressed their devotion to Jefferson and their contempt for Hamilton, who was frequently portrayed as the original "economic royalist." Agriculture Secretary, and later the vice president, Henry A. Wallace (1888–1965) wrote in *Whose Constitution: An Inquiry into the General Welfare* that in the early days of the Republic, "farmers were perhaps outmaneuvered by the commercialists led by Hamilton," though he acknowledged his financial skills and believed his actions were rooted in principle, not self-interest. However, in less scholarly venues Wallace was a vocal champion of New Deal Jeffersonianism. Speaking on Jefferson's birthday in 1935, he claimed that "in the passage of years Hamilton's victory has overshadowed Jefferson's. An economic plutocracy has done its best to scuttle our political democracy, though giving lip service to it." Jefferson served as a guide for those engaged in the "struggle for economic democracy," and were he alive in the

1930s he would not support those forces "who wish to preserve . . . the political and economic pattern of the past."[19]

Throughout much of FDR's presidency the Senate majority leader was Alben W. Barkley (1877–1956) of Kentucky, who later became Harry Truman's vice president. His maiden speech as a young congressman skewered the Republican party for its Hamiltonian roots, particularly its support for "higher-tariff taxation." The conflict between Democrats and Republicans over this issue was first emphasized by the followers of Jefferson and Hamilton, Barkley argued, and this conflict was a "clear-cut fight between right and wrong, between justice and injustice, between the rights of the people and the demands of their despoilers." Democratic National Committee chairman James A. Farley (1888–1976) compared FDR's travails to Jefferson's in a radio address in 1938 in which he described both men as New Dealers. Jefferson "had won for Democracy," though "the die-hards held out and sought by desperate means, even to treason, to wreck the popular government he had created." Just as Jefferson faced "treasonous" Federalists, FDR confronted disloyal Democrats who invoked Jefferson's name while resisting the consolidationist policies of the New Deal. These "so-called 'Jeffersonian Democrats'" did not grasp the entirety of Jefferson's thought, Farley claimed. Jefferson "thundered against the evils of special privilege, and his primary objective was . . . to ensure a type of government that would look out for the civil and economic liberties of the mass of the people."[20]

Roosevelt's Brain Trust, his groups of advisers from academia, included Raymond Moley (1886–1975), a former student and friend of Charles Beard at Columbia University. Moley believed that Beard had created the conditions that allowed for the acceptance of the New Deal by an "educated audience." He admired Jefferson's "uncannily shrewd political technique[s]" and saw him not just as a "man of ideals" but as a "consummately clever and resourceful and successful" leader. After Moley broke with FDR he claimed that one of the reasons for the New Deal's declining popularity was its slighting of a Jeffersonian agrarian political strategy in favor of an urban strategy. Another member of the Brain Trust, Adolph Berle (1895–1971), also from Hamilton's alma mater, drafted much of FDR's Commonwealth Club speech in September 1932. In his original draft Berle had written, "Hamilton was asked what part the people might play in his scheme of things. His famous answer was, 'The people, Sir, are a great beast.'" Though this line was removed from the final draft of the speech, there is little doubt that it reflected the prevailing New Deal opinion of Hamilton. No less an authority than FDR's attorney general, Francis Biddle (1886–1968), lectured an audience at the University of Chicago that Hamilton believed the people were a great beast.[21]

Rexford G. Tugwell (1891–1979), also part of Roosevelt's Columbia Mafia, arrived in Washington in 1933. In a two-part coauthored article written for the *Columbia University Quarterly,* Tugwell the planner and centralizer hailed Hamilton's nation-building skills. "We may well owe" the establishment of the Constitution and the Union to Hamilton more than to "any other single person." His loyalty was to the nation, not to any class or local interest. Tugwell also praised the fact that "the West Indian adventurer" had challenged "the predilection for local advantage" found among many Americans, along with their "resisting dislike for organization and control." His work was incomplete, Tugwell argued, for limitations on the executors of government power still existed, though Hamilton would have removed them from the very beginning "in so far as they interfered with the expansion of the money economy."

Hamilton's failings were rooted in his contempt for democracy and equality, Tugwell contended. He came from a class of West Indian planters and merchants who kept a "precariously maintained white presence" in the islands, with brutal measures directed against "the gay and shiftless blacks" whose "careless attitude toward life in general" could have led to revolts that might have eliminated "the master class." Men raised under these circumstances are "incapable of viewing men as equal" and equally "incapable of viewing the lower classes as men at all . . . at least Hamilton had difficulty in doing so." The slave-owning Jefferson, on the other hand, had an easygoing relationship with his slaves and "looked forward to the elimination not only of slavery but of poverty as a whole." Hamilton concluded that "equality was nonsense," that "economic power could never center in the people." Comparing Hamilton with FDR, Tugwell observed that the former "was not on the side which created difficulties with well-to-do citizens who can be so savage at the betrayal of their class, and so his courage was never tested in that way." Hamilton's degeneration "into reaction after retirement from office" and his "ambition for place and money" were among other failings that his partisans needed to confront. Nonetheless, he concluded that Hamilton's policies served as a model for the 1930s, with the "beginnings of some national control of the whole economy" and the decline of the states' rights doctrine. In a very un-Jeffersonian way, he observed that the qualifications necessary for those officials who conduct "enlarged governmental functions" made clear "the truth that we are not really all of us equal in capacity."[22]

Tugwell's essays appeared shortly after the failure of FDR's Court-packing proposal. Announced in February 1937, the scheme was designed to allow FDR to appoint judges sympathetic to his New Deal initiatives. The Supreme Court had voided some of his regulatory acts, and the president was determined to circumvent this opposition. Tugwell vented the anger felt by Roosevelt's allies toward the Court in his essay on Hamilton. He observed that "one who believes in majority rule and in popular mandates . . . cannot at the same time believe that these divisions [the executive, legislative, judicial powers] should be allowed to check each other even to the point of governmental futility."[23]

At the height of the Court-packing crisis, New Dealer Dean Acheson (1893–1971) criticized the justices for their obstructionist tendencies and Hamilton for his "conception of the Court as the angel with the flaming sword standing at the gate of the Garden of Eden protecting us from the iniquitous intentions of the legislature and the President." Acheson's former boss, Justice Louis D. Brandeis (1856–1941), though usually sympathetic to Roosevelt's initiatives, had a different perspective from Acheson regarding Hamilton and the Constitution. Writing in 1916, Brandeis argued that "Hamilton was an apostle of the living law."[24]

The Court-packing proposal went down to defeat, but over time FDR's appointees tilted the Court away from its opposition to New Deal initiatives. One appointee, Felix Frankfurter (1882–1965), believed that "only gratuitous partisanship" would prevent an American from recognizing the "indispensable share that the genius of Hamilton contributed" to founding the nation. However, "the difference between Jefferson and Hamilton is the vital lesson for us." Hamilton was not a celebrated figure in the American tradition because "he was bounded by fears and distrust." Jefferson's sanguine temperament and conviction that America must rest on "nothing less than the whole American democracy" had rendered him a far more persistent influence in the life of the nation.[25] Another FDR appointee to the Supreme Court, for a brief time, was James F. Byrnes (1879–1972) of South Carolina. As a senator, he blasted the Court and its apologists for invoking the name of Thomas Jefferson in defense of states' rights. Jefferson was "a progressive, a liberal, and, above all, a champion of the masses. . . . If the sage of Monticello were alive today, he would frown upon any effort to use his views of states' rights to block social and economic reforms."[26]

Justice William O. Douglas (1898–1980), perhaps FDR's most liberal appointee to the Court, thought that Hamilton's vision of an industrial America "resulted in great good" but also led to "grave abuses . . . which it took over a century to eradicate." He believed that Hamilton's political philosophy was "bottomed on a class conflict in society," and as a result he held that the "propertied class" should control the government. Hamilton "did more than lure" the propertied class in support of the government through proposals such as the Bank of the United States: "He favored it." At his core, he was no friend of the people: "We think of Hamilton as the champion of a powerful national government. And so he was. He thought monarchy was preferable to republicanism. Failing to obtain a chief executive who was hereditary, he turned to other devices designed to rescue the nation from democracy. He believed that 'the people is a great beast,' not to be trusted. Therefore a coercive state was essential." Hamilton's belief that a Bill of Rights was unnecessary was particularly galling to Douglas, for it demonstrated that he was one "who did not trust the people, who felt that government need keep a firm hand on the citizen if the nation was to survive."[27]

Douglas's colleague, Justice Hugo Black (1886–1971), was a devotee of the works of Charles Beard, Dumas Malone, Claude Bowers, and Madison's biographer and New Deal confidant Irving Brant. Black considered Bowers to be "that matchless and superb democrat, that glorious upholder of the standards of Jackson and Jefferson." Regarding Jefferson, Black observed that "in practically everything . . . he said, I agree with him." As a U.S. senator from Alabama, Black frequently invoked Jefferson's and Bowers's names in the course of Senate debates and inveighed against Hamilton. One biographer noted that the "mere sight or sound of Hamilton's name launched him on a fit of oratory." According to Black, Hamilton was "the darling of wealth and privilege" and had referred to the people as beasts. Hamilton also "admired extravagantly the monarchy of England," but Jefferson, Black argued, was the "instinctive and able champion of the struggling many." The chief issues confronting the Democratic party in 1930 were economic, and Senator Black urged his party to focus on these problems. By so doing, the party could "bring about the liberation of the masses from economic slavery."[28]

Black's sentiments were shared to some extent by a group of writers, the Southern Agrarians, most of whom were faculty members, students, or alumni of Vanderbilt University. Though they differed with one another on many issues, they viewed the South as an enclave of agrarian-oriented Jeffersonianism holding Hamiltonian industrialism at bay. Their most famous work, *I'll Take My Stand: The South and the Agrarian Tradition*, included contributions from Frank L. Owsley (1890–1956), a graduate student of William E. Dodd; Robert Penn Warren (1905–1989); John Crowe Ransom (1888–1974); and Allen Tate (1899–1979), among others. They were united in their distress over "the melancholy fact that the South itself has wavered a little and shown signs of wanting to join up behind the common or American industrial ideal. It is against that tendency that this book is written." Ransom starkly summarized the conflict between Jefferson's and Hamilton's vision for America in a question addressed to President Herbert Hoover: "Do Mr. Hoover and the distinguished thinkers at Washington see how essential is the mutual hatred between the industrialists and the farmers, and how mortal is their conflict?" Ransom held onto the slim hope that the "Democratic party can be held to a principle, and that the principle can now be defined as agrarian, conservative, anti-industrial."[29]

Frank L. Owsley's essay reflected the view of Reconstruction popular among Southern sympathizers such as Claude Bowers. A historian at Vanderbilt, Owsley believed that the cause of the Civil War was rooted in economic differences between a commercial North and an agricultural South. The "passionate ideal for which the South stood and fell was the ideal of an agrarian society," he argued. During Reconstruction the South was "turned over" to freed slaves, "some of whom could still remember the taste of human flesh and the bulk of them hardly three generations removed from cannibalism. These half-savage blacks were armed." They were inspired by "savage" political leaders like Charles Sumner, "whose chief regret had been that his skin was not black." Early in the life of the nation, the conflict between the two societies was delineated by the two men who "defined the fundamental principles of the political philosophy of the two societies, Alexander Hamilton for the North and Jefferson for the South." Owsley contended that over time Big Business sought shelter behind Hamilton's national government and that "the vested interests of industrialism have not had any great use for state rights. They are the founders of the doctrine of centralization, of the Hamiltonian and Republican principles." In a later coauthored work, Owsley praised Hamilton for his financial prowess in restoring the nation's public credit. Nonetheless, his effort to enlist the rich in support of the new government allowed the regime to disregard the common people, or "the despised common man," as the authors put it. Owsley repeated a popular theme among Jeffersonian nativists, that Hamilton was "handicapped by some un-American notions."[30]

Owsley viewed Hamiltonianism as the realization of "the plutocratic philosophy," as he suggested in an essay in *Who Owns America?* coedited by Herbert Agar (1897–1980) and the poet and literary critic Allen Tate. Tate endorsed Owsley's claim that the United States was governed by a plutocracy and that the industrial behemoths of the North had ruined American civilization. In an essay published in 1936, he argued that the struggle of one kind of property against another, between "small ownership, typified by agriculture" and "big, dispersed ownership — the corporation" began in 1787. In this struggle the small property owner was "worsted [by] Big Business." He believed that "the struggle is not new. It is the meaning of American history. Hamilton and Jefferson are the symbols of the struggle. Its story is too well known to need retelling."[31]

Tate had been profoundly impressed with a crude study of American history published by Herbert Agar in 1933, *The People's Choice,* proclaiming it to be "the most brilliant short history of the United States ever written." Agar held that the rise of an American plutocracy was achieved behind a façade of democracy. Alexander Hamilton engineered something akin to a counter-revolution, enticing a befuddled President Washington to support a program he did not fully understand. In the famous quarrel between Jefferson and Hamilton, the latter had the advantage due to his "temperamental affinity" with Washington. Both Washington and Hamilton were authoritarian and possessed a "love of property and a strong tendency to acquire more and more of it." Agar also cited Henry Adams's famous quote from America's founding plutocrat: "Your people, sir — your people is a great beast."[32]

Tate and the other agrarians also admired the work of the historian Ulrich B. Phillips (1877–1934), a graduate of the University of Georgia who taught for most of his life in Northern schools. In a lecture delivered in 1932, Phillips contended that Hamilton distorted the intentions of the framers of the Constitution. While the states had come together to form a "more perfect union," Hamilton "was reshaping it again as a paradise for investors and speculators in bonds and stocks." In order to create the Bank of the United States, he convinced George Washington and the Congress that "what was expedient was 'necessary and proper.'" Both large and small farmers were skeptical of Hamilton's scheme, along with "localists and individualists" who fought the plan to no avail. Nothing could stop the Hamiltonian behemoth, for "an architect of nationality was laying the base of a colossal structure, cementing it with money-baron appetite for profits and privilege. . . . Hamilton, his groundwork mightily done, withdrew from office." Phillips believed that Hamilton was "not far from Napoleonic" and that only John Adams prevented his "personal ambition for exploits" from coming to pass.[33]

John Adams was a hero to the expatriate poet Ezra Pound (1885–1972), whose hatred of Hamilton was exceeded only by his hatred of Jews. Though not a Southern Agrarian, like them he was an economic populist and, oddly for an expatriate, a nativist. Pound had a conspiratorial understanding of history, claiming that the corruption of the Western world was rooted in the practice of usury. The "usurocracy" was the source of what ailed America, particularly during the dramatic bank wars of the early Republic but also in Pound's own time. His heroes were all opponents, to a great extent, of centralized banking, including John Adams, Thomas Jefferson, Andrew Jackson, Martin Van Buren, and Thomas Hart Benton. A graduate of Hamilton College in New York (class of 1905), he spent a good part of his life trying to defame the reputation of his alma mater's namesake.[34]

A reader of Charles Beard and Claude Bowers, Pound greatly admired the latter's *Jefferson and Hamilton* and mentioned Bowers in one of his poems (Canto 81). Pound was a close friend of W. E. Woodward and used him to try to send advice to Franklin Roosevelt. Pound was greatly impressed with Woodward's work and shared his disdain for Hamilton's manoeuvres, one of Pound's more delicate descriptions of his financial policies. Hamilton was the "conservative agent of finance," and in the midst of praising W. E. Woodward as a historian Pound observed that "it is hard enough for me to pardon Burr for not shooting Hamilton sooner. . . . Alex Hamilton served the devil."[35]

Pound corresponded frequently with Massachusetts congressman George H. Tinkham (1870–1956) from the late 1920s until the start of World War II. One letter described the dirty work undertaken by Hamilton and Nicholas Biddle on behalf of the Bank of the United States. Pound was troubled not only by Hamilton's financial policies but also by another aspect of his life — what he described as the "son-in-law racket." In one letter to Tinkham, Pound wrote, "Hamilton (Alex) was I believe a snot, more I read, more it appears so, but back of him was his pa/in/law. The snots when they can't elect someone sure to sign on the dotted line plug for 'YOUTH,' which they think they . . . can bamboozle."[36]

One of Pound's more notable works was *The Cantos*, a massive poem composed between 1915 and 1972. In Canto 37, a rambling tribute to Martin Van Buren, he wrote about Van Buren's struggle with the Bank of the United States:

> "on precedent that Mr Hamilton has
> never hesitated to jeopard the general
> for advance of particular interests.
> "Bank curtailed
> 17 million on a line of
> 64 million credits.

In Canto 62 he compared John Adams and Alexander Hamilton: "and as for Hamilton / we may take it (my authority, ego scriptor cantilenae) / that he was the Prime snot in ALL American history." In 1944 Pound implied that Hamilton was Jewish, observing that his race "was never determined with certainty" although his abilities were comparable to Disraeli's. By 1954 the uncertainty had vanished: "Hamilton WAS a kike. a red headed scotch chew" [*sic*]. In 1969 Pound returned to Hamilton College for the commencement ceremonies and was greeted with a standing ovation from the audience.[37]

One of Pound's pen pals was William Carlos Williams (1883–1963), a New Jersey–born poet whose most notable works included *Paterson*, a five-part poem that portrayed Hamilton in the words of one scholar as "the city's protocapitalist villain." Though not as critical of Hamilton as Pound (a high standard to be sure), Williams viewed him as the instigator of American decline and corruption as typified by Paterson, New Jersey. In writings prior to *Paterson* Williams indicated his displeasure with Hamilton, "a type that needed power." In his *In the American Grain*, he contended that usurpers, particularly Alexander Hamilton, betrayed the promise of the American Revolution by creating a materialistic society. This was "*his* United States: Hamiltonia — the land of the company." Aaron Burr represented the true spirit of the American Revolution, a mixture of the Marquis de Sade and Jean Jacques Rousseau. But for "a sombre Washington — with shrewd dog Hamilton at his side — locking the doors, closing the windows, building fences and providing walls," true liberty could have been realized. Burr "knew what a democracy must liberate," including women, whom he loved and whom they loved in return. Burr "was as immoral as a satyr" but far more moral than the greedy, puritanical types like Hamilton, this "balloon of malice." Hamilton "harness[ed] the whole, young, aspiring genius" of American liberty to "a treadmill" and was "the agent" responsible for replacing one form of tyranny with another "as bad as or worse than the one it left behind."[38]

Williams's epic *Paterson* (1946–1958) portrayed the city founded by Hamilton and his Society for Establishing Useful Manufactures as an exemplar of the spiritual degradation of America. In his *Autobiography*, Williams observed that he selected Paterson because "in the end, the city, Paterson, with its rich colonial history . . . associated with many of the ideas upon which our fiscal colonial policy shaped us through Alexander Hamilton, interested me profoundly — and what has resulted therefrom." In Book Two, published in 1948, he described Hamilton as distrusting the people, "'a great beast' as he saw them," who thought "Jefferson to be little better if not worse than any." Hamilton's spiritless soul was revealed by his reaction to the beautiful Passaic River. "Even during the Revolution Hamilton had been impressed by the site of the Great Falls of the Passaic. . . . Here was water-power to turn the mill wheels and the navigable river to carry manufactured goods to the market centers: a national manufactury." His dream of a model industrial center degenerated into an American nightmare, as the beautiful river by Williams's time was "the vilest swillhole in christendom." Hamilton's vision of a manufacturing nation evolved to the point where Paterson, and mid-twentieth-century America, was a vast wasteland dominated by industrialists, "those guilty bastards . . . trying to undermine us."[39]

In 1933 the Pulitzer Prize–winning poet and author Stephen Vincent Benet (1898–1943) and his wife Rosemary wrote *A Book of Americans,* a collection of verse for children about famous Americans. Thomas Jefferson, in his poem, declares:

> I liked the people,
> The sweat and crowd of them,
> Trusted them always
> And spoke aloud of them.

Alexander Hamilton, on the other hand, is the man who considered his countrymen to be great beasts:

Jefferson said, "The many!"
Hamilton said, "The few!"
Like opposite sides of a penny
Were those exalted two.
If Jefferson said, "It's black, sir!"
Hamilton cried, "It's white!"
But, 'twixt the two, our Constitution started working right.

Hamilton liked the courtly,
Jefferson like the plain, . . .

He came from the warm Antilles
Where the love and the hate last long,
And he thought most people sillies
Who should be ruled by the strong.
Brilliant, comely and certain,
He generally got his way,
— Till the sillies said, "We'd rather be dead."
And then it was up to J.

And he yoked the States together
With a yoke that is strong and stout
(It was common dust that he did not trust
And that's where J. wins out.)[40]

Fellow poet and Pulitzer Prize–winner Carl Sandburg (1878–1967) also had
something to say about Hamilton's alleged contempt for the common man.
In his book-length poem *The People, Yes,* an unnamed Hamilton served as
the foil for Sandburg's paean to the people:

Men of "solid substance" wore velvet knickerbockers
And shared snuff with one another in greetings.
One of these made a name for himself with saying
You could never tell what was coming next from the people:
"Your people, sir, your people is a great beast,"
Speaking for those afraid of the people, . . .

Wherefore high and first of all he would write
God, the Constitution, Property Rights, the Army and the Police,
After these the rights of the people.

This shepherding is a divine decree laid on the betters.
"And surely you know when you are among your betters?"

This and a lot else was in the meaning:
"Your people, sir, is a great beast."[41]

Another disciple of the populist school of historical interpretation was the novelist John Dos Passos (1896–1970), whose work on the American founding was profoundly influenced by Claude Bowers. Dos Passos claimed in 1941 that no other book "opened up so many dynamic possibilities" as Bowers's *Jefferson and Hamilton*. Dos Passos reiterated his praise for it in his 1954 biography, *The Head and Heart of Thomas Jefferson*. In *The Ground We Stand On*, he described Hamilton as a Napoleonic conqueror dreaming of an American empire where "consolidated property interests" ruled "over a stratified society." While impressed with Hamilton's brilliance, Dos Passos cited the obligatory great beast quote and disparagingly referred to "Hamilton and his moneymen" as the guiding force behind "the authoritarian trend" of the 1790s. He dealt again with Hamilton in *The Men Who Made the Nation*, where he muted his earlier populist rhetoric concerning him. Nonetheless, in his account of Hamilton's "inquisition" against the "whiskey boys," he portrayed him as a closet Napoleon. Jefferson's biographer Dumas Malone reviewed the book for the *New York Times* and particularly enjoyed Dos Passos's depiction of Hamilton. "He gives a candid report on the relations between Hamilton, the Colossus of the Federalists, and the aging Washington, who was more a prisoner of the Federalists than most historians are willing to admit."[42]

With poets and novelists voicing the despair of depression-era America and Hamilton branded as the cause of that despair, the 1930s witnessed a hemorrhaging of his reputation the likes of which had not been seen since the age of Jackson. It didn't help Hamilton's standing when Robert I. Warshow published *Alexander Hamilton: First American Business Man* at a time when the image of businessmen was at its nadir. It especially didn't help when Warshow dedicated the book to Andrew W. Mellon, "who has carried on with rare distinction the tradition of Hamilton." It was comments such as Warshow's that prompted a journalist, the future editor of the *Nation*, I. F. Stone (1907–1989), to note that Hamilton "has always been the hero of our upper classes." Stone was skeptical of the claim that a disinterested Hamilton enlisted the support of the wealthy to bolster the new Constitution. It was equally likely that Hamilton's "clients and wealthy family connections" prompted his actions. Hamilton was the "poor boy who married a Schuyler" and "who came to his conclusions on society that coincided with the interests of his clients."[43]

As the depression lingered, political candidates offered simple solutions for ending the ordeal, including abolition of the Federal Reserve System. One such candidate was Congressman William Lemke (1878–1950) of North Dakota, who ran for president in 1936 as the nominee of Father Coughlin's Union party. Lemke saw himself as the heir to the legacy of Jefferson, Jackson, and Lincoln, all of whom fought against economic slavery. This impassioned rhetoric was not confined strictly to the campaign trail. When writing about Alexander Hamilton, depression-era scholars lost all sense of proportion. Lyon Gardiner Tyler (1853–1935), President John Tyler's son, taught at the College of William and Mary and was its president from 1888 to 1919. In 1935, he wrote that no political party since the administration of James Monroe, whether they believed it or not, had "dared to call the people a 'beast' as Alexander Hamilton did." That same year the prominent historian Charles M. Wiltse depicted an authoritarian Hamilton who believed that force was the basis of government and "coercion a necessary instrument of control." Wiltse's neofascist Hamilton was disappointed with the Constitution because it did not "rob the common man of his liberty."[44]

The depression-era works of James Truslow Adams (1878–1949) were littered with anti-Hamilton references, including the claim that he called the people a great beast. Hamilton rose to membership in "the ruling caste" and became more of an aristocrat than those who had allowed him to join their kind. He "stood for strength, wealth and power" while Jefferson stood for "the American dream." Hamilton's philosophy was at odds with the Declaration of Independence, and thus the American economy "developed along the lines of Hamiltonian special privilege and moneyed classes." By the turn of the century his system had "run completely amuck," and the rights of capitalists had become divine rights. The Republican party, Adams asserted, "may well look back to Hamilton as its High Priest" but "would not dare to breathe aloud in any party convention, campaign, or speech . . . 'The People, your People, Sir, is a great Beast.'"[45]

Dumas Malone wrote an essay in the first heady months of FDR's presidency that captured the prevailing spirit of the day. In "Jefferson and the New

Deal," Jefferson, the "Prophet of Democracy," faced a rival who found power "intoxicating," "loved the din of battle," "scorned" the common man, and became the idol of "militarists, industrialists, and bankers." Though Malone conceded the "absolute necessity" of Hamilton's "energetic central government," he discerned a troublesome element in his philosophy. Hamilton's belief in "class-rule" and his "contempt for the stupidity of the lesser orders of mankind" had certain totalitarian connotations. In 1933, Malone argued, this type of philosophy would "lead straight to Fascism." Warren Harding and Calvin Coolidge's utter complacency in dealing with the "rise of a financial oligarchy ... proved themselves spiritual descendants of Hamilton" while Jefferson, the champion of the unfortunate and the enemy of the moneychangers, would favor a "new and fairer deal" for the American people.[46]

The condition of Hamilton's tomb on Wall Street epitomized the declining state of his reputation in the 1930s. His stone had begun to sag and the inscription was barely legible to visitors to the Trinity churchyard, most of whom passed the tomb without realizing who lay beneath. Throughout the decade Hamilton's birthday was often commemorated in token, almost pathetic, ceremonies held at his gravesite, with the occasional Republican party functionary in attendance, along with a representative from Columbia University. The New York Times reported a "brief and simple ceremony" in 1930 that was observed by a "group of several hundred financial workers."[47]

In 1932 the notorious Andrew Mellon laid a wreath at the foot of the Hamilton statue on the Treasury grounds to commemorate the 175th anniversary of his birth. That same year witnessed the celebrations of Washington's 200th birthday, with Hamilton mentioned sporadically in the publicity materials released by the George Washington Bicentennial Commission. The New York Times editorialized in June 1933 that the news of that year "would tickle [Hamilton] to death," with a president empowered to regulate vast sectors of the economy, including running a "fertilizer business at Muscle Shoals [Alabama]." Old-line Hamiltonians like Elihu Root disagreed, arguing that many powers assumed by FDR were taken without the consent of the governed and that the "spirit and tone" of Hamilton's economic writings should serve as a model for a reasoned debate on the future of constitutional government. The fear of New Deal centralization led many Republicans to abandon Hamilton and openly embrace Jefferson and states' rights, though a few valiant souls tried to find a middle path between the two.[48]

In 1936 Republicans chose not to commemorate Hamilton's birthday, and Arthur Krock (1886–1974), writing in the *New York Times*, observed that the "omission was wise," what with Hamilton's approval of the notion of implied powers in the Constitution. Covering the Republican National Convention in 1936, William Allen White predicted that a discerning observer of the party's platform for that year may "find a definite swing to the Jeffersonian ideal and away from the Hamiltonian philosophy." Even that ageless Hamiltonian stalwart Nicholas Murray Butler recognized that Jefferson might have been on to something. Butler called for the Democrats to return to their Jeffersonian roots and abandon their policies of "compulsion" and "governmental regimentation." He believed that Jefferson was "the forgotten man" of the New Deal, whose principles were now being "vigorously preach[ed]" by Republicans. The *New York Times'* editors noted the strange ideological transformation that seemed to be occurring within both parties: despite "all their annual lip service to Jefferson the Democrats are now far more Hamiltonian than Hamilton ever was."[49]

Senator Carter Glass (1858–1946) of Virginia, Woodrow Wilson's secretary of the treasury and a conservative Democrat, violently objected to the New Deal and agreed with the *New York Times* that New Dealers were out-Hamiltoning Hamilton. He wished that there were "some Alexander Hamiltons in the Congress" who would not spend more money than the government received. Glass excepted, most Democrats realized how politically unpalatable it would be to adopt Hamilton as an icon. A century's worth of rhetorical assaults had succeeded in portraying him as a hard-hearted, dictatorially inclined plutocrat. Whatever contradictions there might be in doing so, Democrats were content to be associated with the egalitarian populism of Jefferson and Jackson, or at least some vulgarized image thereof.[50]

Before the 1930s drew to a close, a few die-hard Hamiltonian Republicans undertook another futile effort to celebrate Hamilton as a founder of their party. William Guggenheim (1868–1941) of the famous philanthropic family attempted in 1939 to resurrect the movement begun in the late 1920s to have the party commemorate Hamilton's (and Benjamin Franklin's) birth. The hope was that these celebrations would match the Democrat's Jefferson–Jackson Day festivities. Endorsed by some party leaders as an appropriate statement of the party's devotion to thrift and sound finance, the proposal ultimately came to nothing.[51] As the new decade began, the

Roosevelt-Jefferson juggernaut was poised to leave Hamilton on the ash heap of history.

One prominent author inclined to do so was Van Wyck Brooks (1886–1963). A Pulitzer Prize–winning literary historian, Brooks observed in the *Opinions of Oliver Allston* that he was tired of writers referring to the American people as rabble. There was no such thing as "an American rabble," he contended. Furthermore, "when Alexander Hamilton said, 'The people is a great beast,' he backed himself out of the American door. There is one categorical imperative in American life, that one must respect man as such. Whoever does not respect man as such is, in America, a traitor." The *New York Times* felt compelled to rally to Hamilton's defense, noting that "Hamilton's fate at the hand of present-day writers is not a happy one." Citing Brooks's statement, the *Times* did not question the authenticity of Henry Adams's beast quote but argued that Hamilton intended to criticize only the "excesses of the mob when it gets out of hand." Even if one accepted Brooks's bleak interpretation of Hamilton's alleged statement, the *Times* claimed that Hamilton's arch rival Jefferson was also a bit of an elitist who "detested" the urban "proletariat," being something of a "kulak" of his day.[52]

During winter 1943 the *Times* once again found it necessary to intervene on Hamilton's behalf, this time regarding the often expressed sentiment of the era that he was a fascist. A fascist, according to the *Times,* "is the kind of man that Alexander Hamilton was not." Unlike most fascists, he put his country above ideology; he was "a tory who placed his country first." The general secretary of the American Communist party, Earl Browder, differed with the *Times'* assessment of Hamilton. In *The People's Front,* he argued that Hamilton was the "ideological guide and inspiration of the camp of reaction" and possessed "dictatorial ambitions." Appearing at a Jefferson bicentennial celebration with Claude Bowers shortly after the *Times* editorial appeared, Browder claimed that Hamilton was "the typical statesman of the upper bourgeoisie; shortsighted in the greed for huge and quick profits, fearful of the unruly democracy of the masses" who sought to unite the "defeated forces of feudal aristocracy and reaction." Modern American capitalists worshiped at his shrine, though mistakenly so, for had Hamilton's policies been wholeheartedly adopted they would have retarded the development of capitalism by compromising with "feudalism and slavery." New York congressman Vito Marcantonio (1902–1954) agreed with Browder's interpretation. Though not openly a Communist, Marcantonio promoted the party's agenda in the House of Representatives. He noted in 1948 the "deadly parallels of earlier periods and now . . . [with] Jefferson, say, and Hamilton. The contest is always the same — always the people against the entrenched interests."[53]

A neofascist Hamilton debuted on Broadway on 29 January 1943 in Sidney Kingsley's *The Patriots.* The play was a publicist's dream for a nation at war. Written by a sergeant in the U.S. Army, it was hailed in a review in the *New York Times* as a "moving and inspiring" expression of the effort to preserve the ideals of the Declaration of Independence. A special performance was held at the Library of Congress in April of that year to launch a series of events commemorating the bicentennial of Jefferson's birth. General George C. Marshall, Justice Felix Frankfurter, members of FDR's cabinet, and assorted congressmen witnessed a cigar-smoking Hamilton and his Marie Antoinette–like wife utter nasty comments about the French Revolution, the people (the "drunken swine"), and certain political figures from Virginia. The play opens with the Sage of Monticello returning from Paris with his daughter to a polarized country. A bewildered, grandfatherly George Washington ineffectually presides over the nation's government while his "foppish and affected" aide, Colonel David Humphreys (inexplicably referred to as Billy in the play) acts as a lackey for Hamilton within Washington's inner sanctum. The boyish, hot-blooded Hamilton grapples with accusations surrounding his affair with Maria Reynolds while Jefferson tries to get along with this remarkable young man, as he calls Hamilton. In the midst of a yellow fever outbreak, Hamilton scribbles anonymous assaults against the even-tempered Jefferson, calling him a lunatic and a fanatic. Hamilton is in denial about his common roots and becomes enraged when Jefferson reminds him of his ordinary origins. At key moments in the play Jefferson's daughter Patsy appears, along with the family's happy-go-lucky slave Jupiter ("you just come fum one a dem cabinet meetin's?"). A group of Federalists attacks Jupiter, calling him a nigger, an incident that leads him to remark that his owner will someday free all the slaves.

The core of the play is devoted to Jefferson's heroic crusade to preserve the Republic from Hamilton and his "gang of king-jobbers." It is a struggle between the tribune of the people and the champion of privilege. As Jefferson sees it, the faintly alien Hamilton seeks to bring to the New World "the vices and crimes of the Old World." Jefferson instructs Hamilton that a country can be strong only if its people govern it, to which Hamilton responds, "Very well. Let it be a fight, then. But make it a good one. And, when you stir up the mobs, remember — we who really own America are quite prepared to take it back for ourselves, from your great beast, the People." At the play's conclusion, Jefferson persuades Hamilton not to engage in a coup d'etat during the deadlocked election of 1800 and to support the constitutional process that ultimately leads to Jefferson's elevation to the presidency. Shortly after the performance of the play at the Library of Congress, Kingsley was invited to sit in the president's box at the dedication ceremonies at the Jefferson Memorial, accompanied by President and Mrs. Roosevelt.[54]

Newsweek observed that the play recounted "that smoldering period in American history when Thomas Jefferson was forced to joust again for the truths his country had held to be self-evident." There were Americans at that time, *Newsweek* maintained, "who relished paying homage to a king." As for Alexander Hamilton, *Newsweek* claimed he "favored a ruling aristocracy of wealth." *Time* asserted that the issues contested in the play "still have force" and noted that Jefferson feared Hamilton's "encouragement of a plutocracy and hatred for 'that great beast, the people.'" The production was designated the Best Play of 1943 by the New York Drama Critics' Circle and won awards from the Theatre Club, the New York Newspaper Guild, and the New York Federated Women's Clubs. Because of the popularity of Kingsley's works, *The Patriots* was translated into German, Spanish, Korean, Chinese, Arabic, and numerous languages in India. One of the few dissenting voices in the orgy of tributes paid to the play came from some surviving members of the Hamilton club, who distributed a pamphlet critical of a "non-commissioned upstart, who so brazenly incriminates an intrepid Major-General of the Army of the Revolution." Norman Cousins, the editor of the *Saturday Review of Literature*, was also unimpressed. Cousins was disturbed by the liberties Kingsley took with the historical record, noting that his portrayal of Hamilton as a "hell-bent-for-leather fascist . . . may be good theatre but it certainly isn't good history."[55]

With the prevailing popular and academic opinion of the time relegating Hamilton to a status slightly above Tokyo Rose, his defenders were reduced to attempting to convince the American public that he probably would have opposed Hitler. In 1942, *Fortune* magazine, which one might assume possessed a certain Hamiltonian slant, claimed that he and his followers sought to "make the national debt a steppingstone to wealth and power for the few." However, the magazine was not quite prepared to endorse the popular notion that he was a fascist. The editors described him in December 1943 as a "bit of a social climber" who "hated the people" and saw them as a great beast, but "he was above all a Constitutionalist, and he would have had no sympathy for fascists and Nazis." Many Americans were not entirely sure — Dumas Malone suggested in 1943, in an imaginary letter from Jefferson to FDR, that Hamilton found great joy "in battle for its own sake. . . . I suspected my rival Mr. Hamilton, of valuing governmental power for itself and not merely as a means to human happiness and well-being. To those persons in the world today who value force and power for their own sake, I should be unalterably opposed."[56]

The insinuation that Hamilton had certain fascist inclinations reached its peak at the height of World War II and generally did not persist beyond it, though the idea was resurrected somewhat during the Vietnam era. But the great beast canard flourished both during and after the war years. Two wartime-era college history textbooks repeated the quote as gospel, one going so far as to describe it as indicative of a "reactionary wave" that culminated, among other things, in the drafting of the Constitution. Excerpts from Charles A. Beard's *The Republic* were published in *Life* magazine in 1944 and also helped to keep the great beast alive. The passages included an exchange between Beard and a fictional character, Dr. Smyth. An impatient Smyth argues, "Nobody can say that Hamilton had anything but contempt for the people. He is the fellow who said, 'Your people are a great beast,' or something like that, and thought it, whether he said it or not," to which Beard replies, "Substantially all that you say is true." Author Gerald W. Johnson (1890–1980) cited the beast quote in *American Heroes and Hero-Worship*, but Arthur C. Millspaugh (1883–1955), in *Democracy, Efficiency, Stability* was one of the few scholars with the good sense to write that Hamilton was reported to have dismissed the people as a great beast. The prominent historian Merle Curti (1897–1996) quoted it as fact in *The Growth of American Thought*, for which he was awarded the Pulitzer Prize in history in 1944.[57]

Since the 1790s Jefferson and his adherents had portrayed their struggle with Hamilton as a contest between the apostle of freedom and a scheming monocrat (later plutocrat) — with the monocrat having the added peculiarity of foreign birth. By the end of the New Deal, the Hamilton image in the

American mind was something akin to a hybrid mix of Ebenezer Scrooge and Benito Mussolini. The atmosphere was so hostile that even Charles Beard complained in 1948 that Hamilton's name aroused "choking emotions in the bosoms of all 'right thinkers' who confine their knowledge and thinking to the Anti-federalist tradition."[58] When Franklin Roosevelt succeeded in elevating Thomas Jefferson into the American pantheon, Hamilton was, in a sense, airbrushed out of the founding.

One can understand, and perhaps even endorse, the partisan rationale for Franklin Roosevelt's promotion of all things Jeffersonian, particularly in light of FDR's conflict with the Supreme Court, where he invoked the echoes of Jefferson's and Jackson's clashes with that institution. Less justifiable was the lowering of scholarly standards by the nation's intellectuals, who promoted a simplistic common folk versus plutocrat view of American history. Certainly the impact of a cruel depression and a war against fascism partially explains this phenomenon, but it was also likely that some scholars knowingly proffered these distorted accounts to promote FDR's agenda. A review of New Deal–era scholarship on Hamilton and Jefferson seems to offer a glaring example of historians in the service of a political movement.

The principle of economic equality was invoked to undermine Hamilton's reputation during the New Deal, but the ticking time bomb threatening Jefferson's reputation, and one shortly to explode, was the equally compelling principle of racial equality. Jefferson, and many Jeffersonians, either ignored or in fact were quite comfortable with racial privilege. Sheltered behind Jefferson's states' rights doctrine, Jim Crow was alive and well but would soon be undone by the Hamiltonian institutions of the national government. For the time being, the record of the slave owner of Monticello and author of the disturbing *Notes on the State of Virginia* contrasted to that of a founding member of the Society for Promoting the Manumission of Slaves provided solace to those observers who believed that the contest for America's soul was far from settled.

7

Hail Columbia!
Hamilton and Cold War America

The architect of America's cold war policy, Harry S Truman (1884–1972), viewed Thomas Jefferson as a champion of the forgotten man and often criticized Alexander Hamilton's elitism in both public and private comments. There were, however, rare instances when President Truman praised Hamilton's patriotism and financial prowess. He was impressed by the writings of Claude Bowers, whom he described as a "factual writer" and "one of the most able public men of his generation." He tried to enlist Bowers in an effort to counter what he saw as a biased press and cited his "Jefferson books, *The Tragic Era,* and articles" as fitting him "to do a real service to freedom of speech." On more than one occasion, Truman compared his ordeal as president to Jefferson's and claimed, "There never was a more thoroughly misrepresented man than Thomas Jefferson." He once wrote that "the Adamses and the New England historians made a crook and an atheist out of Thomas Jefferson, until honest research proved 'em in error (to put it mildly)."[1]

Hamilton, Truman believed, "sometimes tended to behave on the autocratic side" and "admired the British ruling classes." It perplexed him that Hamilton was "the spokesman for the aristocrats" in the United States, given that he came from "humbler circumstances" than Jefferson. While writing or commenting in nonpartisan venues, Truman acknowledged some admirable qualities in Hamilton. He praised his contributions to *The Federalist,* and after leaving the White House, observed that Hamilton "came to this country without friends or family and deserves a tremendous amount of credit for making a success of his life by the use of his mind; he had a great brain, and one of the most terrible things that ever happened in this country is that his life ended when he was only forty-nine. He did a lot of good things for the country and would have done many more if he'd lived longer." Ultimately, Jefferson and Jackson's populism appealed more to Truman than Hamilton's elitist policies. Jefferson "made the greatest contribution to our system of government," and Jackson was "my personal favorite among our presidents (after Franklin Roosevelt, of course)." Truman enthusiastically endorsed Jackson's war on the Bank of the United States, noting that it was "a great thing that Jackson did" in challenging and ultimately dissolving the bank. He believed, however, that Jackson had not destroyed Hamilton's bank but a corrupt offspring of the original institution.[2]

Truman saw himself continuing the fight begun by Jefferson and Jackson for the cause of liberalism against reaction. According to him, Jefferson challenged the Federalists because he believed they were "stifling the true democratic concept of the new republic," and Jackson "staged a revolution against the forces of reaction, which once more had entrenched themselves in the federal government." In his campaign for president in 1948, Truman told the assembled delegates at the annual Jefferson–Jackson Day dinner that Hamilton "frankly affirmed his belief that the government should be controlled by the rich and the well born. He believed that government should be aristocratic and that it should operate primarily in the interest of wealth and privilege." The cleavage that existed between Hamilton and Jefferson could "hardly have been a[ny] sharper." Hamilton's modern-day adherents were ensconced in the Republican party: "The followers of Alexander Hamilton also banded themselves together as a political party. This, the party of conservatism, the party of rule by the privileged few, has its counterpart in our national life today." Less than a month before his upset victory over Thomas E. Dewey, Truman accused him of downplaying the differences between Republicans and Democrats. "Thomas Jefferson did not seek unity by concealing the real issues between himself and Alexander Hamilton. He made the issues clear, so that the people could reach a decision. And their decision determined that democracy rather than autocracy should prevail in this great country of ours."[3]

By the late 1940s New Deal and Fair Deal initiatives had dramatically expanded the power of the federal bureaucracy. While most progressive scholars and politicians kept Hamilton at arm's length, one could occasionally discern a certain admiration for him as the founder of American public administration and planning, as could be seen in the writings of New Deal Brain Truster Rexford G. Tugwell. Another admirer was the scholar Leonard White (1891–1958), who wrote in *The Federalists: A Study in Administrative History* that "Alexander Hamilton was the greatest administrative genius of his generation in America, and one of the great administrators of all time." The *New York Times* observed in a 1947 editorial that "an advocate of a planned economy who preceded Joseph Stalin by more than 130 years was Alexander Hamilton." Hamilton's ideas approached Marshal Stalin's in their "fervent conviction that national security demands a strong central Government." The *Times* added that modern defenders of free enterprise distorted the truth when they claimed that economic planning was a recent American phenomenon. Planning had been a feature of American government since the day Hamilton issued his Report on Manufactures, calling for the protection or subsidization of America's infant industries, the *Times* argued.[4] This invocation of Hamilton's name in defense of the modern administrative state led some American conservatives in the last half of the twentieth century to abandon their allegiance to Hamiltonianism.

An additional source of distress for many conservatives, particularly those with isolationist inclinations, was the tendency of Truman-era internationalists to cite Hamilton's principles in support of American involvement in the North Atlantic Treaty Organization (NATO). What some conservatives found particularly disturbing was the contention that the president could unilaterally respond to a Soviet attack on a NATO ally without a congressional declaration of war. In congressional debates held in 1949, some Republican senators expressed concern over this prospect. The controversy inspired James Reston of the *New York Times* to write two columns recounting the quarrels of the early Republic over the scope of executive versus legislative war power. Hamilton's belief in discretionary executive authority was contrasted with Jefferson and Madison's defense of legislative control over the use of force. Supporters of American involvement in NATO tended to embrace Hamilton's position that in the event of an outbreak of hostilities the president could respond without waiting for congressional action.[5]

Isolationists were further horrified by the position taken by some internationalists when Hamilton's principles were recalled in defense of an actual political union among the Western powers. NATO was not enough, these advocates of an Atlantic Union argued. Hamilton's financial plans for infant America could be applied to a new union consisting of the United States, seven European democracies, and the six members of the British Commonwealth. This alliance would deal a devastating blow to communism and accelerate European economic recovery. Proponents argued that the United States should take the lead in inviting the other Western democracies to a convention, where a union would be formed and the debts of the member states assumed by the new regime. Hamilton's plan from 1790 "restor[ed] . . . the foreign credit of the United States" and helped to build a nation. It could work again in 1948 for a new transatlantic federal union. One of the foremost advocates of such a proposal was Harold C. Urey (1893–1981), a professor at the University of California who won the Nobel Prize for Chemistry in 1934. He was involved in the development of the atomic bomb and was a recipient in 1961, along with seven other Nobel winners, of a Hamilton Medal from the alumni association of Columbia College. Urey believed that Hamilton's principles could assist the world in avoiding both the threat of communism and a nuclear holocaust. While the United Nations provided cause for some hope, "Hamilton would have seen an exceedingly familiar pattern" in the difficulties confronting that organization. The inability of the United Nations to reach decisions, or to enforce its decrees when it achieved consensus, was a problem remarkably similar to that confronting the United States under the Articles of Confederation. Urey believed that Hamilton's prescription to address the defects of the Articles could be applied among the Western democracies in 1961. "It is my belief that Hamilton would have . . . seen clearly that what is required" was a union of the Western democracies and that he "would have favored again a strong central government for that union."[6]

Throughout the cold war Hamilton's reputation as a foreign policy theoretician generally won him more praise than his domestic policies. American cold warriors drew inspiration from his counsel that effective foreign policy required executive "secrecy and dispatch." Along with the necessity of granting the president the authority to act with "vigour and expedition," Hamilton advocated a certain tough-mindedness in the conduct of foreign policy. Paul Nitze and the authors of the seminal American cold war document NSC-68 evoked Hamilton's maxim that "the means employed must be proportioned to the extent of the mischief" in urging a policy of containment vis-à-vis the Soviet Union. The influential scholar of American foreign policy Hans J. Morgenthau (1904–1980) considered Hamilton's statecraft worthy of emulation. In his *In Defense of the National Interest* he claimed that Hamilton's thinking was rooted in the idea that "international politics is an unending struggle for power in which the interests of individual nations must necessarily be defined in terms of power." Hamilton's famous debate with Madison in the Pacificus-Helvidius dispute over the issuance of a neutrality proclamation in 1793 established Hamilton's credentials as a realist. The dispute was decided in his favor — in essence, a triumph of his pragmatic foreign policy as opposed to a policy derived from moral and legalistic principles. Hamilton's "realistic position," Morgenthau observed, was "formulated with unsurpassed simplicity and penetration." In response to Madison's moral and legal arguments, he "unswervingly applied one standard: the national interest of the United States." To a great extent Hamilton's principles guided the course of American foreign policy throughout the nation's history, though that policy often operated "under the cover of those moral principles with which from Jefferson onward American statesmen have liked to justify their moves."[7]

The historian Felix Gilbert (1905–1991), like Morgenthau an émigré from Hitler's Germany, endorsed the latter's realist interpretation of Hamilton. Gilbert argued that the passages Hamilton wrote for President Washington's Farewell Address reached "beyond any period limited in time and reveals the basic issue of the American attitude toward foreign policy: the tension between Idealism and Realism." In that famous state paper, "Eighteenth-century power politics spoke authoritatively and decisively through the voice of Alexander Hamilton."[8]

One of the key architects of America's containment policy against the Soviet Union was Arthur H. Vandenberg, who in the early days of the cold war served as chairman of the Senate Foreign Relations Committee. The Republican senator secured his place in history by endorsing the Truman administration's Marshall Plan and other internationalist policies. *Life* magazine referred to him in July 1947 as "a famous modern Hamiltonian." In that same issue Vandenberg published an essay on Hamilton that backtracked to some extent from his earlier adoration. "In my impetuous youth I set out to right an historical wrong . . . but I have lived to realize that no one patriot can be called The Greatest American in a land blessed with so many leaders."

He now believed he had "overshot my mark" and conceded that Jefferson was as "equally needed [by] young America." Nonetheless, he still believed that Hamilton "never has been given his historic due." Hamilton's life remained for Vandenberg a classic American success story. "We Americans love Horatio Alger heroes — brave young men who rise above adversity to win great place and fame. Well — here is the top prodigy of them all." He concluded that an appropriate epitaph for Hamilton could be reduced to five words: "The Republic Is His Monument."[9]

Hamilton and his principles were yet again resurrected during the famous debates in the 1950s over the Bricker amendment. Senator John Bricker (1893–1986) of Ohio introduced a series of constitutional amendments beginning in 1951 that sought to protect American sovereignty from international agreements, particularly the United Nations Charter. Bricker and many conservatives feared the erosion of states' rights, due to an increase in federal power necessary to implement international agreements within the United States. His amendment, which went through many revisions, would have restricted the president's power to make executive agreements (agreements reached with foreign powers not requiring Senate ratification) and stated that "no treaty shall be made abridging any of the rights and freedoms recognized in this Constitution." The issue dogged Dwight Eisenhower (1890–1969) throughout his presidency. Eisenhower first attempted to stall Bricker's efforts, but in the end he decided to fight the amendment. Both men turned to Hamilton's essays in *The Federalist* as well as to his other writings on presidential power to bolster their cases. Eisenhower couched his response to Bricker in Hamiltonian language, much to the surprise of his secretary of state, John Foster Dulles. If Bricker's amendment became the law of the land, Eisenhower argued, it would "put us back" to a situation similar to the Articles of Confederation, with its lack of executive leadership. Bricker found Hamilton's understanding of the treaty power to be "most profound" and argued that Hamilton had a restrictive view of it. More than any other founder, he attempted to reconcile the treaty-making power with other constitutional provisions. He "readily saw that an omnipotent Federal Government could be created if the treaty-making power and the power of legislation were regarded as wholly interchangeable." He reconciled this tension by arguing that "treaties are contracts with foreign nations, which have the force of law, but derive it from obligations of good faith. They are not rules prescribed by the sovereign to the subject, but agreements between sovereign and sovereign." The United Nations, however, was engaged in an "effort to junk Hamilton's theory." This effort would not succeed in the United States, Bricker contended, because Hamilton's theory protected "the liberties of the people" while at the same time allowing the nation "to participate fully and responsibly in foreign affairs."[10] In the end, Eisenhower was able to defeat Bricker's amendment.

Despite some growing uneasiness, mid-twentieth-century Hamiltonians tended to be drawn from conservative ranks. One fervent admirer was the Illinois senator Everett Dirksen (1896–1969). Speaking at the dedication of a Hamilton memorial in Chicago in the midst of the 1952 Republican National Convention, he declared that Hamilton "rolled up a scroll of accomplishment almost unmatched by any American I can name." Hamilton's major achievements included the calling of the Constitutional Convention and the erection of a stable financial system upon which to build a nation. The Republican nominee from that 1952 convention, Dwight Eisenhower, was strangely silent about Hamilton (Bricker amendment excepted), considering his brief service as president of Columbia University, though he once described George Washington as "the greatest human the English-speaking race has produced." Ike's running mate, Richard M. Nixon (1913–1994), was asked during the 1956 presidential campaign whether he was more of a Jeffersonian or a Hamiltonian. Breaking ranks with many Republicans, he described himself as an adherent of Jefferson. His "philosophy of individual rights [and his] philosophy of states' rights [was] a philosophy pretty close to much of what we stand for in this administration." Nixon added, "When Jefferson first ran for the Presidency, he ran as a Republican." Although Nixon admired Hamilton's support for sound fiscal policies, Jefferson's belief in individual rights was "the secret of our prosperity." Nixon reiterated his esteem for Jefferson in his race for president in 1960, criticizing Democrats for abandoning their historic commitment to limited government represented by "Jefferson, Jackson, and Wilson." The opposition party had been captured by "radical federalists . . . [John Kenneth] Galbraith, [Chester] Bowles, and [Arthur M.] Schlesinger." Despite Eisenhower's apparent lack of interest in Hamilton and Nixon's embrace of his Republican predecessor from Virginia, the New York Times, one month into Ike's first term, proclaimed "The Hamiltonians [are] back in power after an absence of twenty years."[11]

Dwight Eisenhower's two-time Democratic opponent Adlai E. Stevenson (1900–1965) was a card-carrying Jeffersonian and somewhat of a believer in the Claude Bowers school of historical interpretation. In the early days of his tenure as governor of Illinois, Stevenson defended the Democratic party against the charge that it eroded states' rights by concentrating power in Washington. "History shows us," he argued, "that the trend toward a strong central government was first advocated by Hamilton," who was "sometimes considered to be philosophically the father of Republican policies." Stevenson presided over a celebration in Chicago in 1950 of the 150th anniversary of Jefferson's election to the presidency, with President Truman as the guest of honor. Jefferson, according to Stevenson, was "the immortal philosopher of democracy," and the main tenets of Jeffersonianism included a "firm faith in the people" and a belief in "special privilege for none."[12]

In his 1952 campaign for president, Stevenson hoped to win the allegiance of the common man by appealing to their "ancient Jefferson faith," but in this election the Sage of Monticello was no match for a war hero. In a speech delivered shortly after President Eisenhower's inauguration in 1953, Stevenson asserted that America could not effectively wage cold war if it played the role of a bully. "We cannot, my friends, enlist the support of ordinary people abroad if we do not trust them at home. The Democratic and Republican parties today are separated by the same old principles which divided Jefferson and Hamilton." While Jefferson had faith in "all the people" Hamilton "felt that only men of wealth and affairs were qualified to understand and conduct government."

Jeffersonian scholars of course were disappointed by Stevenson's defeat. Julian Boyd and his assistants compiling *The Papers of Thomas Jefferson* (1950–) wrote, "We wish again to express our thanks to you for your efforts in furthering, during your campaign, the ideals of American democracy which are vital to our survival." In 1955 Stevenson suggested to Boyd an effort to point out repeatedly Jefferson's "advanced ideas in the context of his time." Claude Bowers wrote to Stevenson and drew certain historical parallels between Jefferson's struggle to save the Bill of Rights with efforts in the 1950s to protect civil liberties from McCarthyite excesses. The advice was unnecessary; Stevenson was already referring to Bowers's *Jefferson and Hamilton* for guidance. Stevenson adopted Bowers's position in a speech that his friend Boyd urged him to deliver on Founder's Day at the University of Virginia in

April 1960. Warning of recent efforts to "suspend political debate," Stevenson drew comparisons with Washington's caution in his (and Hamilton's) Farewell Address "against those self-created societies that had fomented so much political dissent." Washington "spoke warmly of respect for law and order, little upon the subject of liberties, and not at all upon the right to criticize." This dangerous drift culminated, in the name of national security, in the Alien and Sedition Acts. Ironically, only four years after Stevenson's condemnation of the "shameful McCarthy era," Boyd published *Number 7: Alexander Hamilton's Secret Attempts to Control American Foreign Policy,* which accused Treasury Secretary Hamilton of secretly collaborating with a British intelligence agent.[13]

In academic circles the siren song of economic populism continued to attract influential adherents throughout the 1950s. The Princeton history professor Eric Goldman was one such believer, as he confirmed in a Fourth of July essay written for *Saturday Review* in 1953. He contended that *The Federalist* was "the gentlemen's *Common Sense*" and was written primarily by the Virginia planter Madison and "Alexander Hamilton, who had staked his extraordinary brilliance on a marriage with the New York aristocracy." *The Federalist* rallied "the propertied groups" behind the Constitution and became over the years a "steady beacon to men of substance [as it] spelled out the belief that people of substance are more fit to run the nation than propertyless nobodies. . . . Many an American could proudly take his light from such unembarrassed conservatism." Goldman saw indications that some elements of the principles of *The Federalist* and Social Darwinism were at work among Eisenhower's conservative supporters, "riding in on a fear . . . and a grin."[14]

While Goldman's views were typical of the era, the bicentennial celebration of Hamilton's birth in 1957 (some argued that it should have been celebrated in 1955) generated renewed scholarly interest in and reconsideration of the founder. The American Philosophical Society devoted its general meeting in 1957 to a discussion of Hamilton. The conference generated a series of important papers on his legacy written by admirers such as the Rutgers professor Broadus Mitchell and Dr. John Krout, the vice president and provost of Columbia University, and critics such as Dumas Malone. Louis M. Hacker, a dean at Columbia University, released *Alexander Hamilton in the American Tradition* in 1957. He hoped in part to counter Hamilton's image as the tribune of the privileged. A critic in the *Saturday Review* observed that Hacker and other Hamilton biographers had their work cut out for them. Though "closer . . . than we have ever been to this exotic, disturbing creature," Hamilton remained "through the ironic twists of reputation in history [the] symbol of all that is commercial and industrious in the material part of Americans."[15]

The first volume of Broadus Mitchell's exhaustively researched biography of Hamilton also appeared in 1957, *Alexander Hamilton, Youth to Maturity, 1755–1788*. Both Hacker and Mitchell were Hamilton admirers, but they differed in their interpretation of his political economy. Hacker viewed him as something of a free market libertarian, and Mitchell (who had run as the Socialist candidate for governor of Maryland in 1934) saw him as a believer in "organization, association, central planning." A reviewer in the *Nation* recognized the discrepancy between the Hacker and Mitchell accounts but ultimately concluded, "in a sense, Hamilton was the father of the Welfare State."[16]

The Stanford history professor John C. Miller, in *Alexander Hamilton: Portrait in Paradox* (1959), argued that the supreme paradox of Hamilton's career arose from the methods he used to build the American economy, ultimately aggravating regional tensions and undermining the very Union Hamilton loved. The publication of Robert E. Brown's *Charles Beard and the Constitution* (1956) and Forrest McDonald's *We the People: The Economic Origins of the Constitution* (1958) were also important milestones, as Hamilton benefited somewhat from scholarship that recognized sources other than economic self-interest in the principles and practices of the founding fathers.[17]

Nevertheless, Hamilton's negative image persisted in some quarters, even in his bicentennial year. A popular American history textbook released in 1957 and coauthored by the two-time Pulitzer Prize–winning historian Richard Hofstadter (1916–1970) yet again portrayed Hamilton as a plutocrat. He stood on "the extreme conservative side" at the Constitutional Convention and during John Adams's presidency was "aching to lead [the army] into battle," for he "hungered for military glory in a war against France." Subtlety was not the hallmark of this textbook:

Hamilton had no respect for the men who were opening up the vast reaches of the new country. He despised farmers, and he hated westerners as troublemakers. In his plan to unify the nation, he assigned to both groups inferior roles. . . . Hamilton showed, too, that the Federalists controlled the army, and were quite willing to make use of it. A readymade network of chambers of commerce . . .

worked for Federalism on the local level. . . . Every Hamiltonian measure was a capitalist's measure that alienated debtors from creditors, even in the Northeast. Every Hamiltonian attitude was an aristocratic attitude that pleased the "gentlemen of principle and property" and offended the "people of no particular importance."

The authors also considered it important to tell students that Hamilton's father-in-law was rich. This exaggerated view of Hamilton was not confined to professional historians. The Harvard political scientist Louis Hartz, in his classic *Liberal Tradition in America*, referred without the slightest hesitation to "Hamilton's hatred of the people."[18]

In light of textbooks such as Hofstadter's, it was not surprising that the bicentennial festivities chaired by the South Dakota senator Karl Mundt (1900–1974) failed to generate widespread public interest. The 1957 celebration of Hamilton's birth paled in comparison to the Washington (1932) and Jefferson (1943) celebrations, perhaps partly because of Mundt's unfavorable reputation among the nation's intelligentsia. He had served as the acting chairman of the House Committee on un-American Activities during the dramatic confrontation between Alger Hiss and Whittaker Chambers and after being elected to the Senate was involved in the infamous Army-McCarthy hearings. In the 1952 presidential election, Mundt led a Republican truth squad following Adlai Stevenson around the country and repeatedly pointed out that the Communist *Daily Worker* had endorsed Stevenson's nuclear test ban proposals. A polarizing figure on the great issues of his day, as bicentennial chairman he sought to defuse the conflict between Hamiltonians and Jeffersonians: "I, for one, never have believed there were any major irreconcilable differences between Jefferson and Hamilton." He was aware that his commission faced an uphill battle to convince many Americans that Hamilton deserved a party. Some members of Congress apparently sought to limit the celebration, allowing only two hundred thousand dollars for the commission's work, an amount that Mundt later described as "less than was needed to do a complete job."[19]

Another controversial appointee to the bicentennial commission was Treasury Secretary George M. Humphrey (1890–1970), considered by American intellectuals to be the quintessential bland, business-oriented Eisenhower-era Republican. Humphrey had drawn their wrath by comments such as his response to Ernest Hemingway's *The Old Man and the Sea* (1952): "Why would anybody be interested in some old man who was a failure?" Undaunted, Mundt and Humphrey's commission wrote thousands of letters to television and radio stations, newspapers and journals, libraries and museums, in an attempt to generate interest in a Hamilton celebration. Humphrey dispatched Undersecretary of the Treasury W. Randolph Burgess, whose wife was Hamilton's great-great-granddaughter, to a gathering of some two thousand historians at the 1955 meeting of the American Historical Association to urge widespread observance of the bicentennial. From his home in Gettysburg on 16 September 1956, President Eisenhower issued the obligatory proclamation calling on state governors, federal officials, and all citizens to "observe the year commencing January 11, 1957, as the Alexander Hamilton Bicentennial." Eisenhower's proclamation described Hamilton as "one of the principal architects and leaders of the movement for 'a more perfect Union.'" He "served his country well throughout his life," and his role as secretary of the treasury "proved him to be one of the boldest and most farsighted of the founders." Despite the commission's best effort, as the cultural historian Michael Kammen observed, it was "all to little effect." Karl Mundt indicated in his final report to Congress that he was frustrated with his commission's limited success in generating interest in Hamilton. Particularly galling was the reluctance of the entertainment industry to produce films on him: "The commission staff tried hard to persuade individuals and corporations to produce such films but with little success."[20]

On the appointed day, 11 January 1957, observances were held in New York City; Washington; Chicago; Paterson, New Jersey; Baltimore; and Havana, Cuba, where a memorial service was held by a joint session of the Cuban congress. Ceremonies were also held at American army posts around the globe and on the island of Nevis, Hamilton's birthplace, in the British West Indies. New York City and Columbia University in particular served as the focal point, as Dean Louis Hacker opened the celebrations with a nationally broadcast address from the Columbia University Club on Hamilton's relevance to the world of the 1950s. He emphasized Hamilton's usefulness as a guide for the emerging former colonies of the world who needed to "understand that the processes of building are slow and painful; they require the honorable discharge of obligations." America had survived and prospered because an underdeveloped United States followed Hamilton's advice on the importance of responsibility and integrity in government. Senator Mundt delivered an address on the steps of Federal Hall in New York City in front of a statue of Hamilton and praised him for his establishment of a sound national currency. Hamilton understood that "a sound dollar means as much to the poorest man among us as to the richest." The presence of "godless aggressive tyrannies of communism" in 1957 served to remind Americans of the importance of Hamilton's system of individual rights and "orderly Government." Later in the day Mundt spoke to the board of governors of the American Stock Exchange and included an appeal for money to restore Hamilton's proverbially threatened Harlem home, the Grange. Vice President Richard Nixon joined Treasury Secretary George Humphrey in laying a wreath at Hamilton's statue on the Treasury grounds; the ceremony concluded with some brief remarks from Humphrey.[21]

In August 1957, Mundt spoke again at a bicentennial event honoring Hamilton, this time marking his role as the founder of the Coast Guard. True to his concern for internal security, Mundt claimed Hamilton "cut the pattern" for immigrants to the United States who since the founding had embraced "America as their only home and loyalty." Though pleased that he was finally receiving some recognition, the New York Times lamented the fact that Hamilton was one of the "most romantic figures amongst American statesmen" but had never "become a great popular legend in the front rank of our national heroes."[22]

The one event that restored some luster to Hamilton's reputation, and the most important to come out of the bicentennial era, was the publication of The Papers of Alexander Hamilton (1961–1987). The idea for the project originated in 1938 with Hamilton's old promoter Nicholas Murray Butler of Columbia University. Economic conditions and war delayed the project until 1955, when it was formally announced that the Columbia history professor Harold C. Syrett (1914–1984) would edit the series. Syrett believed that both the John C. Hamilton and Henry Cabot Lodge editions of Hamilton's writings fell "short of meeting the needs of scholars and students today." He asked one of his former master's degree students, Jacob E. Cooke, to join him as associate editor for the project. They received grants from the Rockefeller Foundation and from Time, Incorporated, with Columbia University Press serving as the publisher. The editorial board of historians and economists from Columbia included Dumas Malone, Henry Steele Commager, Louis Hacker, and Allan Nevins. In 1955 it was projected that the completed collection would consist of ten volumes, though in fact it ultimately grew to twenty-seven, the first two of which appeared in 1961. In the end the project cost over $1.5 million, with the editors collecting approximately nineteen thousand documents. The Hamilton bicentennial commission contributed to the successful hunt for archival material related to him. Mundt requested in 1956 that Secretary of State John Foster Dulles instruct American embassies around the globe to ask their host governments to search for copies of any foreign Hamiltonia related to Syrett's project. Ultimately, relevant items were found in some thirteen countries.[23]

On the eve of the publication of the first two volumes, Syrett told the *New York Times* that Hamilton was a "ruthless, ambitious hustler on the make" who was always "the right guy at the right place at the right time." Nonetheless, the Cornell professor Clinton Rossiter (1917–1970) claimed that the publication of Hamilton's papers would advance the refurbishment of his reputation. The crises of the cold war had made all Americans "tougher and braver . . . in a word more Hamiltonian," and a reading of his papers could only improve his standing. A 1961 review in *Time* hailed the surge in publication of the founders' papers for contributing to a revision of their "convenient caricatures," especially that of Hamilton. For too long, *Time* argued, "in the great pageant surrounding the birth of the nation, Hamilton clearly played the heavy." The *New Yorker* agreed, claiming that among the men from the founding generation, Hamilton was "obscured by years of political partisanship" and "has been particularly hard to see."[24]

Dumas Malone applauded the publication of Hamilton's papers along with those of the other founders, but he could not resist hurling another veiled criticism at his hero's nemesis. Hamilton was the "first great architect of national power" and would make a magnificent secretary of the treasury in any era, and in a time of national emergency "would be a superb Secretary of Defense." Though uninterested in money for himself, he would nonetheless be "much sought after by business if he were here now, and he might end up at the head of General Motors or the United States Steel Corporation. Unquestionably, he would be a superb business executive." Linking Hamilton with General Motors seemed to be in vogue during the Eisenhower years. In an essay in the *Midwest Journal of Political Science*, one writer observed that "Hamilton is, beyond question, the founding father of the G.M. view of the national interest, of a businessman's government, of the partnership principle, of the conservatism of the present administration." Connecting Hamilton with

General Motors may appear odd, but it stemmed from President Eisenhower's proclivity for appointing business executives to his cabinet. Secretary of Defense (Engine) Charlie Wilson had been president of GM and during his confirmation hearings had uttered the immortal line, "What was good for the country was good for General Motors and vice versa."[25] His comment repulsed many academics and members of the media; and Hamilton, as the father of American capitalism, was thus held responsible for the typical 1950s corporate Republican.

Malone later criticized Hamilton over a different issue in a 1956 *New York Times* book review, charging that he was sympathetic to the "entire body of repressive legislation" found in the Alien and Sedition laws of 1798 to a degree even greater than President Adams. The director of the Hamilton bicentennial commission, J. Harvie Williams, took exception to Malone's criticism in a letter to the *Times*. There was certainly room for legitimate dispute on this issue, but it was symptomatic of the uphill struggle facing the bicentennial promoters in convincing Americans that Hamilton deserved a celebration.[26]

A little noticed but significant achievement of the Hamilton bicentennial staff was its request to the Library of Congress to track down the source of the great beast quote. The commission considered one of its responsibilities to be the "correction of canards and misconceptions of various acts and views of Hamilton." The director of the Legislative Reference Service at the library traced the quote back to Henry Adams and observed that he and other authors had not cited the original source. The commission concluded in its interim report that the quotation was "without basis, according to an exhaustive check by the Library of Congress." At the close of the bicentennial year, one observer suggested that America probably had not seen the last of the great beast. Professor Bower Aly, chair of an advisory committee for the bicentennial, noted that "men who should know better have attacked Hamilton" for his alleged comment. Aly protested that whenever the legitimacy of the quote was called into question, the standard reply was, "well, anyway, it sounds like Hamilton," or, "you can't prove that he didn't say it." The great beast quote proved more resilient than the bicentennial commission's final recommendation to Congress that a suitable memorial to Hamilton be erected in Washington "in keeping with the weight and measure of his accomplishments."[27]

As the 1960s began, some Jeffersonians reluctantly broke from their ancient faith. Weaned on the New Deal, many of these defectors converted out of admiration for Hamilton's conception of a robust national government, though emotionally their hearts remained at Monticello. Charles L. Black Jr. (1915–2000), a professor at Yale University Law School and a leading figure in American legal circles, described his agonizing conversion to Hamiltonianism: "Jefferson, to most of us, is a more attractive figure than is Hamilton. Jefferson made himself a symbol of trust in human nature and of belief in the rights of man. . . . I can and do get as much joy as the next man from calling up to thought the rout which Hamilton and his associates suffered at the polls in 1800. The contemplation of that triumph is as freshly pleasurable as if it happened yesterday." Nevertheless, the time had come for Americans to confess that "Hamilton was right and Jefferson was wrong" on the great issue of constitutional interpretation. Without Hamilton's broad interpretation of the powers of the federal government, "there would have been no T.V.A. [Tennessee Valley Authority] — but alas for those who would count this loss a gain, there would have been no F.B.I." And he concluded in 1960, "We are all Hamiltonians today."[28]

That same year Senator John F. Kennedy (1917–1963) captured the White House. Kennedy extolled Jefferson in his speeches and uttered the famous line at a dinner for Nobel Prize winners that it was "the most extraordinary collection of talent, of human knowledge, that has ever been gathered together at the White House, with the possible exception of when Thomas Jefferson dined alone." Despite his admiration for Jefferson, the presidential historian Henry Graff of Columbia University saw more of Hamilton than Jefferson in Kennedy. With Kennedy in mind, Graff wrote in 1962 that Hamilton's "youthfulness, hardness, and unambiguousness" were considered by many Americans as "de rigueur in an ideal national leader." The political scientist and Kennedy biographer James MacGregor Burns agreed with Graff that there was something Hamiltonian about Kennedy. He led the executive branch "with such vigor and style and imagination that in a sense he was 'tuning high' the whole national government, just as Alexander Hamilton had once done."[29]

Kennedy's Pulitzer Prize–winning *Profiles in Courage* had contributed to his image as a politician with intellectual inclinations and helped him emerge as a national figure. The book briefly discussed Hamilton's concern that senators be insulated from public pressure but noted that they were soon confronted with situations forcing them to choose between their consciences and the wishes of the public. In particular, "the local prejudices which Hamilton

hoped to exclude" intensified as partisan and regional differences arose between the Federalists and the Jeffersonians. In the midst of the most serious
challenge of Kennedy's presidency, the Cuban missile crisis, the *New York
Times* observed that Hamilton's directive issued in 1790 regarding procedures
for boarding foreign vessels was "widely quoted and applied in all naval services." But for the most part Kennedy himself seldom mentioned Hamilton
during his presidency, though at a Fourth of July address from Independence
Hall in 1962 he stated that the United States would be "ready for a Declaration of Interdependence" with America's European partners. Kennedy noted
that while pressing for the adoption of the U.S. Constitution, "Alexander
Hamilton told his fellow New Yorkers 'to think continentally.' Today Americans must learn to think intercontinentally." Kennedy's most effusive praise
for Hamilton came in an August 1962 address when he referred to him as "the
progenitor of so many distinguished acts."[30]

During the Kennedy era, the fate of Hamilton's New York City home, the
Grange, became something of a minor cause célèbre. The house was built in
1801 and 1802 and was designed by John McComb Jr., one of the architects of
New York's city hall. It was the only home Hamilton ever owned and remained in his family's hands until 1833. In 1889 it was moved a short distance
from its original site and was used as a rectory for St. Luke's Episcopal Church.
In 1924 the house was bought by the millionaire financier J. P. Morgan and a
partner and presented to the American Scenic and Historic Preservation
Society, with the condition that it be relocated to a suitable location. The
society was unable to raise the funds needed to maintain the property, and it
fell into disrepair, despite hopes that the Grange would "serve to perpetuate
the memory of Hamilton as Mount Vernon does that of Washington and
Monticello that of Jefferson."[31]

Senators Jacob Javits (1904–1986) and Kenneth Keating (1900–1975) of New
York introduced a resolution in Congress in May 1960 to declare the Grange
a national monument. The Department of the Interior proclaimed the home
eligible for registration as a historic landmark in December 1960, hoping that
this would spur efforts for a federal takeover of the building. A year later Javits
and Representative John Lindsay toured the home and were shocked to see
its dilapidated condition. There was some concern as the delegation made its
way to the second floor that the rickety stairs might collapse. The *New York
Times* later reported that the building was "hardly noticed by the public. Plas-

ter falls from its ceilings, paint peels from its walls, and small boys delight in breaking its windows."[32]

Two perennially contentious issues arose during the fight to save the Grange — the responsibilities of the wealthy in American society and race. Repeated pleas for private funds to restore and relocate the home by Senator Karl Mundt, the *New York Times,* and the American Scenic and Historical Preservation Society went nowhere. The *Times* couldn't resist noting that private efforts to save the only home ever built by the "patriarch of America's fiscal system" failed to generate a "few score thousand dollars — a paltry sum by Wall Street standards." The home "ought to have been rescued long ago by the financial institutions of this city." The fact that the nation's bankers and industrialists were stingy when it came to honoring the founding father of American finance was too much for some congressmen to abide. When Javits's bill came up for consideration in the House these members attacked the business community for not supporting private preservation efforts. Interest groups representing America's banks were invited to congressional hearings on the subject. Representative J. T. Rutherford of Texas hoped that the American Bankers Association would contribute to a private effort because he had heard bankers "complain about members of Congress being loose with [public] money." Representative John Saylor of Pennsylvania wrote to the president of the association, asking that they "pay for the cost of establishing this shrine." The bankers had been "very free on occasion to criticize the expenditure of public funds" and had a unique opportunity "to honor their founder." Saylor's request was rejected. Rutherford and Representative Herbert Zelenko of Manhattan, the House sponsor of the legislation, pushed for a limitation on the amount of federal money to be spent on the memorial at $460,000, a figure that would be reduced even further if the banking community changed its mind.[33]

The race issue emerged after Senate majority leader Mike Mansfield chose to attach a constitutional amendment outlawing the poll tax to the resolution declaring Hamilton's Grange a national monument. It was a highly appropriate action in light of Hamilton's aversion to slavery. In 1962 five states retained the practice of levying a tax as a requirement to vote, including Alabama, Arkansas, Mississippi, Texas, and Virginia. Mansfield's action outraged Senator Strom Thurmond of South Carolina, who observed, "It is indeed significant that this proposed constitutional amendment is to be substituted for a joint resolution to establish Alexander Hamilton's only home as a memorial to his memory. It creates a perplexing state of affairs when a proposal to honor this man, who wrote so eloquently in defense of States rights, is used as a vehicle to further encroach upon them. It is a sad commentary to the memory of Alexander Hamilton that this bill which would establish a memorial . . . must be shunted aside for this purpose, even temporarily." Senator John Sparkman (1899–1985) of Alabama agreed, claiming that while he followed the political philosophy of Thomas Jefferson, he "always had a great admiration for Alexander Hamilton," whom he considered the godfather of the Republican party. Hamilton was a patriot, and though Sparkman was "in favor of the proposed Alexander Hamilton National Monument," he did "not like to see that measure sacrificed by being changed into a vehicle for the proposed poll tax measure." One senator questioned whether there was a genuine desire to honor Hamilton by some opponents of the poll tax amendment. Senator Spessard Holland of Florida recalled, "Some Senators who [we]re not greatly interested in the Alexander Hamilton resolution wept bitter tears over the fact that that resolution was interfered with."[34]

A nine-day Senate filibuster was finally broken in a 62 to 15 vote, the entire minority from the South, save one. The House and the Senate went on to final approval of a bill making Hamilton's home a national shrine and separately approved the poll tax amendment that was sent to the states for ratification. On 30 April 1962 Senator Javits and Representative Zelenko were notified that President Kennedy signed the Hamilton bill sometime over the weekend. Unfortunately, this action did not mark the end of the troubled saga of the Grange.[35]

From his position inside Kennedy's White House, Arthur Schlesinger Jr. wrote in the *New Republic* after the publication of the first two volumes of the Hamilton papers that his philosophy "produced social irresponsibility but economic progress." Despite "its contempt for the mass," the Hamiltonian tradition benefited the people by "increasing output and raising living standards." Schlesinger added, "Hamilton was the first great modernizer in our history. He believed that the development of his adopted country required a national government and an industrial economy; and his policies consisted in transferring authority to the centralizers and income to the entrepreneurs." Conservatives may not have been surprised to read such claims from Arthur Schlesinger, but when the business-oriented magazine *Fortune* published an article in 1957, "Was Hamilton the First Keynesian?" and essentially answered yes, it doubtless prompted more than one conservative to question their allegiance to Hamilton.[36]

This image of Hamilton as a planner and regulator of all things economic had been noted warily in 1953 by the prominent conservative scholar Russell Kirk (1919–1994), when he expressed serious misgivings about Hamilton's legacy. John Adams was "the real conservative" of the American founding, with Hamilton properly understood as the champion of American acquisitiveness and centralization of government power. According to Kirk, Hamilton lacked the foresight to see that a "consolidated nation" might also become a "leveling and innovative nation." Despite the example of Jacobin France, Hamilton proceeded with efforts to create a strong government, unconcerned that this power could be used for ends other than to support a "conservative order." Kirk endorsed the often repeated idea that there was something alien about Hamilton, or as he put it, his "very exoticism" blinded him to the fact that Americans would resist his desire to transplant English ways into their nation. Moreover, Hamilton's pragmatism prevented him from discerning the long-term damage his policies would produce. "The haughty and forceful new aristocrat" failed as a statesman in not anticipating, among other things, the shocking state of modern cities that became breeding grounds for a "newer radicalism" sharply at odds with Hamilton's principles. Preeminently a city man, Hamilton "never penetrated far beneath the surface of politics to the mysteries of veneration" and did not grasp that "veneration withers upon the pavements." Hamilton's fascination with "the idea of a planned productivity" caused drastic changes in America that might have occurred naturally at a far less destructive pace. His "thoroughgoing contempt for the people" led him to hope that his powerful state would be guided by "the rich and well-born," who, through firm enforcement of the laws, "could keep their saddles and ride this imperial system like English squires." Over time Hamilton's powerful consolidationist state fell into the hands of levelers.[37]

Vincent Miller, a critic for *National Review,* was also suspicious of the increasing admiration for Hamilton found among liberals, observing that Jeffersonian battle cries of sweeping out of office the privileged few sounded less appealing to intellectuals, now that "the elite is no longer one of money." Miller was particularly critical of Clinton Rossiter's *Alexander Hamilton and the Constitution* (1964). He noted that Rossiter once referred to Hamilton's constitutional theories as "rightism run riot" but now viewed him as useful to "the garden variety liberal" eager to continue expanding the powers of a "broadly interpreted Constitution." In fact, Rossiter had criticized Hamilton in his earlier *Conservatism in America* for expressing "a high-toned, plutocratic . . . opportunistic brand of Federalism." Modern industrial conservatives, Rossiter claimed, were the true heirs of Hamilton. He branded Hamilton a plutocratic Tory and on another occasion described him as dazzled by plutocracy. But by 1964 Rossiter's new Hamilton was seen as useful to liberals, as Miller put it, because he believed in a living Constitution that favored "federal power, a strong executive, a ruling elite," and control of the economy. Rossiter had speculated in *Alexander Hamilton and the Constitution* that Hamilton's constitutional theory allowed for such actions as President Truman's seizure of the steel industry. Although Miller believed that Hamilton deserved "all the veneration Professor Rossiter wishes to give him," he should not be praised for what he "did to the Constitution."[38]

Despite growing indications that some liberals were converting to Hamiltonianism, it was still generally believed that, as the *Saturday Review* noted in 1962, "when right-wing politicos look for a patron saint of greater antiquity and less radicalism than Lincoln, Hamilton usually gets their votes." There was no way around "the unflinching bluntness of Hamilton's conservatism." One liberal observer who probably would have agreed with that assessment was James MacGregor Burns. He was part of a generation of historians and political scientists who had come into prominence in the post–World War II era and persisted in describing Hamilton as the champion of the rich and well born. He wrote in *The Deadlock of Democracy*, an influential book among those interested in getting America moving again, that Hamilton "looked on the mass of people as grasping, ignorant, slavish, in short, as incapable of self government." Despite the fact that years had elapsed since the authenticity of the great beast statement had been called into question, Burns noted that "opposition to majority rule is not so blatant today as when Hamilton uttered his famous malediction on the people as a 'great Beast.'"[39]

Three of Burns's contemporaries, Richard N. Current, T. Harry Williams, and Frank Freidel, wrote a popular 1960s college history textbook that abandoned the great beast canard but asserted that Hamilton, toward the end of his life, believed the United States was sinking into chaos. Proceeding to intuit Hamilton's innermost thoughts, the authors claimed, "Then, he thought, the country would need a military dictator, a sort of American Napoleon, to bring order out of chaos, and he imagined that he himself would emerge as the man of the hour."[40]

Ironically, one of the premiere right-wing politicos of the day, Senator Barry Goldwater (1908–1998), probably would not have contested these disturbing depictions of Hamilton. Goldwater considered himself a Jeffersonian, as did many of his supporters. The publication of his *Conscience of a Conservative* played a significant role in his emergence as the spokesman for the Republican party's conservative wing, and his chapter "Freedom for the Farmer" cited a passage from Hamilton's *Federalist* no. 17. Hamilton had claimed that it was improbable that the national government would be interested in the "supervision of agriculture": if the national government did so, "the attempt to exercise these powers would be as troublesome as they were nugatory." Goldwater contended that "Hamilton was wrong in his prediction as to what men would do, but quite right in foreseeing the consequences of their foolhardiness." In "A Conservative's Creed" Goldwater condemned "the siren call of material goods" and urged a "rededication to the national goals that Jefferson set." During his presidential campaign in 1964 one of Goldwater's followers, Frank Donovan, wrote an election-year biography, *The Americanism of Barry Goldwater*, which contended that Hamilton and his allies considered the people a mob. As a result, the Hamiltonians sought a national government with "wider latitude so that the upper class which they favored to dominate the government would have more leeway to rule." As he revealed in a memoir published in 1979, Goldwater shared the concern of the early populists regarding the power of "international moneylenders" — "how they acquired this vast financial power and employ it is a mystery to most of us." Jefferson "opposed Alexander Hamilton's scheme" for a Bank of the United States, and rightly so. Goldwater observed that "the powerful European banker Anselm Rothschild once said, 'Give me the power to issue a nation's money, then I do not care who makes the laws.'" The Bank of the United States' collateral descendant, the Federal Reserve, was "beyond the reach of any president" and operated "outside the control of Congress." Despite Goldwater's allegiance to Jeffersonianism, I. F. Stone claimed in 1964 that the "authentic springs of Goldwaterism" could be found in the conservative tradition dating back to Hamilton, for whom "the people . . . were 'a great beast.'"[41]

The most prominent Jefferson scholars of the 1960s were uncomfortable with the tendency of Goldwater and other states' rights advocates to describe themselves as Jeffersonians. In the historical community Merrill Peterson, the author of *The Jefferson Image in the American Mind,* Julian Boyd, and Dumas Malone, the author of the six-volume Pulitzer Prize–winning *Jefferson and His Time,* acted as the principal guardians of Jefferson's legacy. Peterson took particular exception to the Goldwater-Jefferson comparison, arguing that "American history is grossly distorted when the shock which Hamilton's nationalism gave to the Jeffersonians is bracketed with the perturbations now felt by Goldwater Republicans." Peterson was the most balanced of the trio when it came to interpreting Hamilton, but unlike Malone, he seemed skeptical of any chance of reconciling Hamilton's legacy with Jefferson's. Citing Henry Adams on Hamilton and Jefferson, Peterson wrote in 1965 that "whatever shading was supplied by historians, 'no compromise between them ever was or ever will be possible.'" "It is inescapable," he observed, that the two remain in the realm of "historical Manicheanism." Peterson strongly objected to Clinton Rossiter's claim that Hamilton was "the first full-blooded American," believing instead that he was not a true exemplar of Americanism. Peterson's Hamilton was "a faint hearted republican at best, 'unquestionably a man of the Right.' . . . little involved in the feelings, attachments, and aspirations of the American people, Hamilton's commitment was not to America but to his own glorious image of a great nation." He "operated on principles that were more European than American." Peterson shared the view of many historians of his day, that Hamilton was, as he put it, the founder who "never understood the liberal principles that defined American nationality itself" and who won the "confidence of the privileged classes." While acknowledging the plausibility of various favorable interpretations of Hamilton, Peterson seemed allied with those who saw him as a champion of soulless materialism. This was the Hamilton whose "bust and portrait have long graced Chambers of Commerce, and whose statue before the Treasury Building in Washington was dedicated by President Harding and Secretary Mellon."[42]

Boyd and Malone tended to give little credit to Hamilton and often refused to acknowledge any defects in Jefferson. When Jefferson's spotty record as a civil libertarian was highlighted in 1963 by Leonard Levy in his *Jefferson and Civil Liberties: The Darker Side,* Boyd, who read only the concluding chapter of the work, stated that Jefferson could only be measured, according to Levy's account, "sympathetically and uncritically." Boyd told Levy that if his account was accurate, then he had "wasted his best years in the wrong profession." In fact, President Jefferson had advised that a few wholesome state prosecutions be directed against his Federalist enemies and often used tactics that Boyd and Malone tended to condemn in Hamilton but excused in Jefferson.[43]

As Clinton Rossiter observed, Malone's Jefferson series was riddled with references to Hamilton that put the author squarely in the tradition of Claude Bowers. Malone alluded to Hamilton's "aggressiveness, . . . imperiousness, . . . lust for power" and used the terms "intrigue, potential dictator, officious, natural prima donna, and egotism" to describe him. These qualities stood in sharp contrast to Jefferson, a "true and sure symbol of the rights of man." In 1962, with Hamilton's legacy seen in a somewhat more favorable light and Jefferson's states' rights doctrine linked with racial discrimination, Malone delivered an address at Rice University in which he offered the theory that whatever mistakes Jefferson made were really Hamilton's fault. Malone believed that Hamilton was a patriot, had "constructive talents in the realm of government," was a creative financier, and "performed magnificent service" in the fight to ratify the Constitution. But — and there always was a but — Hamilton was "exceedingly aggressive, inordinately ambitious, and undeniably arrogant. . . . He was indifferent to, even contemptuous of, the ordinary individual." Malone claimed that Jefferson adopted his states' rights positions and his rigid interpretation of the Constitution because Hamilton provoked resistance. Jefferson wouldn't have adopted these unyielding positions if Hamilton hadn't "pressed things so far and so hard." In essence, Malone's Jefferson had responded in desperation to a power-hungry Hamilton by advocating policies he really did not support. Malone was determined to preserve Jefferson's image as a champion of human rights, even at the cost of questioning the man's fortitude. There was, however, no reason to doubt the sincerity of Dumas Malone's beliefs. "Above all," as Peterson described it, Malone believed "in the greatness of 'the great generation' in Virginia." Though Malone sought to reconcile himself with Hamilton, too much was at stake to allow for an authentic reassessment of the great adversaries. This was particularly true in the case of Jefferson's states' rights doctrine and its relationship to America's tawdry legacy of racial discrimination.[44]

Although most defenders of states' rights turned to Jefferson for inspiration, Senator Sam J. Ervin (1896–1985) of North Carolina looked instead to Hamilton. A prominent critic of the activist Warren Court of the 1950s and 1960s, Ervin cited Hamilton to make his case that the court was legislating instead of interpreting the law. Prompted by the desegregation of Southern schools, Ervin claimed in 1955 that the Supreme Court had exceeded its constitutional authority by nullifying acts of Congress and the states. He contended that Alexander Hamilton had assured opponents of the Constitution that "the supposed danger of judicial encroachments . . . is, in reality, a phantom." In his address to the Harvard Law School Association of New York City, Ervin cited at length Hamilton's claims that members of the Supreme Court would exercise restraint due to their lifelong immersion in the laborious study and practice of the law. "The people had no reason to doubt the accuracy of Hamilton's assurance" of judicial restraint, which held throughout most of the history of the United States. Ervin claimed that the justices of the Warren Court had violated Hamilton's pledge to the American people. By substituting their consciences for the law, as *Brown v. Board of Education* and other decisions revealed, the Warren Court rendered Hamilton's assurance moot. Ervin suggested that perhaps a constitutional amendment was the vehicle necessary to restore Hamilton's promise of judicial restraint, restricting service on the Court to those who had legal as opposed to political backgrounds.[45]

The social upheaval associated with the civil rights movement of the 1960s was matched if not exceeded by the turmoil surrounding the Vietnam War. Hamilton's advocacy of an energetic executive, once warmly welcomed by some liberal academics and politicians, was now rendered suspect. In an essay written at the peak of the cold war, Adrienne Koch (1912–1971) bluntly summarized the anxiety many Americans felt regarding the national security state and its executive overseers. Koch claimed that "never was the role of the state and its military defense system a greater problem for freedom" than in the cold war. A professor of history and an author of numerous favorable works on Jefferson, Koch viewed Hamilton as Curtis LeMay in a waistcoat and breeches. She contended that Hamilton was a man of "secret ambition and unscrupulous hopes" with a "private vision of himself as a Caesar." She was disturbed by what she labeled "Hamilton's militant, wealth-oiled nationalism" and argued that in the absence of the tempering effects of Jeffersonian and Madisonian principles, "There would have been little in a Hamiltonian tradition to withstand the appeals of totalitarian 'efficiency.'"[46]

Echoes of Koch's fear of Hamilton's militarism could be found in the work of Richard H. Kohn, who began in the mid-1960s to examine the origins of the American military establishment. Kohn believed that at no other time, except perhaps during Reconstruction and the cold war, had militarism threatened the United States to the extent that it did during the early years of the Republic. Alexander Hamilton was a key player in this saga, as he was "infected with dreams of lasting historical fame." Military command in the service of empire building provided the best avenue for him to realize that ambition. During the Quasi-War with France he yearned for the type of fame awarded a "great general in battle." Kohn's Hamilton "lusted for military command" and "was the personification of American militarism. . . . No one posed a greater danger to the nation's emerging military traditions." John Adams prevented Hamilton's "dream of power and glory" from coming to pass when he "disassociated himself from a Hamiltonian cancer that might consume his administration." Though Kohn believed that Hamilton had done more than any other man to create an administratively sound American military establishment, his leadership contributed greatly to the destruction of a Federalist party "consumed by militarism."[47]

Douglass Adair (1912–1968) held similar concerns about Hamilton's incipient Caesarism. An editor of the *William and Mary Quarterly* and a professor at Claremont Graduate School, Adair claimed that Hamilton had a "demonic passion for fame" and by 1798 his "once laudable ambition had become dangerous." He had a craving for the presidency and on realizing he was unelectable, "an alternative road" to power appeared during the Quasi-War with France. He cherished this crisis, but it was a situation fraught with peril for the young nation: "Give an army to any man who lusts for supreme power and who sees no legitimate road to power under existing institutions, and existing institutions are at once in danger. . . . Was not Alexander Hamilton the one major leader among our Founding Fathers who had the desire, the will, and the capacity to attempt a policy of Caesarism in which he was destined the Caesar?"[48]

By 1800 Hamilton was suffering from a "species of political insanity." That year he "invited" Governor John Jay of New York to "stage a legislative coup d'etat," an indication of how "dangerously irresponsible Hamilton had become." He later proposed a "rather terrifying project" for a Christian Constitutional Society to oppose "the devilish Jeffersonians." Though a kinder, gentler Hamilton emerged near the end of his life, this proposal for a "repulsive pressure group" capable of fanning "the fires of religious intolerance" reflected the Hamilton of old, the Hamilton of unbridled ambition.[49]

Adair considered Hamilton to be "the prophet of capitalism" and argued that he unequivocally favored a "moneyed aristocracy and a hierarchical society." He "expected a continual use of military force would be required to keep the rebellious poor in their place." While his *Federalist* coauthor James Madison favored union to prevent "class war from being declared in America," Hamilton cherished it "as an instrument guaranteeing that the rich would win every class struggle."[50]

A note of dissent from this antagonism toward Hamilton could be found in an influential work by Gerald Stourzh, *Alexander Hamilton and the Idea of Republican Government*. A professor at the University of Vienna, Stourzh was a research associate at the University of Chicago in the late 1950s, where he was influenced by Hans J. Morgenthau and to a lesser extent by Leo Strauss (see chapter 8). Stourzh also viewed Felix Gilbert, another scholar of Hamilton's statecraft, as one of his mentors. In his book Stourzh examined the impact of Montesquieu, Machiavelli, David Hume, William Blackstone, and other political philosophers on Hamilton's thought and statesmanship. Stourzh hoped to contribute to the discussion about republican government and the founders "by analyzing both Alexander Hamilton's understanding of republican government and the direction he wished to give it in America." Reflecting the influence of Morgenthau and Gilbert, Stourzh devoted great attention to Hamilton's foreign policy and his understanding of the interrelationship between domestic and foreign initiatives. Hamilton's arguments on behalf of an energetic government, Stourzh maintained, stemmed primarily from his concern over foreign threats, with domestic matters a secondary concern. For Stourzh, Hamilton was "one of America's first great statesmen," and his enduring achievement could be found "in his fight to establish . . . a new nation, a new empire."

Perhaps the most controversial aspect of Stourzh's book was his contention, borrowing from Abraham Lincoln, that Hamilton belonged to "the family of the lion, or the tribe of the eagle" — a man ideally suited for founding but disdainful of the regular day-to-day politics of a settled constitutional regime. Hamilton failed "as a servant of the Constitution," Stourzh claimed, and this could be seen in his "treasonable role" in the Beckwith affair, recounted by Julian Boyd in *Number 7*. In this instance and in his later attempt to "disregard constitutional provisions" in New York during the selection of presidential electors in 1800, Hamilton revealed a certain contempt for constitutional democracy. Nevertheless, both efforts arose from high motives, reflecting his desire to steer "the new nation in the right direction." As the "self-appointed founder of an empire," he did not feel bound by a "strict adherence to constitutional rules." Both his triumph as the founder of an empire and his failure as a constitutional servant were attributable to his love of fame, "the ruling passion of the noblest minds."[51]

In characterizing Hamilton as something of a noble, farsighted statesman, albeit a potentially dangerous one, Stourzh drew the wrath of Adrienne Koch, one of the chief proponents of a one-dimensional image of Hamilton. Koch bridled at the suggestion that a foreign commentator such as Stourzh could offer a more objective perspective on American politics and political figures than his American counterparts. She was irked by his apparent presumption that "those who are free of American democratic faith are in a better position to grasp Hamilton's true greatness." In keeping with her fellow Jeffersonians, she implied that this particular foreign observer was impatient with the American desire for "the good society and for reins on power." She suggested that Stourzh viewed these "American concern[s]" as "an undue tenderness for civil liberty." His brusque challenge "to virtually all other scholars who have written on Hamilton" was of some interest, she noted, but common sense revealed a Hamilton afflicted with an "incurable love of and pursuit of political power" who was guilty of "grave irregularities" as treasury secretary and Federalist party leader.[52]

Grave irregularities marked the presidencies of Lyndon Johnson and Richard Nixon, including the Vietnam War, the Watergate scandal, and charges of misdeeds by the Central Intelligence Agency. These events bolstered the arguments of those observers who sought a return to a constitutional presidency along the lines of Jefferson and Madison. The alleged aversion of these two presidents to executive secrecy and dispatch and their supposed willingness to defer to Congress (far more the case with Madison than with Jefferson) were held up as the ideal for post-Vietnam America. The unpopular and divisive presidential war in Vietnam led many prominent academics who once hailed the activist presidencies of FDR, Truman, and Kennedy to modify their position.

Arthur Schlesinger Jr., the influential author of the post-Vietnam classic *The Imperial Presidency*, was one such convert. He confessed that he too had been wrong to belong to what he called "the uncritical cult of the activist presidency." To the extent that Hamilton was seen as the founder who promoted an energetic executive, this revisionist view of an imperial presidency exposed him to a line of scholarly attack muted since the New Deal. However, most critics of the imperial presidency tended to cite excerpts from Hamilton's writings indicating that even he favored a restrained or constitutional presidency. They generally avoided attacking Hamilton but softened his position by neglecting passages that broadly interpreted executive power.[53]

Senator Thomas Eagleton, one of the prime sponsors of the War Powers Act of 1973, noted that "even Alexander Hamilton, hardly a populist," acknowledged "the superior weight and influence of the legislative body in a free government." Eagleton continued, "It is often said that during this formative period in our history, one voice, that of Alexander Hamilton, spoke for broader presidential authority." He disagreed with this assessment, citing Hamilton's criticism of Jefferson's restraint during the conflict with the Barbary States. He argued that "Hamilton's position in this instance cannot reasonably be read as a brief for the right of a President to initiate hostilities."[54] Nonetheless, Hamilton's broad definition of defensive war probably would have led him to oppose the War Powers Act as an infringement on the president's role as commander in chief.

During the Vietnam era a number of prominent Americans joined with Arthur Schlesinger in reassessing their support for an activist presidency. Henry Steele Commager (1902–1998), something of an unofficial dean of the historical community, joined the chorus of those condemning the rogue presidencies of Lyndon Johnson and Richard Nixon. Commager had studied under the tutelage of the great Jeffersonian William E. Dodd and to a certain extent adopted his conception of the historian as political activist. The young Commager found Claude Bowers's *Jefferson and Hamilton* absolutely fascinating and deemed it the best account of the conflict between the two men. "Bowers is an out and out Jeffersonian, for which thank God . . . and this is the cleverest defense of Jefferson I have seen in so short a compass." Commager was moved by Bowers's jeremiad and embraced his version of Jefferson. "Certainly there never was in this country a statesman of more talent, more genius, more admirable versatility than Jefferson. . . . This country has seldom seen Jefferson's equal in any walk of life." Hamilton, however, "was a much overpraised individual." Commager allowed that he "was possibly the most brilliant intellect of his age, possibly of America," but he was "quite out of spirit with the whole trend of that nascent nation which he, strangely enough, did so much to make and maintain." In keeping with mid-twentieth-century historical scholarship, Commager dismissed Hamilton as "essentially a class-legislator." He once wrote that "my sympathies have always gone to . . . the dissenters" and that he wanted to "live with . . . Jefferson, not Hamilton, or with Tom Paine, not Burke." A defender of the New Deal, Commager refused to admit that there were any Hamiltonian elements in FDR's conception of the presidency or in his policies. FDR was not a Hamiltonian because Hamilton had no concern for the common man — it was Herbert Hoover who was the real Hamiltonian.

The young Commager had celebrated the activist presidency, or at least strong progressive presidencies. He wrote in 1941 that "all the 'strong' presidents were 'great' Presidents, and all the 'great' Presidents were 'strong' Presidents" and argued that the threat to liberty in America was more likely to emerge from Congress than from the executive branch. However, the Vietnam War changed all that. Commager denounced the imperial presidencies of Johnson and Nixon, welcomed congressional attempts to restrain presidential power, and enthusiastically endorsed the student protests of the 1960s. He wrote in *The Defeat of America* that even Hamilton, "always ardent for power," would not have approved of the broad exercise of authority assumed by America's cold war presidents. Nonetheless, "It is Madison, not Hamilton, who has a just claim to be considered not only the father of the Constitution but its most authoritative interpreter," and it was Madison who believed only Congress can make the decision to go to war.[55]

Commager's friend Allan Nevins (1890–1971) also championed strong presidential leadership along the lines practiced by Franklin Roosevelt. A journalist turned historian, Nevins differed with Commager in that he was less of an activist scholar and somewhat more sympathetic to Alexander Hamilton, despite his friendship with his colleague at the *New York World,* Claude Bowers. Nevins admired Bowers's practical experience in politics and considered him to be one of the nation's best historical writers. Nevins appeared to accept some of the mid-twentieth-century gospel on Hamilton, including the validity of the great beast quote. However, in 1922 he published an exhaustive history of the *New York Evening Post*, the newspaper started by Hamilton and some of his lieutenants, and portrayed the founder in a favorable light. Referring to Hamilton as a statesman he added, "No other leader approached him in brilliance, but his genius was not unmixed with an erratic quality."

Nevins supported the New Deal and praised what he saw as FDR's Hamiltonian conception of the powers of the national government. He admired the humane ideas of Jefferson but criticized him for not realizing "as Hamilton realized, that liberty and democracy are bound to suffer if they do not have a strong government to protect them. A powerful central government . . . was set up despite Jefferson and in defiance of his wishes." Nevins's respect for Hamilton was based partly on the fact that, unlike many of his contemporaries, he did not view businessmen and entrepreneurs as villains. He wrote respectfully of John D. Rockefeller, Henry Ford, and Eli Whitney and was seen by his students at Columbia as "very conservative" and as an "apologist for capitalism." When the Vietnam War came, Nevins was far more restrained than Commager in offering support for the student movement.[56]

The same cannot be said for the more radical historian Howard Zinn, who taught for many years at Boston University. His account of American history made Charles Beard sound like a publicist for the Daughters of the American Revolution. He had a penchant for interpreting American history as a squalid tale of oppression and exploitation. An activist who participated in the civil rights movement and in protests against the Vietnam War, Zinn believed that the preservation of economic privilege animated the principles and practices of the founders. This was particularly true of the Federalists, and in that sense Zinn was not that far removed from Beard, Claude Bowers, William E. Dodd, and other mainstream twentieth-century historians. However, Zinn diverged from them in viewing racism and sexism as an equally powerful force in the creation of nation. In his popular *People's History of the United States*, he depicted Hamilton as the originator of the "alliance between big business and the government" and erroneously described him as a "merchant from New York." Hamilton "was one of the most forceful and astute leaders of the new aristocracy" and "an up-and-coming member of the new elite." His efforts at the Constitutional Convention were influenced by his "connections . . . to wealthy interests through his father-in-law and brother-in-law." This new aristocracy was jolted by Shays's Rebellion into writing a Constitution "that serves the interests of a wealthy elite" while doing just enough for small property owners and middle-income Americans who acted as "buffers against the blacks, the Indians, the very poor whites."[57]

Zinn's fellow 1960s activist Staughton Lynd, a professor at Yale and an occasional visitor to North Vietnam during the war, offered a "new (perhaps New Left) American history," which emphasized "economic causes, while avoiding the caricature that limits 'the economic factor' to conscious pursuit of pecuniary advantage." A Quaker pacifist whose parents had authored the sociology classic *Middletown: A Study in Contemporary American Culture* (1929), Lynd saw the Constitution as a compromise between "Northern Capitalists and southern plantation owners." He believed that Hamilton was part of a group of brilliant New York Federalist leaders who were public-spirited and devoted to their country more than to their private concerns. Yet these same New York conservatives, clustered around the Schuyler and Livingston families, "functioned throughout the Revolution as something very similar to an 'executive committee of the ruling class.'" At stake for Hamilton and his fellow wealthy New Yorkers was "what kind of society would emerge from revolution when the dust settled, and on which class the political center of gravity would come to rest." They "took it for granted that society was a hierarchy of ranks, with a wealthy and leisured elite at its head and the 'lower orders' and 'the peasants' under their rule." These men were also "conservative . . . in the very modern sense of resisting fiercely government intrusions on free enterprise," with Alexander Hamilton serving as "the principal spokesman of the nation's investors in fluid capital."[58]

As one might expect, the late 1960s and early 1970s witnessed a return to the tradition of debunking figures from America's past in a manner not seen since the heyday of W. E. Woodward. Sidney Lens (1912–1986), a onetime editor of *Progressive Magazine* and leader of the New Mobilization to End the War in Vietnam, claimed that Hamilton was "the spokesman for the wealthy of America." The charge was made in *Radicalism in America,* in which he also argued that Hamilton envisioned a society where the "interests of the 'rich and well born' were paramount." Questions related to "freedom or the common man were distinctly secondary" in Hamilton's mind, Lens added. Ferdinand Lundberg (1902–1995) in *The Rich and the Super-Rich* echoed Lens's assertions.

Lundberg had fashioned a lifelong career out of writing scathing exposés of the rich, and in this work he portrayed Hamilton as "a self-appointed spokesman for plutocracy and outright corruption in politics" and the "political father of American plutocracy."[59]

The great beast canard continued to flourish throughout the 1960s. A member of Vice President Hubert Humphrey's staff did his part to keep the beast alive, citing the quote in a history of the Democratic party published in 1967. Comedian-turned-activist Dick Gregory, who left the comedy circuit to run for president in 1968, also kept Henry Adams's tale in circulation. It was not "a wonderful life" in Gregory's America, and Alexander Hamilton was Henry Potter. Gregory believed that the core of the American experience since Hamilton's time was the struggle for money — "how to get it for the have-nots, and how to keep and increase it for the haves." One of the first acts of the American government was "the establishing of the privilege of the wealthy few at the expense of the many." According to Gregory, "When Hamilton's 'great beast,' the people, rose up in Pennsylvania . . . Hamilton got his man George Washington to send in government troops." It was no surprise that a writer for the *New York Times* noted on the Fourth of July 1967 that if a popularity poll were taken that day "as to where Alexander Hamilton stands in the regard of the townspeople, the answer very likely would be low. . . . Those who know little else of his career will remember something about a remark he made (if he made it) about equating the people with a 'great beast.'"[60]

Hamilton's Columbia University was the site of some of the more highly publicized confrontations between students and administrators during the Vietnam era. The 1960s marked the beginning of a ritual at the university — students liberating Hamilton Hall. In 1968 they occupied the hall, demanding that the university end its participation in defense-related research and halt plans to build a gymnasium; in 1972 the hall was seized again over demands for an end to the war in Vietnam; in 1985 over demands that the university divest itself of stocks from companies engaged in business in South Africa; and in 1996 over demands that the university establish a department of ethnic studies. The symbolic import of seizing Hamilton Hall was not lost on some observers of the day. One letter writer to the *New York Times* in 1968 reminded the Columbia community that Hamilton had single-handedly managed to disperse an unruly group of students threatening to burn the house of the college's Tory president. Hamilton's "amazing powers of persuasion" were more effective than the "large force of police" required two hundred years later, an example the writer apparently hoped would be heeded by the university's president, Grayson Kirk. The *New York Times* in 1975 ran a story describing Hamilton as a "radical Columbia dropout who went on to make it big" and recounted his efforts to stop the mob from harming the college president. This hip Hamilton was one student rebel who became part of the establishment — when the school reopened in 1784 as Columbia College, Hamilton was named to the board of trustees.[61]

In a remarkably brief span of time both Columbia University and the nation had undergone a radical transformation. It was hard to imagine that in 1957 Dean Louis Hacker had launched the Hamilton bicentennial with a nationally broadcast address from the university. At that time Hacker, author of *The Triumph of American Capitalism* (1940), had claimed that Hamilton's America served as a model for the rest of the world. He also declared that "revolutionary fervor is one thing; public responsibility is another." In 1970, Andrew Hacker, who followed his father into academia, published *The End of the American Era*. Nothing more vividly captured the rapid demoralization of the nation than this collapse of confidence within the Hacker family.[62]

That "the times were a changin'" was undoubtedly true. But nothing was changing for the Hamilton image in the American mind, for he continued to be seen as the personification of the nation's dark side. As the editors of a sixties reader saw it, he was part of a tradition that "despised both change and equality and concocted arguments to refute them." Hamilton and other conservatives "defended hierarchy and the status quo against democrats and apostles of progress." As the nation staggered out of the 1960s, it appeared unlikely that this "enemy of progress" would ever emerge as something more than a poster boy for privilege and militarism. His situation was so dire that one sympathetic scholar, Gilbert L. Lycan, who had challenged much of the accepted wisdom regarding Hamilton, wrote in 1973, "Every writer for several years past has been attacked for writing an objective, balanced and fair book about Hamilton. People who review books are generally liberals, and American liberals have long since resolved to categorize H[amilton] falsely, and they defy anybody to write truthfully about him."[63]

As the 1970s dawned, the Jefferson-Hamilton blood feud reached new depths of ferocity. Julian Boyd, whose earlier accusation that Hamilton served as an intelligence source for the British generated considerable controversy, launched a new salvo against him in 1971. Despite complaints that *The Papers of Thomas Jefferson* was being issued at a remarkably slow pace, Boyd somehow found the time to write a seventy-eight-page appendix in volume 18 of that series, attempting to confirm the old Jeffersonian accusation that Hamilton used his high office for personal gain. Merrill Peterson had earlier criticized Boyd for including in Jefferson's papers an account of Hamilton's actions as agent Number 7. Peterson suggested that it was "more properly a chapter in Hamilton's history than in Jefferson's" and that it "astonishes belief when no one can foresee [the Jefferson papers'] completion in a hundred volumes." Undaunted, Boyd pressed on in another attempt to discredit Jefferson's rival. In essence he argued that Hamilton was involved in speculation while serving as treasury secretary and had revealed his adultery with Maria Reynolds as a cover story to conceal serious financial misconduct. Boyd alleged that Hamilton's dramatic admission of an affair served as a smoke screen to keep congressional inquisitors at bay and that he forged letters from James and Maria Reynolds as part of his cover-up. The alleged extortion letters were the "palpably contrived documents of a brilliant and daring man who . . . tried to imitate what he conceived to be the style of less literate persons." Boyd believed that the events associated with the Reynolds affair marked the "first symbolic clash between Hamilton and Jefferson" and involved questions of high philosophic import. But it also revealed "the sordid level of reality to which the head of a great department permitted it to descend." Not surprisingly, he concluded that Hamilton "took his guidance from the old order, Jefferson from the new."[64]

A more ambitious cover-up, and a real one at that, captured the nation's attention during President Richard Nixon's second term. Hamilton's name was invoked frequently throughout the Watergate scandal, occasionally as a founding sage who spoke wisely of impeachment but at other times to demonstrate that Hamilton possessed certain Nixonian qualities. Congressman Peter Rodino, who chaired the House Judiciary Committee's investigation of possible impeachable offences, had been a member of the Alexander Hamilton Bicentennial Commission. Rodino and his committee members often turned to Hamilton's *Federalist* essays for his perspective on impeachment. Congresswoman Barbara Jordan from Texas cited Hamilton's remarks in *Federalist* no. 65 as she formally announced her intention to vote to impeach the president. She added, "I was not included in . . . 'We, the people.' I felt somehow for many years that George Washington and Alexander Hamilton just left me out by mistake. . . . I have finally been included in 'We, the people.'" A bewildered Congressman William Cohen, another member of Rodino's committee, asked, "How in the world did we ever get from the Federalist papers to the edited transcripts," referring to Nixon's White House tape recordings.[65]

One Watergate-related investigation focused on reports that President Nixon used government funds to improve his private residences. Congressional investigators drew heavily from Hamilton's *Federalist* no. 73 in arguing that the president's salary remained fixed and could not be increased or diminished while in office without violating the Constitution. Eleven members of the House Judiciary Committee believed that Nixon's home improvements were impeachable offenses and cited no. 73 in their committee's final report to bolster their case. Oddly, Hamilton also emerged as a bit player in the drama surrounding Vice President Spiro Agnew. When the vice president became the subject of a criminal investigation over corruption charges dating back to his time as governor of Maryland, his lawyers challenged the authority of the investigation taking place in Maryland and claimed that only Congress had jurisdiction over a sitting vice president. There was precedent, of course, in Vice President Aaron Burr's murder indictment in New Jersey for killing Hamilton, plus a separate New York indictment stemming from the duel. The Burr case became the subject of inquiries by interested members of Congress. Both Agnew and the Burr precedent were soon forgotten after the vice president chose to resign and pled no contest to some of the charges against him.[66]

Throughout the impeachment saga the media also consulted Hamilton's *Federalist* writings. An essay in *Time* observed that "Alexander Hamilton, the most persuasive apostle of a strong Chief Executive," believed that impeachment was the "ultimate device for checking power in a democracy." The *New York Times* was fond of quoting Hamilton to bolster the case for impeachment, in one instance citing passages in 1973 from his *Federalist* no. 65 that the editors believed "treat impeachment in a perfectly matter-of-fact fashion." Welcoming evidence that the nation's fear of impeachment appeared to be ebbing, the *Times* noted that "185 years ago, Alexander Hamilton summed up both the relevance and the dangers of impeachment in the present crisis." A favorite passage of Hamilton's cited repeatedly by the media and by members of Congress justified the use of impeachment for "those offenses which proceed from the misconduct of public men, or in other words from the abuse or violation of some public trust. They are of a nature which may with peculiar propriety be denoted political, as they relate chiefly to injuries done immediately to the society itself." The *Times* contended that President Nixon "can fairly be charged with abusing his public trust in the way that Hamilton describes."[67]

While Hamilton was seen by many people as a font of constitutional wisdom during the Nixon impeachment saga, there was also the perception in some quarters that he planted the seed for the imperial presidency and its Watergate offspring. Senator Lowell Weicker of Connecticut, a member of Sam Ervin's Senate Watergate Committee, claimed that "the modern theory of Presidential power was conceived by Hamilton," although he believed that the founder did set certain qualifications on that power. The trend toward expanding presidential power established by him was "irrevocably set" when the Jeffersonian "strict constructionists came to power in 1801 and did not curb Executive power, but rather enlarged it." The columnist Carl Rowan saw Nixon's dirty tricks as part of the "meanness and madness perpetrated in the name of what Alexander Hamilton called, 'checking the unsteadiness of the people.'" According to Rowan, Hamilton "was the advocate of the notion that if you just put things in the hands of a rich, wellborn elite, they'll take care of the status quo and you won't have to worry about the mass of the people upsetting anything. . . . Those wonderful people who gave us Watergate considered themselves the modern day elite, even those who weren't rich and wellborn." Rowan claimed that Thomas Jefferson personified an alternative tradition in America that had confidence in the masses.[68]

In the midst of the Watergate crescendo, Stanley Cloud, writing in *Time* in 1973, had the ghosts of Hamilton and Jefferson engage in a dialogue at the base of the Washington Monument. Hamilton sounded much like G. Gordon Liddy, Jefferson a mix of Sam Ervin and Bob Woodward. According to Cloud, Jefferson was "the noble idealist who symbolizes the dream of the American Revolution" while Hamilton "represented the business interests of New York . . . and mistrusted the electorate and was not above using questionable tactics to shape policies and institutions." Hamilton is pleased that America in August 1973 is powerful and rich but disturbed by the demoralized state of the American people. Jefferson argues that although the country is "bigger and richer and more powerful . . . the soul of our Revolution has been lost." There is a "paucity of spirit" in the nation because "the White House has become a royal palace . . . inhabited by a new American sort of monarch." Hamilton retorts that this is "Jacobin nonsense" and asserts that if there is a distance between Nixon and the people, "well, so much the better."

Stanley Cloud's Hamilton believes that it is "the emotions of the uninspired mob . . . that plague America today." President Nixon is "hounded ceaselessly by the rabble," and the presidency itself is endangered. Jefferson has heard this before, noting that Hamilton served as a role model not just for Richard Nixon but also for Senator Joseph McCarthy by "denouncing those who opposed [his] 'system' as 'subversives.'" There are parallels between Hamilton's actions and the drafting of an enemies list in the Nixon White House. At one point in the exchange, Hamilton, as is his wont, becomes angry. "The people, the people, the people! . . . I fully understand how Mr. Nixon felt. . . . A mob — not unlike the Paris mob or the St. Petersburg mob — was baying in the streets of America. . . . Mr. Nixon seemed to believe that extraordinary methods were called for, and I for one cannot blame him." A sad Jefferson reminds Hamilton that these are the arguments of tyrants and that "the people are sovereign," to which Hamilton replies, "The people are children to be instructed and led." Hamilton remains confident that the people will reject impeachment and "will support the Government's efforts to root out subversives." At dawn the two ghosts return to their monuments, but not before Jefferson dubs Hamilton "most deserving of the title 'Founding Father' in 1973."[69]

Cloud's caricature of Hamilton reflected the cynicism of the day, although he retained enough optimism to believe that a return to Jeffersonian principles could restore the Republic's health. The same cannot be said for a bestselling book published that year by Gore Vidal, *Burr: A Novel. Burr* was a publicist's dream, released at a time when many Americans questioned the legitimacy of their system of government. Vidal portrayed the founders as a group of schemers not far removed from Richard Nixon. A reviewer in the *New York Times* hailed *Burr* as a diabolically well-timed novel that "says in effect that all the old verities were never much to begin with." The *New Republic* noted that Vidal depicted Hamilton as a brilliant and shrewd operator as well as a "lecher, careerist and manipulator of men." The magazine added that Hamilton's absence of scruple and gentlemanliness made him "hardly worth killing." At one point in *Burr* the title character exclaims, "What would [Hamilton] think now when 'the beast,' as he used to call the generality, governs, or at least we flatter it into thinking that it governs." Vidal's Hamilton accuses Burr of an incestuous relationship with his daughter, thus the duel. In the ensuing showdown Hamilton fires first, although he concocts a scheme to convince the world he will hold his fire. But Burr observes, "Hamilton realized better than anyone that the world — our American world at least — loves a canting hypocrite."[70]

If there was one element of Alexander Hamilton's life that continued to intrigue Americans it was the duel. The 1970s saw Hamilton's showdown with Burr commemorated on a number of fronts. The *Reader's Digest* ran a story at the start of the decade that painted Hamilton in a most favorable light, willing to sacrifice his own life to save the Union from Burr's "ruthless ambition." When cynical Nixon-era journalists decided to name the pressroom in the Treasury Department the "Aaron Burr Memorial Room" in honor of Hamilton's slayer, irate citizens wrote bitter letters demanding that Treasury officials remove the "small government-issue plaque" outside the pressroom door (which they did). An opera, *The Duel,* was written by a cigar-smoking, "sweatshirted, unshaven, thirty-seven-year-old Methodist minister" and produced by the New York Metropolitan Opera Guild in 1974 for younger audiences. The author stated that Hamilton had "a feeling that is outdated today — a real concept of public honor," but he was determined that his production not romanticize him, as "young people are hip to so much . . . no authority is beyond probing." The opera included "a calypso number, since Hamilton was born in the West Indies." Weehawken's bicentennial celebrations of 1976 included a reenactment of the duel with the town's mayor, portraying Hamilton, squaring off against a member of his bicentennial commission. It was reported that Hamilton lost again. Not all Weehawken residents were pleased with the reenactment, particularly Lillie Stokes, the spunky octogenarian head of the Weehawken Historical Society. "Why bring that up anyway? . . . It was not one of our better moments. . . . As far as I know, I haven't heard of one person who attended it."[71]

One of the more peculiar commemorations took place at Hamilton College in New York when Samuel E. Burr Jr., the seventy-eight-year-old president of the Aaron Burr Association and a Burr descendant, was invited to speak at the college on the occasion of Hamilton's 220th birthday in 1977. Burr was honored to be invited to the college that bore Hamilton's name, for the students needed to know "the real villain was Hamilton, not Burr. Perhaps I can show them the light." The students were told that "Hamilton, contrary to popular belief, was not ruthlessly gunned down by Burr. In fact, Hamilton's insulting comments to Burr provoked the duel; he was the culprit." Burr's descendants were most likely encouraged by bicentennial-era essays in *American Heritage* and *Smithsonian* that raised doubts about Hamilton's actions prior to and during the duel. The *Smithsonian* suggested that Hamilton engaged in foul play by using a hair trigger pistol that would give him "a theoretical advantage by allowing him to shoot very quickly." By the 1980s, Burr's descendants felt comfortable enough to come out of the closet. Burr was "just as good a guy as Alexander Hamilton," said a spokesman for the Aaron Burr Association, which claimed to have eleven hundred members in 1981 dedicated to refurbishing Burr's reputation. "We were sort of embarrassed to be related," said one descendant at a ceremony honoring Burr in 1986; "it was like a cloud on us, the idea that Aaron Burr had disgraced the family generations earlier." Those days were over, claimed descendant Dorothy Peterson: "Aaron was no worse and probably a lot better than Thomas Jefferson or Alexander Hamilton."[72]

The unease produced in the 1970s by Watergate and the ensuing Nixon resignation was probably less disturbing to most Americans than the financial tremors of the era. At various times throughout the decade Hamilton the political economist was called upon for advice on monetary matters. The Nobel Prize–winning economist Milton Friedman examined, through the lens of Hamilton's *Federalist* no. 15, the rising European economic union and remained skeptical of its chances for success. Hamilton's essay "contains a more cogent analysis of the European Common Market than any I have seen from the pen of a modern writer." Friedman believed that Hamilton's criticisms of the American Articles of Confederation were applicable to the Common Market.[73]

Although Americans rejected Senator George McGovern in his 1972 race for the White House, his proposals were seen by some people as a continuation of the populist effort to curtail Hamiltonian economic elites. During the campaign McGovern's pledge to redistribute income was described in the *New York Times* as a sign that another clash between Hamiltonians and Jeffersonians might be on the horizon. If McGovern personified a truly resurgent populism, then Richard Nixon and "the Hamiltonians . . . will feel outflanked. Fewer voices will be raised . . . in preferring Hamilton to Jefferson." Hamilton's economic views appeared malleable enough that a conservative newspaper in the United States could cite him in 1976 as an opponent of government welfare and regulatory measures. That same year a reviewer in the *Economist* claimed that Hamilton had something to say to the English public about his "rejecting Adam Smith's individualism in favour of government planning in cooperation with finance and industry."[74]

The financial capital of the United States, Hamilton's New York City, found itself on the verge of bankruptcy in 1975. President Gerald Ford was urged by many Americans to provide a federal bailout for the city. When Ford rejected the idea (which produced probably the most famous tabloid headline in the history of American journalism, "Ford to City: Drop Dead"), an exchange took place in the *New York Times* speculating as to Hamilton's stance on the bailout. His biographer, Broadus Mitchell, claimed that Ford and his treasury secretary William Simon (a Hamilton admirer from Paterson, New Jersey) acted contrary to Hamilton's beliefs. Mitchell argued that Hamilton halted a financial panic in New York City in 1792 by "using Treasury money to purchase public securities." Though the situation was not exactly parallel to 1975, there was enough similarity to persuade Mitchell that Hamilton would have sanctioned some form of federal intervention. Another Hamilton biographer, Robert A. Hendrickson, disagreed, commending the administration for its "courage to stand for responsible Hamiltonian fiscal and monetary policies against the tide of popular clamor for unfunded bailouts." The MIT economist Franklin Fisher took issue with Hendrickson's "curious" comments, charging that Hamilton's program to have the federal government assume the state debts left from the Revolutionary War was a controversial act in his day that would "doubtless be termed a 'Federal bail-out' in ours."[75]

New York City eventually recovered, and in 1976 the United States celebrated the bicentennial of its birth. It was Thomas Jefferson's party, and rightly so. He graced the cover of national magazines and was the subject of praise across the political spectrum. The columnist Hugh Sidey wrote "Oh for Another Stargazing Gardener," a paean to Jefferson published in *Time*. President Gerald Ford made a pilgrimage to the Tidal Basin to lay a wreath in honor of Jefferson's birthday and proclaimed 13 April 1976 Thomas Jefferson Day. His celebration was overshadowed somewhat by the publication of Fawn

Brodie's *Thomas Jefferson: An Intimate History*, which revitalized the ancient allegation that he had an amorous relationship with his slave Sally Hemings. It was never clear which element of the Hemings story most disturbed Jefferson's admirers. Whatever the reason for their discomfort, the reaction to Brodie's book demonstrated once again the unwillingness of those Jefferson scholars who believed in "the greatness of the 'great generation' of Virginia" to countenance any suggestion of improper behavior. While some of these scholars were quick to raise allegations of immoral or corrupt behavior by Hamilton, his candid confession to an extramarital affair stood in stark contrast to 170 years of stonewalling, to borrow a Watergate-era term, surrounding Jefferson and Hemings.[76]

Dumas Malone found the "more titillating passages" of Brodie's account of Jefferson "unrecognizable." The testimony of Madison Hemings recorded in 1873 was undertaken and published, Malone argued, "in the tradition of political enmity and abolitionist propaganda." He added that he was also disturbed by the portrayals of Washington and Jefferson in Vidal's *Burr*, conspicuously not mentioning Hamilton. Julian Boyd accused Brodie, of all things, of "manipulat[ing] the evidence." He claimed, "Mrs. Brodie's Jefferson never existed . . . he is as fictional as the Jefferson in Vidal's *Burr*." Merrill Peterson believed that Fawn Brodie had not proved her case, and he saw no reason to "charge off in defense of Jefferson's integrity when we have no solid grounds for doubting it." Peterson's comments on the Hemings affair in the 1970s were far more restrained than when he first wrote about the issue in *The Jefferson Image in the American Mind* in 1960. At that time he noted that no serious Jefferson scholar ever believed the story, and with only "Jefferson's own history and the memories of a few Negroes to sustain it, it faded into the obscure recesses of the Jefferson image." Peterson also observed in 1960 that the Hemings story originated partly from "the Negroes' pathetic wish for a little pride."[77]

For the time being, Brodie's allegations were dismissed, and the bicentennial proceeded apace. The government-sponsored celebration of 1976 was criticized by some observers as far too reliant on corporate contributions and dominated by modern-day Tories. The Peoples Bicentennial Commission hoped to offer an alternative to those who would "commercialize, trivialize, and vandalize" the revolutionary promise of the Declaration of Independence. One task undertaken by the counterbicentennial group was the publication of a "planning and activity guide for citizens." It included a suggestion that the reader "put together a King George exhibit, showing what kind of people have been opposed to a free press — King George III, Alexander Hamilton, Adolf Hitler." The text also provided a history of the founding of the nation and described Hamilton as "the intellectual leader and principal figure of the wealthy Federalist coalition" and a proponent of "authoritarian beliefs." He was part of a school of thought consisting of "intellectual embroiders of the old fabric." The authors added a new twist to the great beast story, citing Thomas Jefferson as the cause of Hamilton's outburst. "When Jefferson expressed confidence in the sense of the People, his powerful opponent Alexander Hamilton snarled, 'Your People, sir, is a great beast!'"[78]

This view of Hamilton was not confined exclusively to the American left. A bicentennial history edited by Henry Steele Commager with contributions from prominent mainstream historians portrayed Hamilton in somewhat similar terms. It described him as "the great defender of birth and connection. Of poor origins, he believed that government was the preserve of 'the rich and the well born.' . . . Nor did he hide his contempt for democracy. 'Your people, Sir, is a great Beast.'" The popular historian Nathan Miller in *The Founding Finaglers* demonstrated that the debunking tradition was alive and well during the bicentennial. "Like most of the plutocracy spawned by the struggle for independence," Miller intoned, "Hamilton was an offspring of revolution who quickly forgot his origins." Hamilton and the rest of "America's new aristocracy" trundled off to Philadelphia in 1787 to "make the nation safe for profits and property." Hamilton in particular sought to check the riotous spirit of the people, whom he regarded as a great beast.[79]

As the bicentennial year drew to a close, Governor Jimmy Carter of Georgia captured the presidency. Carter admired Thomas Jefferson, particularly for the simple republican style he brought to the White House. During the campaign, Carter frequently compared himself to Jefferson by observing, "It's been a long time since we've had a farmer in the White House. I think Thomas Jefferson was the last one. It's time we had another one." He vowed to be a leader who stood for compassion and who understood the people's "hopes, ideals, dreams, patriotism, self-confidence, dignity," an understanding "first expressed by Thomas Jefferson." At the end of his first year in office, Carter told reporters that the "pomp and ceremony of office does not appeal to me, and I don't believe it is a necessary part of the Presidency. . . . I am no better than anyone else. And the people that I admire most who have lived in this house have taken the same attitude. Jefferson, Jackson, Lincoln, Truman have minimized the pomp and ceremony. . . . I don't think we need to put on the trappings of a monarchy in a nation like our own."[80]

President Carter might have been relieved to have identified himself as a Jeffersonian after reading James Thomas Flexner's *Young Hamilton: A Biography*. The author pronounced Hamilton the "most psychologically troubled of the founding fathers." Flexner rose to prominence in the late 1960s and early 1970s as the author of an award-winning four-volume biography of George Washington. He believed that Hamilton was "one of the greatest of the founding fathers" and a "brilliant and almost unbelievably efficient substitute brain" for Washington, but he was nonetheless capable of "hysterically" changing at any moment "into an imperiled, anguished child." This deeply divided man was in part a "semimadman who sought from the world an ever-denied release from inner wounds." Part of Hamilton's "uncontrolled mind" was haunted by "megalomania." His psychological disorders were traceable to his lack of maternal care, for "a mother's betrayal is the worst blow a child can receive." This "whore child" carried his "psychic wounds" into his effort to build a nation, and although he did as much as anyone, possibly excepting Washington, to unify the country, he also "sowed disunion." In his great conflict with Jefferson, Hamilton bore the lion's share of responsibility, for he "relished hand-to-hand fighting." His pugnacious character arose from his view that "the human race was not only unworthy, but to him a personal enemy that must be fought and conquered."[81]

Flexner intended to deflate the myths surrounding Hamilton that he believed were "more preposterous than those that trailed after Washington and Jefferson." The hype surrounding Hamilton stemmed from the desire of Northern capitalists during the Civil War era to point to a founder they could call their own. "The capitalists who were finally conquering America were being attacked by the agrarians as interloping outsiders." Authors rushed in to meet the demand for pro-Hamilton biographies "for sales to capitalists with heavy pocketbooks." While Southern Jeffersonians complained about Hamiltonian myth making, Northerners simply ignored the rebels.[82]

Generally, Flexner's book was well received, though with some reservations expressed about the whole genre of psychohistory. Arthur Schlesinger Jr., described it as "a brilliant picture"; *Newsweek* claimed that Flexner had written a biography "that even the most rabid Jeffersonian can applaud" and that it was "hard to see how Flexner's Hamilton could be improved." *Newsweek's* book critic maintained that Hamilton would feel quite comfortable in post-Watergate America, for after all he had "urged a strong executive on a coerced republic." The reviewer added that Hamilton had allied "rich industrialists with the government" and concluded, "Poor Hamilton, he wanted the presidency; today he would have had it." John Leonard observed in the *New York Times* that "the heart sinks on being told that *The Young Hamilton* is a 'psychological biography,'" but he nonetheless found the book to be "meticulous and feisty." Leonard added that Hamilton had a "distrust of individuals (the 'great beast' of the people)." Most scholarly journals shied away from reviewing Flexner's book, though a critique in the *American Historical Review* noted that while Thomas Jefferson "would have approved of this book . . . this reviewer remains not only unconvinced but also appalled at Flexner's interpretations."[83]

Flexner's semimadman received far better, but nonetheless controversial, treatment in Forrest McDonald's *Alexander Hamilton: A Biography.* The publication of this book in 1979 was an important development in Hamilton historiography. McDonald challenged, in a rather blunt fashion, much of the accepted wisdom surrounding Hamilton and his great adversary from Virginia. McDonald was something of a maverick in the historical community, serving as chairman of the Goldwater for President Committee in Rhode Island while a professor at Brown University and frequently contributing essays to William F. Buckley's *National Review.* McDonald found much to admire in Hamilton, less in Washington, far less in Jefferson. In *The Presidency of George Washington* he portrayed the first chief executive as something of a bit player to "the most brilliant bastard in American history," Alexander Hamilton. Hamilton was "the most powerful man in the government," and Washington "provided the shield for Hamilton, and knew — or at least sensed — what he was doing." McDonald's *Presidency of Thomas Jefferson* was highly critical of Jefferson's attempt to repeal the legacy of twelve years of Federalist rule. Though Jefferson "humanized the presidency," McDonald disapproved of his effort to dismantle the nation's military and "destroy the complex financial mechanism that Hamilton built." He was also disturbed by the Jeffersonian contempt for "due process of law and for law itself." In the end the Jeffersonians "failed calamitously" because "their system was incompatible with the immediate current of events, with the broad sweep of history, and with the nature of man and society."[84]

McDonald was well prepared for his work on Hamilton, having reviewed the Hamilton papers for the *William and Mary Quarterly* on numerous occasions. His knowledge of the works of the great political economists was second to none, and thus one finds a large portion of the biography devoted to Hamiltonomics. What made McDonald's book controversial was its unabashed debunking of the myth of Hamilton as plutocrat. Turning the Jeffersonian mythology on its head, McDonald claimed that it was Hamilton who sought a social revolution to overturn the power and privileges of the "oligarchs who dominated the American republic." In this regard Hamilton was far more radical than his Virginia contemporaries, beneficiaries of a highly stratified class system resting on slave labor. Jefferson "idealize[d] the serene, secure life of the plantation gentry," and "the only privilege he ever seriously opposed was privilege that threatened the security of his own little world." Hamilton sought to transform an America where "status . . . derived from birthright" was replaced by status based on "the marketplace, where deeds and goods and virtues could be impartially valued."

Hamilton wanted to reward industry, and the provincial squirearchies and slave plantation gentries who seldom allowed outsiders to break into their circles and accumulate wealth were a major obstacle to his plan. As an immigrant, he appreciated these difficulties, even though he had managed to break into one of these prominent circles by marrying into the Schuyler family of New York. Nonetheless, he dedicated himself to opening the process by which men of talent could accumulate wealth. His goal was simply "to promote industry, both in the sense of industriousness and in the sense of large scale manufacturing." As McDonald noted, Hamilton believed the function of government was "to promote a general spirit of improvement. It should reward productivity and punish dissipation, idleness, and extravagance. . . . If such policies were adhered to, every member of society would gain — the poor as well as the rich, the farmer as well as the manufacturer and merchant, the South as well as the North — and the gains would be justly distributed, for rewards would be proportionate to ability, integrity, and industry."[85]

McDonald's radical assault on the accepted wisdom regarding Hamilton was greeted with mixed reviews. One critic claimed, "McDonald believes that business aims are correct. One of his first books was a biography of Samuel

Insull, another financial genius like Hamilton, who also never did anything wrong. Speculation and corruption were not their doing, though perhaps that of their associates." The Lincoln scholar David Herbert Donald praised the "exceptional skill and learning" that McDonald applied to his reexamination of Hamiltonomics but thought the author damaged his case by excessive partisanship. Harold C. Syrett, the editor of *The Papers of Alexander Hamilton*, agreed with Donald that McDonald was too partisan, arguing that "in certain areas it takes us back to the good guy/bad guy [era of] Vernon L. Parrington and Claude Bowers." Both Donald and Syrett noted a passage in McDonald's epilogue, where he claimed that America's greatness peaked "in the middle of the twentieth century: after that time it became increasingly Jeffersonian . . . its decline candy coated with rhetoric of liberty and equality and justice for all." The same passage was cited in a 1979 review in *Business Week* that urged McDonald not to despair. "It could be that neo-Jeffersonianism is already in eclipse: Look at the low regard in which the public holds Jimmy Carter, its principal exponent. At the same time, the main tenets of Hamiltonianism — incentives, fiscal responsibility, and deregulation of the economy — have become popular political issues."[86]

Jimmy Carter was turned out of office, no doubt to the delight of the *Business Week* critic. In the past, the rise of a more conservative American electorate generally coincided with an improvement in Hamilton's stature. But the new president, and many of his supporters, had cut their political teeth in the Goldwater insurgency of 1964, with its embrace of Jefferson's vision of states' rights and strict constitutional interpretation. Suspicious of centralized authority and committed to restraining a runaway judiciary, Ronald Reagan appeared to be the consummate Jeffersonian. "Government is not the solution to our problem," President Reagan argued in his first inaugural address, "government is the problem." Yet the Reaganites were far more in the tradition of Hamilton than of Jefferson in their advocacy of a muscular American foreign policy. The new president also understood the symbolic hold the presidency had on the American imagination. When it came to using the trappings of the White House as a stage with which to impress the people, Reagan's presidential style was high-toned Hamiltonian. Gone was the relaxed, Jeffersonian atmosphere of the president carrying his own bags onto Air Force One.[87]

The historian and onetime librarian of Congress Daniel J. Boorstin had observed in the early days of the cold war that "it is still taken for granted the proper arena of controversy was marked off once and for all in the late eighteenth century: we are either Jeffersonians or Hamiltonians. In no other country has the hagiography of politics been more important." As America entered the concluding stages of its long, twilight struggle with the Soviet Union, Boorstin's observation still held.[88]

8

At Century's End
A Hamilton Restoration on the Horizon?

During the last twenty years of the twentieth century, there were indications that Hamilton's long national nightmare might be over, that a balanced reassessment of his importance as a founder was under way. In part this was due to a decline in Jefferson's standing, as a nation increasingly sensitive to racial matters reexamined the Sage's record and found it wanting. Liberal critics, who once considered Hamilton to be the founding plutocrat, reconsidered their stance in light of his support for national power. This was partly a response to Ronald Reagan's proposals to devolve power to the states, proposals that were endorsed and partially enacted in the 1990s under a Republican-controlled Congress. Most conservative scholars, particularly neoconservatives, remained on the Hamilton bandwagon, but for reasons different from those of their liberal brethren. They feared the erosion of executive power that began under Richard Nixon and that seemed to accelerate under Jimmy Carter. These conservatives contended that a strong presidency, unencumbered by congressional restrictions and capable of moving with secrecy and dispatch, was vital if America was to win the cold war.

Ronald Reagan's landslide victory in 1980 was viewed by some observers as a rejection of the New Deal. Ironically, the new president admired Franklin Roosevelt and shared with him a propensity for citing Thomas Jefferson in his speeches. Reagan's sunny optimism also drew him to Thomas Paine's comment that "we have it in our power to begin the world over again," a remark rarely quoted by American conservatives. Reagan invoked Hamilton's maxims less frequently but referred to him while criticizing welfare programs or assailing an activist judiciary. Speaking to an organization of African-American Republicans in 1982, Reagan quoted *Federalist* no. 79, noting that "Alexander Hamilton, one of our greatest Founding Fathers," observed that "a power over a man's subsistence amounts to a power over his will." Too many people in America's inner cities suffered from "a new kind of bondage" brought on by government welfare programs that fostered a "state of dependency."[1]

Reagan also drew from Hamilton in his attempt to move the Supreme Court in a strict constructionist direction. His elevation of William H. Rehnquist to chief justice and the appointment of Antonin Scalia as an associate justice were part of this effort. At their swearing-in ceremony, Reagan observed that Hamilton had referred to the judiciary as the "least dangerous" branch, possessing "neither force nor will, but merely judgement." Reagan claimed that while Hamilton and Jefferson disagreed on many great issues, beginning "our long tradition of loyal opposition," they both believed "as should be — on the importance of judicial restraint." When the Senate rejected his Supreme Court nominee Robert Bork in 1987, Reagan blamed the defeat on a confirmation process that had become a "spectacle of misrepresentation and single-issue politics." According to Reagan, Alexander Hamilton would not have been pleased, for he wrote that "the complete independence of the courts of justice is . . . essential in . . . [the] Constitution." Reagan repeated the remark just weeks later in an attempt to save another nominee, Douglas Ginsburg, who came under fire after revelations of marijuana use. When he finally succeeded in getting Justice Anthony Kennedy on the Court, Reagan again recalled Hamilton's vision of a restrained court exercising merely judgment.[2]

Hamilton was also part of Reagan's proverbial comic routine, where he would make light of his advanced age by claiming he knew the founders. On greeting his new treasury secretary Nicholas F. Brady in 1988, Reagan said, "Well, Nick, I'm delighted to turn over the keys to the Treasury Department to you. Don't lose them. Alexander Hamilton gave them to me personally." Toward the end of his public life, Reagan called for the repeal of the Twenty-second Amendment to the Constitution, which limited the president to two terms in office. In an essay advocating the Amendment's repeal, he referred to "the wisdom of Hamilton's insight" and called him "the ever perspicacious Hamilton." The former president repeatedly cited Hamilton's arguments in *The Federalist* for executive duration and reeligibility.[3]

As Reaganomics became a household word in the 1980s, and budget deficits ballooned, Hamilton was inevitably drawn into the debate over the rapid increase in the national debt. He had referred to the debt as a national blessing, if it were not excessive. By the mid-1980s many Americans believed that, as the *Washington Post* put it, "the national debt has finally, in Hamilton's words, become 'excessive.'" One prominent Wall Street economist recommended in 1984 that the government adopt Hamilton's sinking fund as a solution. This fund would exist outside the budget and be devoted exclusively to retiring the debt. The economist claimed Hamilton's proposal avoided the pitfalls associated with unpopular spending cuts or with tax increases likely to be spent on new programs. In desperation, before the red ink eased in the mid-to-late-1990s, some members of Congress, along with President Reagan, proposed an amendment to the Constitution mandating a balanced budget. Opponents cited passages from Hamilton and Madison in *The Federalist,* which appeared to argue against the kind of supermajority the amendment would have required in Congress to raise taxes or to authorize more government borrowing.[4]

On the two hundredth anniversary in 1989 of Hamilton's swearing in as the nation's first treasury secretary, *U.S. News and World Report* paid tribute to his financial prowess. The magazine concluded that "with an endemic federal budget gap and a yawning trade deficit" it was fortunate that the government's "'full faith and credit' backing on its debt is still considered a blue chip guarantee. . . . That it remains so is just one measure of the gratitude Americans owe Alexander Hamilton." The *American Banker* agreed, woefully noting that "not since Alexander Hamilton sat alone in a room has anyone been able to get his arms around the entire U.S. financial system."[5]

The worst crisis of Ronald Reagan's presidency, the Iran-Contra affair, tarnished the celebration of the Constitution's bicentennial in 1987. This bicentennial failed to interest the American people in any way comparable to the 1976 festivities. Framing a Constitution simply could not compete with Revolutionary War battles and the drama of pledging one's life and sacred honor for independence. Nonetheless, Alexander Hamilton's role in drafting and ratifying the Constitution was the subject of numerous essays and books recounting the events of 1787. In keeping with the predominant trend of the twentieth century, Hamilton received more than his share of bad press during the bicentennial. He was frequently portrayed as a fringe member of the Constitutional Convention, to which no one paid any particular attention, an often repeated claim with some validity. What was not true was the notion that Hamilton hoped to design a government to "protect the few from the many," as a 1987 essay in the *Washington Post* argued. This assertion ignored the fact that Hamilton had said, "Give all power to the many, they will oppress the few. Give all power to the few, they will oppress the many. Both therefore ought to have power, that each may defend itself against the other."[6]

One prominent American corporation sponsored a series of essays on the Constitution in national newsmagazines. Written by the popular historian and playwright Charles L. Mee Jr., one essay claimed that Hamilton left the Constitutional Convention in a huff after being outvoted on "issue after issue" but returned to "deliver a six hour speech in favor of aristocracy, to which almost no one paid the least attention." Another entry in this series alleged that "the would-be aristocrat Alexander Hamilton . . . took every opportunity to express his contempt for the people." In his book *The Genius of the People* Mee described Hamilton at the Constitutional Convention as a "connoisseur of elegant clothes and houses and fine wine and fine prints and land." He added, "just to the right of center, at the New York table, was another of the most notable delegates to the convention: Alexander Hamilton — his coat open to show cascades of white ruffles at his chest, his long reddish hair swept back like a cockatoo's crest . . . drawn up in a posture of military correctness, his chin elevated just so. He believed that the best form of government was monarchy and that the people were a 'great beast.'"[7]

In *The Struggle for Democracy*, a companion volume to a PBS documentary, authors Benjamin Barber and Patrick Watson claimed that "Alexander Hamilton, the New York banker . . . regarded the people as howling masses." None of the founders particularly trusted the people — Hamilton and most of his comrades sought deliverance from "the 'mobocrats and democrats and all the other rats.'" Even the official bicentennial commission contributed to reinforcing a somewhat caricatured view of Hamilton. The nation's schools were sent copies of *A Musical Skit for Children on the Constitution Convention* that had been developed by a teacher in Maryland. In *We Are All a Part of It: U.S.A. 1776–1840*, Hamilton played the now-familiar role of the founding heavy. At one point in the musical the Anti-Feds were to sing, "Oh Mister Ham-il-ton, just listen to me. Your plan reminds me of roy-al-ty. Oh we fought the Rev-o-lu-tion for our liber-ty. Now each state wants its sovereignty.

We don't want all that pow-er vested in one place, For we want ru-lers whom we can re-place. Other nations think with-out a king we're bound to fail. But we'll show them de-mocra-cy will pre-vail."[8]

There were accounts of Hamilton published during the bicentennial era that struck a more positive tone. The *New York Times* columnist James Reston paid tribute to Hamilton's remarkable letter written in 1780 contending that the thirteen states were unfit to govern the country either in war or peace. He argued that the remedy for the nation's problems lay in calling a convention of the states, an observation made seven years prior to the Constitutional Convention. *Time* recounted Hamilton's effort in "hatch[ing] the idea" for *The Federalist,* "so penetrating an explication that fifty years later Alexis de Tocqueville described it as a tour de force that 'ought to be familiar to the statesmen of all countries.'" *Time* added, "Nobody told it better than Madison, Hamilton and Jay." *Time* also reported in its special bicentennial issue that President Reagan, "while no constitutional scholar" had "read a lot" from *The Federalist* during his conversion to conservatism in the 1950s. In a fitting conclusion to a project that had finally allowed Hamilton to speak for himself, the last volume of *The Papers of Alexander Hamilton* was released during the bicentennial year. This final tome consisted of additional material discovered since the publication began, as well as addenda and errata, and a cumulative index. Harold Syrett had finished much of his labor of love before he died in 1984; his wife Patricia, who had also devoted much of her life to the publication, died in 1986.[9]

Opinion polls taken during the bicentennial era indicated that the American public had much to learn about the founding and the role of framers such as Hamilton. A 1986 survey of seventeen-year-old Americans revealed that 39 percent of them could not place the writing of the Constitution in the correct half century, though this was a far better showing than the 68 percent who could not place the Civil War in the correct half century. That same year a survey of one hundred college students at California State University at Fullerton revealed that only 10 percent had heard of Alexander Hamilton, yet 60 percent could identify the main character on the television soap opera *All My Children.* In September 1986, NBC News and the *Wall Street Journal* sponsored an opinion poll that asked over twenty-one hundred Americans, "Who do you think played the biggest roll in writing the nation's Constitution?" The choices were Jefferson, Franklin, Washington, Madison, Hamilton, someone else, or not sure. Not sure was the big winner at 50 percent; Jefferson took 31 percent of the tally although he was in Paris at the time the Constitution was written. Someone else polled 8 percent, followed by Franklin at 6 percent and Washington at 3 percent. Tied for dead last were Hamilton and Madison at 1 percent apiece.[10]

Perhaps the American public learned more about their Constitution from the ongoing Iran-Contra saga than from the official bicentennial celebration. Congressional hearings took place throughout summer 1987 that highlighted the worst dispute between the legislature and the executive since Watergate. Both critics and defenders of Ronald Reagan turned to *The Federalist* to bolster their case. A special board named by Reagan to investigate the scandal, the Tower Commission, included former U.S. senator Edmund Muskie. He argued that "Alexander Hamilton . . . was at pains to emphasize the modest nature of presidential authorities" and cited Hamilton's statement in *Federalist* no. 67 that the president's powers were "in some instances less" than the governor of New York. Muskie endorsed "the recent efforts to restore a more wholesome balance between the branches." Reagan, while denying direct knowledge of some of the scandal's more egregious violations, sought to deflect congressional attempts to legislate further restrictions on presidential power. "Our government has no higher duty than the defense of the freedom of the American people," he maintained. He referred members of Congress to Hamilton's argument in *Federalist* no. 23 that "the circumstances [that] endanger the safety of nations are infinite" and thus "no constitutional shackles can wisely be imposed on the power to which the care of it is committed." The congressional committee investigating Iran-Contra recommended strengthening some preexisting oversight mechanisms and was sharply critical of the president's apparent contempt for congressional foreign policy prerogatives. A small minority of members, all Republicans, disagreed, arguing that although the president made mistakes, to some extent his administration's actions epitomized Hamilton's energetic executive. The minority report was laced with references from Hamilton's writings on presidential power from *The Federalist* nos. 70 through 75 and his writings as Pacificus in his famous debate with James Madison over Washington's neutrality proclamation of 1793.[11]

The Pacificus essays were just one example of the founding generation's reliance on newspapers as a vehicle to disseminate their views and influence public opinion. During the Reagan years, one of the president's more vocal supporters was Hamilton's old *New York Post*. In 1801 Hamilton and some of his associates founded the *New York Evening Post* and hired William Coleman as its first editor. The *Post* was proud of being the oldest continuously published newspaper in the United States and having eminent editors such as William Cullen Bryant and Carl Schurz and writers such as Walt Whitman and Washington Irving. By the 1970s the *New York Post* (sans *Evening*) was in something of a constant state of upheaval that lasted for nearly twenty years. In 1976 it was sold to Rupert Murdoch, an Australian millionaire with a media empire whose daily fare tended toward sex, scandal, sports, and crime.[12]

Murdoch brought a conservative, pro-Reagan slant to the *Post*'s editorial page, but its news coverage had a distinctly sensationalist slant that probably would have repulsed both Reagan and Hamilton. Headlines from the Murdoch era included "SEX-TRIAL SOCIALITE'S SHOCKER: 'I SLEPT WITH A TRUMPET,'" "500 POUND SEX MONSTER GOES FREE," and "FIEND DERAILS TRAIN." When Murdoch was forced to sell the paper in 1988, the new owners ran a series of television advertisements: "A reassuring word to the founder of the *Post*, Alexander Hamilton. Don't worry, Mr. Hamilton, your newspaper is in good hands." Despite these assurances, the paper continued to hemorrhage money, until Murdoch repurchased it in 1993. Prior to his second bout of ownership, Abraham Hirschfeld, a parking garage mogul with a reputation for spitting on reporters, briefly owned the newspaper. The *Post*'s editors and writers devoted an entire issue to insulting their new owner. On the cover was a weeping Alexander Hamilton; inside was a cartoon showing Hirschfeld in a padded cell wearing a straitjacket.[13]

In a 1983 essay in *Harper's*, "LINK FOUNDING FATHER TO SLEAZE KING," Ron Rosenbaum observed that Hamilton would have approved of the *Post*'s feisty take on the news. While acknowledging that some people "may wonder how stories headlined STOVE TOP EXORCISM . . . contribute to the health of the Hamiltonian republic," Rosenbaum contended that Hamilton's *Federalist* essays revealed an intellectual kinship with the modern *Post*. In *Federalist* no. 6, his "wise and useful meditation on the corruption of human nature," he related "the dark passions, the 'inflammable humors' within the individual body, to the factional passions that inflame the body politic." If self-government and liberty were to prevail, governments must be so designed as to take into account the momentary passions and inflammable humors that can render both citizens and leaders subject to "impulses of rage, resentment, jealously, ava-rice." He contended that "each classic *Post* story is a reenactment of the drama of self-government that goes on within every fallen soul." He believed that the *Post*'s extensive coverage of the divorce of a prominent Palm Beach, Florida, couple had "obvious Hamiltonian implications." Anyone who had read *The Federalist* could see that the "marriage is a maimed confederation, the exact embodiment of Hamilton's dark vision of the strife, jealously, an-archic self-destructive collapse that would be the fate of the states . . . should they not adopt the binding union their new constitution offered."[14]

Writers at the *Post* might well have been intrigued by an account circulat-ing in the early 1980s that their newspaper's founder had committed suicide in his duel with Aaron Burr. Building on the work of James Thomas Flexner, the authors of an essay in *The Journal of Psychohistory* claimed that Burr was not the instrument of Hamilton's death but that Hamilton himself was re-sponsible — "or rather, Hamilton's distorted perception of Burr as his evil self." Hamilton "hated his origins and he constantly lied about them," partly because he viewed his mother as a slut. He believed his life "would have been so much better had he not been born a bastard." Toward the end of his life he saw his dreams of glory dashed as certain Federalists turned to Aaron Burr for leadership. According to the psychohistorians, this abandonment left Hamilton once again "the helpless bastard before the court." Yet he did not really hate Burr, but he did hate the Burr who became Hamilton's "vile self." Suicide had never been far from his mind, and when he fell at Weehawken and cried, "I am a dead man," he fulfilled his death wish.[15]

A somewhat more restrained description of Hamilton's neuroses appeared in Jacob E. Cooke's *Alexander Hamilton.* The author was an associate editor of *The Papers of Alexander Hamilton* and thus came fully prepared for the task of writing his biography. Cooke noted that his eclectic approach to writ-ing the book included heavy reliance on "Freudian theory and on the intel-lectually most impressive neo-Freudian of our day, Erik H. Erikson," whose standards "no historian has yet matched." Cooke's book was an insightful ac-count of Hamilton's career, but it was marred by his affinity for psychohistorical conjecture. Hamilton's affair with Maria Reynolds was most likely the result of his "unconsciously acting out unresolved conflicts of his early life." Cooke suggested that when Hamilton looked at Maria Reynolds he saw his mother, who had been similarly accused of promiscuous behavior. Cooke implied that

Hamilton committed suicide in the duel with Burr, perhaps abandoning his family in a manner comparable to the way his father had abandoned him.[16]

On a deeper level, Cooke challenged the gospel according to the Jeffersonians and his book was a formidable successor to Forrest McDonald's *Alexander Hamilton*. McDonald claimed that Cooke "demolishe[d] myth after myth propagated by historians partial to Jefferson" and hoped that "textbook writers, if they are to keep their work honest and up to date, will be impelled to make a thorough overhaul" of their chapters dealing with the Federalist era. One such myth summarily dismissed by Cooke was that Hamilton possessed Napoleonic dreams of conquest during the crisis with France in the late 1790s. Cooke noted that this charge "appears to be cemented onto the pages of American history books." Moreover, he argued that Hamilton did not intend to use military force "to stamp out democracy" but sought adequate military strength to impress potential European opponents. Though Hamilton's support for American expansion into Louisiana and Florida was expressed "between the lines of letters to [Francisco de] Miranda," he distanced himself from the effort to liberate Latin America. Nevertheless, he desired to see the United States ascendant in the Americas, and this longing was shared and ultimately realized by Thomas Jefferson and his Louisiana Purchase. Hamilton believed the Louisiana territory could be acquired only by force, though Jefferson succeeded through diplomacy. By so doing, he was "crowned with laurel for accomplishing a design that earned Hamilton notoriety as an incipient imperialist, the would-be Napoleon of the New World."[17]

Cooke contended that the indictment of Hamilton for dealing with the British agent George Beckwith by the "Virginian's historical partisans" was misguided. The facts, Cooke averred, "dictate a rather more lenient verdict" than that handed down by Julian Boyd in *Number 7*. Hamilton acted at the behest of President Washington in meeting Beckwith and submitted a report on their conversations, albeit abridged. In his talks Hamilton repeatedly emphasized that he was speaking for himself and that the secretary of state was the appropriate contact for formal diplomacy. If Hamilton was guilty of anything in talking to Beckwith, it was his inability to restrain his "compulsive self-expression in a situation that called for silence." Hamilton in effect was showing off. The charge that he was guilty of gross misrepresentation of the facts to President Washington and overall duplicity was itself a gross misrepresentation.[18]

Cooke also defended Hamilton's financial policies against the charge of corruption, noting the odd double standard of Hamilton's generation: "Speculation in public and bank stock was somehow unethical; speculation in land was merely one of the risk enterprises of the day. . . . For every stockjobber there were countless land speculators." Cooke endorsed McDonald's thesis that although Hamilton "cherish[ed] tradition," he was the symbol of "the thrust toward modernity" and in an important way was the most radical of the founders. In contrast, Jefferson could reasonably be described as a "prototypical American conservative," a Virginia aristocrat whose quest to preserve an idealized vision of an agrarian America made him a "steadfast supporter of the status quo."[19]

The revisionist account of Hamilton promulgated by Cooke and McDonald was supported to a great extent by an emerging though somewhat marginalized cadre of political scientists. A circle of scholars linked to the school known as Straussianism tended to view Hamilton as a statesman of the highest order. Leo Strauss (1899–1973) was a German émigré to the United States who taught at the New School for Social Research in New York City and later at the University of Chicago. Strauss through his approach emphasized the study of the great works of political philosophy and rejected the quantitative and behavioralist methodology that dominated the field of political science in the mid-to-late twentieth century.

Though most Straussians devoted their attention to classic texts in the Western canon, some Straussian fellow travelers with an interest in American politics focused on the nation's founding. Although not viewing Hamilton and Madison as philosophers, they did see them as statesmen animated by a devotion to principle. These scholars rejected modern notions that the Constitution and the Declaration of Independence were antiquated works with little or no impact on the real world of politics. Professors Herbert Storing, Martin Diamond, Morton Frisch, Walter Berns, and Harvey Flaumenhaft were students of Strauss who attempted to reinvigorate serious study of the American founding, rejecting the fashionable notion that the founders sought the establishment of a plutocratic regime hostile to popular majorities. Instead, the founders' Constitution created a democratic republic where "moderate, deliberate popular majorities" would prevail. As Diamond put it, the framer's representative democracy was "perfectly consistent with the principle of popular government, that is, lodging sovereignty with the many."

Though Storing, Diamond, Frisch, Berns, and Flaumenhaft disagreed on some issues, they shared a core belief that the progressive interpretation of American politics that opened the century and continued to dominate it at the end was misguided.[20]

Herbert Storing praised the broad constitutional understanding that Hamilton and Madison brought to bear on the framing of the presidency. Hamilton's essays in *The Federalist* dealing with the executive branch were the "first and best general treatment" of the American executive, Storing contended, and Hamilton's case for an energetic presidency was argued "in a way that would be difficult to improve upon." He added, "It is not going too far to say that in his treatment in *The Federalist* Hamilton brings the creation of the presidency to completion, so far as the founding generation was concerned." Echoing Forrest McDonald, Storing disagreed with the claim that Hamilton played an insignificant role at the Constitutional Convention. Hamilton's controversial speech in which he advocated a strong, well-mounted government helped secure the passage of the vigorous Virginia plan, in part by making it the moderate or centrist alternative to his extreme plan for centralization. Storing also differed with proponents of the modern administrative state who proclaimed Hamilton as their founder. "The old Hamiltonianism," though related to modern "scientific management, . . . had a common-sense quality [and a] breadth and soundness" that contemporary administration lacked. Most important, Storing argued that Hamiltonianism "was not antidemocratic, but it was concerned with the problematic character of democracy."[21]

Martin Diamond was perhaps the most influential Straussian of his generation in shaping the thought of American public intellectuals toward their regime. Senator Daniel Patrick Moynihan, Ambassador Jeane Kirkpatrick, columnist George Will, and Education Secretary William Bennett attested to his influence. Diamond rejected the prevailing textbook account of American history that portrayed a "conflict between a crabbed old-world liberalism and a generous democratic outlook . . . with Hamilton and Jefferson starring as rival champions." In an essay written on the eve of the 1976 bicentennial celebrations, Diamond condemned the tendency to break American history into three acts. Act one was the Revolution and its "Declaration of democratic equality"; act two was the constitutional counterrevolution based in part on preserving economic privilege; act three was the successful but still incomplete struggle to overcome "the confining Constitution." A fourth act always remained to be written, chronicling the "final triumph of democracy." Diamond admired James Madison more than Hamilton, viewing the former's *Federalist* no. 10 as "the most important original political writing by an American." He dedicated his coauthored textbook, *The Democratic Republic*, "to the spirit of James Madison, Founder, Theorist, Statesman." Diamond sought to counter the notion of an undemocratic American regime and appeared uncomfortable with some of Hamilton's prescriptions. The latter's hope that the electoral college might act, independent of popular will, for instance, placed Hamilton somewhat outside "any reasonable democratic standard." But Diamond disapproved of the stigmatization of Hamilton and other framers as "the aggressive representatives of urban commercial interests." He could not conceive of a "single author of the Declaration or a leading framer of the Constitution" who would have disagreed with Hamilton's belief that popular government was subject to weakness and disorders. The drafters of the Constitution sought a novel system designed to ameliorate those defects, or as Hamilton put it, the framers were employing means "by which the excellencies of republican government may be retained and its imperfections lessened or avoided." Though Hamilton may have differed with the other founders over the forms and instruments of government, he shared their faith in the "priority of liberty as the end of government."[22]

Martin Diamond's friend and colleague Morton Frisch edited the *Selected Writings and Speeches of Alexander Hamilton* and wrote *Alexander Hamilton and the Political Order*. Frisch contended that "Hamilton was not a political philosopher, but rather a statesman who . . . had thoughts of such a high order as to constitute the nearest approximation to political philosophy in the proper and full sense of the word." Frisch rejected Jefferson's accusation that Hamilton favored a monarchical or aristocratic form of government, noting that all the officials in his plan of government were to be elected directly or indirectly by the people and hold those offices during good behavior. Jefferson's charge was "manifestly unfair," for Hamilton contemplated "neither a 'constitutional dictatorship' nor an 'Imperial Presidency.'" Hamilton's political thought, despite decades of Jeffersonian suggestions to the contrary, "belongs to America, not England."[23]

Walter Berns of Georgetown University observed, as only an admirer can, that Hamilton had not received his due from his countrymen:

Alexander Hamilton has never been a popular hero among his fellow citizens. When visiting the capital city . . . few of them visit, or probably have ever heard of, Hamilton's statue in front of the Treasury building. The name of his great adversary, Thomas Jefferson, is attached not only to a Memorial but to a hotel, a "corner," an Institute for Justice, a condominium, and a host of other institutions. . . . Hamilton rates only an insurance company and (perhaps significantly) an Income Tax Service, and one lonely street. It's as if he were only a minor figure in this country's history, rather like Elbridge Gerry or Roger Sherman.

To some extent Berns believed that Hamilton's neglect relative to Jefferson was warranted, for unlike Jefferson, Hamilton was not a philosophic politician and left no aphorism that one would be inclined to memorialize. Jefferson also had a "local cottage industry to commemorate his every act." And the neglect shown Hamilton from his fellow citizens was partly the result of his unwillingness to court public favor. One of Jefferson's lasting legacies, Berns claimed, was labeling Hamilton a monocrat, a charge Hamilton never successfully countered. Hamilton played into Jefferson's hands with his praise for the British constitution as a form of government capable of protecting the rights of man, though Berns noted that Jefferson appeared to express the same belief in the Declaration of Independence. Berns believed that Hamilton's wartime role was "second only to that of Washington" and that no one did more to bring about the Constitutional Convention or "set in motion the machinery of American government." Hamilton "can rightly claim the title of Founding Father," Berns argued, for "more than anyone else, [Hamilton] launched the country on its way to becoming a great commercial republic."[24]

Harvey Flaumenhaft also contributed to the burgeoning revisionist interpretation of Hamilton's statesmanship. A student of Herbert Storing and Leo Strauss, Flaumenhaft was the author of *The Effective Republic: Administration and Constitution in the Thought of Alexander Hamilton*. He believed that Forrest McDonald's book was unequaled in its examination of Hamilton's "achievements and intentions, particularly in political economy." But he sought to fill a gap by providing a "systematic and analytic account" of the principles underlying Hamilton's deeds, an examination of "Hamilton's political science" that no historian had undertaken. In a sense, Flaumenhaft undertook a task that Hamilton himself had once contemplated, writing a treatise on his understanding of the "history and science of civil government."

Hamilton's early death meant that others would have to discover what animated his work, and Flaumenhaft combed through his scattered writings on this quest.

One of Flaumenhaft's important contributions to the study of Hamilton's political science was his emphasis on the founder's concern with "efficacious administration." Hamilton sought to make government "flowing from the people . . . *work* for the people." Hamilton and other framers endeavored to "energize government even while they sought safeguards for the citizenry against abuses in the exercise of that great power which they thought they needed to establish." The Jeffersonian criticism that Hamilton was an enemy of republicanism was unfounded, Flaumenhaft claimed, for his public life was devoted to the creation of administrative supports that would allow popular government to flourish. The conventional understanding of the American system held that the separation of powers was designed to prevent government from oppressing the people. But this understanding, Flaumenhaft contended, ignored a key element in Hamilton's plan. Partitioning power also ensured that those institutions best equipped to deal with a particular problem could respond in an effective manner. In other words, there was an element of specialization in Hamilton's design.[25]

These prominent Straussians in turn taught a new generation of students to take the Constitution seriously, and in effect, Hamilton and Madison as well. As the twentieth century drew to a close, succeeding generations of Straussians or neo-Straussians rejected the distorted Hamilton of Bowers, Boyd, and other progressive historians. Karl Walling from the University of Chicago published *Republican Empire: Alexander Hamilton on War and Free Government*, a rebuttal to Richard Kohn's thesis that Hamilton was a militarist. Walling argued that more than any other founder Hamilton "reflected most deeply and comprehensively on preserving freedom in a world all too frequently at war." This understanding of the threat to liberty presented by external threats led Hamilton to design institutions that allowed the United States to remain free and conduct war, a truly unique historical achievement. Walling rejected the simplistic morality play that pitted a monarchical Hamilton, intent on destroying American liberty to further his dreams of foreign conquest, against Thomas Jefferson, the defender of republican virtue. Hamilton emphasized responsibility — "that those responsible for the nation's defense had to be granted the powers necessary to serve that end," while Jefferson emphasized vigilance — encouraging popular suspicion of power. Hamilton had seen such vigilance degenerate into "a spirit of narrow and illiberal distrust," capable of incapacitating a government even when the security of the nation was at risk. Walling concluded that the tension between these two virtues allowed the United States to remain free and powerful while a complete triumph of either virtue would end in tragedy.[26]

Peter McNamara, another scholar partial to Strauss, focused on Hamilton's political economy, questioning the assumption that he would have approved of the innumerable tasks undertaken by modern government. Hamilton believed that the focus of government should be "commerce, finance, negotiation, and war" and would be perplexed to see the government stoop to undertake anything other than "the great objects of state." McNamara claimed that Hamilton "valued the habits of industry, frugality, and enterprise" generated by a free market and believed a spirit of enterprise animating the populace was good for the economy, for the polity at large, and for the individual citizen. "There is little doubt," McNamara wrote, that Hamilton "would have recoiled at the rise of the entitlement state since the New Deal," in good measure due to its demoralizing effect on the recipients of the state's largesse.[27]

These Straussian-influenced accounts of Hamilton tended to receive a warmer reception from political scientists, particularly those inclined toward political philosophy, than from historians. Beyond the academy, American politicians from both major parties continued to wrap themselves in Jefferson's mantle in the 1990s. The most dominant political figure of the decade, President William Jefferson Clinton, carried on his party's tradition of celebrating his namesake, as did many Republicans hostile to big government.

Clinton considered Jefferson to be "perhaps the most brilliant of our Founding Fathers," and began his inaugural ceremonies in 1993 at Monticello, where he and Vice President Al Gore departed in a bus caravan to the gala in the nation's capital. Shortly after his inauguration, *U.S. News and World Report* described Thomas Jefferson as "Bill Clinton's Muse." The president once claimed that the deaths of John Adams and Thomas Jefferson on the fiftieth anniversary of the Declaration of Independence were the best evidence the modern world had for the existence of God. In his first year in office Clinton paid the now obligatory visit to the Jefferson Memorial on the Virginian's birthday and even enlisted him in his effort to enact national health insurance, claiming that Jefferson would be "appalled to think that the United

States is the only advanced country where every person doesn't have access to affordable health care."[28]

The president hailed Hamilton's economic prowess during one of his appeals for the country to accelerate its entry onto the information superhighway. The United States was founded in a period similar to the 1990s, Clinton argued, and Hamilton helped guide the young nation to prominence. The late eighteenth century was a period of "enormous economic upheaval when the world was beginning to move from an agrarian to an industrial economy. Alexander Hamilton . . . understood these changes well. . . . Hamilton identified new ways to harness the changes then going on so that our nation could advance."[29]

The bulk of Bill Clinton's presidency was marked by bitter partisan struggles with a Republican-controlled Congress. Although Republicans might have appeared as a monolithic force to the White House, congressional leaders, along with conservative columnists in the media, engaged in a sometimes rancorous debate over the party's post-Reagan agenda. At its core the debate focused on the merits of pursuing Jeffersonian or Hamiltonian goals. Republicans were divided over whether they should embrace a "limited government, states' rights" conservatism or a "national greatness" conservatism. William Kristol and David Brooks of the Weekly Standard, a conservative journal that began publishing in 1995, championed the latter position, arguing that "something is missing at conservatism's core." The missing element was an "appeal to American greatness," and the authors urged that conservatives reinvigorate American nationalism, "the nationalism of Alexander Hamilton and Henry Clay and Teddy Roosevelt." Conservatives were advised to support a limited but energetic government capable of conducting a robust foreign policy and enhancing competition and opportunity at home.[30]

House majority whip Tom Delay dismissed the Kristol-Brooks appeal as "Rockefeller Republicanism," and Senator Phil Gramm of Texas claimed that "Hamilton's views are anachronistic to our views." Gramm added, "We are Jeffersonians," a rallying cry echoed by Republican congressman David McIntosh of Indiana, who argued, "We have to be the party of less government, Jeffersonian, not Hamiltonian." McIntosh viewed Speaker of the House Newt Gingrich as a Hamiltonian who brought the Republicans to power, but he believed the future of the party belonged to the Jeffersonians. (Alexander Hamilton was one of Speaker Gingrich's heroes, along with John Wayne,

Kemal Ataturk, and Father Flanagan.) Although Gingrich admired Hamilton, his deputies Tom Delay and Majority Leader Dick Armey were devoted Jeffersonians. On one level, the party's takeover of Congress in 1994 was a bold revolution, Armey wrote a year later, "scrapping an entrenched, arrogant political order" and "tossing out the moneychangers." On another level, it was a revolution in "the humbler, Jeffersonian sense of revolving back to our points of origin."[31]

Michael Lind, a conservative turned liberal, dismissed the Kristol-Brooks call for national greatness conservatism but from a perspective quite different from that of Dick Armey or Tom Delay. Lind, the author of *Hamilton's Republic: Readings in the American Democratic Nationalist Tradition*, claimed that 1990s conservatives were "the heir of the Southern Jefferson-Jackson tradition" and that the "real vehicle for the Hamiltonian tradition in the twentieth century was the New Deal/Cold War Liberal Democratic coalition." There was no serious possibility that Hamiltonian nationalism could be revived in the Republican party, Lind asserted, because the "populists and plutocrats of the Republican right" would immediately denounce it as liberalism or socialism.[32]

While the battle for the Republican party's soul raged in the editorial pages, congressional Republicans had a more immediate concern at hand — impeaching President Clinton. Hamilton was resurrected again to offer sage counsel on impeachment, but he was also a witness, of sorts, in defense of the president's contention that private behavior should not be a subject of public inquiry. In 1998 an independent counsel, along with some Republican congressmen, alleged that the president had perjured himself while testifying about his relationship with a White House intern, Monica Lewinsky. In response, the president's lawyers presented a thirty-page brief to the House Judiciary Committee citing Hamilton's affair with Maria Reynolds and the reluctance of Congress to pursue the issue after concluding it was a private matter. The White House special counsel Greg Craig claimed, "Hamilton paid hush money, destroyed evidence and got (Mr. Reynolds) out of town. But it was considered a personal matter and didn't reflect an abuse of power." The editorial writers of the *St. Louis Post-Dispatch* agreed there were lessons to be learned in comparing the Lewinsky and Reynolds affairs. "When Alexander Hamilton was found to have paid hush money to cover up an adulterous love affair, none of the founding fathers suggested impeachment." The

Harvard law professor Alan Dershowitz also cited the Reynolds affair in defense of President Clinton, noting that "Washington and Madison agreed" with Hamilton's defending himself by "saying it was sex." At one point it seemed as if the duel would be replaced by the Reynolds affair as the event in Hamilton's life familiar to most Americans. In fall 1998, *Gentlemen's Quarterly* ran an article with the subtle title, "America's First Lecher," and *Harper's* reprinted lengthy excerpts from Hamilton's confession of his affair in the article "Foundering Father."[33]

Conservative politicians and columnists rejected any comparison of Clinton's and Hamilton's travails. Congressman Charles Canady, a Republican member of the House Judiciary Committee, argued that "the defenders of the president have sought to smear Hamilton. Hamilton was never accused of perjury or obstruction of justice." Hamilton's biographer and the *National Review*'s senior editor Richard Brookhiser contended that unlike Monica Lewinsky, Maria Reynolds was not Hamilton's employee and added that "when a garbled account appeared in the press, Hamilton did not consult his legal team, but published the full story" and "never lied about it under oath." David Frum in the *Weekly Standard* accused the White House of smearing Hamilton's reputation and charged that "Clinton chose the opposite course from Hamilton's: He disdained his public trust and broke the law, rather than suffer the exposure of his false pretenses as a father, husband, and national leader." Other observers were less outraged; as one writer for the *San Antonio Express-News* put it, "I've discovered even Republicans can get too horny — starting with Alexander Hamilton and on through to Dwight Eisenhower."[34]

Cable News Network's program *Inside Politics* named Hamilton the recipient of its "Political Play of the Week" for 9 October 1998, not for his renewed fame for having an affair but for his role as every congressman's favorite source for impeachment quotes. *The Federalist* became something of a best-seller as politicians and pundits once again turned to Hamilton's essays for guidance. Senator Daniel Patrick Moynihan of New York was seen toting his dog-eared copy of *The Federalist* and marveling at how prescient Hamilton could be — "the most extraordinary things are being written about what this new office of President will be." Both Clinton's critics and his defenders found passages in *Federalist* no. 65 to bolster their case, with Republicans claiming that Hamilton broadly construed the impeachment power to include any "violation of some public trust." Democrats focused on Hamilton's statement that impeachment proceedings, particularly in the House, "will be regulated more by the comparative strength of parties, than by the real demonstrations of innocence or guilt." Not all observers of the impeachment proceedings were impressed. A columnist for the *New York Post* questioned the sincerity of senators and congressmen who "bounce around the name of Alexander Hamilton" and "drop the words 'The Federalist Papers' the same way that some presidents drop their pants."[35]

The attention accorded Hamilton by politicians and journalists during the Clinton impeachment saga did not always translate into a more profound understanding of the man. A caricature of Hamilton still prevailed, as could be seen in repeated references to the great beast quote in the news media. Some forty years had elapsed since its veracity had been called into question, but the beast would not die. The *New Republic*'s David Grann described Republican frustrations with the people's support for Bill Clinton during the impeachment struggle and noted, "Alexander Hamilton once called the public a 'great beast.'" An impeachment-related essay in the *Buffalo News* claimed that Hamilton "tried to protect the country from . . . the workings of the mob. 'The people is (*sic*) a great beast,' warned the great New Yorker." A 1998 book review in the *Washington Times* asserted that Hamilton labeled the mass of common people the beast. A columnist in the *St. Petersburg Times* criticized Speaker Newt Gingrich and the radio talk-show host Rush Limbaugh for encouraging "the Great Beast to devour the good along with the bad." The writer noted that the original source of the great beast quote was attributed to Alexander Hamilton "in a debate with Thomas Jefferson." The beast crept into the Canadian consciousness when one writer in the *Ottawa Citizen* observed that modern Canadian leaders were comparable to Hamilton, who "said to Thomas Jefferson: 'Your "People," sir, is a great monster.'" An editorialist in the *Vancouver Sun* who apparently read the same history texts as the writer from Ottawa claimed that the great beast was the name "that Alexander Hamilton, one of the founders of the American republic, nervously gave to 'the people.'" Back in the States, those who had some inkling of the quote's tainted lineage often cited it nonetheless. The syndicated columnist Paul Greenberg wrote that Hamilton's supposed response to the idea of popular government was to claim that the people were a great beast and added, "it does sound just like him, even if historians have never been able to verify the comment."[36]

There were other misrepresentations of Hamilton published throughout the closing decade of the century. An essay in *U.S. News and World Report* described him as having meddled "in everything with an arrogance undiluted by any tincture of humility." He was pictured as "ablaze with satin and lace, the model of aristocratic elegance. . . . At any moment [he] had multiple schemes up his ruffled sleeve, concealed by layers of guile." The Pulitzer Prize–winning historian Gordon S. Wood of Brown University contended in the *New Republic* that Hamilton led a faction in the 1790s that "was promoting the interests of financiers and monarchists at the expense of the general public."[37]

In 1993 the award-winning playwright Arthur Miller *(Death of A Salesman, The Crucible)* brought to the stage in London and New York *The Last Yankee.* All the characters in this play, rich and poor, appear trapped in an empty, materialistic American wasteland. The ideals of the early Republic are dead, or perhaps they were deformed at birth. The title character is Leroy Hamilton, a carpenter descended from Alexander Hamilton, whose lack of ambition is a source of despair for his pill-popping, perpetually depressed wife. At one point in the play Leroy engages in a dialogue with a wealthy businessman, John Frick, whose equally depressed wife is confined to the same psychiatric hospital as Mrs. Hamilton. Leroy reprimands John for denigrating the carpentry profession and wonders aloud about the state of equality in America. At another point Leroy announces, "Maybe I am a failure; but in my opinion no more than the rest of this country." Leroy Hamilton is the only character in the play who is somewhat stable and contented, having rejected the notion that he needs a bigger car or a better house than his neighbor. The wealthy Mr. Frick admires Alexander Hamilton, but Leroy, whose father disliked his founding ancestor's philosophy, appears to disapprove of his famous forebear also. Alexander Hamilton and his commercial republic, Arthur Miller has suggested, doomed America from the start.[38]

It was perhaps inevitable that after decades of Hamilton-bashing, Aaron Burr's reputation would begin to revive. Three books sympathetic to Hamilton's killer were released in the late 1990s. Arnold Rogow's *A Fatal Friendship: Alexander Hamilton and Aaron Burr,* Thomas Fleming's *Duel: Alexander Hamilton, Aaron Burr and the Future of America,* and Roger Kennedy's *Burr, Hamilton, and Jefferson: A Study in Character* portrayed Hamilton in a most unflattering light. Arnold Rogow contended that Hamilton had earned his reputation "for coldness and cruel indifference" by advocating the employment of women and children in manufacturing. In an interview given shortly after his book was published, Rogow claimed that Aaron Burr was "much maligned" and "was quite an impressive man" — the "first feminist in this country." Hamilton was "brilliant [but psychologically] unstable . . . ruthless . . . capable of dishonesty on . . . a massive level, [and] dangerous" to American ideals and "had no use for ordinary people." Rogow was almost certain that Hamilton passed inside Treasury Department information to his family and friends, who "were able to make a great deal of money." Hamilton's hatred for Burr was based in part on a "homoerotic attraction" to Burr that he found threatening to his "macho image of himself." Perhaps not surprisingly, Rogow announced in his interview that he had joined the Aaron Burr Association.[39]

Thomas Fleming argued that Hamilton was intensely aware toward the end of his life that "in a world shadowed by Napoleon Bonaparte . . . election was not the only way a man could achieve power." Hamilton's antipathy to Burr resulted from the former's reserving "for himself the part that Bonaparte had played in restoring order to revolutionary France," and he "could not let Aaron Burr, of all people, usurp this last hope of ultimate fame." Roger Kennedy agreed with Fleming's account of a dictatorially inclined Hamilton, claiming that he was a "voluptuary [who was] enraptured by the prospect of another army to lead to glory." Kennedy found Burr to be something of a Renaissance man, a charismatic figure with a great sense of humor that made him "the Adlai Stevenson of the eighteenth century." Hamilton, however, was "full of self-loathing" and saw in the talented Burr "everything he feared most in himself." Kennedy added, "Self-disgust is the propellant of projection," and Hamilton "projected upon Burr his own sexual and financial profligacy." Hamilton could have averted the showdown with Burr at Weehawken but instead "arranged to have Burr kill him."[40]

Although such caricatures of Hamilton were clearly still in vogue, polling data indicated that a stereotyped understanding of him was hardly his most serious problem. Many Americans simply had no idea who he was. A 1998 opinion poll conducted by the Opinion Research Corporation asked 1,004 adults aged thirty-five to fifty-four, "Who was not one of our country's 'founding fathers'?" The respondents were given four names to choose from: Washington, Jefferson, Hamilton, and Lincoln. Three percent answered George Washington, 4 percent Thomas Jefferson; the correct answer, Abraham Lincoln, received 55 percent of the responses. Thirty-three percent of Americans believed Alexander Hamilton was not a founding father.[41]

Yet as the twentieth century drew to a close, in some scholarly and media circles Hamilton's reputation began to improve, partly due to a decline in his rival's status. Questions concerning Jefferson's attitude toward slavery, his apparent relationship with Sally Hemings, his expressions of support for mass executions during the French Revolution, his endorsement of prerogative power, his states' rights doctrine, and his record on civil liberties had produced dissembling responses from the Monticello Mafia, as Jefferson's biographer Joseph Ellis dubbed the old Charlottesville clique. By the mid-1990s Jeffersonian controversies were finally being addressed in scholarship published in the shadow of Monticello by the University Press of Virginia. Younger, more skeptical scholars with a particular interest in Jefferson and race replaced the old cadre of Jefferson boosters associated with that university. Ellis's *American Sphinx: The Character of Thomas Jefferson* was but one indicator that the era of Jeffersonian myth making was over. The historian Robert Middlekauff observed in a review of Ellis's book that Jefferson was "no longer in good repute among professional historians." Middlekauff added that Daniel Boorstin wrote *The Lost World of Thomas Jefferson* in 1948; in 1998 Jefferson's "reputation has also been lost."[42]

It was not simply a result of Jefferson's declining reputation that Hamilton experienced something of an end-of-century revival. In some vague way he benefited from the renewed appeal of capitalism that occurred with the collapse of communism in Eastern Europe. (*Forbes* magazine published an article in 1990, "Lech Walesa, Meet Alexander Hamilton.") The economic boom of the 1980s and 1990s and the increasing public respect for entrepreneurs also contributed to Hamilton's improved standing. In 1995 he was inducted into the Junior Achievement National Business Hall of Fame and entered the Gallery of Laureates at the Chicago Museum of Science and Industry, alongside Frederick Maytag and Frank Woolworth. "If it can be said that free enterprise as we know it was born after the American Revolution," *Fortune* claimed in announcing Hamilton's induction, then he was "the doctor who delivered and spanked the baby."[43]

Hamilton had always been a popular figure in business and financial circles. But now there was a growing tendency beyond these traditional Hamiltonian enclaves to acclaim him as the personification of the American experience. One of the nation's first immigrant success stories, Hamilton, like millions after him, embraced his new homeland with a nationalistic fervor, despite an often chilly reception from native Americans. Both Richard Brookhiser on the right and Michael Lind on the left of the political spectrum saw these elements in Hamilton's life and bemoaned the fact that he had not been properly honored. Brookhiser observed that the Hamilton Grange, unlike the Virginia temples to Washington and Jefferson, was hardly visited, despite Hamilton's opposition to slavery, his understanding of the "persistence of nationalism as a world force," and his role as a "great apostle of capitalist enterprise as a catalyst for human potential." Lind lamented the absence of a Hamilton memorial on the Washington Mall but noted that "until one is built, we will have to make do with the existing monuments to the Hamiltonian vision: West Point and the Pentagon, the Federal Reserve, the interstate highway and air travel systems, Detroit and the Silicon Valley." In 1997 the *Economist* observed that Hamilton had been "eclipsed for a century" by Thomas Jefferson but was making a comeback. A New York organization working from the site of Hamilton's former law firm began campaigning for a national monument to Hamilton in Washington, and a group of African-American capitalists organized an annual memorial at the Grange.[44]

In 1960 Merrill Peterson observed that "the spacious grandeur of Monticello" stood in stark contrast to the "shabby disrepair and virtual anonymity" of the Grange in crowded Harlem. It was, he said, a "true reflection of the two rivals' contemporary reputations."[45] The spacious grandeur of Monticello, brought about by the toil of hundreds of slave laborers, is a truly fitting monument to Thomas Jefferson. For decades Monticello served as a Potemkin Village, where evidence of the existence of Jefferson's slaves was hidden from visitors. Monticello was, in a larger sense, emblematic of the twentieth-century airbrushing of history by Jeffersonian politicians and scholars. The crowded, slighted Grange, in the midst of New York's poverty and in the shadow of its great wealth, is the appropriate destination for Americans seeking the truth about their country's mixed record of triumph and failure.

In the future, a more diverse nation is apt to focus on race as the crucial issue in the American experience. Race has always been Jefferson's Achilles heel, and in the twenty-first century it could well be his undoing. If the past holds any lessons, then Hamilton's standing should continue to improve; for it appears to be an iron law that as one falls, the other rises. Jefferson and the Jeffersonians would have it no other way; as the Sage himself once put it, "opposed in death as in life."[46]

9

Getting Right with Hamilton
"The Public Good Must Be Paramount"

In the twentieth century, the contest between Hamilton and Jefferson for the soul of America was largely a lopsided affair, for with the exception of the century's first quarter and its last few years, all honor went to Jefferson and his rhetoric. Although Theodore Roosevelt viewed Hamilton as far superior to Jefferson as an American statesman, this perception was not widely shared by Roosevelt's successors. Other than TR, Hamilton's principal admirers in the twentieth-century White House were Warren G. Harding and Calvin Coolidge, two chief executives whose opinions are dismissed by most historians and political scientists. Jefferson's champions, however, included John F. Kennedy and the beloved Franklin Roosevelt.

The celebration of Jefferson was prompted by Franklin Roosevelt's desire to secure the support of the South for a transitory political coalition and to confer on it the legitimacy of a founder; making Jefferson a national icon was a brilliant political move by a Northern patrician eager for Southern support. FDR received considerable assistance from a group of progressive historians and political scientists, most especially Claude Bowers, Dumas Malone, and Julian Boyd. Hamilton was the champion of "the rule of the favored few," as Malone put it, while Jefferson was portrayed as the crusader for liberty and protector of the common man. The decline of Hamilton's reputation in the twentieth century was in good measure the result of a partisan effort to advance a progressive political agenda and to a lesser extent to highlight the primacy of Virginia in the American founding. As a result, the real Hamilton became shrouded behind a caricature of the man and his principles.

Hamilton was aware toward the end of his life that this caricature had already taken hold in the minds of many of his fellow citizens. It is no surprise that in 1802 he wrote, "What can I do better than withdraw from the Scene? Every day proves to me more and more that this American world was not made for me."[1] Perhaps it is not an overstatement to say that he became something of a victim of a form of internal exile, for all practical purposes labeled by substantial numbers of his countrymen as un-American.

At the dawn of the new millennium, it is difficult to predict whether his internal exile will continue, or if the American public will abandon entirely the old myths regarding Hamilton and Jefferson. However, though his authorship of the Declaration of Independence has forever secured his place in the nation's pantheon, there appears the gradual realization that, at the very least, the twentieth-century celebration of Jefferson was excessive. Americans seem perhaps ready to reassess him: whether this will be coupled with a reappraisal of Hamilton's legacy remains to be seen, although there are disturbing suggestions that his image as a reactionary member of the founding generation will not quickly be erased. Yet the shroud of myth may be receding, and the door opening, to a more objective appraisal of the accomplishments of both men. A sober assessment may reveal that beneath his highly colored reputation, Hamilton was the most forward looking of the framers, responsible in many ways for creating the innovative American institutions that have flourished for over two centuries. For the concluding section of this book, I shall briefly recount some of the misinterpretations of Hamilton's record and describe his important contributions to building the American nation.

Reclaiming Hamilton's Record

For many Americans, Alexander Hamilton remains a somewhat ominous figure from the past, his alleged contempt for the people being the main source of his poor standing. The stamina of the great beast quote caused the most damage to his reputation and shows no sign of flagging. Whether through sloppiness or malice, and it is more likely the latter, Henry Adams succeeded in tarnishing Hamilton's image for decades. The beast saga is yet one more reminder to scholars of the necessity of approaching the great works of prestigious authors with some degree of skepticism. It is truly sobering to recall the number of talented writers who repeated Henry Adams's tale without the slightest hesitation. Those authors who continue to cite the beast remark as something that "sounds like Hamilton" and who dismiss concerns about its provenance reveal a stunning disdain for the integrity of scholarship and journalism.

Although the great beast tale is the most egregious example of Hamiltonian myth making, other misrepresentations deserve mention. Critics have often cited, as evidence of his tepid Americanism, Hamilton's remark that from the "very beginning I am still labouring to prop the frail and worthless fabric [the Constitution]." But this was more likely a reflection of the despair he felt toward the end of his life at living in Jefferson's America with a president disposed to dismantling the props he erected to make the Constitution work. Hamilton's anguish was misguided, for he underestimated the gap between Jefferson's public posturing and his actions: concealed beneath layers of rhetoric, Jefferson was a Hamiltonian chief executive. In this same letter, in a passage seldom cited by his critics, Hamilton expressed guarded optimism about America's future, anticipating that "the time may ere long arrive when the minds of men will be prepared to make an offer to recover the Constitution."[2]

It is frequently claimed that Hamilton did not believe in liberty, that he was, in fact, a closet Caesar, a view promulgated by many historians, including Dumas Malone, Julian Boyd, Adrienne Koch, and Douglass Adair. Malone's belief that Hamilton "loved command for its own sake" and cared little "for the liberal ideas of the Enlightenment" was based in part on Jefferson's report of a dinner held in 1791 where Hamilton allegedly claimed that Julius Caesar was "the greatest man that ever lived." Jefferson first recounted the episode in 1811, twenty years after Hamilton supposedly uttered the remark. As Thomas P. Govan observed, "Hamilton's extant papers do not confirm" Jefferson's assertion that Hamilton admired the Roman leader. At the Constitutional Convention of 1787 Hamilton professed that he was "as zealous an advocate for liberty as any man whatever, and trusted he should be as willing a martyr to it." He shared the belief of the other founders in natural rights, writing in 1775 that "the sacred rights of mankind are not to be rummaged for, among old parchments, or musty records. They are written, as with a sun beam, in the whole *volume* of human nature, by the hand of the divinity itself; and can never be erased or obscured by mortal power." In some measure his image as a defender of liberty is blurred because he saw no distinction between property and liberty, and the defense of property rights in the twentieth century has been tagged with the patina of greed and selfishness. But — in agreement with both John Locke and the author of the Declaration of Independence — Hamilton believed the right to property was essential if liberty were to flourish. In 1795 he defended his plan for funding the nation's debt and observed that, in the absence of such measures, "adieu to the security of property adieu to the security of liberty. Nothing is then safe — all our favourite notions of national & constitutional rights vanish. Every thing is brought to a question of power."[3]

Alexander Hamilton never spoke of enlisting the rich and wellborn simply to benefit that class; he believed that without the support of this powerful group, the American experiment would collapse. Govan effectively dealt with the issue of Hamilton and the rich and wellborn in an essay published in 1950. He cited a number of prominent historians who interpreted a comment recorded by Robert Yates at the Constitutional Convention of 1787 as indicative of Hamilton's belief in the innate virtue of the rich and wellborn. These accounts claimed that Hamilton believed that the wealthy few "could be safely entrusted with political power," a conclusion with which Govan firmly disagreed, arguing that Hamilton was "under no such delusion." Govan rightly noted that Hamilton saw all individuals — regardless of class — as subject to the passions of "avarice, ambition, interest" and did not "assign priority" to any group. He wanted a government where the national interest prevailed, not the interest of any one group. Govan concluded that Hamilton "feared absolute and despotic power whether exercised in the name of the people, the aristocracy, or the crown, and would balance the passion of each over against that of the others."[4]

Hamilton did not hate the people, as is often asserted. Stories abound of his personal generosity toward his fellow citizens, many of whom he did not know. He also was blessed with many friends who cherished his company and to whom he remained a devoted companion. Nor did he accept the accusation that he was an aristocrat. When Hamilton and other proponents of the

Constitution were accused of attempting to create an American aristocracy, he replied, "I hardly know the meaning of this word as it is applied. . . . Who are the aristocracy among us? Where do we find men elevated to a perpetual rank above their fellow citizens; and possessing powers entirely independent of them? . . . There are men who are rich, men who are poor, some who are wise, and others who are not . . . indeed every distinguished man is an aristocrat." As Jacob Cooke correctly observed, "In Hamilton's own experience, privilege and distinction were earned by brilliance and diligence, not conferred by birth."[5]

It is true that Hamilton was not an advocate of participatory democracy: he believed — along with almost the entire founding generation — that history confirmed the dangers of direct popular rule. However, he believed that popular government could succeed with the adoption of a system filtered by representation and restrained by anchors of stability and permanence. Whatever misgivings he had about the final document produced in Philadelphia in 1787, and he had some, he worked as hard as any American to ensure the ratification and implementation of the Constitution. Yet Jefferson and subsequent generations of Jeffersonians succeeded in labeling Hamilton a monarchist, a highly incendiary charge designed to curtail debate and destroy Hamilton's viability in the political arena. "It is doubtful," Hamilton's biographer John C. Miller observed, "if Jefferson could have found an issue more calculated than was 'monarchism' to undermine Hamilton's position before the country and, incidentally, to obscure the real issues between himself and the Secretary of the Treasury." Accusing a public figure of being a monarchist or monocrat was the 1790's equivalent of accusing someone of being a Communist in 1950. It was a propaganda weapon as Miller noted, wielded by Jefferson with "consummate skill." Hamilton's colleague Fisher Ames astutely called the charge "a substitute for argument, and its overmatch."[6]

Over time the monarchist charge no longer resonated with the public, and the Jeffersonians resorted to the accusation that Hamilton and his philosophical heirs sought the creation of a plutocracy. Jefferson was already gravitating in this direction, realizing the great rewards that could accrue to the party that championed the common man. Writing a few years after Hamilton's Bank of the United States was chartered, Jefferson claimed that "immense sums were . . . filched from the poor and ignorant." Jefferson's demagoguery about banks knew no bounds. "I have ever been the enemy of banks," he wrote John Adams and noted the derision directed at him "by the tribe of bank-mongers" who were "seeking to filch from the public their swindling, and barren gains." Another example of Hamilton's alleged heartlessness toward the vulnerable elements of society was his proposal in his "Report on Manufactures" recommending the employment of women and children in manufacturing, a comment often cited by latter-day Jeffersonians as indicative of his lack of compassion. As Jacob Cooke noted, however, Hamilton made this statement "at a time when children were put to work on the farm at a young age and forced to labor long hours in the fields," and the proposal that they work in factories "was neither novel nor callous."[7] One could add that the use of women and children as slave laborers by Hamilton's Virginia contemporaries was a far more grievous injustice than a proposal for employing them as wage earners.

Hamilton's role in suppressing the Whiskey Rebellion of 1794 is yet another commonly cited example of his alleged disregard for the citizenry. There is an odd tendency among Hamilton's critics to romanticize this event, to portray the distillers of whiskey as God's chosen people. Although one can differ on the question of whether producing and consuming whiskey is a noble calling, the fact remains that President Washington, not Hamilton, approved the military operation to enforce the law and restore the government's authority. Hindsight might allow one to dismiss the seriousness of the affair, but the threat was quite plausible to a newborn government whose viability was still open to question. In an effort to appease the citizens in western Pennsylvania upset with the law, Hamilton proposed alterations to the legislation authorizing the whiskey excise. Nonetheless, repeated acts of violence against authorities persisted. It was, as Hamilton saw it, a question of whether law or force would prevail in America, the former being the definition of liberty, the latter the definition of despotism. As Hamilton put it, "A sacred respect for the constitutional law is the vital principle, the sustaining energy of a free government." The difficulty of instilling in the citizenry the notion that obedience to law is liberty appears perennial in popular government: a similar situation would confront Abraham Lincoln on a much larger scale in less than four-score years. Hamilton saw the rebellion as posing in unambiguous terms the question, "Shall the majority govern or be governed?" and concluded that "those who preach doctrines, or set examples, which undermine or subvert the authority of the laws, lead us from freedom to slavery."[8]

Hamilton is also frequently criticized for his actions in and around the Quasi-War with France, labeled a warmonger and accused of viewing the crisis as an opportunity to crush dissent at home and to engage in the conquest of Latin America. Hamilton urged vigorous preparations for war with France, yet he also urged the Adams administration to leave "the door to accommodation open and not [proceed] to final rupture." Moreover, he objected, although not vigorously, to certain aspects of both the Alien and Sedition Acts. He urged that the execution of the former "not be cruel or violent," and of the latter he warned, "Let us not establish a tyranny. Energy is a very different thing from violence." As Jacob Cooke reminds us, in the face of a perceived crisis Hamilton was no civil libertarian: but in this he was joined by such eminent personages as Thomas Jefferson, Abraham Lincoln, Woodrow Wilson, and Franklin Roosevelt. (Jefferson once observed that there were "extreme cases where the laws become inadequate even to their own preservation, and where the universal recourse is a dictator, or martial law.") The often repeated idea that Hamilton intended to use the military to crush partisan dissent in Virginia and elsewhere runs counter to his frequently stated rationale, the defense of the nation against possible French attack. Seeking peace from a position of strength is sound policy, not a plan for a military coup d'etat. Samuel Eliot Morison noted that there was not "the slightest evidence" to support the allegation that Hamilton intended to use the military to "suppress democracy," a charge that nonetheless continues to haunt his reputation. Concerned, along with many Federalists and many Virginians, about the situation in Virginia in 1798 and 1799 in the wake of the Kentucky and Virginia Resolutions, he hoped "to give time for the fervor of the moment to subside" and for reason to prevail but supported if necessary a show of force to restore order as had been done in the Whiskey Rebellion. As Jacob Cooke concluded, even if "the incipient Caesar" was intent on snuffing out democracy, the "pygmy army" that was assembled was "woefully inadequate" to the task.[9] Nevertheless, it would have been John Adams's decision to authorize the use of force, not Hamilton's, unless one accepts a coup d'etat as part of Hamilton's scheme. Although he never, of course, attempted such an action and directed the disbanding of the army when the French threat subsided, the idea persists to this day that Hamilton intended to use this force for nefarious purposes.

One final event proverbially cited by Hamilton's critics as evidence of his Caesarian tendencies was his proposal in 1800 to change the rules after his candidates lost their races for the New York state legislature. These results were favorable to Aaron Burr's machine and allowed the Republicans to control the legislature and thus select the state's presidential electors. Hamilton believed that Burr had united Republican factions in New York, as Forrest McDonald put it, through "a devious scheme that fattened their purses." Burr also persuaded many prominent figures in New York to allow their names to be placed on the ballot for the state legislature, even though none of them was genuinely committed to holding such an undignified position. The purpose of this exercise was to elect these state legislators who would in turn select Republican electors and open the way for Burr's party to win the White House. Hamilton believed that Burr's deceitful practices in the election warranted a response. He urged Governor John Jay to call the outgoing Federalist legislature into special session and change the election laws to provide for popular elections of presidential electors by district. Hamilton suggested that Jay not be overscrupulous at such a time, but Jay rejected Hamilton's advice, and the Republicans carried New York and the nation.

It is important to note that the alteration of the selection process for presidential electors for partisan reasons was the norm at this time. Five states changed their election laws in 1800 to make them less democratic, including Virginia. Jefferson and his lieutenants opted for a statewide system that ensured that no electors were selected from a Federalist district in Virginia, even though Jefferson once argued that "the minority is entirely unrepresented" in such a system. Forrest McDonald observed that Hamilton has been universally condemned for his proposal to John Jay, despite the fact that the process he sought to overturn did not directly represent the will of the people. Hamilton's plea to Governor Jay was consistent with his lifelong support for the direct election of electors by district, and two years later he recommended the adoption of a constitutional amendment allowing for such a method.[10]

Hamilton's actions throughout 1800 were a source of distress to Aaron Burr, who, it is important to remember in light of recent attempts at rehabilitation, was deeply distrusted by Jefferson, Hamilton, Monroe, Washington, and many others. These men saw a flaw in Burr's character that modern revisionist authors have missed: a remarkably disparate group of early American statesmen reached a consensus that he was an unprincipled man guided only by ambition and unworthy of high office. In an act of exceptional states-manship, Hamilton, who justly observed that "if there be a man in the world I ought to hate it is Jefferson," urged his fellow Federalists in the House of Representatives to break the deadlocked presidential election between Burr and Jefferson and to vote for the latter. It was a seminal moment, an illustra-tion of Hamilton's tendency to put the national interest first. As he observed, "With Burr I have always been personally well. But the public good must be paramount to every private consideration."[11]

One contemporary who had complete confidence in Hamilton's charac-ter, talents, and devotion to the public good was George Washington. Little over a year before he died, Washington wrote that Hamilton filled "one of the most important departments of Government with acknowledged abili-ties and integrity" and had established himself as "a conspicuous character in the United States, and even in Europe." Hamilton was "enterprising, quick in his perceptions," and his judgment was "intuitively great." Writing at a time when Washington was shunning Hamilton's great rival, the former president observed, "By some he is considered as an ambitious man, and therefore a dangerous one. That he is ambitious I shall readily grant, but it is of that laud-able kind which prompts a man to excel in whatever he takes in hand."[12] No person worked as closely with George Washington throughout years of war and nation building than Alexander Hamilton, and this historic relationship saw Washington and Hamilton in accord on the great issues of their day. A man of towering integrity, Washington saw qualities in his young confidant unnoticed by Jefferson and his philosophical heirs. Or perhaps they did notice. But the Jeffersonians understood that attacking Hamilton was far more pal-atable to the public than attacking the father of their country and that tying Washington to Hamilton would undermine a main tenet of their faith. In recovering the bond that linked the two, one makes a compelling case that Alexander Hamilton was about as American as one can get.

Building a Nation: The Spirit of Enterprise

These controversial actions generally obscure Hamilton's substantial record of achievement. They are diversions, interesting sideshows that allow one to dismiss Hamilton without delving deeper into the more difficult issues sur-rounding his theoretical principles and his practical statesmanship. Hamilton's statesmanship is evident in a variety of areas, including his endeavor to transform America from a sleepy, unproductive agrarian backwater into a commercial power.

Hamilton's economic program involved three central tenets: first, that the federal government should assume the debts contracted by the states during the American Revolution; second, that a national bank be created to facilitate the fiscal policies of the federal government and serve as a catalyst for national economic growth; third, that the federal government should take steps to transform America into a manufacturing power, thus ending its reliance on Europe for these goods. The first two proposals became law, although not without heated opposition, led primarily by James Madison. Madison understood that Hamilton's proposal of debt assumption was designed not merely to retire debts and obligations from the war but stemmed from his desire to "bind the states' creditors to the central government with hoops of gold." Passage was achieved only after Hamilton struck a deal with Jefferson and Madison allowing the U.S. capital to be located on the Potomac in exchange for the passage of the assumption bill. The act creating a Bank of the United States also passed, but only after Hamilton authored a ringing defense of the implied powers of the Constitution that may have persuaded President Washington to sign the bill into law. Whatever the impact on President Washington, Hamilton's constitutional arguments certainly influenced later interpretations of that document, particularly those of future Supreme Court Chief Justice John Marshall. A national bank, Hamilton believed, would become a "nurser[y] of national wealth" and would provide "greater facility to the government in obtaining pecuniary aids, especially in sudden emergencies."[13] The bank debate exposed Hamilton to the charge that he was the champion of the wellborn, but his true goal was the creation of national instruments of economic and political power necessary for greatness.

By far the most ambitious of Hamilton's economic proposals was his "Report on the Subject of Manufactures." Years ahead of his time, Hamilton viewed an American manufacturing capability as a means of rendering the United States "independent [of] foreign nations," particularly "for military and other essential supplies," and thereby completing the task begun in 1776. Hamilton noted in his report that "to cherish and stimulate the activity of the human mind, by multiplying the objects of enterprise, is not the least considerable of the expedients, by which the wealth of a nation may be promoted. . . . Every new scene, which is opened to the busy nature of man to rouse and exert itself, is the addition of a new energy to the general stock of effort."[14] Though Congress refused to adopt his proposals, he alone among the principal founders championed an American spirit of enterprise that eventually transformed a Third World nation into the greatest economic power ever known.

In time, Thomas Jefferson came to accept the idea that political independence was inextricably linked with economic self-sufficiency, though he reached this conclusion long after Hamilton was dead. In *Notes on the State of Virginia*, written in 1781, Jefferson had declared, "For the general operations of manufacture, let our work-shops remain in Europe." But by 1816, he had undergone another Hamiltonian transformation. In a letter to Benjamin Austin, he admitted "that to be independent for the comforts of life we must fabricate them ourselves. We must now place the manufacturer by the side of the agriculturist. . . . Experience has taught me that manufactures are now as necessary to our independence as to our comfort."[15]

Judicial Legacy

Alexander Hamilton's influence in creating a respected national judiciary and in shaping American jurisprudence was somewhat indirect, but nonetheless significant. His legal education consisted of reading the works of such scholars as William Blackstone, Edward Coke, and Emmerich de Vattel. Though he took to the law somewhat reluctantly, his legal training proved beneficial to his career as a nation builder, for "he learned that liberty and compliance with prescribed rules of behavior are not opposites that must somehow be balanced . . . but are complementary and inseparable."[16]

In *The Federalist*, Hamilton identified the crowning defect of the Articles of Confederation as "the want of a judiciary power" and clearly stated his belief in the necessity for "one Supreme Tribunal" to "avoid the confusion which would unavoidably result from the contradictory decisions of a number of independent judicatories." This was essential to nation building, for "all nations have found it necessary to establish one court paramount to the rest — possessing a general superintendance" and authorized in the last resort to declare a "uniform rule of civil justice." Perhaps his most important contribution to building a formidable American legal structure was his authorship of *Federalist* no. 78, in which he argued that the federal judiciary, appointed to lifetime positions during good behavior, would act as a bulwark against legislative encroachments on liberty. Permanently appointed judges in a monarchy act as a barrier against a despotic prince; in a republic they act as a bar against the "oppressions of the representative body." Possessed of neither force nor will, the judiciary is dependent on the executive to carry out its judgments; and since it is the weakest of the three branches, "liberty can have nothing to fear from the judiciary alone." Nonetheless, the "interpretation of the laws is the proper and peculiar province of the courts. A constitution is in fact, and must be, regarded by the judges as a fundamental law."[17]

Though an independent federal judiciary exists to "guard the constitution and the rights of individuals," Hamilton was aware of the potential for the judiciary to "substitute their own pleasure" for that of the legislature. Permanency in office would help to restrain this tendency, he believed. "To avoid an arbitrary discretion in the courts, it is indispensable that they should be bound down by strict rules and precedents, which serve to define and point out their duty in every particular case that comes before them." This knowledge of precedent and procedure is gained only from years of experience, and if appointments were made with an eye to finding judges with integrity, knowledge, and moderation, the courts would refrain from interpreting the Constitution in an ill-defined manner.[18]

The impact of Hamilton's judicial writings can be seen in the jurisprudence of the greatest chief justice, John Marshall. In three of his landmark decisions, *Marbury v. Madison* (1803), *Fletcher v. Peck* (1810), and *McCulloch v. Maryland* (1819), Marshall turned to Hamilton for guidance. In *Marbury*, Marshall's argument that "it is emphatically, the province and duty of the judicial department, to say what the law is" was rooted in the arguments of *Federalist* no. 78. In *Fletcher* (the Yazoo Land Grant case), the Supreme Court determined that public grants were contracts protected by the contract clause, an argument advanced fifteen years earlier by Hamilton in a private legal opinion. In *McCulloch*, Marshall borrowed from Hamilton's defense of implied powers advanced during the debate over a national bank and also adopted much of Hamilton's interpretation of the necessary and proper clause. As the editor of *The Papers of John Marshall* has noted, "Scarcely a passage in the first part of *McCulloch* could not be traced to Hamilton's advisory opinion" on the bank.[19]

Military Power

Hamilton believed that the creation of a professional American military establishment was a necessary prerequisite to establishing respect for the new
nation. As General Washington's favorite aide-de-camp, he had witnessed
firsthand the costs of conducting a war without sufficient levels of military
professionalism and preparedness, an experience that gave him a deeper
understanding of military matters than either Jefferson or Madison. His hard-
earned wartime lessons found their way into *The Federalist* and were the
source of many of his actions as leader of the Federalist party. As with many
of his other proposals, his opponents assumed his advocacy of military
strength was part of a grand scheme to further his monarchical designs on
the country.

One of the main objections of the antifederalists to the proposed Constitution was the absence of a provision prohibiting the existence of peacetime
standing armies. Hamilton attempted in *The Federalist* to allay these concerns,
noting in no. 24 that the presence of a permanent corps in the pay of the
government might be necessary to defend the western frontiers from the
depredations of the British, the Spanish, and the Indian tribes. He contended
that the decision to establish such a corps should be left to the discretion of
the legislature and not prohibited by the Constitution. Hamilton found the
militia system to be a poor substitute for a professionally trained military; he
could barely contain himself when dealing with this issue in *The Federalist*
and attempted to convince his fellow countrymen that the notion of a yeoman farmer who dropped his plow to take arms and then defeated the British during the Revolution was a myth.

We shall be told, that the Militia of the country is its natural bulwark, and would
be at all times equal to the national defence. This doctrine in substance had like
to have lost us our independence. . . . The steady operations of war against a regular and disciplined army, can only be successfully conducted by a force of the same
kind. The American Militia . . . know, that the liberty of their country could not
have been established by their efforts alone. . . . War, like most other things, is a
science to be acquired and perfected by diligence, by perseverance, by time, and
by practice.[20]

In light of these beliefs, Hamilton argued that the creation of a military
academy was indispensable. Indeed, he sought to establish four separate acad-

emies, one for cavalry and infantry, a school for artillerists and engineers, a naval academy, and a "fundamental school" at West Point. He later noted that "in proportion as the circumstances and policy of a country forbid a large military establishment, it is important that as much perfection as possible should be given to that which may at any time exist." In a debate over this issue during the Washington administration, Jefferson argued that "none of the specific powers given by the Constitution would authorize" the creation of a national military academy. As president, he reversed course and agreed to the establishment of a military academy at West Point, one of many instances where he demonstrated a penchant for adopting Hamiltonian proposals he had vehemently opposed in the 1790s.[21]

The establishment of American naval power was particularly disturbing to the antifederalists and later to the Jeffersonian Republicans. One prominent Republican, Samuel McKee, exclaimed, "Show me a nation possessed of a large navy and I will show you a nation always at war." Navies were tools of imperialism, difficult to control due to the problems involved with communications, and constantly in harm's way. But Hamilton argued that an American fleet would help the United States "influenc[e] the conduct of European nations towards us," and he foresaw the day when the nation would "create a navy, which, if it could not vie with those of the great maritime powers, would at least be of respectable weight." Hamilton believed a navy essential to America's rise as a commercial power: "If we mean to be a commercial people or even to be secure on our Atlantic side, we must endeavor as soon as possible to have a navy. To this purpose there must be dock-yards and arsenals, and, for the defence of these, fortifications and probably garrisons." Hamilton's advocacy of maritime power insinuated itself into many of the key proposals of the Washington administration, including the president's Farewell Address, and was explicitly stated in Washington's last annual message to Congress in December 1796: "To an active commerce, the protection of a Naval force is indispensable." In a warning apparently lost on Jefferson and Madison, Washington cautioned, "To secure respect to a Neutral Flag, requires a Naval force, organized, and ready to vindicate it from insult and aggression." And he warned of a more immediate threat on the horizon: "Our trade to the mediterranean, without a protecting force, will always be insecure. . . . These considerations invite the United States, to look to the means, and set about the gradual creation of a Navy."[22]

The policies begun at Hamilton's urging under the Washington administration, and continued under John Adams, saw the peacetime military grow
from 843 men in 1789 to 5,400 men in 1801. The American navy, which had
been scrapped after the Revolutionary War, consisted of thirteen frigates in
1801 with six more under construction. Much of the navy was gutted for both
ideological and economizing reasons under Jefferson and Madison, which left
the United States ill-prepared for the War of 1812.[23] But Hamilton's larger
principles ultimately prevailed in the way America thinks about foreign affairs
and military preparedness. The belief that respect in the international arena
is dependent in great measure on military power guided the United States to
international preeminence in the twentieth century.

An Energetic Executive

Both in principle and in practice, Alexander Hamilton laid the foundation
for a strong presidency. Although he never held the office himself, his authorship of the essays in The Federalist dealing with presidential power provided the theoretical underpinnings for assertive executive conduct. As the
most trusted member of President Washington's inner circle, Hamilton's
influence over that important precedent-setting first presidency cannot be
overstated.

Hamilton's president would possess "all the requisites to energy" that "republican principles would admit." He argued in Federalist no. 70 that an
energetic executive ensured the steady administration of the laws, protected
property "against those irregular and high handed combinations, which sometimes interrupt the ordinary course of justice," and provided for "the security of liberty" against the "assaults [of] faction." Hamilton believed that
energy in the executive was particularly important in the conduct of foreign
policy, especially during conflicts. "The direction of war," he asserted, "im-
plies the direction of the common strength; and the power of directing and
employing the common strength, forms an usual and essential part in the
definition of executive authority."[24]

As secretary of the treasury in Washington's administration, Hamilton was
frequently embroiled in foreign policy controversies, much to the chagrin of
Secretary of State Jefferson. In the controversy over the Neutrality Proclamation of 1793, Hamilton argued that the question of American obligations

under the treaty of 1778 with France was by its nature an executive decision: the Constitution in Article 2 gave the president a general grant of power by vesting in him the executive power. As Robert Scigliano has noted, Hamilton's argument followed this line of thought: "The power to declare war is given to Congress and the powers to consent to treaties and appointments are given to the Senate. Otherwise the grant is complete [to the president]. . . . It would have been difficult for the document to have contained a 'complete and perfect specification of all cases of executive authority,' and so it left the rest 'to flow' from the general grant." The differing methods of expression in Articles 1 and 2 of the Constitution were deemed significant by Hamilton; Article 1 refers to "all legislative powers herein granted," and the more loosely worded Article 2 vests "the executive power" in the president. Apparently influenced by the works of Locke and Montesquieu on the nature of executive primacy in foreign affairs, Hamilton propounded an interpretation that has been followed by most nineteenth- and twentieth-century American presidents. This includes Thomas Jefferson, whose actions as chief executive reveal an affinity for the Hamiltonian belief that shrewd and coherent foreign policymaking requires "decision, activity, secrecy, and dispatch."[25]

Hamilton wanted a government capable of responding to crises that threatened the nation's security. For instance, in *Federalist* no. 23, he argued that "the authorities essential to the care of the common defence . . . to raise armies . . . to direct their operations . . . ought to exist without limitation: Because it is impossible to see or define the extent and variety of national exigencies, or the corresponding extent & variety of the means which may be necessary to satisfy them. The circumstances that endanger the safety of nations are infinite; and for this reason no constitutional shackles can wisely be imposed on the power to which the care of it is committed." Later, in *Federalist* no. 25, he stated that "wise politicians will be cautious about fettering the government with restrictions, that cannot be observed" when necessity dictates.[26] In interpreting broadly the executive power to deal with national security, Hamilton laid a foundation of constitutional thought that would bolster the actions of such presidents as Abraham Lincoln and Franklin Roosevelt. This manner of forceful executive leadership was a contributing factor in the twentieth-century triumph of the United States over fascism and communism.

Alexander Hamilton was no saint. He cheated on his wife, directed intem-
perate remarks against his opponents, came off as haughty, and was a lousy
political tactician. But he was far removed from the caricature presented by
Thomas Jefferson, assorted Jacksonians, populist demagogues, Henry
Adams, Vernon Parrington, Claude Bowers, William E. Dodd, Franklin
Roosevelt, Dumas Malone, Julian Boyd, Adrienne Koch, and others.

Fisher Ames's hope that over time the public would recognize Hamilton's
greatness has not come to pass. A partial explanation for our neglect of
Hamilton can be found in the successful Jeffersonian effort to portray him as
un-American. It was only a short time ago that Merrill Peterson could write
about the "faintly alien . . . odor of [Hamilton's] character and politics." It is
also probably true that most Americans find it difficult to admire someone
who refused to flatter the people. And it is surely true, as Richard Brookhiser
has observed, "Nobody loves his accountant." Hamilton was, of course, more
than our national accountant, but it is his economic system whose fruits we
enjoy. As Brookhiser also noted, "Had Hamilton not done his job so well,
the United States might have become a maple republic."[1]

The manner in which thoughtful Americans react to Alexander Hamilton
often reveals their sense of pride or guilt in America's economic and military
power as well as their attitude toward their own prosperity. Most Americans
love the comforts generated by their economic system and enjoy the fact that
they are citizens of the world's only superpower. But at the same time, they
do not want to appear overly enamored with their wealth and power. Though
it is unlikely that many Americans would opt for a life of subsistence farm-
ing or seek a return to the days when the nation had a smaller military than
Poland, holding on to the lost world of Thomas Jefferson helps us salve our
consciences. Throughout the nation's history, Hamilton's critics expressed
disdain for the man's obsession with power, a luxury afforded by the fact that
his principles prevailed.

Thomas Jefferson's vision might be America's vision, but it was Hamilton's
institutions that gave us the greatness and the power that allowed Americans
to pursue happiness. To borrow from John Adams,[2] Hamilton studied the
science of government so that his children might study mathematics and

philosophy and his grandchildren painting, poetry, and music. The pursuit of happiness might well have been the preserve of the favored few without a strong central government able to repel external threats to liberty or internal threats from racial, economic, or religious factions. It is also worth considering the nature of the American pursuit of happiness in the absence of some greater national purpose. It is conceivable that without Hamilton's energetic nationalism, the United States of America would resemble a collection of cantons inhabited by atomized individuals drawn to nothing beyond themselves. Free yes, assuming the absence of internal or external threats, but free to do what? The America that explored the outer reaches of space, welcomed millions of immigrants, led the effort to defeat fascism and communism, produced countless technological advances, and abolished slavery and Jim Crow is Hamilton's America. It is difficult to envision Massachusetts or Virginia, or any subdivision thereof, accomplishing these great endeavors.

It would be a mistake, however, to view Hamilton simply as the founder of a great republican empire. The fate of liberty was also one of his primary concerns. In light of this, he shared James Madison's fear of the destructive potential of majority faction. Though it may insult contemporary sensibilities, Hamilton believed that the public "sometimes err[s]." It was a "just observation" that the people "commonly intend the public good," but they did not always "reason right about the means of promoting it." This was partly due to their susceptibility to the siren call of demagogues "who flatter their prejudices to betray their interests."[3] Hamilton's understanding of history led him to conclude that the death of republics often occurred when demagogues secured the loyalty of the people through such flattery, including the promise of economic rewards obtained by trampling on the right to property.

In looking at contemporary American politics and government, it would appear that the nation has discarded much of Hamilton's counsel. His high-toned republican government was grounded in popular consent but capable of promoting the long-term interests of the nation. "The deliberate sense of the community should govern" the actions of those entrusted to manage the people's affairs, Hamilton argued, and thus public officials were obligated to resist "temporary delusion[s]" and "every sudden breeze of passion," allowing time for "more cool and sedate reflection." Stable and sufficiently empowered institutions would help secure these purposes. Hamilton envisioned an electoral college selecting presidents of "ability and virtue" and capable of "good administration." Although he believed in an energetic executive and considered "decision, activity, secrecy, and dispatch" to be fundamental qualities of the office, he also acknowledged the importance of the more deliberative institutions of government. He saw a Senate composed of men of moderate and judicious temperament, along with a judiciary equipped to check the boisterous and fluctuating House of Representatives. He sought a national government sufficiently empowered but limited to conducting the great affairs of state, "commerce, finance, negotiation, and war," and thus respected at home and abroad.[4]

Our major institutions no longer function as Hamilton or any of the framers intended, with the exception of the House of Representatives. American presidents are now selected in a process that places a premium on media skills and fund-raising potential rather than on character and ability. Once a president is elected, the role of party leader often eclipses the chief executive's responsibility as head of state, and his greatness is frequently measured by his success in rallying the public with rhetoric appealing to emotion rather than to reason. Some chief executives seem averse to their educative role as leaders, instead relying on input from focus groups to shape both their public appeals and their policies. A Senate now directly elected is in many ways as boisterous and poll-driven as the House it was designed to temper; the judiciary routinely engages in policymaking and is often in the forefront of social change rather than an anchor of tradition.

The divergence of American institutions from the founders' intent was accompanied by a rapid decline in the quality of the nation's politics in the twentieth century. Resorting to base appeals to mobilize the citizenry became common practice, as flattering the people and feeling their pain was adopted by public figures at all levels of government. Hamilton believed that a government that perpetually pandered to the people would ultimately lose their respect. He feared this sort of populist politics, and he presents us with an alternative mode of leadership, though certainly not one without political risk. He was the personification of the antiflatterer, and both he and his party suffered from his propensity for frankness. Hamilton was intellectually honest to the core and would have been appalled, although not surprised, to see political discussion in our day degenerate into a contest of sound bites and spin. When dealing with great issues of his time, Hamilton did not condescend, nor did he direct emotional appeals to the public. He would marshal his arguments logically and publish lengthy treatises for whoever wished to peruse them, hoping that an appeal to reason would cause his fellow citizens to abandon parochial interests and think continentally.

We still have much to learn from Hamilton, particularly as the nation enters the new millennium. A strong case can be made that much of the public's disaffection with American politics can be traced to an increasingly democratized, poll-driven politics that seldom inspires the citizenry. Presidential candidate Ross Perot's proposal for national referendums through use of interactive technology is but one example of the drive to democratize America, to substitute electronic town meetings for a republican mode of government. Former president Bill Clinton's consultant Dick Morris has also suggested that the Internet be used as a vehicle to move the nation toward a direct democracy. Through interactive web sites, Internet referendums, though not legally binding, will be politically binding in that the millions of participants will compel their elected representatives "to heed their message."[5] This is not the kind of government Hamilton would have endorsed.

Hyperdemocracy is the term the political scientist Hugh Heclo has used to describe this phenomenon of the displacement of the Constitution and the deliberative process of policymaking with a politics of "participatory openness" that has all but eliminated thoughtful decision making. An appreciation for the complexity of problems is lost in the din of this new politics that places a premium on "publicity, exposure, investigation, revelation." Confounding the hopes of its advocates, this courting of public opinion and the rejection of elitist deliberation has produced even greater mistrust and alienation.[6]

A return to Hamiltonianism could help fix much of what ails modern American politics by restoring the possibility for statesmanship and deliberation, thereby leading to a rebirth of pride among the people in their political system. Granted, the likelihood of this happening is remote. However, the prospects for this American renewal would be enhanced if a grateful nation began by acknowledging all it owes to Hamilton.

ABBREVIATIONS
AHR   American Historical Review
AM   Atlantic Monthly
APSR   American Political Science Review
AR   American Review
FED   Federalist
JAH   Journal of American History
LD   Literary Digest
MVHR   Mississippi Valley Historical Review
NAR   North American Review
NAT   Nation
NEQ   New England Quarterly
NR   New Republic
NYT   New York Times
PAH   Papers of Alexander Hamilton
PPP   Public Papers of the Presidents of the United States
PSQ   Presidential Studies Quarterly
SR   Saturday Review of Literature
USNWR   U.S. News and World Report
VQR   Virginia Quarterly Review
VSD   Vital Speeches of the Day
WMQ   William and Mary Quarterly
WP   Washington Post
WSJ   Wall Street Journal

DEATH AND REMEMBRANCE

1. Forrest McDonald, *Alexander Hamilton: A Biography* (New York: W. W. Norton, 1982), p. 361. After the duel a letter was written by Hamilton's physician, David Hosack, providing a detailed account of Hamilton's wounds. In 1989, Marc Mappen, a chronicler of all things New Jersey for the *New York Times*, asked Stanley Trooskin, M.D., director of Trauma Services at Kings County Hospital, New Jersey, to examine the letter and make a diagnosis of Hamilton's injuries. Trooskin had treated numerous gunshot wounds and from Hosack's account concluded that a 1989 death certificate for Hamilton would read, "cardiac arrest secondary to spinal shock following a gunshot wound." Trooskin stated that with modern medical care Hamilton's survival would have been a reasonably safe bet but that he would have been a paraplegic. This diagnosis bolstered the peculiar claim made in 1969 by Dr. Samuel E. Burr Jr., president of the Aaron Burr Association, that Aaron Burr "didn't really kill Alexander Hamilton. . . . I really think Hamilton died because of poor medical attention." See Marc Mappen, "Alexander Hamilton in the Emergency Room," in *Jerseyana: The Underside of New Jersey History* (New Brunswick, N.J.: Rutgers University Press, 1992), pp. 63–66, and "Burr Is Defended by a Loyal Band," *NYT,* 14 September 1969, p. 58.

2. Forrest McDonald, *Alexander Hamilton*, pp. 355–56. See also, Arnold A. Rogow, *A Fatal Friendship: Alexander Hamilton and Aaron Burr* (New York: Hill and Wang, 1998), p. 209; *New York Evening Post*, 12 July 1804, no. 825, p. 3, and 13 July 1804, no. 826, pp. 1–2. News of Hamilton's death caused a considerable stir, not only in the United States but in England as well. The *Times* of London devoted extensive coverage to the story, running lengthy pieces on 11 August 1804, p. 2; 13 August 1804, p. 2; "Duel Between Gen. Hamilton and Col. Burr," 17 August 1804, p. 3 (entire page), and to p. 4; 18 August 1804, p. 3; "From the American Papers," 13 September 1804, p. 3.

3. Alexander Hamilton, *The Papers of Alexander Hamilton*, ed. Harold C. Syrett, 27 vols. (New York: Columbia University Press, 1961–1987), "Bill for Alexander Hamilton's Coffin," 26: 317 (hereafter *PAH*). Professor Leo Hershkowitz, director of the Queens College Historical Documents Collection, recovered the bill for Hamilton's coffin and other documents from the city coroner's office in the 1970s. A 1974 *New York Times* article on Hershkowitz's efforts to preserve New York City's records noted, "Hamilton's mahogany coffin cost $25 in 1804 and notwithstanding his views on personal enterprise, the state paid." See Ralph Blumenthal, "Early Files Depict a Grim but Familiar City," *NYT*, 29 March 1974, p. 37.

4. Morris, whose reflections on Hamilton provide an early assessment of the man's strengths and flaws, had been "wholly unmanned" after arriving at Hamilton's bedside on the twelfth and witnessing his demise. When he was asked to deliver the eulogy, he noted in his diary that certain observations would "be proper to avoid." Hamilton's illegitimacy would remain unmentioned, along with Morris's belief that he was "indiscreet, vain, and opinionated," though the latter points Morris believed could be broached in a more polite manner. Hamilton "was in principle opposed to republican and attached to monarchical government," and Morris further observed that "the most important part of his life was his administration of the finances. The system he proposed was in one respect radically wrong; moreover, it has been the subject of some just and much unjust criticism." He also noted in his diary that "I must not . . . dwell on his domestic life; he has long since foolishly published the avowal of conjugal infidelity." Some observers thought that Morris was overcome with emotion when he began his remarks. See Gouverneur Morris, *The Diary and Letters of Gouverneur Morris, Minister of the United States to France, Member of the Constitutional Convention, etc.*, ed. Anne Cary Morris, 2 vols. (New York: Charles Scribner's Sons, 1888), 2: 456–57.

5. *National Intelligencer and Washington Advertiser* (triweekly edition) 55 (20 July 1804): 2, and (18 July 1804): 2; (Worcester, Mass.) *National Aegis* 3 (18 July 1804): 2; *PAH*, 26; 322–29. See also William Coleman, *A Collection of the Facts and Documents Relative to the Death of Major General Alexander Hamilton; With Comments: Together with the various Orations, Sermons, and Eulogies that Have Been Published or Written on His Life and Character* (Austin, Tex.: Shoal Creek Publishers, 1972), facsimile reproduction, p. 59.

6. McDonald, *Alexander Hamilton*, p. 7.

7. *PAH*, 1: 4. This quote is often cited by those who see a Napoleonic streak in Hamilton, although frequently they neglect to add that it was written by a youth of twelve or perhaps fourteen years.

8. Ibid., pp. 45–78 and 81–165.

9. Although hotly debated among scholars, it is at least plausible, for instance, that Hamilton's proposal for a president and senate elected for life (18 June 1787) so astonished the delegates to the convention as to make the proposals for a president with strong executive powers, which eventually was accepted, appear moderate by contrast.

10. For readers interested in a more comprehensive account of Hamilton's life, Broadus Mitchell's massive two-volume study, *Alexander Hamilton: Youth to Maturity, 1755–1788* (New York: Macmillan, 1957), and *Alexander Hamilton: The National Adventure, 1788–1804* (New York: Macmillan, 1962), is highly recommended. Also, McDonald's *Alexander Hamilton* offers a more concise account of Hamilton's career, placing particular emphasis on his political economy and his various financial proposals. General readers may find Richard Brookhiser's *Alexander Hamilton: American* (New York: Free Press, 1999) to be the most accessible account of Hamilton's life.

11. Hugh Sidey, "We're Still Jefferson's Children," *Time*, 13 July 1987, p. 14, and George F. Will, *Restoration: Congress, Term Limits, and the Recovery of Deliberative Democracy* (New York: Free Press, 1992), p. 167.

12. Consider, for instance, Jefferson's actions against the Barbary pirates (and his careful and selective reporting of those actions to Congress) and his implementation of the stringent embargo of 1807–1808 to halt trade between the United States and European belligerents.

1. "AND NIGHT RETURNING BRINGS ME NO RELIEF"

1. Dumas Malone, *Jefferson and His Time*, (Boston: Little, Brown, 1970), vol. 4, *Jefferson the President, First Term, 1801–1805*, p. 425. The "Mr. Randolph" Jefferson refers to is his son-in-law, Thomas Mann Randolph Jr. Philip Mazzei was the recipient of the famous Jefferson letter written in spring 1796 that appeared to accuse George Washington of abandoning his principles while under the spell of the "harlot England."

2. Merrill D. Peterson, *The Jefferson Image in the American Mind* (New York: Oxford University Press, 1960), p. 33, and Thomas Jefferson, *Thomas Jefferson, Writings*, ed. Merrill Peterson (New York: Library of America, 1984), p. 1530.

3. Thomas Jefferson, *The Writings of Thomas Jefferson*, ed. Andrew A. Lipscomb, 10 vols. (Washington, D.C.: Thomas Jefferson Memorial Association, 1903), 1: 271, 278–79, 311, 347, 432–33; John C. Miller, *Alexander Hamilton: Portrait in Paradox* (New York: Harper and Brothers, 1959), p. 534. Ironically, Albert Gallatin is buried a short distance from Hamilton in the Trinity Church graveyard in Manhattan.

4. Thomas Jefferson, *The Papers of Thomas Jefferson*, ed. Julian Boyd, Charles T. Cullen, and John Catanzariti, 28 vols. (Princeton: Princeton University Press, 1950–), vol. 27, *1 September–31 December 1793*, p. 62.

5. Ibid., vol. 24, *1 June–31 December 1792*, p. 358; Gilbert Chinard, *Thomas Jefferson: The Apostle of Americanism* (Boston: Little, Brown, 1929), p. 270.

6. Martin Van Buren, *Inquiry into the Origin and Course of Political Parties in the United States* (New York: Augustus M. Kelly, 1967), pp. 116–17.

7. Max Farrand, ed., *The Records of the Federal Convention of 1787*, 4 vols. (New Haven: Yale University Press, 1966), 3: 534, and Lipscomb, ed., *The Writings of Thomas Jefferson*, 10: 77.

8. Irving Brant, *James Madison, Secretary of State, 1800–1809* (Indianapolis: Bobbs-Merrill, 1953), p. 246; Noble E. Cunningham Jr., *The Presidency of James Monroe* (Lawrence: University Press of Kansas, 1996), p. 4; McDonald, *Alexander Hamilton,* pp. 243–44, 334–36. John Beckley, clerk of the House of Representatives and a Jefferson functionary, was most likely Callendar's source for information on the Reynolds affair.

9. Brant, *James Madison, Secretary of State,* p. 246. In a letter to Jefferson written a week after the duel, Gallatin repeated his belief that "to the natural sympathy and sincere regret excited by Mr. Hamilton's death, much artificial feeling, or semblance of feeling, has been added by the combined Federal and anti-Burrite party spirits." See *The Writings of Albert Gallatin,* ed. Henry Adams, 3 vols. (Philadelphia: J. B. Lippincott, 1879), 1: 201. In the months following the duel, Jefferson gave Gallatin the task of maintaining cordial relations between the administration and Aaron Burr. As vice president, Burr was required to preside over the trial of Judge Samuel Chase, the first step in an effort designed to cleanse the Federalist judiciary. Gallatin had numerous cordial meetings with Burr, though the effort to convict Chase failed. See Raymond Walters Jr., *Albert Gallatin: Jeffersonian financier and Diplomat* (New York: Macmillan, 1957), p. 167. While Burr presided over the trial, Washingtonians were invited in newspaper advertisements to view a new display at the Museum of Wax-Works featuring "a striking likeness and representation of the late unfortunate duel between Col. Aaron Burr . . . and Gen. Alexander Hamilton." See Claude Bowers, *Jefferson in Power: The Death Struggle of the Federalists* (Boston: Houghton Mifflin, 1936), p. 279.

10. C. Edward Skeen, *John Armstrong, Jr., 1758–1843: A Biography* (Syracuse, N.Y.: Syracuse University Press, 1981), pp. 52–53.

11. James Madison, *The Writings of James Madison,* ed. Gaillard Hunt, 9 vols. (New York: G. P. Putnam's Sons, 1908), 7: 163–64. Webster had been an ally of Hamilton's until the latter attempted to block the reelection of President John Adams.

12. Milton Lomask, *Aaron Burr: The Years from Princeton to Vice President, 1756–1805* (New York: Farrar Straus Giroux, 1979), pp. 356–57; Henry Adams, *John Randolph* (Greenwich, Conn.: Fawcett, 1961), p. 83.

13. Andrew Jackson, *The Papers of Andrew Jackson,* ed. Harold D. Moser and Sharon Macpherson (Knoxville: University of Tennessee Press, 1984), vol. 2, *1804–1813,* pp. 25–26, 83. The spelling is left as found in the original letters.

14. Some Jackson biographers believe that on his way to his duel with Charles Dickinson in 1806, Jackson regaled a member of his party with stories of Burr and Hamilton. "Personally, no gentleman could help liking Hamilton. But his political views were all English. . . . Why, did he not urge Washington to take a crown!" The story is probably apocryphal. See Marquis James, *Andrew Jackson: The Border Captain* (Indianapolis: Bobbs-Merrill, 1933), p. 124.

15. Malone, *Jefferson the President, First Term,* 4: 427; Daniel J. Boorstin, *The Americans: The National Experience* (New York: Random House, 1965), pp. 207–8. As of the year 2000, the Commonwealth of Kentucky still required all state officeholders and attorneys to swear under oath that they had "not fought a duel with deadly weapons within this state nor out of it . . . nor . . . acted as a second in carrying a challenge." An effort was made in 1999 to prevent state representative Ricky Cox from taking his

seat in the Kentucky House of Representatives for challenging a newspaper publisher to a duel with "pistols, knives, fists and skulls, wet corncobs or banjos." See Michael Quinlan, "Jousting Grows over State Lawmaker's Offer to Duel Ideological Foe," *(Louisville) Courier–Journal*, 11 November 1998, p. 1A; Christopher Swope, "Fighting Words and Unintended Consequences," *Governing Magazine*, February 1999, p. 10. I am grateful to Lance Banning for this observation.

16. Coleman, *Alexander Hamilton: A Collection of Facts and Documents*, pp. 162–75, 192; Martin R. Zahniser, *Charles Cotesworth Pinckney: Founding Father* (Chapel Hill: University of North Carolina Press, 1967), pp. 245–47; Paul Leicester Ford, *Bibliotheca Hamiltoniana: A List of Books Written by, or Relating to Alexander Hamilton* (New York: Knickerbocker Press, 1886), p. 71; James H. Broussard, *The Southern Federalists, 1800–1816* (Baton Rouge: Louisiana State University Press, 1978), p. 110.

17. Samuel Eliot Morison, *Harrison Gray Otis, 1765–1848: The Urbane Federalist* (Boston: Houghton Mifflin, 1969), pp. 90, 238. According to Claude Bowers, "More memorial services were held in New England than ever had been held for a native son." A brief flap occurred at Harvard University when it was reported that the Harvard administration had prevented its students from attending a eulogy on Hamilton. The administration responded that the students had not been invited to it but that they did attend their classes wearing mourning badges (Bowers, *Jefferson in Power*, p. 252).

18. Fisher Ames, *Works of Fisher Ames, Compiled by a Number of His Friends* (Boston: T. B. Watt, 1809), p. 97; Winfred E. A. Bernhard, *Fisher Ames: Federalist and Statesman, 1758–1808* (Chapel Hill: University of North Carolina Press, 1965), pp. 342–43. Bernhard lists the publication date of the Ames eulogy as 7 August 1804, Ford and Seth Ames as July 1804. See Ford, *Bibliotheca Hamiltoniana*, pp. 69–71, and Seth Ames, *Works of Fisher Ames*, ed. William B. Allen (Indianapolis: Liberty Classics, 1983), pp. 510–11.

19. Robert Ernst, *Rufus King: American Federalist* (Chapel Hill: University of North Carolina Press, 1968), pp. 282–83.

20. John Marshall, *The Papers of John Marshall*, ed. Charles F. Hobson, 10 vols. (Chapel Hill: The University of North Carolina Press, 1974–), vol. 6, *Correspondence, Papers, and Selected Judicial Opinions, November 1800–March 1807*, pp. 343, 530, and vol. 9, *Correspondence, Papers, and Selected Judicial Opinions, January 1820–December 1823*, p. 200.

21. John Marshall, *An Autobiographical Sketch by John Marshall, Written at the Request of Joseph Story and Now Printed for the First Time from the Original Manuscript Preserved at the William L. Clements Library, Together with a Letter from Chief Justice Marshall to Justice Story Relating Thereto*, ed. John Stokes Adams (Ann Arbor: University of Michigan Press, 1937), p. 14.

22. McDonald, *Alexander Hamilton*, p. 314; James McClellan, *Joseph Story and the American Constitution: A Study in Political and Legal Thought* (Norman: University of Oklahoma Press, 1971), p. 79 n. 67.

23. See *PAH*, 25: 169–234, for a complete account of this low point in Hamilton's career. The anger of the Adams family toward Hamilton for writing this criticism of John Adams persisted for generations. In 1836, Adams's grandson, Charles Francis Adams, wrote in his diary, "We discussed today the old pamphlet of Alexander Hamilton against my Grandfather, one of the series of belligerent measures in which we have

for two generations been involved. When I reflect upon this state of war and turbulence which has heretofore attended us, I do not think I can pursue it. The task is so painful a one." See Charles Francis Adams, *Diary of Charles Francis Adams,* ed. Marc Friedlaender and L. H. Butterfield (Cambridge: Belknap Press of Harvard University Press, 1974), vol. 6, *November 1834–June 1836,* pp. 358–59.

24. Phyllis Lee Levin, *Abigail Adams: A Biography* (New York: St. Martin's Press, 1987), pp. 407–8. On 18 August 1804, Abigail Adams wrote President Jefferson and made a passing reference to the duel. Defending laws designed to restrict press attacks on public figures, Adams observed that without such restraints "will not Man become the judge and avenger of his own wrongs, and as in the late instance, the sword and pistol decide the contest?" Lester Cappon, ed., *The Adams-Jefferson Letters: The Complete Correspondence Between Thomas Jefferson and Abigail and John Adams,* 2 vols. (Chapel Hill: University of North Carolina Press, 1959), vol. 1, *1777–1804,* p. 277.

25. Marie B. Hecht, *John Quincy Adams: A Personal History of an Independent Man* (New York: Macmillan, 1972), pp. 155–56, and John Quincy Adams, *The Writings of John Quincy Adams,* ed. Worthington Chauncey Ford (New York: Greenwood Press, 1968), vol. 3, *1801–1810,* pp. 41–43, 42 n. 1. Adams's opinion of Hamilton softened as he grew older. In 1839 he delivered a speech to the New York Historical Society in which he lauded Hamilton as "one of the first financiers of his age." Hamilton's financial plan, especially the national bank, had, he judged, "operated like enchantment for the restoration of public credit" and provided for "the encouragement of industry and the active exertions of enterprise." See Lynn Hudson Parsons, "Continuing Crusade: Four Generations of the Adams Family View Alexander Hamilton," *NEQ* 37 (March 1964): 53.

26. John Adams, *Diary and Autobiography of John Adams,* ed. L. H. Butterfield (Cambridge: Belknap Press of Harvard University Press, 1961), vol. 3, part 1, *Diary 1782–1804, Autobiography Part One to October 1776,* pp. 234, 240, 386–87, 434–35, 446–47; see also Joseph Ellis, *Passionate Sage: The Character and Legacy of John Adams* (New York: W. W. Norton, 1993), pp. 60, 62; Cappon, ed. *The Adams-Jefferson Letters, 1812–1826,* 2: 488.

27. Benjamin Rush, *The Autobiography of Benjamin Rush: His 'Travels Through Life' together with his Commonplace Book for 1789–1813,* ed. George W. Corner (Princeton: Princeton University Press, 1948), p. 313; David Hackett Fischer, *The Revolution of American Conservatism: The Federalist Party in the Era of Jeffersonian Democracy* (New York: Harper and Row, 1965), p. 152. Hamilton, a trustee of the college, was able to prevent Columbia from hiring Benjamin Rush. Columbia awarded Hamilton an honorary degree in 1788. See Broadus Mitchell, *Heritage from Hamilton* (New York: Columbia University Press, 1957), p. vii.

28. Jack Fruchtman Jr., *Thomas Paine: Apostle of Freedom* (New York: Four Walls Eight Windows, 1994), pp. 412–14; Thomas Paine, *Life and Writings of Thomas Paine,* ed. Daniel Edwin Wheeler, 10 vols. (New York: Vincent Parke, 1908), 7: 160; John Keane, *Tom Paine: A Political Life* (Boston: Little, Brown, 1995), pp. 502–3; Wheeler, ed., *Life and Writings of Thomas Paine,* 10: 176–77.

29. See Leonard W. Levy, *Jefferson and Civil Liberties: The Darker Side* (Chicago: Ivan R. Dee, 1989), pp. 58–59; McDonald, *Alexander Hamilton,* p. 358. Ambrose Spencer later said of Hamilton that he was "the greatest man this country ever produced. . . . It was

he, more than any other man, who thought out the Constitution of the United States and the details of the government. . . . He, more than any man, did the thinking of the time." Quoted in Henry Cabot Lodge, *Alexander Hamilton* (Boston: Houghton, Mifflin, 1898), pp. 273–74.

30. Frank Luther Mott, *American Journalism, A History: 1690–1960* (New York: Macmillan, 1962), p. 170; Bernard A. Weisberger, *The American Newspaperman* (Chicago: University of Chicago Press, 1961), p. 61; Coleman, *Alexander Hamilton: A Collection of Facts and Documents*, p. 149.

31. Coleman, *Alexander Hamilton: A Collection of Facts and Documents*, introduction to 1972 edition, and p. 1.

32. See Mitchell, *Alexander Hamilton: The National Adventure, 1788–1804*, pp. 553–54; Gerald H. Clarfield, *Timothy Pickering and the American Republic* (Pittsburgh: University of Pittsburgh Press, 1980), pp. 268–69; Peterson, *The Jefferson Image in the American Mind*, pp. 224–25. Betsey Hamilton was quite thorough in her efforts to document her husband's life; for instance, she wrote a letter in 1832 to Chancellor James Kent asking that he address eight questions, covering "your early acquaintance with my husband — when, and the circumstances of it?" "any facts connected with his history at the Bar before he went into the Treasury," and "any anecdotes illustrative of his character or strong expressions?" James Kent, *Memoirs and Letters of James Kent, LL.D.*, ed. William Kent (Boston: Little, Brown, 1898), pp. 281–82.

33. It is possible that William met a young Illinois militia captain named Abraham Lincoln while serving in this war. See Earl Schenck Miers, ed., *Lincoln Day by Day: A Chronology, 1809–1865* (Washington, D.C.: Lincoln Sesquicentennial Commission, 1960), vol. 1, *1809–1848*, p. 21. William Hamilton is probably the Mr. Hamilton who surveyed the town of New Salem, Illinois, and produced one of the earliest maps of the town where Abraham Lincoln lived from 1831 to 1837. See *Abraham Lincoln, an Exhibition at the Library of Congress in Honor of the 150th Anniversary of His Birth* (Washington, D.C.: Library of Congress, 1959), p. 12. Sylvan J. Muldoon, in *Alexander Hamilton's Pioneer Son: The Life and Times of Colonel William Stephen Hamilton, 1797–1850* (Harrisburg, Penn.: Aurand Press, 1930), states categorically that William Hamilton "met and hobnobbed" with Abraham Lincoln and Jefferson Davis during the Black Hawk War (see pp. 125–26).

34. Mitchell, *Alexander Hamilton: The National Adventure*, pp. 554–55, 773 n. 34, and James Grant Wilson and John Fiske, eds., *Appletons' Cyclopaedia of American Biography*, 7 vols. (New York: D. Appleton, 1892), 3: 60. See also Alice Curtis Desmond, *Alexander Hamilton's Wife: A Romance of the Hudson* (New York: Dodd, Mead, 1953), p. 259.

35. David Hackett Fischer, *The Federalist Party in the Era of Jeffersonian Democracy* (New York: Harper and Row, 1965), pp. 185–87.

36. Donald H. Stewart, *The Opposition Press of the Federalist Period* (Albany: State University of New York Press, 1969), pp. 487–89, 538–41; McDonald, *Alexander Hamilton*, pp. 239–41. See also Emory Elliott, *Revolutionary Writers: Literature and Authority in the New Republic, 1725–1810* (New York: Oxford University Press, 1982), p. 133.

37. See *PAH*, 4: 178–211, especially pp. 192–95 and 213. There are five different versions of Hamilton's 18 June speech, including his own notes as well as those of James Madison, Robert Yates, John Lansing Jr., and Rufus King. See also McDonald, *Alexander Hamilton*, pp. 99–105, for a helpful discussion of Hamilton's speech.

2. HAMILTON AND THE JACKSONIAN ERA

1. Interestingly, many members of this second generation of leaders were born in the same year, 1782, including Daniel Webster, John C. Calhoun, Martin Van Buren, Thomas Hart Benton, and Lewis Cass. The Revolutionary War was still unfinished when these men were born, and most would live long enough to see the cracks in the Union begin to emerge, or in the case of Cass and Van Buren, the Civil War itself. See Donald B. Cole, *Martin Van Buren and the American Political System* (Princeton: Princeton University Press, 1984), p. 3.

2. Marvin Meyers, *The Jacksonian Persuasion: Politics and Belief* (Stanford: Stanford University Press, 1957), p. 7.

3. Robert V. Remini, *Andrew Jackson and the Course of American Empire, 1767–1821* (New York: Harper and Row, 1977), p. 145, and *Andrew Jackson and the Course of American Freedom, 1822–1832* (New York: Harper and Row, 1981), p. 32; James D. Richardson, ed., *A Compilation of the Messages and Papers of the Presidents, 1789–1897* (Washington, D.C.: U.S. Government Printing Office, 1896), 2: 448; Robert V. Remini, *Daniel Webster: The Man and His Time* (New York: W. W. Norton, 1997), p. 353 n.26.

4. Remini, *Andrew Jackson and the Course of American Empire*, pp. 92–94; William Graham Sumner, *Andrew Jackson* (Boston: Houghton, Mifflin, 1899), pp. 13–14; Remini, *Andrew Jackson and the Course of American Freedom*, pp. 33, 100, 114.

5. Jefferson's biographer Dumas Malone writes that Jefferson was on "the best of personal terms" with General Jackson and had approved of Jackson's controversial operations in Florida that almost ignited a war with Great Britain. However, Malone also notes that "two Adams" men, Daniel Webster and George Ticknor, both reported conversations with Jefferson in which he stated that Jackson was a man of violent passions temperamentally unsuited to be president (*Jefferson and His Time* [Boston: Little, Brown, 1981], vol. 6, *The Sage of Monticello*, 436–37, 437 n. 42).

6. Meyers, *The Jacksonian Persuasion*, pp. 10–11.

7. Remini, *Andrew Jackson and the Course of American Democracy, 1833–1845* (New York: Harper and Row, 1984), p. 98.

8. Whatever other attributes Jackson may have possessed, knowledge of the founding fathers was not one of them. He told James Hamilton that his father "was not in favor of the Bank of the United States," though perhaps one must allow for the possibility that Jackson saw Nicholas Biddle's bank as a mutant offspring of the one envisioned by Hamilton. See Robert V. Remini, *Andrew Jackson and the Bank War: A Study in the Growth of Presidential Power* (New York: W. W. Norton, 1967), pp. 49, 61–64.

9. Quoted in Arthur M. Schlesinger Jr., "An Impressive Mandate and the Meaning of Jacksonianism," in *Andrew Jackson: A Profile*, ed. Charles Sellers (New York: Hill and Wang, 1971), p. 135. One responsible member of Congress who attempted to temper the rhetoric surrounding the BUS debate was Congressman George McDuffie of South Carolina, the chairman of the House Ways and Means Committee. In April 1830 McDuffie's committee issued a report, drawing from Hamilton's 1791 opinion to President Washington urging the creation of a national bank, that defended the bank's record and rejected Jackson's fear-mongering. Despite this defense, however, the forces that Jackson had unleashed were too powerful to be countered. See Frank Otto Gatell, *The Jacksonians and the Money Power, 1829–1840* (Chicago: Rand McNally, 1967), pp. 7–9.

10. Van Buren, *Inquiry into the Origin and Course of Political Parties in the United States*, p. 120.

11. Oddly, his friendship with Burr and Van Ness did not prevent Van Buren and James A. Hamilton from becoming close political allies later in life, though the memories of the senior Hamilton constantly loomed over their relationship. When President Jackson appointed James Hamilton as U.S. attorney for southern New York, Van Buren told James that he could not support the nomination due to party opposition based on James's lineage (Cole, *Martin Van Buren and the American Political System*, pp. 16–17, 19, 193–94). See also Donald B. Cole, *The Presidency of Andrew Jackson* (Lawrence: University Press of Kansas, 1993), p. 46.

12. Van Buren, *Inquiry into the Origin and Course of Political Parties in the United States*, pp. 74, 79, 87–88, 92, 97, 99, 110, 123, 137–38, 166.

13. The quote can be found in Martin Van Buren, *The Autobiography of Martin Van Buren*, published in the *Annual Report of the American Historical Association for the Year 1918* (Washington, D.C.: U.S. Government Printing Office, 1920), 2: 471. Van Buren stated in his *Autobiography* that Hamilton was born in England. Though it was an inaccurate statement, in Van Buren's mind there was no doubt Hamilton was "British" (see p. 470).

14. Remini, *Andrew Jackson and the Bank War*, p. 63, and Cole, *Martin Van Buren*, p. 234.

15. Cole, *Martin Van Buren*, p. 27. Cole is convinced that Van Buren's position was more "political than ideological."

16. Quoted in John Ashworth, *"Agrarians" and "Aristocrats": Party Political Ideology in the United States, 1837–1846* (Cambridge: Cambridge University Press, 1987), p. 216.

17. Remini, *Andrew Jackson and the Course of American Democracy*, pp. 165, 540 n. 21; Thomas Payne Govan, *Nicholas Biddle, Nationalist and Public Banker, 1786–1844* (Chicago: University of Chicago Press, 1959), p. 12; Bray Hammond, "Jackson, Biddle, and the Bank of the United States," in *Essays on Jacksonian America*, ed. Frank Otto Gatell (New York: Holt, Rinehart and Winston, 1970), p. 161.

18. Decades later at a dinner, Benton was asked by the governor general of Canada whether he had known Andrew Jackson. Though the reply is possibly apocryphal, Benton is said to have answered, "Yes sir, I knew him, sir. I shot him, sir. Afterwards he helped me in my battle with the United States Bank, sir" (cited in Arthur Schlesinger Jr., *The Age of Jackson* [New York: Book Find Club, 1945], p. 473).

19. Ibid., pp. 81 and 473; Thomas Hart Benton, *Thirty Years' View; or, A History of the Working of the American Government for Thirty Years, from 1820 to 1850* (New York: Greenwood Press, 1968), 1: 2–3. See also Major L. Wilson, *The Presidency of Martin Van Buren* (Lawrence: University Press of Kansas, 1984), p. 88. Surprisingly, Benton did express some admiration for Hamilton, whom he did not know but came to appreciate through his friendship with Hamilton's ally Rufus King. Benton and King were colleagues in the Senate, and the elder King counseled Benton on its ways and mores. See William M. Meigs, *The Life of Thomas Hart Benton* (Philadelphia: J. B. Lippincott, 1904), pp. 135–37.

20. Charles Grier Sellers Jr., *James K. Polk, Jacksonian, 1795–1843* (Princeton: Princeton University Press, 1957), p. 280. In February 1846, Polk gave a dinner party at the White House that included Hamilton's eighty-eight-year-old widow. Polk recorded in his

diary for that day, "Mrs. General Hamilton, upon whom I waited at table, is a very remarkable person. She retains her intellect and memory perfectly, and my conversation with her was highly interesting." Unfortunately, Polk did not provide an account of the conversation. See James K. Polk, *Polk: The Diary of a President, 1845–1849,* ed. Allan Nevins (London: Longmans, Green, 1952), p. 52.

21. James K. Polk, *The Diary of James K. Polk During his Presidency, 1845–1849,* ed. Milo M. Quaife, 4 vols. (Chicago: A. C. McClurg, 1910), 2: 305; Roy Franklin Nichols, *Franklin Pierce: Young Hickory of the Granite Hills* (Philadelphia: University of Pennsylvania Press, 1931), p. 122.

22. Arlin Turner, *Hawthorne as Editor: Selections from His Writings in the American Magazine of Useful and Entertaining Knowledge* (Baton Rouge: Louisiana State University Press, 1941), pp. 29–37; Robert L. Gale, *A Nathaniel Hawthorne Encyclopedia* (New York: Greenwood Press, 1991), p. 7; F. O. Matthiessen, *American Renaissance: Art and Expression in the Age of Emerson and Whitman* (New York: Oxford University Press, 1968), p. 318. Turner points out that the bulk of the Hawthorne essay on Hamilton was written by his sister Elizabeth, but the quotations I have cited here are considered to be his work. Hawthorne had a streak of a latter-day debunker in him; he once wrote of George Washington, "Did anybody ever see Washington naked? It is inconceivable. He has no nakedness, but I imagine was born with his clothes on and his hair powdered" (quoted in Steven Jaffe, *Who Were the Founding Fathers? Two Hundred Years of Reinventing American History* [New York: Henry Holt, 1996], p. 42).

23. James Fenimore Cooper, *The Letters and Journals of James Fenimore Cooper,* ed. James Franklin Beard, 6 vols. (Cambridge: Harvard University Press, 1960), 1: xx, xxiv, and Meyers, *Jacksonian Persuasion,* p. 58.

24. Beard, ed., *The Letters and Journals of James Fenimore Cooper,* 2: 180.

25. James Fenimore Cooper, *Gleanings in Europe, Switzerland* (Albany: State University of New York Press, 1980), p. 248.

26. Beard, ed., *The Letters and Journals of James Fenimore Cooper,* 2: 32.

27. Meyers, *The Jacksonian Persuasion,* chap. 4. Meyers's account of the somewhat tenuous relationship between Cooper and Jacksonianism is impressive.

28. Washington Irving, *Washington Irving, Letters,* ed. Ralph M. Aderman, Herbert Kleinfield, Jenifer S. Banks, 4 vols. (Boston: Twayne, 1978–), vol. 1, *1802–1823,* p. 105. Irving was an acquaintance of Hamilton's widow and children and often socialized with members of the Hamilton family. When President Tyler and Secretary of State Daniel Webster chose Irving to be the American ambassador to Spain in 1842, Irving selected Alexander Hamilton Jr., Hamilton's grandson, to be the secretary of the legation (see, for instance, vol. 3, *1839–1845,* p. 155).

29. Stanley T. Williams, *The Life of Washington Irving* (New York: Oxford University Press, 1935), 1: 97.

30. Irving, *Letters,* 1: 287, 288 n. 2. The Weehawken monument to Hamilton has had as turbulent a history as the subject it memorializes. The monument that Washington Irving visited in 1810, an eight-foot-high white-marble obelisk topped by a flaming urn on a four-foot pedestal, was later destroyed by local citizens upset that the site continued to serve as a mecca for duelers. It was "thrown into the river," according to one account, sometime prior to 1822, on orders from the New Jersey legislature.

The legislature was concerned that "the honor thus paid him [Hamilton] would tend to encourage the dreadful practice by which he came to his untimely end." Other less dramatic accounts state that the monument was destroyed over time by souvenir seekers, dismantled to allow the installation of railroad tracks, or destroyed by the owner of the property on his own initiative because of its use as a dueling site. In October 1934 someone stole Hamilton's marble head from a memorial designed to replace the original and ignominiously tossed his shoulders onto the rocks two hundred feet below the Palisades in Weehawken. A bronze replacement bust was installed in July 1935. See "A Monument to Alexander Hamilton," *NYT*, 20 March 1882, p. 5; "Hamilton Monument," *NYT*, 21 June 1903, p. 36; "More Business Efficiency," *NYT*, 29 December 1916, p. 7; "Home Growth on Weehawken Cliff," *NYT*, 29 August 1926, sect. 10, p. 1; "New York's Memory," *NYT*, 9 January 1932, p. 16; "Head of Hamilton Bust Is Stolen in Weehawken," *NYT*, 15 October 1934, p. 1; "Hamilton Bust Unveiled," *NYT*, 13 July 1935, p. 7; "People," *Time*, 22 July 1935, p. 38.

31. Irving, *Letters*, 3: 746.
32. Washington Irving, *Life of George Washington*, Part 2 (New York: Peter Fenelon Collier, 1897), pp. 114, 431. The *Life of George Washington* was Irving's last work, a plea to preserve the Union. He had worked sporadically on the biography for eleven years and saw the final volume published in 1859, the year he died. His death spared him the agony of witnessing the Civil War (*Part 4*, p. 175). See also, Mary Weatherspoon Bowden, *Washington Irving* (Boston: Twayne, 1981), pp. 179–82, and Dumas Malone and Allen Johnson, eds., *Dictionary of American Biography*, 20 vols. (New York: Charles Scribner's Sons, 1932), 9: 505–11.
33. Remini, *Daniel Webster: The Man and His Time*, p. 53.
34. Daniel Webster, *The Papers of Daniel Webster, Correspondence*, ed. Charles M. Wiltse (Hanover, N.H.: University Press of New England, 1974), vol. 1, *1798–1824*, p. 31.
35. Daniel Webster, *The Papers of Daniel Webster, Legal Papers*, ed. Alfred S. Konefsky and Andrew J. King (Hanover, N.H.: University Press of New England, 1982), vol. 1, *The New Hampshire Practice*, pp. 55–56. Nott's eulogy made a lasting impression on a number of Webster's contemporaries. Congressman Leverett Saltonstall of Massachusetts wrote to his wife in 1839 (thirty-five years after reading Nott's address), "I have just returned from the Capitol, where I heard a very beautiful and eloquent discourse from President Nott, of Union College Schenectady. He obtained celebrity when quite a young man, by a brilliant discourse upon the ever to be lamented death of General Hamilton. It was spread through the Country. No one could read it without emotion. I remember just where I was . . . when I read it, and how I felt. It filled me with admiration for the talents and services of Hamilton" (*The Papers of Leverett Saltonstall, 1816–1845*, ed. Robert E. Moody [Boston: Massachusetts Historical Society, 1981], vol. 2, *1831–June 1840*, p. 257). Paul Leicester Ford in his *Bibliotheca Hamiltoniana* states that Nott's sermon was the most popular of all those delivered in the wake of Hamilton's death (see p. 77).
36. Remini, *Daniel Webster: The Man and His Time*, pp. 164–65, and McDonald, *Alexander Hamilton*, p. 207; *McCulloch v. Maryland* 4 Wheat. (17 U.S.) 316 (1819).
37. Daniel Webster, *The Papers of Daniel Webster, Correspondence*, ed. Charles M. Wiltse and Harold D. Moser (Hanover, N.H.: University Press of New England, 1976), vol. 2, *1825–1829*, pp. 46–48, 65.

38. Ibid., vol. 4, *1835–1839*, p. 173. Excerpts from Kent's remarks can be found in George Shea, *The Life and Epoch of Alexander Hamilton, A Historical Study* (Boston: Houghton, Osgood, 1879), p. 435. See also John T. Morse, *The Life of Alexander Hamilton*, 2 vols. (Boston: Little, Brown, 1876), 2: 344.

39. Daniel Webster, *The Works of Daniel Webster*, ed. Edward Everett, 6 vols. (Boston: Charles C. Little and James Brown, 1851), 1: 198–200.

40. Ibid., p. 203, and Remini, *Daniel Webster: The Man and His Time*, p. 353.

41. Robert Allen Rutland, *The Presidency of James Madison* (Lawrence: University Press of Kansas, 1990), pp. 197–98, and John Niven, *John C. Calhoun and the Price of Union: A Biography* (Baton Rouge: Louisiana State University Press, 1988), pp. 52–53. Madison, reversing course, began to appreciate the necessity for some type of central bank, much to the distress of die-hard strict constructionists such as John Randolph of Roanoke, who lamented that Madison "out-Hamiltons Alexander Hamilton."

42. Irving H. Bartlett, *John C. Calhoun: A Biography* (New York: W. W. Norton, 1993), p. 92. Indicative perhaps of Calhoun's early admiration for Hamiltonian nationalism, Hamilton's son Alexander chaired a meeting in New York City in August 1831 that nominated Calhoun for president. See John C. Calhoun, *The Papers of John C. Calhoun*, ed. William E. Hemphill, Robert L. Meriwether, and Clyde N. Wilson, 25 vols. (Columbia: University of South Carolina Press, 1959–), vol. 11, *1829–1832*, p. 142n.

43. Merrill D. Peterson, *The Great Triumvirate: Webster, Clay, and Calhoun* (New York: Oxford University Press, 1987), pp. 252–53; Hemphill et al., eds., *The Papers of John C. Calhoun*, vol. 15, *1839–1841*, pp. 228–29.

44. Hemphill et al., eds., *The Papers of John C. Calhoun*, vol. 12, *1833–1835*, pp. 132, 159.

45. Ibid., vol. 14, *1837–1839*, pp. 240–41, 412, 566, 575.

46. Ibid., vol. 15, *1839–1841*, pp. 267, 271, 649.

47. John C. Calhoun, *Union and Liberty: The Political Philosophy of John C. Calhoun*, ed. Ross M. Lence (Indianapolis: Liberty Fund, 1992), pp. 79, 244–45, 250–53.

48. It may be, as Merrill Peterson argues, that it never occurred to Clay that his advocacy of "an enlarged role for the government in the promotion of economic development . . . was surrendering Jeffersonian principles for Hamiltonian ones." However, this perspective is more likely the result of Peterson's unwillingness to concede Hamilton's influence than an accurate assessment of Clay's own understanding of his political transformation. See Peterson, *Great Triumvirate*, pp. 14, 68–69; Niven, *John C. Calhoun and the Price of Union*, p. 226; Alexander Hamilton, James Madison, and John Jay, *The Federalist*, ed. Jacob E. Cooke (Middletown, Conn.: Wesleyan University Press, 1961), no. 11, p. 73 (hereafter *FED*). Clay wrote a spirited defense of his actions in the Burr case in a letter to Richard Pindell in October 1828. See Henry Clay, *The Papers of Henry Clay*, ed. James F. Hopkins and Robert Seager II, 11 vols. (Lexington: University Press of Kentucky, 1959–1992), vol. 7, *Secretary of State, January 1, 1828–March 4, 1829*, pp. 501–2.

49. Glyndon G. Van Deusen, *The Life of Henry Clay* (Boston: Little, Brown, 1937), p. 22.

50. Bernard Mayo, *Henry Clay: Spokesman of the New West* (Boston: Houghton Mifflin, 1937), pp. 82–83, 176–77.

51. Hopkins and Seager, eds., *The Papers of Henry Clay*, vol. 1, *The Rising Statesman*, pp. 530–31; Van Deusen, *The Life of Henry Clay*, pp. 111–13; Peter McNamara, *Politi-*

cal Economy and Statesmanship: Smith, Hamilton, and the Foundation of the Commer-cial Republic (DeKalb: Northern Illinois University Press, 1998), p. 176 n. 1; Hopkins and Seager, eds., *The Papers of Henry Clay*, vol. 3, *Presidential Candidate, 1821–1824*, p. 718, and vol. 6, *Secretary of State, 1827*, p. 320 n. 8.

52. Hopkins and Seager, eds., *The Papers of Henry Clay*, vol. 3, *Presidential Candidate, 1821–1824*, p. 506.

53. Ibid., Supplement, *1793–1852*, p. 281.

54. Ibid., vol. 10, *Candidate, Compromiser, Elder Statesman, 1844–1852*, p. 169.

55. John Ashworth, *"Agrarians" and "Aristocrats,"* pp. 117–18, 118 n. 63; Philip Hone, *The Diary of Philip Hone*, ed. Allan Nevins (New York: Kraus Reprint, 1960), vol. 1, *1828–1851*, pp. 486–87; Dorothy Burne Goebel, *William Henry Harrison: A Political Biography* (Indianapolis: Historical Bureau of the Indiana Library and Historical Department, 1926), p. 39; Lee Benson, *The Concept of Jacksonian Democracy: New York as a Test Case* (Princeton: Princeton University Press, 1961), p. 244.

56. Steven Jaffe, *Who Were the Founding Fathers?* p. 51.

57. John Quincy Adams, *The Diary of John Quincy Adams, 1794–1845, American Diplomacy, and Political, Social, and Intellectual Life, from Washington to Polk*, ed. Allan Nevins (New York: Charles Scribner's Sons, 1951), pp. 477–78.

3. HAMILTON RISES AGAIN

1. For a discussion of Jefferson as one of Virginia's largest slaveholders, see Gordon S. Wood, "The Ghosts of Monticello," in *Sally Hemings and Thomas Jefferson: History, Memory, and Civic Culture*, ed. Jan Ellen Lewis and Peter S. Onuf (Charlottesville: University of Virginia Press, 1999), p. 21; for the travails of Jefferson's statue, see Philip B. Kunhardt Jr., Philip B. Kunhardt III, Peter W. Kunhardt, *The American President* (New York: Riverhead Books, 1999), p. 415; the Curtis quote is from Peterson, *The Jefferson Image in the American Mind*, p. 223.

2. James Garfield, *The Works of James Abram Garfield*, ed. Burke A. Hinsdale (Boston: James R. Osgood, 1882), 1: 71, and *The Wild Life of the Army: Civil War Letters of James A. Garfield*, ed. Frederick D. Williams (Lansing: Michigan State University Press, 1964), pp. 19, 21. Hamilton's grandson, Dr. Allan McLane Hamilton, physician and alienist, was an expert witness at the trial of President Garfield's assassin, Charles Guiteau, whom he described as a "shrewd scamp." He also testified at the trial of President McKinley's assassin Leon Czolgosz. See "Dr. A. M'L. Hamilton, Alienist, Dies at 71," *NYT*, 24 November 1919, p. 15.

3. Benjamin F. Butler, *Butler's Book, A Review of His Legal, Political, and Military Career* (Boston: A. M. Thayer, 1892), pp. 85–86.

4. The term "Ivy League" was not used until the twentieth century, an observation of Forrest McDonald's for which I am grateful. I have chosen this designation to assist the modern reader.

5. Wilson and Fiske, eds., *Appletons' Cyclopaedia of American Biography*, 1: 12–13; Worthington Chauncey Ford, ed., *A Cycle of Adams Letters, 1861–1865* (Boston: Houghton Mifflin, 1920), 1: 67–68; Charles Francis Adams, "The Madison Papers," *NAR* 53 (July 1841): 70–72.

6. Edward Everett, *Orations and Speeches on Various Occasions by Edward Everett*, 4 vols. (Boston: Charles C. Little and James Brown, 1850–1868), 1: 396, 480, and 2: 99.

7. Edward G. Parker, *Reminiscences of Rufus Choate, The Great American Advocate* (New York: Mason Brothers, 1860), pp. 253, 317; Rufus Choate, *Addresses and Orations of Rufus Choate* (Boston: Little, Brown, 1891), p. 234.

8. Richard Henry Dana, *The Journal of Richard Henry Dana, Jr.*, ed. Robert F. Lucid, 3 vols. (Cambridge: Belknap Press of Harvard University Press, 1968), 2: 528–29.

9. "Hamilton on Coercing a State," *NYT*, 31 January 1861, p. 4; "The Union and the States — Real Nature of Our Perils," *NYT*, 9 June 1863, p. 4.

10. Wilson and Fiske, eds., *Appletons' Cyclopaedia of American Biography*, 6: 592–93; Hon. Fernando Wood, *An Address on the Genius, Public Life, and Opinions of Alexander Hamilton, Delivered at Richmond, Va., May 9, 1856, by the Request of the Ladies of the Central Mount Vernon Association, and in Aid of the Purchase of Mount Vernon* (New York: Evander Childs, Steam Book and Job Printer, 1856), pp. 36–37.

11. Jaffe, *Who Were the Founding Fathers?* p. 56.

12. William Lloyd Garrison, *The Letters of William Lloyd Garrison*, ed. Walter M. Merrill (Cambridge: Belknap Press of Harvard University Press, 1971), vol. 1, *I Will Be Heard, 1822–1835*, pp. 23 n. 1, 27–28. On 23 October 1857, Garrison's abolitionist newspaper, the *Liberator* covered its entire front page with statements from various founders, including Hamilton's, "what are the relations and compromises of the U.S. Constitution appertaining to American slavery?" (*Letters*, ed. Louis Ruchames [Cambridge: Belknap Press of Harvard University Press, 1975], vol. 4, *From Disunionism to the Brink of War, 1850–1860*, p. 497 n. 21).

13. Carl Brent Swisher, *Roger B. Taney* (Hamden, Conn.: Archon Books, 1961), p. 586; Don E. Fehrenbacher, *The Dred Scott Case: Its Significance in American Law and Politics* (New York: Oxford University Press, 1978), p. 347.

14. Frederick Douglass, *The Frederick Douglass Papers*, ed. John W. Blassingame (New Haven: Yale University Press, 1985), vol. 3, *1855–1863*, series 1, pp. 180, 474. The editor of this series states with unwarranted certainty that "Hamilton held slaves throughout his life, occasionally buying and selling them for his friends" (see p. 180 n. 24). Even the National Park Service's official brochure for the Hamilton Grange National Memorial in New York City claims that Hamilton "continued to hold slaves throughout his life" (Hamilton Grange National Memorial, New York, National Park Service, U.S. Department of the Interior [Washington, D.C.: U.S. Government Printing Office, 1992]). The editors of *The Papers of Alexander Hamilton* argued that one sentence from a letter Hamilton wrote in 1781 to George Clinton "provides one of the few pieces of extant evidence that either H or his wife owned slaves." Hamilton wrote: "I am told it has lately risen something [the exchange rate with France], and I expect by Col Hay's return to receive a sufficient sum to pay the value of the woman Mrs. H had of Mrs. Clinton." I am persuaded by Forrest McDonald's argument that although this passage could be referring to the purchase of a slave, "given Hamilton's limited means at the time, and given that the reference to Lt. Col. Udny Hay, deputy quartermaster general, could concern only Hamilton's back pay, much less than enough to buy a slave, it is far more likely that Betsey, in keeping with common practice at the time, had merely hired a servant employed by or belonging to Mrs. Clinton." Some historians have also cited a 1797 transaction in which Hamilton was involved in the purchase of a slave woman and child as proof that Hamilton owned slaves. McDonald correctly points out, however, that Hamilton was acting as an agent and attorney for

John B. Church and not purchasing the slaves for himself. Evidence that Hamilton did not own slaves can be found in a letter written by his sister-in-law in June 1804, bemoaning the fact that Hamilton and his wife did not have a slave to help them with a social function they hosted. Hamilton's family steadfastly denied allegations that he was a slave owner, and considering his efforts on behalf of manumission in New York, it is my belief that Hamilton probably did not own slaves. See *PAH*, 2: 642–43, 643 n. 2; McDonald, *Alexander Hamilton*, p. 373 n. 12; and Brookhiser, *Alexander Hamilton, American*, p. 176.

15. C. Edwards Lester, *Life and Public Services of Charles Sumner* (New York: United States Publishing Company, 1874), pp. 601–2.

16. Frank Freidel, *Francis Lieber, Nineteenth-Century Liberal* (Baton Rouge: Louisiana State University Press, 1947), pp. vii, 52, 67–71, 89–90, 215, 231–32, 324–25, 392, 415; Merle Curti, *Probing Our Past* (New York: Harper and Brothers, 1955), pp. 142 and 142 n. 96. Lieber's son was named for Alexander Hamilton.

17. Abraham Lincoln, *Abraham Lincoln, Speeches and Writings, 1859–1865*, ed. Don E. Fehrenbacher (New York: Library of America, 1989), pp. 18–19; Allen C. Guelzo, *Abraham Lincoln: Redeemer President* (Grand Rapids, Minn.: Wm. B. Eerdmans, 1999), p. 4.

18. Guelzo, *Abraham Lincoln: Redeemer President*, pp. 9, 195; see also pp. 453–60 for his incisive comments on Lincoln's antipathy toward Jeffersonian and Jacksonian Democracy. Guelzo asserts "that Abraham Lincoln grew and matured as an American political thinker into an adversary of almost every practical aspect of Thomas Jefferson's political worldview" (p. 5).

19. Abraham Lincoln, *The Collected Works of Abraham Lincoln*, ed. Roy P. Basler, 9 vols. (New Brunswick, N.J.: Rutgers University Press, 1953–1955), index, pp. 68, 108, 131. Two of the references to Hamilton are in editorial footnotes and two are included in speeches by Stephen Douglas. There are only two Lincoln speeches in which he mentions Hamilton by name. The *Collected Works* also includes one letter to the editor written by an observer of Lincoln's tariff address in March 1844 describing the scene mentioned (hereafter *Lincoln's Collected Works*).

20. Ibid., 1: 334, 502–3.

21. Ibid., 3: 531. William Cullen Bryant (1794–1878), editor of Hamilton's old *New York Evening Post*, introduced Lincoln at the Cooper Institute in 1860 and gave an account of the address the next day. Bryant noted in the *Post* that "in this great controversy the Republicans are the real conservative party. They simply adhere to a policy which had its origin with George Washington of Virginia, Benjamin Franklin of Pennsylvania, Abraham Baldwin of Georgia, Alexander Hamilton of New York, and other men from other states worthy to be named with them" (Herbert Mitgang, ed., *Lincoln: As They Saw Him* [New York: Rinehart, 1956], p. 156).

22. Lincoln's "beau ideal" quote can be found in *Lincoln's Collected Works*, 3: 29.

23. Guelzo, *Abraham Lincoln: Redeemer President*, pp. 193–94; Phillip S. Paludan, *A Covenant with Death: The Constitution, Law, and Equality in the Civil War Era* (Urbana: University of Illinois Press, 1975), pp. 185–86, 186 n. 25. Guelzo suggests that Lincoln adopted this "convenient Whig tactic" to lambaste a Democratic party dominated by slave interests and distancing itself from its own founder's most notable work.

24. Hay's comment can be found in Henry Adams, *The Letters of Henry Adams*, ed. J. C. Levenson, Ernest Samuels, Charles Vandersee, Viola Hopkins Winner, 6 vols. (Cam-

bridge: Belknap Press of Harvard University Press, 1982), vol. 2, *1868–1885*, p. 456 n. 4; Seward's remarks are in William H. Seward, *An Autobiography, from 1801 to 1834; Memoir of His Life, and Selections from His Letters, 1831–1846*, ed. Frederick W. Seward (New York: Derby and Miller, 1891), pp. 68, 197; Chase's comment is in J. W. Schuckers, *The Life and Public Services of Salmon Portland Chase* (New York: D. Appleton, 1874), p. 278.

25. Stephen B. Oates, *With Malice Toward None: The Life of Abraham Lincoln* (New York: Harper and Row, 1977), p. 30.

26. J. G. Randall, *Lincoln the President: Springfield to Gettysburg* (New York: Dodd, Mead, 1945), 1: 23–24, and *Lincoln the Liberal Statesman* (New York: Dodd, Mead, 1947), p. 179. It is important to note that Randall's account of Reconstruction was distinctly pro-Southern and warmly welcomed there. He was hostile to the Radical Republicans and dismissed Lincoln's reputation as a Great Emancipator as a myth. One African-American reviewer correctly found in Randall's work "unconcealed antipathy" to the emancipation tradition. Oddly, Randall's Hamilton was even less of an antislavery advocate than the slave-owning Jefferson. See Merrill Peterson, *Lincoln in American Memory* (New York: Oxford University Press, 1994), pp. 298–304, 308–9 and Randall, *Lincoln the President*, p. 24.

27. Edgar Lee Masters, *Lincoln the Man* (New York: Dodd, Mead, 1931), pp. 24–27, 485–86, 494, 497–98. In Masters's *Aaron Burr and Madam Jumel* (1934), Burr was portrayed as a man who killed Hamilton because the latter was showing "despotism . . . how to make entrance and destroy the charters" of liberty. Burr's empire-building scheme in the West was designed to "build a separate realm" and "lift again . . . the banner of freedom" (quoted in Charles J. Nolan, *Aaron Burr and the American Literary Imagination* [Westport, Conn.: Greenwood Press, 1980], pp. 100–101).

28. Jefferson Davis, *The Papers of Jefferson Davis*, ed. Haskell M. Monroe Jr. and James T. McIntosh, 7 vols. (Baton Rouge: Louisiana State University Press, 1971–), vol. 3, *July 1846–December 1848*, pp. 266–67 (hereafter *Davis Papers*).

29. Jefferson Davis, *Jefferson Davis, Constitutionalist, His Letters, Papers and Speeches*, ed. Dunbar Rowland, 10 vols. (Jackson: Mississippi Department of Archives and History, 1923), 2: 478, 502. See especially Scott to Davis, 21 May 1856, for another example of the acrimonious tone of their relationship (3: 39).

30. Ibid., vol. 4, *1849–1852*, p. 209; vol. 5, *1853–1855*, p. 141; *Davis Papers*, vol. 6, *1856–1860*, p. 365; Rowland, ed., *Jefferson Davis, Constitutionalist*, 3: 170, and 323, 571.

31. Rowland, ed., *Davis, Constitutionalist*, 4: 259; this speech was delivered on 8 May 1860.

32. Ibid., 4: 170.

33. *Davis Papers*, vol. 7, *1861*, p. 43.

34. George C. Rable, *The Confederate Republic: A Revolution Against Politics* (Chapel Hill: The University of North Carolina Press, 1994), pp. 147, 249.

35. Jefferson Davis, *The Rise and Fall of the Confederate Government*, 2 vols. (New York: Thomas Yoseloff, 1958), 1: 144, 150–51, 162–63, 178–79, and 2: 5.

36. Rudolph Von Abele, *Alexander H. Stephens: A Biography* (New York: Alfred A. Knopf, 1946), p. 73; Burton J. Hendrick, *Statesmen of the Lost Cause: Jefferson Davis and His Cabinet* (Boston: Little, Brown, 1944), p. 58.

37. Alexander Stephens, *A Constitutional View of the Late War Between the States; Its Causes, Character, Conduct and Results* (Philadelphia: National Publishing Company,

1870), p. 25; *FED*, no. 54, p. 368. Jacob Cooke states that as to no. 54, "the presumption . . . must be in favor of Madison's claim" (see p. xxvii).

38. Rowland, ed., *Jefferson Davis, Constitutionalist*, 8: 406–7; Schlesinger, *The Age of Jackson* (New York: Book Find Club, 1945), pp. 371–73, 496–97.

39. Andrew Johnson, *The Papers of Andrew Johnson*, ed. Leroy P. Graf and Ralph W. Haskins (Knoxville: University of Tennessee Press, 1970), vol. 2, *1852–1857*, pp. 172, 304, 417–19. The Know-Nothings were a political party of the 1850s concerned with the immigration of Irish and other European Catholics to the United States.

40. Edmund Ruffin, *The Diary of Edmund Ruffin*, ed. William Kauffman Scarborough (Baton Rouge: Louisiana State University Press, 1976), vol. 2, *The Years of Hope, April, 1861–June, 1863*, pp. 617–18; Wilson and Fiske, eds., *Appletons' Cyclopaedia of American Biography*, 1: 648; Jeremiah Clemens, *The Rivals: A Tale of the Times of Aaron Burr, and Alexander Hamilton* (Philadelphia: J. B. Lippincott, 1860), p. viii. Southern discomfort with Hamilton persists to this day. Former congresswoman and U.S. ambassador Lindy Boggs of Louisiana recounted in her 1994 memoir a discussion with the artist Howard Chandler Christy about his painting, *Scene at the Signing of the Constitution of the United States* (1940). Christy had used live models to "flesh out actual people," prompting Boggs to ask, "Who is that handsome Alexander Hamilton?" Christy responded, "You wouldn't be interested . . . he's a worker in the Navy Yard." This prompted Boggs to observe, "I enjoyed the knowledge that in this democratic society of ours, a laborer could portray the elegant Mr. Hamilton" (*Washington Through a Purple Veil: Memoirs of a Southern Woman* [New York: Harcourt, Brace, 1994], p. 91).

41. John C. Hamilton, *The Life of Alexander Hamilton*, 2 vols. (New York: Halsted and Voorhies, 1834), 1: iv, and *The Works of Alexander Hamilton Comprising His Correspondence, and His Political and Official Writings, Exclusive of the Federalist, Civil and Military*, ed. John C. Hamilton, 7 vols. (New York: John F. Trow, Printer, 1850–1851). Writing in the 1940s, Hamilton's biographer Nathan Schachner described John C. Hamilton's work as a collection of "elisions, distortions and downright falsehoods," which were "slavishly copied by generations of succeeding historians" ("Alexander Hamilton Viewed by His Friends: The Narratives of Robert Troup and Hercules Mulligan," *WMQ* 3d series, 4 [April 1947]: 203).

42. John Braeman, "Richard Hildreth (1807–1865)," in *American Historians, 1607–1865*, ed. Clyde N. Wilson (Detroit: Gale Research Company, 1984), pp. 116–17, 128; Harvey Wish, *The American Historian: A Social-Intellectual History of the Writing of the American Past* (New York: Oxford University Press, 1960), p. 65; Richard Hildreth, *The History of the United States of America*, 6 vols. (New York: Harper and Brothers, 1851), 5: 527. See also Arthur M. Schlesinger Jr., "The Problem of Richard Hildreth," *NEQ*, 13, 2 (June 1940): 223–45.

43. George Ticknor Curtis, *History of the Origin, Formation, and Adoption of the Constitution of the United States; with Notices of Its Principal Framers*, 2 vols. (New York: Harper and Brothers, 1860), 2: 114, 570–71, 577. See also Clinton Rossiter, *Alexander Hamilton and the Constitution* (New York: Harcourt, Brace, and World, 1964), p. 333 n. 19.

44. Samuel M. Schmucker, *The Life and Times of Alexander Hamilton* (Philadelphia: J. W. Bradley, 1857), pp. vi–viii, 383–84, 393. A lengthy review of Schmucker's book

appeared in *North American Review* in April 1858. The reviewer, Henry T. Tuckerman, never once mentioned the book in forty-three pages. Tuckerman said of Hamilton: "'Persecution' is a mild term to designate the opprobrium and vindictiveness he incurred as a political and public man" (review of *The Life and Times of Alexander Hamilton*, by Samuel Schmucker, *NAR* 86 [April 1858]: 368–411). See also Ford, *Bibliotheca Hamiltoniana*, p. 95.

45. Ford, *Bibliotheca Hamiltoniana*, pp. 95–97; Peterson, *The Jefferson Image in the American Mind*, pp. 224–25; Frank Shuffelton, *Thomas Jefferson: A Comprehensive, Annotated Bibliography of Writings About Him (1826–1980)* (New York: Garland, 1983), pp. 205, 241.

46. Christopher Riethmuller, *Alexander Hamilton and His Contemporaries, or The Rise of the American Commonwealth* (London: Bell and Daldy, 1864), p. 440; C. C. Hazewell, "Alexander Hamilton," *AM*, November 1865, p. 625. Riethmuller's book was also published as *The Life and Times of Alexander Hamilton, Aide-De-Camp, Secretary, and Minister of General Washington*.

47. Joseph Jay Rubin, *The Historic Whitman* (University Park: Pennsylvania State University Press, 1973), p. 9; T. J. Whitman, *Dear Brother Walt: The Letters of Thomas Jefferson Whitman*, ed. Dennis Berthold and Kenneth M. Price (Kent, Ohio: Kent State University Press, 1984); Newton Arvin, *Whitman* (New York: Macmillan, 1938), p. 14; Van Wyck Brooks, *The Times of Melville and Whitman* (New York: E. P. Dutton, 1947), p. 127; Walt Whitman, *Walt Whitman: The Correspondence*, ed. Edwin Haviland Miller (New York: New York University Press, 1969), vol. 4, *1886–1889*, p. 396; Thomas L. Brasher, *Whitman as Editor of the Brooklyn Daily Eagle* (Detroit: Wayne State University Press, 1970), p. 101.

48. William Leggett, *Democratick Editorials, Essays in Political Economy by William Leggett*, ed. Lawrence H. White (Indianapolis: Liberty Press, 1984), p. 244. Whitman retained an admiration for Leggett to the end of his life. See his *Gathering of the Forces, Editorials, Essays, Literary and Dramatic Reviews and Other Material Written by Walt Whitman as Editor of the Brooklyn Daily Eagle in 1846 and 1847*, ed. Cleveland Rogers and John Black, 2 vols. (New York: G. P. Putnam's Sons, 1920), 1: 10. Ironically, Leggett too fought a duel at Weehawken. See Wilson and Fiske, eds., *Appletons' Cyclopaedia of American Biography*, 3: 679.

49. Rubin, *The Historic Whitman*, pp. 4–5, 39–44; Van Wyck Brooks, *The Times of Melville and Whitman*, p. 127; Whitman, *The Gathering of the Forces*, 1: 8, 219, and 2: 192–94; Horace Traubel, *With Walt Whitman in Camden (November 1, 1888–January 20, 1889)* (New York: Rowman and Littlefield, 1961), p. 139. The government purchased Hamilton's papers from his heirs for twenty thousand dollars by an act of 12 August 1848, which also authorized a twenty thousand dollar payment for the papers of Thomas Jefferson. The papers were stored in the historical archives of the Department of State until they were transferred to the Library of Congress in 1903. See Gaillard Hunt, "The History of the Department of State," *American Journal of International Law 6*, 4 (October 1912): 911–12.

50. Ralph Waldo Emerson, *The Letters of Ralph Waldo Emerson*, ed. Ralph L. Rusk, 6 vols. (New York: Columbia University Press, 1939), 2: 357; Daniel Aaron, *Men of Good Hope: A Story of American Progressives* (New York: Oxford University Press, 1951), p. 17.

51. Ralph Waldo Emerson, *The Journals and Miscellaneous Notebooks of Ralph Waldo Emerson*, ed. William H. Gilman et al., 16 vols. (Cambridge: Belknap Press of Harvard University Press, 1960–1982), 5: 47; 6: 236; 11: 385; and 16: 90. Emerson, apparently along with anyone of note who lived during the first half of the nineteenth century, met Hamilton's widow in August 1845. See Rusk, ed., *The Letters of Ralph Waldo Emerson*, 3: 295. The Civil War diarist and Hamilton family attorney George Templeton Strong exclaimed in 1848, "I don't believe that old lady [Hamilton's widow] has the slightest intention of ever going to a better world: such a specimen of juvenile antediluvianism I never encountered" (see *The Diary of George Templeton Strong: Young Man in New York, 1835–1849*, ed. Allan Nevins and Milton Halsey Thomas [New York: Macmillan, 1952], p. 334).
52. "Alexander Hamilton," *NYT*, 25 January 1869, p. 5.

4. HAMILTON'S GILDED AGE

1. Richard B. Hovey, *John Jay Chapman: An American Mind* (New York: Columbia University Press, 1959), p. 23. Chapman's writings had a significant impact on the thought of Herbert Croly, the influential progressive author and editor. See Arthur M. Schlesinger Jr.'s introduction to Croly's *The Promise of American Life* (Cambridge: Belknap Press of Harvard University Press, 1965), p. xiv.
2. James A. Garfield, *The Diary of James A. Garfield*, ed. Harry James Brown and Frederick D. Williams (Lansing: Michigan State University Press, 1981), vol. 4, *1878–1881*, pp. 436–37 and 437 n. 223; Benjamin Harrison, *This Country of Ours* (New York: Charles Scribner's Sons, 1897), pp. 85, 208–9; James G. Blaine, *Twenty Years of Congress from Lincoln to Garfield, with a Review of the Events Which Led to the Political Revolution of 1860* (Norwich, Conn.: Henry Bill, 1884), 1: 186, 483. See also George F. Parker, *Recollections of Grover Cleveland* (New York: Century, 1909), pp. 286–87, and Rutherford B. Hayes, *Diary and Letters of Rutherford Birchard Hayes, Nineteenth President of the United States*, ed. Charles Richard Williams, 5 vols. (Columbus: Ohio State Archaeological Society, 1922–1926), vol. 1, *1834–1860*, pp. 156, 160–161; vol. 4, *1881–1893*, p. 164.
3. Theodore P. Cook, *The Life and Public Services of Hon. Samuel J. Tilden, Democratic Nominee for President of the United States* (New York: D. Appleton, 1876), p. 20; William A. Wallace, "The Mission of the Democratic Party," *NAR* 132 (January 1881): 96–98; Colleen McGuiness, ed., *American Leaders, 1789–1994* (Washington, D.C.: Congressional Quarterly, 1994), p. 380.
4. "Alexander Hamilton," *NYT*, 6 February 1876, p. 4; "A Statesman of Genius," *NYT*, 4 April 1876, p. 8; letters to the editor, *NYT*, 6 April 1876, p. 4; letters to the editor, *NYT*, 10 April 1876, p. 4; "A Statue to Hamilton," *NYT*, 12 November 1876, p. 6. See also Wilson and Fiske, eds., *Appletons' Cyclopaedia*, 4: 25.
5. "A Statue to Hamilton," *NYT*, 12 November 1876, p. 6; editorial, *NYT*, 13 August 1878, p. 4.
6. "Alexander Hamilton," *NYT*, 20 November 1880, p. 4; "The Statue of Hamilton," *NYT*, 23 November 1880, pp. 1–2.
7. Morse *The Life of Alexander Hamilton*, 2: 19, 221, 274, 331–32, 336, 344, 371. See also David Alan Lincove, "John T. Morse, Jr. (1840–1937)" in *American Historians, 1866–1912*, ed. Clyde N. Wilson (Detroit: Gale Research Company, 1986), p. 185.

8. Lincove, "John T. Morse, Jr.," pp. 183–92.

9. John A. Garraty, *Henry Cabot Lodge: A Biography* (New York: Alfred A. Knopf, 1953), pp. 38–39, 56–59, 58 n. 1. Henry Cabot Lodge, "The Life of Alexander Hamilton," *NAR*, 123 (July 1876): 113–44. See also William C. Widenor, "Henry Cabot Lodge (1850–1924)," in Wilson, ed., *American Historians, 1866–1912*, pp. 157–62.

10. Garraty, *Henry Cabot Lodge*, pp. 39, 55, 58–59. While working on a book about his great-grandfather George Cabot, he interviewed John C. Hamilton, who wrote Lodge after the publication of the *Life and Letters of George Cabot* (1877) that he was surprised to notice "the ill feelings towards my venerated father." Nonetheless, it was the work on George Cabot that, as Lodge put it, "acquainted me with Hamilton." Brooks Adams once wrote of Hamilton that if the Constitutional Convention had followed his advice, "consolidation, indeed, might have come" and his system might "have ended in despotism," but at least it would have been openly acknowledged and sustained as opposed to the country's unacknowledged drift in that direction in 1874. (See Brooks Adams, "The Platform of the New Party," *NAR* 119 [July 1874]: 47.)

11. Henry Cabot Lodge, *Alexander Hamilton*, pp. vii, 280.

12. Ibid., pp. 273–79. Lodge's admiration for Hamilton's nationalism is apparent throughout his biography. At one point he noted that Hamilton's fame as a writer rested in good measure on his contributions to *The Federalist*, which "has been turned to as an authority by the leading minds of Germany intent on the formation of the Germanic empire" (p. 67).

13. Lodge had been warned that the first collection of Hamilton's writings, assembled by John Church Hamilton, had been subjected to "manipulations and mutilations." Nonetheless, Hamilton's biographer Nathan Schachner later stated that Lodge's "editing of the letters was sloppy. Dates and attributions are wrong in too many instances; he omitted sections of letters that in some cases might be interpreted to the detriment of his hero." One of Lodge's biographers stated that his pro-Hamilton bias was partly responsible for this, in addition to the fact that Lodge did not personally examine the Hamilton manuscripts and seems to have been more concerned with his political obligations at the time. See Garraty, *Henry Cabot Lodge*, pp. 88–89, and Alexander Hamilton, *The Works of Alexander Hamilton*, ed. Henry Cabot Lodge, 12 vols. (New York: G. P. Putnam's Sons, 1904), 1: ix. The *New York Times* celebrated the release of Hamilton's *Works* by praising Lodge for his "workmanlike spirit" and "excellent judgment" and observed that "Hamilton was a genius, if there ever was one" ("Alexander Hamilton," *NYT*, 24 October 1886, p. 12).

14. Garraty, *Henry Cabot Lodge*, p. 56; William C. Widenor, *Henry Cabot Lodge and the Search for an American Foreign Policy* (Berkeley: University of California Press, 1980), p. 28.

15. Though Lodge and Adams differed in their estimation of Hamilton, they both understood that his reputation had come full circle from the early decades of the century, when his name and his principles were under constant attack. By the latter half of the nineteenth century, as Adams told Lodge, it was "always safe to abuse Jefferson" (see *Letters of Henry Adams [1858–1891]*, ed. Worthington Chauncey Ford [Boston: Houghton Mifflin, 1930], pp. 284–85, and Widenor, "Henry Cabot Lodge [1850–1924]," p. 160).

16. Levenson et al., eds., *The Letters of Henry Adams*, vol. 2, *1868–1885*, pp. 455–56, 476; Henry Adams, *The Life of Albert Gallatin* (Philadelphia: J. B. Lippincott, 1880), pp. 159, 268. Parsons's "Continuing Crusade: Four Generations of the Adams Family View Alexander Hamilton," pp. 43–63, is an excellent description of the attitude of the Adams family toward Hamilton. I am indebted to it for this account of Henry Adams.

17. Ernest Samuels, *Henry Adams: The Middle Years* (Cambridge: Belknap Press of Harvard University Press, 1958), p. 56.

18. Henry Adams, *History of the United States of America During the First Administration of Thomas Jefferson*, 2 vols. (New York: Charles Scribner's Sons, 1889), 1: 85, 109, and William Ander Smith, "Henry Adams, Alexander Hamilton, and the American People as a 'Great Beast,'" *NEQ* 48 (June 1975): 216–30; ironically, Henry Adams referred to the people as a beast in a letter to his brother in 1867 (p. 230). For a description of Theophilus Parsons senior and junior, see Wilson and Fiske, eds., *Appletons' Cyclopaedia of American Biography*, 4: 664–65.

The full passage in Parsons's *Memoir* reads: "That was a day of violent language, and, I suppose, of violent feeling; but, with it all, there was some wisdom left. Then, as always, extremes produced extremes; and, in the excitement and exasperation of political antagonism, words were sometimes used which were more extreme than the speaker's thought. At a dinner party in New York, soon after the adoption of the Federal Constitution, the conversation turned upon the prospects of the country. One gentleman, whose name I never heard, was an earnest 'friend of the people,' and descanted with much enthusiasm upon the glorious future then opening upon this new-born nation, and predicted the perpetuity of our institutions, from the purity and intelligence of the people, their freedom from interest or prejudice, their enlightened love of liberty, &c., &c. Alexander Hamilton was among the guests; and, his patience being somewhat exhausted, he replied with much emphasis, striking his hand upon the table, 'Your people, sir, — your people is a great beast!' I have this anecdote from a friend, to whom it was related by one who was a guest at the table. After-dinner utterances have little value, unless, perhaps, their very levity makes them good indicators of the wind. We do not know the qualifying words which may have followed, or the tone and manner of that which was, perhaps, in part or in whole, a jest. And it is fair to suppose that the remark, if it had any serious meaning, meant only that the people might be corrupted by prosperity and adulation, until they would lose all wisdom, and all principles of right, and all guidance of reason. But after every possible allowance is made, the remark was a mistake; for the people is not a beast, but a MAN. It is no uncommon thing to hear it said of an individual, that he is a beast, or no better than a beast; and certainly nothing will so confirm in him the degrading propensities which brutalize him, as treating him like a beast. But, after all, he is a great deal more than a beast, even if a great deal worse; for he cannot cast off if he will the infinite possibilities and equal responsibilities which belong to him as a man" (*Memoir of Theophilus Parsons, Chief Justice of the Supreme Judicial Court of Massachusetts; with Notices of Some of His Contemporaries. By His Son, Theophilus Parsons, Jr.* [New York: Da Capo Press, 1970], pp. 109–10; this edition is an unabridged republication of the original 1859 first edition).

19. Smith, "Henry Adams, Alexander Hamilton, and the American People as a 'Great Beast,'" p. 229 n. 33. Thomas Jefferson, *Writings, Notes on the State of Virginia* (New

York: Library of America, 1984), p. 272. I am indebted to Lorna Knott for this observation.

20. John Fiske, *The Critical Period in American History, 1783–1789* (Boston: Houghton, Mifflin, 1902), pp. 147–48, 411, and *Essays Historical and Literary*, 2 vols. (New York: Macmillan, 1903), 1: 142.

21. Malone and Johnson, eds., *Dictionary of American Biography*, 18: 217–19; William Graham Sumner, *Alexander Hamilton* (New York: Dodd, Mead, 1890), pp. 13, 184–85, 190; John William Ward, "Andrew Jackson: The Majority Is to Govern," in *An American Primer*, ed. Daniel J. Boorstin (Chicago: University of Chicago Press, 1966), p. 275.

22. Kirk Wood, "George Bancroft (1800–1891)" in Wilson, ed., *American Historians, 1607–1865*, pp. 6–22; Lillian Handlin, *George Bancroft: The Intellectual as Democrat* (New York: Harper and Row, 1984), p. 332; N. H. Dawes and F. T. Nichols, "Revaluing George Bancroft," *NEQ* 6 (June 1933): 281; George Bancroft, *History of the United States of America, From the Discovery of the American Continent*, 6 vols. (New York: D. Appleton, 1888), 4: 110–11.

23. George Bancroft, *History of the Formation of the Constitution of the United States of America*, 2 vols. (New York: D. Appleton, 1903), 2: 338; George Bancroft and Stephen Salisbury, "Report of the Council," *Proceedings of the American Antiquarian Society*, n. s., 3 (October 1883–April 1885): 40–50; Bancroft, *History of the United States of America*, 5: 447.

24. Wish, *The American Historian: A Social and Intellectual History of the Writing of the American Past*, pp. 213–14; James Schouler, *History of the United States of America, Under the Constitution*, 7 vols. (New York: Dodd, Mead, 1894), vol. 1, *1783–1801*, p. 189, and *Alexander Hamilton* (Boston: Small, Maynard, 1901), pp. 40, 42, 49, 56–57, 61, 64, 68–69.

25. John Bach McMaster, *A History of the People of the United States, From the Revolution to the Civil War* (New York: D. Appleton, 1914), vol. 1, *1784–1790*, pp. 125–26; see also E. Stanly Godbold Jr., "John Bach McMaster (1852–1932)" in Wilson, ed., *American Historians, 1866–1912*, p. 173.

26. Hermann Von Holst, *The Constitutional and Political History of the United States* (Chicago: Callaghan, 1877), vol. 1, *1750–1833, State Sovereignty and Slavery*, pp. 61, 83, 134, 159, and Michael Kraus, *A History of American History* (New York: Farrar and Rinehart, 1937), pp. 338–41.

27. John Franklin Jameson, *John Franklin Jameson and the Development of Humanistic Scholarship in America*, ed. Morey Rothberg and Jacqueline Goggin (Athens: University of Georgia Press, 1993), vol. 1, *Selected Essays*, p. 41; James Bryce, *The American Commonwealth*, 2 vols. (New York: Macmillan, 1911), 2: 8; Walter Bagehot, *The Collected Works of Walter Bagehot*, ed. Norman St. John-Stevas, 15 vols. (London: Economist, 1968), vol. 4, *The Historical Essays*, p. 287.

28. Gertrude Atherton, review of *Alexander Hamilton: An Essay on American Union*, by Frederick Scott Oliver, *NAR* 183 (7 September 1906): 408; Howard K. Beale, *Theodore Roosevelt and the Rise of America to World Power* (Baltimore: Johns Hopkins University Press, 1956), p. 505 n. 33; William A. Robinson, *Thomas B. Reed, Parliamentarian* (New York: Dodd, Mead, 1930), p. 322; Theodore Roosevelt, *The Letters of Theodore Roosevelt*, ed. Elting E. Morison, 8 vols. (Cambridge: Harvard University Press, 1951–1954), vol. 5, *The Big Stick, 1905–1907*, pp. 393–94; Theodore Roosevelt,

The New Nationalism (New York: Outlook, 1910), p. 205. Writing in 1921, Arthur H. Vandenberg observed that the Hamilton Club of Chicago "has done more than any other American group to perpetuate the memory and doctrines of 'The Greatest American.'" The Chicago club was quite assertive in its efforts to commemorate Hamilton: in the 1920s they sought to move his home, the Grange, from New York City to Chicago. See Arthur H. Vandenberg, *The Greatest American: Alexander Hamilton, an Historical Analysis of His Life and Works Together with a Symposium of Opinions by Distinguished Americans* (New York: G. P. Putnam's Sons, 1921), dedication page; "Hamilton Grange Becomes Memorial," *NYT*, 18 November 1924, p. 12.

29. "Heroic Statue of Hamilton," *NYT*, 5 October 1893, p. 8; Booker T. Washington, *The Booker T. Washington Papers*, ed. Louis R. Harlan (Urbana: University of Illinois Press, 1975), vol. 4, *1895–98*, pp. 97–98, 98 n. 1; Melancthon Woolsey Stryker, *Hamilton, Lincoln, and Other Addresses* (Utica, N.Y.: William T. Smith, 1896), pp. 15, 21; Booker T. Washington, *Black-Belt Diamonds: Gems from the Speeches, Addresses, and Talks to Students of Booker T. Washington*, ed. Victoria Earle Matthews (New York: Fortune and Scott, 1898), p. 98; Woodrow Wilson, *The Papers of Woodrow Wilson*, ed. Arthur Link, 69 vols. (Princeton: Princeton University Press, 1966–1993), vol. 25, *1912*, p. 514. Stryker's Hamilton College was located in Clinton, New York. It evolved from the Hamilton-Oneida Academy founded in 1793 by a missionary, Samuel Kirkland, to educate both white and Iroquois youth. Alexander Hamilton was a trustee of the academy that was rechartered as a college in 1812 and named after him. Over the years the college maintained sporadic ties with Hamilton's descendants, conferring an honorary degree in 1861 on one of Hamilton's sons, James Alexander, and another on his grandson, Allan McLane Hamilton, in 1912. In 1864 the college began the practice of awarding a prize to a senior essay focusing on the character and career of Alexander Hamilton. According to Frank K. Lorenz, curator of Special Collections at Hamilton College, there is still a prize for "the best senior essay upon a theme relating to Alexander Hamilton," but as of the year 2000 "there has been no entry submitted for it in recent years." Nonetheless, the college's namesake has not been completely forgotten. A statue of Hamilton remains in a prominent location on the campus in front of the college chapel, and in 1997 a group of alumni, a professor, and one student traveled to Hamilton's birthplace at Nevis, British West Indies, to commemorate his 240th birthday. The group announced the establishment of a scholarship fund to assist high school students from Nevis to attend Hamilton College. In April 2001, the college hosted a three-day conference examining Hamilton's life and legacy. See Walter Pilkington, *Hamilton College, 1812/1962* (Clinton, N.Y.: Hamilton College, 1962), chap. 1 and pp. 28–29, 64; "Hamilton's Desk Shown," *NYT*, 18 December 1953, p. 27; Melvin Gilbert Dodge, ed., *Alexander Hamilton, Thirty-one Orations Delivered at Hamilton College from 1864 to 1895 upon the Prize Foundation Established by Franklin Harvey Head, A.M.* (New York: G. P. Putnam's Sons, 1896), pp. ix–x; e-mail correspondence with Frank K. Lorenz, curator of Special Collections, Hamilton College, 13–14 January 2000; "In Nevis, Hamilton College Marks a Birthday," *Chronicle of Higher Education* 43, 22 (7 February 1997): A-10.

30. "Plan a Hamilton Memorial," *NYT*, 22 February 1908, p. 14; Marian C. McKenna, *Borah* (Ann Arbor: University of Michigan Press, 1961), p. 97; William E. Borah, *American Problems; A Selection of Speeches and Prophecies by William E. Borah*, ed.

Horace Green (New York: Duffield, 1924), pp. 1–7. William Borah's admiration for Hamilton seems to have persisted over time; in a book review written in 1925 he referred to Hamilton as "the supreme genius of the Federalist party." See William E. Borah, "Jefferson and Hamilton," NR 45 (23 December 1925): 140.

31. "Statue of Hamilton to Be Gift to Grange," NYT, 21 June 1936, sec. 2, p. 2; "A Statue Makes an Interborough Move," NYT, 20 July 1936, p. 9; Peterson, The Jefferson Image in the American Mind, p. 346.

32. This rhetoric was, apparently, her trademark: so vociferous were her pronouncements that her critics changed her middle name to Ellen — so they could call her "Mary Yellin."

33. McGuiness, ed., American Leaders, 1789–1994, p. 167; H. W. Brands, The Reckless Decade: America in the 1890s (New York: St. Martin's Press, 1995), p. 186; Jaffe, Who Were the Founding Fathers? pp. 90, 92–93.

34. McGuiness, ed., American Leaders, 1789–1994, p. 383; Michael Kazin, The Populist Persuasion: An American History (New York: Basic Books, 1995), pp. 9–10, 19.

35. Kazin, The Populist Persuasion, p. 10; G. Jack Gravlee, "Tom Watson: Disciple of 'Jeffersonian Democracy,'" in The Oratory of Southern Demagogues, ed. Cal M. Logue and Howard Dorgan (Baton Rouge: Louisiana State University Press, 1981), p. 96.

36. Thomas E. Watson, The Life and Times of Thomas Jefferson (New York: D. Appleton, 1903), pp. 311–12; C. Vann Woodward, Tom Watson: Agrarian Rebel (New York: Macmillan, 1938), p. 351.

37. Jaffe, Who Were the Founding Fathers? p. 94; Brands, The Reckless Decade, pp. 254–59; Boorstin, ed., An American Primer, p. 573.

38. William Jennings Bryan, "Jeffersonian Principles," NAR 168 (June 1899): 670–78; Paul W. Glad, The Trumpet Soundeth: William Jennings Bryan and his Democracy, 1896–1912 (Lincoln: University of Nebraska Press, 1960), p. 126.

39. Lawrence W. Levine, Defender of the Faith, William Jennings Bryan: The Last Decade, 1915–1925 (Cambridge: Harvard University Press, 1987), p. 222; William Jennings Bryan, The Real Bryan, Being Extracts from the Speeches and Writings of "A Well-Rounded Man," ed. Richard L. Metcalfe (Des Moines, Iowa: Personal Help Publishing Company, 1908), p. 207; Jaffe, Who Were the Founding Fathers? p. 94.

40. Robert M. La Follette, La Follette's Autobiography: A Personal Narrative of Political Experiences (Madison Wis.: Robert M. La Follette, 1913), pp. 103–4; Allan Nevins, Grover Cleveland, A Study in Courage (New York: Dodd, Mead, 1932), p. 392; George F. Hoar, Autobiography of Seventy Years, 2 vols. (New York: Charles Scribner's Sons, 1903), 1: 250, and 2: 244; William Rea Gwinn, Uncle Joe Cannon: Archfoe of Insurgency, A History of the Rise and Fall of Cannonism (New York: Bookman Associates, 1957), p. 24.

41. Samuel S. Cox, Three Decades of Federal Legislation, 1855 to 1885 (Providence, R.I.: J. A. and R. A. Reid, 1885), p. 680; Carl Schurz, Speeches, Correspondence and Political Papers of Carl Schurz, ed. Frederic Bancroft (New York: G. P. Putnam's Sons, 1913), vol. 4, July 1880–15 September 1888, pp. 241–42.

42. McGuiness, ed., American Leaders, 1789–1994, pp. 186; William Maxwell Evarts, Arguments and Speeches of William Maxwell Evarts, ed. Sherman Evarts, 3 vols. (New York: Macmillan, 1919), 3: 154–56.

43. McGuiness, ed., American Leaders, 1789–1994, p. 171; William H. Riker, The Art of Political Manipulation (New Haven, Conn.: Yale University Press, 1986), pp. 10–17.

44. Chauncey M. Depew, *Addresses and Literary Contributions on the Threshold of Eighty-two* (N.P., 1916?), p. 107; "The Statue of Hamilton," *NYT*, 23 November 1880, p. 2. The complete text of Chauncey Depew's address at the 1880 unveiling of a Hamilton statue in New York's Central Park can be found in Margaret Esther Hall, ed., *Alexander Hamilton Reader, A Compilation of Materials by and Commenting on Hamilton* (New York: Oceana Publications, 1957), pp. 21–29.
45. William Ander Smith, "Henry Adams, Alexander Hamilton, and the American People as a 'Great Beast,'" p. 218. Smith cites Charles G. Sellers as his source for this comment.

5. THE TWILIGHT OF HAMILTONIANISM

1. Emily Wortis Leider, *California's Daughter: Gertrude Atherton and Her Times* (Stanford: Stanford University Press, 1991), p. 4; Edward Sandford Martin, *The Life of Joseph Hodges Choate, as Gathered Chiefly from His Letters* (New York: Charles Scribner's Sons, 1920), 2: 252; Gertrude Atherton, *Adventures of a Novelist* (New York: Blue Ribbon Books, 1932), 49, 352–53, and "The Hunt for Hamilton's Mother," *NAR* 175 (August 1902): 229–42. Many prominent African Americans have claimed that Hamilton was black. The scholar and activist W. E. B. DuBois (1868–1963) frequently referred to him as "our own Hamilton." In 1903 he wrote that Hamilton's "drop of African fire quite recently sent Mrs. Gertrude Atherton into hysterics." William Pickens (1881–1954), an educator and a prominent figure in the early days of the NAACP, also believed Hamilton was black. Writing in 1916, he observed that "Hamilton was a Negro. He was a Negro according to the definition accepted in our day. That is, he was a man whose blood was mixed black and white." See W. E. B. DuBois, *Writings in Periodicals Edited by W. E. B. DuBois: Selections from The Horizon*, ed. Herbert Aptheker (White Plains, N.Y.: Kraus-Thomson Organization, 1985), p. 27, and *Writings by W. E. B. Dubois in Periodicals Edited by Others*, ed. Herbert Aptheker (Millwood, N.Y.: Kraus-Thomson Organization, 1982), vol. 1, *1891–1909*, pp. 163, 362; William Pickens, *The New Negro, His Political, Civil and Mental Status and Related Essays* (New York: Negro Universities Press, 1969), p. 103; Rayford W. Logan and Michael R. Winston, eds., *Dictionary of American Negro Biography* (New York: W. W. Norton, 1982), pp. 491–92. It has also been alleged that Hamilton was the father of William Hamilton (1773–1836), a leader of New York City's African-American community who was involved in antislavery and anticolonization movements. See C. Peter Ripley, ed., *The Black Abolitionist Papers* (Chapel Hill: University of North Carolina Press, 1991), vol. 3, *The United States, 1830–1846*, p. 359 n. 1.
2. Gertrude Atherton, *The Conqueror, Being the True and Romantic Story of Alexander Hamilton* (New York: Macmillan, 1914), pp. 345, 358–59, 375, 393, 418, 451. In a letter to the *New York Times* written in April 1902, Atherton wrote of Jefferson's "contemptible character, of his lying, traitoring, and hypocrisy" and concluded that "his character . . . is the most despicable in history." See "Mrs. Atherton Writes of Her Book," *NYT, Saturday Review of Books and Art*, 19 April 1902, p. 265.
3. Malone and Johnson, eds., *Dictionary of American Biography*, 8: 179–80; Allan McLane Hamilton, *The Intimate Life of Alexander Hamilton* (New York: Charles Scribner's Sons, 1910), pp. vii, 52, 281–82, 430–31.
4. Theodore Roosevelt, *New York* (New York: Charles Scribner's Sons, 1924), pp. 362–67; Bancroft, ed., *Speeches, Correspondence and Political Papers of Carl Schurz*, 4; 241–

42; J. W. Cooke, "Theodore Roosevelt (1858–1919)" in Wilson, ed., *American Historians, 1866–1912*, pp. 242–49. In light of TR's love for Hamilton, it is ironic that Hamilton's grandson and biographer Dr. Allan McLane Hamilton wrote an essay in the pages of the *New York Times* in 1912 questioning Roosevelt's sanity, along with the sanity of other progressive politicians. See "The Peril of an Insane Administration," *NYT*, 12 May 1912, pt. 5, p. 2.

5. H. W. Brands, *T.R.: The Last Romantic* (New York: Basic Books, 1997), p. 132; Carleton Putnam, *Theodore Roosevelt* (New York: Charles Scribner's Sons, 1958), vol. 1, *The Formative Years, 1858–1886*, pp. 381–82.

6. Theodore Roosevelt, *Gouverneur Morris* (Boston: Houghton, Mifflin, 1898), preface; Morison, ed., *The Letters of Theodore Roosevelt*, vol. 5, *The Big Stick, 1905–1907*, p. 407, and vol. 7, *The Days of Armageddon, 1909–1914*, p. 175. See also Henry Cabot Lodge, ed. *Selections from the Correspondence of Theodore Roosevelt and Henry Cabot Lodge, 1884–1918*, 2 vols. (New York: Charles Scribner's Sons, 1925), 1: 50, and 2: 282. TR's other volume in the American Statesman series was *Thomas Hart Benton* (Boston: Houghton, Mifflin, 1886).

7. Theodore Roosevelt, *New York*, p. 366; Putnam, *Theodore Roosevelt*, p. 224; Joseph Bucklin Bishop, *Theodore Roosevelt and His Time, Shown in His Own Letters*, 2 vols. (New York: Charles Scribner's Sons, 1926), 2: 27–28.

8. Theodore Roosevelt, *Gouverneur Morris*, p. 119; Bishop, *Theodore Roosevelt and His Time*, 2: 27–28; Theodore Roosevelt, *New York*, p. 367.

9. Theodore Roosevelt, *New York*, pp. 370–71; Morison, ed., *The Letters of Theodore Roosevelt* vol. 1, *The Years of Preparation, 1868–1898*, p. 491; Albert Bushnell Hart and Herbert Ronald Ferleger, eds., *Theodore Roosevelt Cyclopedia* (New York City: Roosevelt Memorial Association, 1941), p. 179.

10. Morison, ed., *The Letters of Theodore Roosevelt*, vol. 5, *The Big Stick, 1905–1907*, pp. 349, 368, 693; Lodge, ed., *Selections from the Correspondence of Theodore Roosevelt and Henry Cabot Lodge*, 2: 225.

11. Frederick Scott Oliver, *Alexander Hamilton, An Essay on American Union* (New York: G. P. Putnam's Sons, 1923), pp. 5, 225–26; Henry F. Pringle, *Theodore Roosevelt, A Biography* (New York: Harcourt, Brace, 1931), pp. 260–61.

12. Link, ed., *The Papers of Woodrow Wilson* 20: 339; Nicholas Murray Butler, *Across the Busy Years, Recollections and Reflections*, 2 vols. (New York: Charles Scribner's Sons, 1940), 2: 228; Walter Lippmann, "Integrated America," *NR* 6 (19 February 1916): 64; Vandenberg, *The Greatest American: Alexander Hamilton*, p. xvi; Atherton, review of *Alexander Hamilton: An Essay on American Union*, by Frederick Scott Oliver, pp. 407–10.

13. Charles Forcey, *The Crossroads of Liberalism: Croly, Weyl, Lippmann, and the Progressive Era, 1900–1925* (New York: Oxford University Press, 1961), pp. xxviii, 123, 129; Nathan Miller, *Theodore Roosevelt: A Life* (New York: William Morrow, 1992), p. 514; Walter Lippmann, "Notes for a Biography," *NR* 63 (16 July 1930): 250–51. See also, Arthur M. Schlesinger Jr.'s introduction in Croly, *The Promise of American Life*, p. xxiii.

14. Theodore Roosevelt, *The New Nationalism*, pp. 3–33; Croly, *The Promise of American Life*, chap. 2, and pp. 53, 168–69. Croly repeated his preference for Hamilton over Jefferson in later writings, arguing that "the nationalism of Hamilton, with all its aris-

tocratic leaning, was more democratic, because more constructively social, than the indiscriminate individualism of Jefferson." See Herbert Croly, *Progressive Democracy* (New York: Macmillan, 1915), pp. 54–55.

15. *Who Was Who in America* (Chicago: A. N. Marquis, 1960), vol. 1, 1897–1942, pp. 218, 1020, 1056, and *Who Was Who in America* (Chicago: A. N. Marquis, 1950), vol. 2, *1943–1950*, pp. 94–95; Butler, *Across the Busy Years*, 1: 60, 363; "The Founders of the Republic," *NYT*, 3 June 1907, p. 6; Hall, ed., *Alexander Hamilton Reader*, 9–20; Alexander Hamilton, *Papers on Public Credit, Commerce and Finance by Alexander Hamilton*, ed. Samuel McKee Jr. (New York: Columbia University Press, 1934), p. ix.

16. McKee, ed., *Papers on Public Credit*, p. vi; Philip C. Jessup, *Elihu Root* (New York: Dodd, Mead, 1938), vol. 2, *1905–1937*, pp. 145, 159, 493.

17. Joseph Hodges Choate, *Arguments and Addresses of Joseph Hodges Choate*, ed. Frederick C. Hicks (St. Paul, Minn.: West Publishing, 1926), pp. 938, 954; Whitelaw Reid, *One Welshman: A Glance at a Great Career* (London: Macmillan, 1912), pp. 26, 31–32, 54.

18. Forcey, *The Crossroads of Liberalism*, pp. 3–4, 52, 56, 295; Walter E. Weyl, *The New Democracy: An Essay on Certain Political and Economic Tendencies in the United States* (New York: Macmillan, 1912), pp. 1, 4, 13–15.

19. Larry L. Adams, *Walter Lippmann* (Boston: Twayne, 1977), pp. 23–24, 28; Edward L. Schapsmeier and Frederick H. Schapsmeier, *Walter Lippmann, Philosopher-Journalist* (Washington, D.C.: Public Affairs Press, 1969), pp. 18–19; Walter Lippmann, *A Preface to Politics* (Ann Arbor: University of Michigan Press, 1962), pp. 16–17; Lippmann, "Integrated America," pp. 64–65.

20. Walter Lippmann, *Public Opinion* (New York: Macmillan, 1936), pp. 218–19, 280, 292; idem, *Men of Destiny* (New York: Macmillan, 1927), p. 186; idem, "Is Harding a Republican?" *NR* 23, (21 July 1920): 219.

21. Lippman, *A Preface to Politics*, pp. 10–11; idem, "The Greatness of Andrew Mellon," *NR* 38 (16 August 1924): 195–96.

22. For a concise account of the 1912 election and the absence of sharp differences between Wilson and TR on most economic matters, see Kendrick A. Clements, *The Presidency of Woodrow Wilson* (Lawrence: University Press of Kansas, 1992), chap. 2. President Taft told a friend that "[John] Marshall is certainly the greatest jurist America has ever produced and Hamilton our greatest constructive statesman. There you have my opinion of our greatest men." See Archibald Butt, *Taft and Roosevelt: The Intimate Letters of Archie Butt, Military Aide* (Garden City, N.Y.: Doubleday, Doran, 1930), p. 294.

23. Clements, *The Presidency of Woodrow Wilson*, p. 15; Stockton Axson, *"Brother Woodrow," A Memoir of Woodrow Wilson*, ed. Arthur S. Link (Princeton: Princeton University Press, 1993), pp. 71–72; Link, ed., *The Papers of Woodrow Wilson*, 2: 150, 228; Henry Wilkinson Bragdon, *Woodrow Wilson: The Academic Years* (Cambridge: Belknap Press of Harvard University Press, 1967), p. 126.

24. Link, ed., *The Papers of Woodrow Wilson*, 8: 368–70; 12: 216; and 15: 537.

25. Ibid., 19: 377, 467; 22: 444; 23: 108; 24: 374; and 25: 83–84.

26. Ibid., 29: 448, and 38: 326.

27. Sidney A. Pearson Jr., "Herbert Croly and Liberal Democracy," *Society* 35 (July/August 1998): 67.

28. George Coleman Osborn, *John Sharp Williams, Planter-Statesman of the Deep South* (Gloucester, Mass.: Peter Smith, 1964), pp. 442–43; Morison, ed., *The Letters of Theodore Roosevelt*, vol. 5, *The Big Stick, 1905–1907*, p. 349; "An Elder Statesman Takes Stock of America," *NYT*, 11 September 1927, sec. 9, p. 3.

29. "Says Hamilton Failed," *NYT*, 5 December 1912, p. 9; John Sharp Williams, *Thomas Jefferson: His Permanent Influence on American Institutions* (New York: AMS Press, 1967), pp. 36, 51, 144–45, 153, 159, 193–94. Former President William Howard Taft criticized Senator Williams for his silence when Woodrow Wilson restored the practice of delivering a State of the Union address in person as opposed to submitting a written message. Jefferson had discontinued the practice of delivering a personal address because of its monarchical overtones. Taft claimed that if a Republican president had reinstated such a practice he could imagine the "eloquent sentences that would have resounded" from Senator Williams and those other "faithful followers of Jefferson" vigorously denouncing "the introduction of 'such a royal ceremony in a speech from the Throne.'" See William Howard Taft, *Our Chief Magistrate and His Powers* (New York: Columbia University Press, 1938), p. 40.

30. Howard E. Dean, "J. Allen Smith: Jeffersonian Critic of the Federalist State," *APSR* 50, 4 (December 1956): 1095; Stanley Elkins and Eric McKitrick, "The Founding Fathers: Young Men of the Revolution," *PSQ* 76, 2 (June 1961): 187; Charles A. Beard, review of *The Spirit of American Government*, by J. Allen Smith, *PSQ* 23, 1 (March 1908): 136–37; J. Allen Smith, *The Growth and Decadence of Constitutional Government* (New York: Henry Holt, 1930), p. 108.

31. Beard, review of *The Spirit of American Government*, pp. 136–37; Frederick L. Bergmann, "Symposium Marks the Birth of Charles A. Beard," in *Charles A. Beard: An Observance of the Centennial of His Birth*, ed. Marvin C. Swanson (Greencastle, Ind.: DePauw University Press, 1976), pp. 5–8; John Braeman, "Charles A. Beard: Historian and Progressive," also in Swanson, ed., *Beard*, pp. 49–50. After his resignation, Beard told Senator Albert Beveridge that it was "certainly a relief" to "be out of Mr. [Nicholas Murray] Butler's asylum."

32. Eric F. Goldman, "The Origin of Beard's Economic Interpretation of the Constitution," *Journal of the History of Ideas* 13, 2 (April 1952): 244; Charles A. Beard, *An Economic Interpretation of the Constitution of the United States* (New York: Macmillan, 1967), pp. 100–114, 188.

33. "The Constitution," *NYT Review of Books*, 23 November 1913, sec. 7, p. 637; Walter Lippmann, "Mr. Beard on Property and Politics," *NR* 26 (2 August 1922): 282; Raymond Moley, *Twenty-seven Masters of Politics, In a Personal Perspective* (New York: Funk and Wagnalls, 1949), p. 12; Richard Hofstadter, *The Progressive Historians: Turner, Beard, Parrington* (New York: Alfred A. Knopf, 1968), p. 212.

34. Nonetheless, the book had many errors or overstatements that would be highlighted decades later by Forrest McDonald and Robert E. Brown. At the very least, the book stressed, to borrow a phrase from Robert A. McCaughey, the size of the founders' investment portfolios at the expense of their rhetoric. See Robert A. McCaughey, *Josiah Quincy, 1772–1864: The Last Federalist* (Cambridge: Harvard University Press, 1974), p. 24. For a full discussion of the many flaws in Beard's account, see Robert E. Brown, *Charles Beard and the Constitution: A Critical Analysis of "An Economic In-*

terpretation of the Constitution" (Princeton: Princeton University Press, 1956), and Forrest McDonald, *We The People: The Economic Origins of the Constitution* (Chicago: University of Chicago Press, 1958).

35. Beard, *An Economic Interpretation of the Constitution of the United States,* p. vi; John Braeman, "Charles A. Beard: Historian and Progressive," pp. 50, 54, 64–65.

36. "New Plan to Revise U.S. Constitution," *NYT,* 18 January 1915, p. 6; Charles A. Beard, "Reconstructing State Government," *NR,* pt. 2, vol. 4 (21 August 1915): 1.

37. Charles A. Beard, "Jefferson and the New Freedom," *NR* 1 (14 November 1914): 19; idem, *The American Party Battle* (New York: Book League of America, 1929), p. 41; idem, "Making the Fascist State," *NR,* 57 (23 January 1929): 277. Beard again drew parallels between the founders' view of Democracy and that of the Fascists (and Bolsheviks) in "Government by Technologists" (*NR* 63 [18 June 1930]: 117). Herbert Croly, Lincoln Steffens, and Ida Tarbell shared Beard's temporary admiration for Il Duce. See John P. Diggins, "Flirtation with Fascism: American Pragmatic Liberals and Mussolini's Italy," *AHR* 71 (October 1965): 487–506.

38. Charles A. Beard, with the collaboration of G. H. E. Smith, *The Open Door at Home: A Trial Philosophy of National Interest* (New York: Macmillan, 1935), p. 158; Allan L. Benson, *Our Dishonest Constitution* (New York: B. W. Huebsch, 1914), p. 5; Eugene V. Debs, *Letters of Eugene V. Debs,* ed. Robert J. Constantine, 3 vols. (Urbana and Chicago: University of Illinois Press, 1990), vol. 1, *1874–1912,* p. 394.

39. Justin Kaplan, *Lincoln Steffens, A Biography* (New York: Simon and Schuster, 1974), p. 32; Stanley K. Schultz, "The Morality of Politics: The Muckrakers' Vision of Democracy," *JAH* 52, 3 (December 1965): 539–40; Lincoln Steffens, *The Autobiography of Lincoln Steffens* (New York: Harcourt, Brace, 1931), pp. 495, 516–17.

40. John Braeman, *Albert J. Beveridge, American Nationalist* (Chicago: University of Chicago Press, 1971), p. 246; Albert J. Beveridge, *The Life of John Marshall,* 3 vols. (Boston: Houghton Mifflin, 1916–1919), 1: 396; 2: 82, 527–28; and 3: 277 n. 1; Morison, ed., *The Letters of Theodore Roosevelt,* vol. 8, *The Days of Armageddon, 1914–1919,* pp. 1352–53. In the midst of writing the Marshall biography, Beveridge wrote to J. Franklin Jameson, "I am, as you know, about as familiar as it is possible to be with the politicians and demagogues of our own day; but is there an example in the history of our own or any other country of so shifty a politician and so reckless a demagogue as Jefferson?" See Elizabeth Donnan and Leo F. Stock, eds., "Senator Beveridge, J. Franklin Jameson, and John Marshall," *MVHR* 35, 3 (December 1948): 478–79.

41. C. David Tompkins, *Senator Arthur H. Vandenberg: The Evolution of a Modern Republican, 1884–1945* (Lansing: Michigan State University Press, 1970), p. 29; Vandenberg, *The Greatest American: Alexander Hamilton,* p. vi; Charles A. Beard and Mary R. Beard, *The Rise of American Civilization* (New York: Macmillan, 1941), vol. 3, *America in Midpassage,* p. 302; Steve Neal, *Dark Horse, A Biography of Wendell Willkie* (Garden City, N.Y.: Doubleday, 1984), p. 58. When Vandenberg was suggested as a possible Republican candidate for president in 1936, the *New York Times* editorialized that despite "their annual lip-service to Jefferson the Democrats are now far more Hamiltonian than Hamilton ever was . . . a disciple of Hamilton as the chief adversary of the actual Hamiltonians piques the imagination." See "A Michigan Hamiltonian," *NYT,* 11 April 1936, p. 14.

42. Vandenberg, *The Greatest American: Alexander Hamilton,* pp. xii, xiv–xv, 69, 347.
43. Arthur H. Vandenberg, *If Hamilton Were Here Today: American Fundamentals Applied to Modern Problems* (New York: G. P. Putnam's Sons, 1923), pp. 30–31, 106–7, 335–37; Tompkins, *Senator Arthur H. Vandenberg,* p. 29. A streak of xenophobia runs through Vandenberg's book, a phenomenon more commonly found in the works of Jeffersonian nativists. Vandenberg claimed, "Run down the average cabal of communism, and you'll find here in America that it speaks a foreign tongue" (see *If Hamilton Were Here Today,* p. 219; also p. 365).
44. Andrew Sinclair, *The Available Man: The Life Behind the Masks of Warren Gamaliel Harding* (New York: Macmillan, 1965), p. 13; Francis Russell, *The Shadow of Blooming Grove: Warren G. Harding in His Times* (New York: McGraw-Hill, 1968), pp. 146, 160–61; Robert K. Murray, *The Harding Era: Warren G. Harding and His Administration* (Minneapolis: University of Minnesota Press, 1969), p. 171.
45. "Need of a Dictator Urged by Harding," *NYT,* 12 August, 1917, sec. 6, p. 1; Francis Russell, *The Shadow of Blooming Grove,* pp. 294–95.
46. James M. Cox, *Journey Through My Years* (New York: Simon and Schuster, 1946), pp. 412, 416–17. See Vandenberg's *The Greatest American: Alexander Hamilton,* p. 54, for Cox's nomination of Jefferson as the greatest American.
47. "Harding Deplores Growth of Factions and Strikes at Klan," *NYT,* 18 May 1923, pp. 1, 8. See also *Time,* 28 May 1923, p. 13. In his address, Harding mistakenly attributed to Hamilton passages written by James Madison from *The Federalist,* no. 10. The funds for the Hamilton statue were supplied by a gift from an anonymous woman from New York, while a congressional appropriation along with some additional private donations paid for the pedestal and the preparation of the site. The sculptor was James Earle Fraser of New York, who was noted for his design of the Indian-head nickel. Fraser stated, "I wanted to express the force of a man who wore lace ruffles and yet had to combat Jefferson and Madison." Fraser saw Hamilton as a man with "the mind and nature of an aristocrat" who bested his opponents by "the sheer power of his superiority of mind." Henry Bacon, architect of the Lincoln Memorial, designed the pedestal; its inscription reads, "first Secretary of the Treasury, Soldier, Orator, Statesman, Champion of Constitutional Union, Representative Government, and National Integrity." See Vandenberg, *The Greatest American, Alexander Hamilton,* pp. 339–43, and "As Hamilton Went to a Cabinet Meeting," *LD* (21 May 1921): 26. James Earle Fraser also sculpted the statue of Albert Gallatin that faces Pennsylvania Avenue on the north side of the Treasury building, a far more prominent location than Hamilton's southside location. Democrats raised private funds for the Gallatin statue in the 1930s after Republicans in Congress refused to appropriate money for the memorial. It was erected in 1947 at the height of New Deal and Fair Deal hostility to Hamilton. See Sarah Booth Conroy, "That Treasure, the Treasury," *WP,* 4 March 1988, p. N-54. There is also a statue of Hamilton in the Great Rotunda of the Capitol. Appropriately, a sculpture of George Washington stands between the Hamilton and Jefferson statues. These Hamilton memorials pale in comparison with other Washington-area monuments.
48. "Mr. Harding on Hamilton," *NYT,* 19 May 1923, p. 12.
49. Kenneth Campbell MacKay, *The Progressive Movement of 1924* (New York: Columbia University Press, 1947), p. 37; Harvey O'Connor, *Mellon's Millions: The Biography of a Fortune* (New York: John Day, 1933), p. 138.

50. "Hamilton and Public Credit," *NYT*, 4 December 1924, p. 20; "Mellon Hailed Here as Second Hamilton," *NYT*, 5 December 1924, p. 3.

51. "Hamilton Explains," *NAT* 128 (20 March 1929): 336; Lippmann, "The Greatness of Andrew Mellon," pp. 195–96, and *Men of Destiny*, pp. 184–89; Harvey O'Connor, *Mellon's Millions*, pp. 327–28. See also "Capital Pays Tribute to Hamilton," *NYT*, 12 January 1932, p. 25, for further evidence of Mellon's admiration for Hamilton.

52. William Allen White, *A Puritan in Babylon: The Story of Calvin Coolidge* (New York: Macmillan, 1938), p. 43; Calvin Coolidge, *The Autobiography of Calvin Coolidge* (New York: Cosmopolitan Book Corporation, 1929), pp. 61–62. Coolidge's teacher, Anson D. Morse (1846–1916), published an essay on Hamilton in *Political Science Quarterly* in 1890, one year before Coolidge arrived at Amherst. Morse lamented the fact that Hamilton had not been "properly appreciate[d]" by the American people, in part because the people "misunderstood" him and he misunderstood the people. Morse hailed Hamilton's nationalism as well as his aversion to demagoguery and his opposition to "the seductive policy of France." His major failing was his distaste for democracy, but ultimately he bequeathed to the people a "safe" republic. "No one," Morse contended, "had done more than he to make it so." See Anson Daniel Morse, *Parties and Party Leaders* (Boston: Marshall Jones, 1923), p. vii, and "Alexander Hamilton," *PSQ* 5 (1890): 1–23.

53. "Coolidge Commends Harding as Leader," *NYT*, 12 January 1922, p. 13; Calvin Coolidge, *The Price of Freedom: Speeches and Addresses* (New York: Charles Scribner's Sons, 1924), pp. 101–16. Coolidge's vice president and a Nobel Peace Prize recipient, Charles G. Dawes (1865–1951) considered Hamilton his "old hero" and visited his grave in Trinity churchyard while vice president. See Charles G. Dawes, *Notes as Vice-President, 1928–1929* (Boston: Little, Brown, 1935), pp. 116–17, and Claude Bowers, *My Life: The Memoirs of Claude Bowers* (New York: Simon and Schuster, 1962), pp. 138–39. Coolidge's opponent in the 1924 presidential election, John W. Davis (1873–1955), considered himself a Jeffersonian but also admired Hamilton. He noted in 1926 that "without Hamilton [America] might have perished in the quagmire of false finance." See John S. Pancake, *Thomas Jefferson and Alexander Hamilton* (Woodbury, N.Y.: Barron's Educational Series, 1974), p. 388.

54. Vernon L. Parrington, introduction to J. Allen Smith's *The Growth and Decadence of Constitutional Government*, p. xvi; Daniel Aaron, "The Mid-American Scholar," *NR* 211 (5 September 1994): 47–49; Vernon L. Parrington, *Main Currents in American Thought: An Interpretation of American Literature from the Beginnings to 1920*, 3 vols. (New York: Harcourt, Brace, 1927–1930), 1: 295, 298–99, 307.

55. William E. Dodd, *Statesmen of the Old South, or From Radicalism to Conservative Revolt* (New York: Macmillan, 1929), pp. 43, 65; Robert Dallek, *Democrat and Diplomat: The Life of William E. Dodd* (New York: Oxford University Press, 1968), pp. 61, 147, 151, 334; Wayne Mixon, "William E. Dodd," in Wilson, ed., *Twentieth-Century American Historians*, pp. 135–41; Fred Arthur Bailey, *William Edward Dodd: The South's Yeoman Scholar* (Charlottesville: University Press of Virginia, 1997), pp. 51–53, 87, 132–33; William E. Dodd, "Washington Meets New Ordeal," *NYT*, 21 November 1926, sec. 4, p. 1.

56. W. E. Woodward, *The Gift of Life: An Autobiography* (New York: E. P. Dutton, 1947), pp. 253, 295–96; idem, *George Washington: The Image and the Man* (New York: Boni

and Liveright, 1926), pp. 83, 370–71; idem, *A New American History* (New York: Farrar and Rinehart, 1936), pp. 264–65. Woodward claimed that if George Washington were alive in the 1920s, "He would be the head of a large corporation." For progressives of the day, this was the ultimate insult. See "Woodward Answers Hart," *NYT,* 24 December 1926, p. 8.

57. Johan J. Smertenko, *Alexander Hamilton* (New York: Greenburg, 1932), p. 5; Kazin, *The Populist Persuasion,* p. 130; Charles E. Coughlin, *A Series of Lectures on Social Justice* (Royal Oak, Mich.: The Radio League of the Little Flower, 1935), p. 63; Arthur M. Schlesinger Jr., *The Age of Roosevelt: The Politics of Upheaval* (Boston: Houghton Mifflin, 1960), p. 27.

6. SLOUCHING TOWARD OBLIVION

1. During the latter years of the depression (1936–1940), the chairman of the Republican National Committee was John D. M. Hamilton of Kansas (apparently no relation). See Donald R. McCoy, *Landon of Kansas* (Lincoln: University of Nebraska Press, 1966), pp. 261, 446–47, 537.

2. Francis Pendleton Gaines, *Southern Oratory: A Study in Idealism* (Huntsville: University of Alabama Press, 1946), pp. 12–13.

3. Bowers, *My Life,* pp. 1, 39; "Jefferson: Third President Relives in New Book by Bowers," *Newsweek,* 5 September 1936, p. 25; Michael Bordelon, "Claude G. Bowers," in Wilson, ed., *Twentieth-Century American Historians,* pp. 86–92.

4. Claude Bowers, "Washington at Last?" *NAT* 123 (27 October 1926): 431–32.

5. Claude Bowers, "Lincoln the Man," *SR,* 21 February 1931, pp. 609–10.

6. Constantine, ed., *Letters of Eugene V. Debs,* vol. 3, *1919–1926,* pp. 444–45.

7. Claude Bowers, *Jefferson and Hamilton: The Struggle for Democracy in America* (Boston: Houghton Mifflin, 1925), pp. 23, 33–35, 41, 69, 109, 135, 511.

8. Merrill D. Peterson, "Dumas Malone: An Appreciation," *WMQ,* 3d ser., vol. 45, no. 2 (April 1988): 239, 249; Samuel Flagg Bemis, review of *Jefferson and Hamilton: The Struggle for Democracy in America,* by Claude Bowers, *AHR* 31, 3 (April 1926): 543–45; Arthur N. Holcombe, review of *Jefferson and Hamilton: The Struggle for Democracy in America,* by Claude Bowers, *APSR* 20, 1 (February 1926): 215–17; Claude Bowers, *The Founders of the Republic* (Chicago: American Library Association, 1927), p. 7.

9. Bowers, *My Life,* pp. 192–98; "Text of Keynote Speech by Claude G. Bowers at Democratic Convention," *NYT,* 27 June 1928, p. 8; Bowers, *My Life,* p. 196, and "Lincoln the Man," p. 610. The same year that Bowers attacked Republicans for claiming to be the party of Hamilton and Lincoln, Henry A. Minor published *The Story of the Democratic Party* (New York: Macmillan, 1928), which took issue with Republican assertions that Hamilton was the intellectual founder of their party. "Beginning about 1880 Alexander Hamilton, displacing all others, was put forward as the founder, fountainhead and father of the Republican party, making the party a posthumous child by fifty years, and ignoring the fact that it (the party) had been really founded by Jeffersonians and Jacksonians [such] as Lincoln" (pp. 366–67).

10. "Hamilton and the Constitution," *NYT,* 17 September 1928, p. 22; "Plan Annual Hamilton Day," *NYT,* 13 January 1928, p. 12; "Gather at Hamilton Grave," *NYT,* 12 January 1928, p. 45; "A Son of the West Indies," *NYT,* 16 January 1928, p. 20.

11. Jonathan Daniels, "Franklin Delano Roosevelt and Books," in *Three Presidents and Their Books: The Reading of Jefferson, Lincoln, F. D. Roosevelt* (Urbana: University of Illinois Press, 1955), p. 95; Claude Bowers, *The Tragic Era: The Revolution After Lincoln* (Cambridge: Houghton Mifflin, 1929), pp. 307–9; Peterson, *The Jefferson Image in the American Mind*, p. 387.

12. Bowers, *My Life*, pp. 250, 260, 297, 303, 316.

13. Claude Bowers, "Jefferson and Civil Liberties," *AM*, January 1953, pp. 52–58.

14. Bowers, *My Life*, p. 127; Daniel R. Fusfeld, *The Economic Thought of Franklin D. Roosevelt and the Origins of the New Deal* (New York: Columbia University Press, 1956), pp. 85–86; Franklin D. Roosevelt, *The Roosevelt Reader, Selected Speeches, Messages, Press Conferences, and Letters of Franklin D. Roosevelt*, ed. Basil Rauch (New York: Rinehart, 1957), pp. 43–47. Bowers editorialized on FDR's behalf after the review appeared, although he probably would have been on Roosevelt's bandwagon regardless of the review. Newly elected Governor Roosevelt wrote Bowers in 1929, "Please let me tell you how very grateful I am for all the splendid editorials in the Evening World. They are a bulwark of strength" (Bowers, *My Life*, p. 250).

15. Frank Freidel, *Franklin D. Roosevelt: The Apprenticeship* (Boston: Little, Brown, 1952), p. 61 n. 56; Arthur Schlesinger Jr., *The Age of Roosevelt: The Crisis of the Old Order, 1919–1933* (Boston: Houghton Mifflin, 1957), pp. 102–3; Frank Freidel, *Franklin D. Roosevelt: The Ordeal* (Boston: Little, Brown, 1954), pp. 205–6 and 206n. See the skeptical reaction in the *New Republic* to FDR's proposal to "recover and realize the Jeffersonian idea" in "The Great Jefferson Joke," 47 (9 June 1926): 73–74.

16. Franklin D. Roosevelt, *The Public Papers and Addresses of Franklin D. Roosevelt*, ed. Samuel I. Rosenman, 13 vols. (New York: Random House, 1938–1950), vol. 1, *The Genesis of the New Deal, 1928–1932*, pp. 631–32, 745; vol. 7, *The Continuing Struggle for Liberalism* (New York: Macmillan, 1941), p. 40; and vol. 9 *War — and Aid to Democracies* (New York: Macmillan, 1941), pp. 435–37.

17. Geoffrey C. Ward, *Before the Trumpet, Young Franklin Roosevelt* (New York: Harper and Row, 1985), pp. 17n–18n; Peterson, *The Jefferson Image in the American Mind*, pp. 360–61.

18. Peterson, *The Jefferson Image in the American Mind*, pp. 360, 377, 430; Rosenman, ed., *The Public Papers and Addresses of Franklin D. Roosevelt* (New York: Macmillan, 1941), vol. 8, *War — and Neutrality*, pp. 577–79; Dumas Malone, "The Jefferson Faith," *SR*, 17 April 1943, p. 4. Merrill Peterson documents the many efforts undertaken by FDR to memorialize Jefferson, including the issuance of postage stamps and the Jefferson nickel (see *The Jefferson Image in the American Mind*, pp. 360–63).

19. Henry A. Wallace, *Whose Constitution: An Inquiry into the General Welfare* (New York: Reynal and Hitchcock, 1936), pp. 36 and 188; "Speaks on Jefferson," *NYT*, 14 April 1935, p. 24. Though antipathy toward Hamilton was common among New Dealers, FDR's secretary of war, Republican Henry L. Stimson (1867–1950), was an admirer of Hamilton. "It was the great genius of Alexander Hamilton," he argued, "that he enlisted on the side of the doers, the Federalists, and in behalf of the progressive doctrine of a liberal construction of the Constitution . . . the business interests of our young nation." See Elting E. Morison, *Turmoil and Tradition: A Study of the Life and Times of Henry L. Stimson* (Boston: Houghton Mifflin, 1960), pp. 129, 129 n. 4, 140.

20. Alben W. Barkley, *That Reminds Me* (Garden City, N.Y.: Doubleday, 1954), pp. 100–101; "Roosevelt Victory Sure, Says Farley," *NYT*, 14 April 1938, p. 10; James A. Farley, *Behind the Ballots: The Personal History of a Politician* (New York: Harcourt, Brace, 1938), pp. 357–58. When necessity required it, New Dealers were not above turning to Hamilton for theoretical support. Some Democrats cited Hamilton's arguments for unlimited presidential reeligibility in *The Federalist*, no. 72, when controversy erupted over Roosevelt's decision to run for a third term. See, for instance, *Congressional Digest* 19, 10 (October 1940): 255–56.

21. Moley, *Twenty-seven Masters of Politics*, pp. 11–16; Raymond Moley, "The Wisdom of a Ghost," *Newsweek*, 21 November 1938, p. 44. FDR offered to appoint Charles Beard to the commission to celebrate the sesquicentennial of the Constitution, but Beard declined the offer (see Braeman, *Charles A. Beard, Historian and Progressive*, p. 50). Adolf A. Berle, *Navigating the Rapids, 1918–1971: From the Papers of Adolf A. Berle*, ed. Beatrice Bishop Berle and Travis Beal Jacobs (New York: Harcourt Brace Jovanovich, 1973), p. 63; Francis Biddle, *The World's Best Hope: A Discussion of the Role of the United States in the Modern World* (Chicago: University of Chicago Press, 1949), p. 60.

22. Rexford Guy Tugwell and Joseph Dorfman, "Alexander Hamilton: Nation-Maker," *Columbia University Quarterly* 29 (December 1937): 209–26, and 30 (March 1938): 59–72. These essays also appeared in book form in Tugwell and Dorfman's *Early American Policy, Six Columbia Contributors* (New York: Columbia University Press, 1960), pp. 7–42. In their introduction, the authors noted that "our study of Hamilton was made when his achievement was given lower appraisal than at any other time since his death" (p. 1).

23. Tugwell and Dorfman, "Alexander Hamilton: Nation-Maker," 30: 71.

24. Dean Acheson, *Among Friends, Personal Letters of Dean Acheson*, ed. David S. McLellan and David C. Acheson (New York: Dodd, Mead, 1980), p. 31; Louis D. Brandeis, *The Curse of Bigness: Miscellaneous Papers of Louis D. Brandeis*, ed. Osmond K. Fraenkel (Port Washington, N.Y.: Kennikat Press, 1965), p. 324.

25. Felix Frankfurter, *Of Law and Men: Papers and Addresses of Felix Frankfurter, 1939–1956*, ed. Philip Elman (New York: Harcourt, Brace, 1956), pp. 234–35.

26. Schlesinger *The Age of Roosevelt: The Politics of Upheaval*, p. 488. Later in his life Byrnes had no objection to using Jefferson's views on states' rights to argue against the social reforms inherent in the *Brown v. Board of Education* decision (1954). In a lengthy dissent written for *U.S. News and World Report*, Byrnes wrote, "It is agreed that the average Negro child, having had little training at home, does not possess the training of the average white child in the same grade and age group. Shall the white children be held back to help the Negroes progress? . . . Tragic as may be the consequences in destroying the public-school system in the South, more frightening are the consequences of the trend of the present Court to destroy the powers of the forty-eight States" ("The Supreme Court Must Be Curbed," *USNWR*, 18 May 1956, pp. 50–58).

27. William O. Douglas, *An Almanac of Liberty* (Garden City, N.Y.: Doubleday, 1954), p. 164, and *The Right of the People* (Garden City, N.Y.: Doubleday, 1958), p. 19.

28. Bowers, *My Life*, pp. 180, 198, 324; Roger K. Newman, *Hugo Black: A Biography* (New York: Pantheon Books, 1994), pp. 129, 143–44, 278, 363, 405n, 449, 452–53, 659 n. 1. Ironically, despite his rhetoric in favor of liberating the masses from economic slav-

ery, Black had joined the Ku Klux Klan in 1923 and was elected to the Senate in 1926 with their backing. He eventually left the Klan but was never completely forthright in his explanation for joining the group and in recalling their critical electoral support (pp. 89–100, 256–61).

29. Paul K. Conkin, *The Southern Agrarians* (Knoxville: University of Tennessee Press, 1988), pp. 1–2, and chap. 3; John Crowe Ransom, "Reconstructed but Unregenerate," in Twelve Southerners, *I'll Take My Stand: The South and the Agrarian Tradition* (New York: Peter Smith, 1951), pp. x, 19, 26–27; Robert Bain, Joseph M. Flora, and Louis D. Rubin Jr., eds., *Southern Writers: A Biographical Dictionary* (Baton Rouge: Louisiana State University Press, 1979), pp. 114, 369, 444.

30. Frank Lawrence Owsley, "The Irrepressible Conflict," in *I'll Take My Stand*, pp. 62, 69, 85–87; Oliver Perry Chitwood and Frank Lawrence Owsley, *A Short History of the American People* (New York: D. Van Nostrand, 1945), vol. 1 *(1492–1865)*, pp. 279–80, 286, 290. In fairness it should be noted that Owsley's views on racial matters were not necessarily shared by the other contributors to *I'll Take My Stand* (see Conkin, *The Southern Agrarians*, pp. 64, 169–71). For further evidence of Owsley's harsh views on racial matters see his "Scottsboro: the Third Crusade, the Sequel to Abolition and Reconstruction," *AR* 1 (June 1933): 257–85.

31. Frank Lawrence Owsley, "The Foundations of Democracy," in *Who Owns America?: A New Declaration of Independence*, ed. Herbert Agar and Allen Tate (Boston: Houghton Mifflin, 1936), p. 54; Allen Tate, "Where Are the People?" *AR* 2 (December 1933): 231–37, and "Notes on Liberty and Property," *AR* 6 (March 1936): 598, 607–8. A slightly altered version of this essay appeared in Agar and Tate, eds., *Who Owns America?* pp. 80–93.

32. Michael O'Brien, *The Idea of the American South, 1920–1941* (Baltimore: Johns Hopkins University Press, 1979), p. 156; Herbert Agar, *The People's Choice: From Washington to Harding, a Study in Democracy* (Boston: Houghton Mifflin, 1933), pp. 19–28, 41.

33. Allen Tate, "Life in the Old South," *NR* 59 (10 July 1929): 211–12; Ulrich Bonnel Phillips, *The Course of the South to Secession: An Interpretation by Ulrich Bonnel Phillips*, ed. E. Merton Coulter (Gloucester, Mass.: Peter Smith, 1958), pp. viii, 60–61. Phillips shared the racist tendencies of many Jeffersonians, writing in 1909 that "Thomas Jefferson, in his *Notes on Virginia* (Query 14), characterized negroes as improvident, sensuous, inconstant, well endowed in memory, poor in reasoning power and dull in imagination. Few, aside from Jefferson, thought it necessary to describe the obvious" (*The Economic and Political Essays of the Ante-Bellum South* [New York: Burt Franklin, 1970], p. 10).

34. Christopher Caldwell, "The Poet as Con Artist," *Weekly Standard*, 15 March 1999, pp. 29–39; Noel Stock, *Poet in Exile: Ezra Pound* (New York: Barnes and Noble, 1964), pp. 194–99.

35. J. J. Wilhelm, *Ezra Pound, The Tragic Years: 1925–1972* (University Park: Pennsylvania State University Press, 1994), pp. 80–81, 97, 135, 242; Ezra Pound, "America and the Second World War," in *Impact: Essays on Ignorance and the Decline of American Civilization*, ed. Noel Stock (Chicago: Henry Regnery, 1960), pp. 188, 194; Pound, "An Introduction to the Economic Nature of the United States," in Stock, ed., *Impact*, pp. 35–36; Pound, "W. E. Woodward, Historian," also in Stock, ed., *Impact*, p. 258.

36. Wilhelm, *Ezra Pound, The Tragic Years*, p. 79; Ezra Pound, *"Dear Uncle George": The Correspondence Between Ezra Pound and Congressman Tinkham of Massachusetts*, ed.

Philip J. Burns (Orono: National Poetry Foundation, University of Maine, 1996), pp. 73, 112.

37. Ezra Pound, *The Cantos of Ezra Pound* (New York: New Directions Books, 1948), pp. 31–36; William M. Chace, *The Political Identities of Ezra Pound and T. S. Eliot* (Stanford: Stanford University Press, 1973), p. 69; Tim Redman, *Ezra Pound and Italian Fascism* (Cambridge: Cambridge University Press, 1991), p. 246; Ezra Pound, *"I Cease Not to Yowl": Ezra Pound's Letters to Olivia Rossetti Agresti*, ed. Demetres P. Tryphonopoulos and Leon Surette (Urbana and Chicago: University of Illinois Press, 1998), p. 169; "Pound Gets Standing Ovation on Nostalgic Visit to Hamilton," *NYT*, 9 June 1969, p. 67.

38. David Haven Blake, "Exile and the Republic: Thomas McGrath and the Legacy of Jefferson's America," *Prospects, an Annual Journal of American Cultural Studies* 23 (1998): 28; William Carlos Williams, *In the American Grain* (Norfolk, Conn.: New Directions, 1939), pp. 143, 190–205.

39. William Carlos Williams, *The Autobiography of William Carlos Williams* (New York: Random House, 1951), p. 391; idem, *Paterson* (New York: New Directions, 1992), pp. 67, 70; idem, *In the American Grain*, p. 195; Robert Lowell, "Paterson II," *NAT* 166 (19 June 1948): 692–94. In October 1945, the city of Paterson acquired for $450,000 the property owned by the Society for Establishing Useful Manufactures. The city had attempted for almost a century to dissolve the state charter that granted the corporation a perpetual exemption from taxes on assessments up to $4 million. The original seven hundred–acre site selected by Hamilton was purchased for $8,320 from Dutch farmers and named in honor of New Jersey's Governor William Paterson, who signed the corporation's charter. The project was a failure and Hamilton withdrew from the effort after one year. "Paterson Buys Society Hamilton Founded and Ends Long Fight on Its Tax Exemption," *NYT*, 25 October 1945, p. 23.

40. Rosemary and Stephen Vincent Benet, *A Book of Americans* (New York: Farrar and Rinehart, 1933), pp. 39, 42–43. Of Burr, the authors wrote, "He shot great Hamilton, 'tis true / (He had some provocation, too.) / And as Vice-President he sat / (But men are seldom hanged for that)." See p. 45. In *America* (1944), Stephen Vincent Benet described Hamilton as "brilliant, fluent, attractive, a brave soldier, an able writer, a great financier." Hamilton's mind "turned toward industry and capital. He had no particular belief in the people — he thought they should be guided and ruled by men more intelligent than they. He admitted his liking for 'the rich, the well-born, and the well-bred.'" While Hamilton was "not an equalitarian," it would be an error to think of him as "anything but the revolutionary which he was." Benet argued that "the adoption of the Constitution which made the United States possible owes as much to Hamilton as it does to any one man." See Stephen Vincent Benet, *America* (New York: Farrar and Rinehart, 1944), p. 54.

41. Carl Sandburg, *The People, Yes* (New York: Harcourt, Brace, 1936), pp. 52–53. A sizable number of writers disposed to admire Jefferson over Hamilton have won the Pulitzer Prize; this would have pleased Joseph Pulitzer, for whom it is named. Claude Bowers, whose *Jefferson and Hamilton* as well as *The Tragic Era* narrowly missed winning the prize, observed that Pulitzer "revered" Jefferson (see Bowers, *My Life*, pp. 111, 127–28).

42. John Dos Passos, *The Ground We Stand On: Some Examples from the History of a Political Creed* (New York; Harcourt, Brace, 1941), pp. 385, 404–5; idem, *The Head and the Heart of Thomas Jefferson* (Garden City, N.Y.: Doubleday, 1954), pp. 363, 367, 381, 407, 418; idem, *The Men Who Made the Nation* (Garden City, N.Y.: Doubleday, 1957), pp. 285–95; Dumas Malone, "While American History Was Marching On," *NYT Book Review,* 10 February 1957, p. 4. The inquisition against the whiskey boys refers to the effort of Washington and Hamilton in 1794 to enforce an excise tax against farmers in western Pennsylvania who were refusing to pay a tax on whiskey and briefly engaged in violent acts of protest.

43. Robert Irving Warshow, *Alexander Hamilton: First American Business Man* (New York: Greenberg, 1931), p. v; I. F. Stone, "Patroon Schuyler's Son-in-Law," *NAT* 149, 20 (11 November 1939): 530–31.

44. William Lemke, *You and Your Money* (Philadelphia: Dorrance, 1938), dedication page and author biography; Peterson, *Lincoln in American Memory,* pp. 252–53; Lyon Gardiner Tyler, "William and Mary College as Expressing in Its Origin, and in Its Subsequent Influences, the American Principle of Democracy," *WMQ,* 2d ser., vol. 15, no. 3 (July 1935): 292; Charles Maurice Wiltse, *The Jeffersonian Tradition in American Democracy* (Chapel Hill: University of North Carolina Press, 1935), pp. 99, 101.

45. Alexander Hamilton, *Hamiltonian Principles: Extracts from the Writings of Alexander Hamilton,* ed. James Truslow Adams (Boston: Little, Brown, 1928), p. xii; James Truslow Adams, *The March of Democracy: A History of the United States* (New York: Charles Scribner's Sons, 1965), vol. 1, *The Rise of the Union,* pp. 266–67; idem, *The Epic of America* (Garden City, N.Y.: Blue Ribbon Books, 1941), pp. 112–13, 134–35, 347; idem, "Jefferson and Hamilton Today: The Dichotomy in American Thought," *AM,* April 1928, p. 447.

46. Dumas Malone, "Jefferson and the New Deal," *Scribner's Magazine,* June 1933, pp. 356–59.

47. "Inscription Is Recut on Hamilton's Tomb," *NYT,* 12 September 1935, p. 28; "Hamilton Honored on 173d Anniversary," *NYT,* 11 January 1930, p. 36.

48. "Capital Pays Tribute to Hamilton," *NYT,* 12 January 1932, p. 25; U.S. George Washington Bicentennial Commission, *Special News Releases Relating to the Life and Times of George Washington* (Washington, D.C.: U.S. Government Printing Office, 1932), 1: 450–54; "Topics of the Times: Hamilton Much at Home," *NYT,* 21 June 1933, p. 16; "Elihu Root Warns of Recovery Plan," *NYT,* 1 July 1934, sec. 2, p. 6.

49. Arthur Krock, "In Washington: Some Contrasts of Jackson and Roosevelt Noted," *NYT,* 14 January 1936, p. 20; William Allen White, "White Sees Party Ready for Rebirth," *NYT,* 8 June 1936, p. 2; "Butler Calls Tax on Rich Malicious," *NYT,* 2 September 1935, pp. 1, 3; "A Michigan Hamiltonian," *NYT,* 11 April 1936, p. 14.

50. "Glass Is Honored; Praises Hamilton," *NYT,* 31 October 1937, p. 5.

51. "Republican Ideals Found in Patriots," *NYT,* 27 November 1939, p. 12. See also "Not Quite Forgotten," *NYT,* 28 November 1939, p. 24; "Republicans Push 'Party-Ideal' Drive," *NYT,* 2 December 1939, p. 10; John H. Davis, *The Guggenheims: An American Epic* (New York: William Morrow, 1978), p. 192.

52. Van Wyck Brooks, *Opinions of Oliver Allston* (New York: E. P. Dutton, 1941), p. 146; "Topics of the Times," *NYT,* 21 November 1941, p. 16. In 1950 Brooks suggested again that Hamilton was not a true American, arguing that he "retained the political and

social ideals of England, and he represented those who wished to maintain the system of England" (*The World of Washington Irving* [New York: E. P. Dutton, 1950], p. 40). In his *Makers and Finders: A History of the Writer in America, 1800–1915*, Brooks wrote that Hamilton regarded the people as a great beast while Jefferson believed in freedom and the brotherhood of man (see *The Confident Years: 1885–1915* [New York: E. P. Dutton, 1952] 5: 584.

53. "Topics of the Times," *NYT*, 6 February 1943, p. 12; Earl Browder, *The People's Front* (New York: International Publishers, 1938), pp. 254–56; Earl Browder, "Jefferson and the People's Revolution," in *The Heritage of Jefferson*, Claude G. Bowers, Earl Browder, and Francis Franklin (New York: International Publishers, 1944), pp. 36–37; Alan Schaffer, *Vito Marcantonio, Radical in Congress* (Syracuse, N.Y.: Syracuse University Press, 1966), p. 199. Vito Marcantonio's mentor, New York mayor Fiorello LaGuardia, admired the "distinguished" Hamilton. LaGuardia noted in 1941 that "we are closer now to the Hamiltonian theory than ever before" and blamed Jefferson's states' rights doctrine for the confusion "from which we have not yet emerged." See "Mayor Pays Tribute to Hamilton, Clinton," *NYT*, 15 January 1941, p. 25, and "Topics of the Times," *NYT*, 16 January 1941, p. 20.

54. Lewis Nichols, "The Play," *NYT*, 30 January 1943, p. 11; "Sgt. Kingsley Detached," *NYT*, 6 April 1943, p. 24; Sidney Kingsley, *The Patriots: A Play in a Prologue and Three Acts* (New York: Random House, 1943), passim, and Nena Couch, ed., *Sidney Kingsley: Five Prize-winning Plays* (Columbus: Ohio State University Press, 1995), pp. 172–73. In the aftermath of the play's critical success, Warner Brothers Studios announced that they were planning to produce a film version of *The Patriots*, but it was never made. It was produced for television in 1963 with Charlton Heston as Jefferson (see Couch, ed., *Sidney Kingsley: Five Prize-winning Plays*, pp. xxv–xxvi).

Hamilton has been a central figure in a surprising number of plays and films. Two plays focusing on him were produced in the first half of the twentieth century. The first, *Hamilton: A Play in Four Acts*, opened at the Apollo Theater in Atlantic City, New Jersey, on 6 September 1917 and then made its New York City debut on 17 September 1917. Written by the noted actor George Arliss (1868–1946) and Mary P. Hamlin, it revolves around Hamilton's relationship with Maria Reynolds and the courage Hamilton demonstrates in dealing with the incident. It includes a ludicrous scene where Jefferson praises "Citizen" Hamilton's response to the affair as "the bravest thing a man ever did" and "a display of personal courage that will rouse the admiration of the world." According to the authors, Hamiltonphiles Henry Cabot Lodge and Nicholas Murray Butler approved of the story line. It was adapted as a film in 1931 by Warner Brothers, with Arliss playing the role of Hamilton. A review of the film in the *New York Herald Tribune* observed that it was "hardly likely" to "appeal to such ardent Jeffersonian Democrats as Claude Bowers." Toward the end of his life Arliss wrote, "I had always had a great admiration for the man. I think he did more for his country than many of the others of his period whose names are better remembered, including Thomas Jefferson." Before the film was produced, Arliss decided to quiz a group of Americans to gauge their knowledge of Hamilton. He found that the name "meant nothing . . . only one of them seemed to know anything about him and he said he wasn't sure what Hamilton did." See Mary P. Hamlin and George Arliss, *Hamilton: A Play in Four Acts* (Boston: Walter H. Baker, 1918), pp. v–vii, 160; "Early

American Bigwigs on the Screen," *LD* 111, 1 (3 October 1931): 20–21; George Arliss, *Up the Years from Bloomsbury, An Autobiography* (Boston: Little, Brown, 1928), pp. 271–74, and Arliss, *My Ten Years in the Studios* (Boston: Little, Brown, 1940), p. 155.

The second play was *Hamilton: A Poetic Drama in Three Acts,* written by Chard Powers Smith. Smith wanted to portray Hamilton's "passionate political idealism" and the "fatal effect" that it had on his family and friends. This same idealism, Smith believed, ultimately cost Hamilton his life. "It is a portrait of a man, in whom one of the most spectacular careers of public service in history was exactly the measure of the depth of his personal tragedy." The focus of the play is Hamilton's rivalry with Burr, but it also includes passages dealing with his struggles with Jefferson, the Reynolds affair, and his financial plans for the new nation, all of which the author attempts to raise to the level of a Shakespearean tragedy. The *New York Times* concluded that Smith wrote "very good verse" but that "the fire necessary for poetic historical drama simply is not latent in the material." See Chard Powers Smith, *Hamilton: A Poetic Drama in Three Acts* (New York: Coward-McCann, 1930), foreword and passim; "Poetic and Other Drama," *NYT Book Review,* 10 August 1930, p. 10.

In the late 1930s, Dorothy Thompson sold a screenplay to MGM Studios about the life of Hamilton. It was never produced, though she described it as "the kind of motion picture America ought to be seeing." Hamilton's other film appearances include *The Beautiful Mrs. Reynolds* (1918); *My Own United States* (1918); *Janice Meredith* (1924); *Magnificent Doll* (1946), with Ginger Rogers as Dolley Madison; *The Duel* (1957), an NBC television movie with E. G. Marshall as Hamilton; *The Adams Chronicles* (1976), a PBS television miniseries; *George Washington* (1984, 1986), a CBS television miniseries; *Liberty! The American Revolution* (1997), a PBS miniseries; *The Crossing* (2000), an Arts and Entertainment Network television movie; and *The Duel* (2000), a PBS documentary. See Peter Kurth, *American Cassandra: The Life of Dorothy Thompson* (Boston: Little, Brown, 1990), p. 298, and the Internet Movie Database <http://us.imdb.com>.

55. "The Patriots," *Newsweek,* 8 February 1943, p. 82; "New Play in Manhattan," *Time,* 8 February 1943, p. 36; "Critics Prize Won by 'The Patriots,'" *NYT,* 14 April 1943, p. 25; Couch, ed., *Sidney Kingsley: Five Prize-winning Plays,* pp. xiv, xxv; Norman Cousins, "Jefferson and Hamilton," *SR,* 17 April 1943, p. 26.

56. "Albert Gallatin," *Fortune,* November 1942, p. 128; "The Reluctant Democrat," *Fortune,* December 1943, p. 154; Dumas Malone, "Mr. Jefferson to Mr. Roosevelt, an Imaginary Letter," *VQR* 19, 2 (Spring 1943): 168, 172–73.

57. Jeanette P. Nichols and Roy F. Nichols, *The Republic of the United States: A History* (New York: D. Appleton-Century, 1942), vol. 1, *1493–1865,* p. 287; Harold Underwood Faulkner, *American Political and Social History* (New York: Appleton-Century-Crofts, 1952), p. 289 (this text, which included the reference to the reactionary wave, was published in various editions throughout the 1940s); Charles A. Beard, "We, the People," *Life,* 17 January 1944, p. 47; Gerald W. Johnson, *American Heroes and Hero-Worship* (New York: Harper and Brothers, 1943), p. 73; Arthur C. Millspaugh, *Democracy, Efficiency, Stability: An Appraisal of American Government* (Washington, D.C.: Brookings Institution, 1942), p. 6; "Merle Curti, Pulitzer Prize–Winning Historian," *Los Angeles Times,* 14 March 1996, p. 20; Merle Curti, *The Growth of American Thought* (New York: Harper and Brothers, 1943), p. 192. The great beast quote emigrated to Europe in 1955, when it appeared in a book written for British undergraduates by Frank

Thistlethwaite, a professor at Cambridge University; see *The Great Experiment: An Introduction to the History of the American People* (Cambridge: Cambridge University Press, 1955), p. 56.

58. Charles Beard, quoted in Saul K. Padover, *The Genius of America: Men Whose Ideas Shaped Our Civilization* (New York: McGraw-Hill, 1960), p. 69.

7. HAIL COLUMBIA!

1. Herbert Lee Williams, *The Newspaperman's President, Harry S. Truman* (Chicago: Nelson-Hall, 1984), pp. 12, 101; Bowers, *My Life*, jacket cover; Harry S. Truman, *The Autobiography of Harry S. Truman*, ed. Robert H. Ferrell (Boulder: Colorado Associated University Press, 1980), p. 30.

2. Harry S. Truman, *Where the Buck Stops: The Personal and Private Writings of Harry S. Truman*, ed. Margaret Truman (New York: Warner Books, 1989), pp. 178, 180, 211, 214, 272, 300–302; Harry S. Truman, *Off the Record: The Private Papers of Harry S. Truman*, ed. Robert H. Ferrell (New York: Harper and Row, 1980), p. 248.

3. Harry S. Truman, *Memoirs by Harry S. Truman* (Garden City, N.Y.: Doubleday, 1956), vol. 2, *Years of Trial and Hope*, p. 172; *PPP, Harry S. Truman, Containing the Public Messages, Speeches, and Statements of the President, January 1 to December 31, 1948* (Washington, D.C.: U.S. Government Printing Office, 1964), pp. 147–48, 770–71.

4. Leonard White, *The Federalists: A Study in Administrative History, 1789–1801* (New York: Macmillan, 1948), pp. 125–26; "Topics of the Times," *NYT*, 12 February 1947, p. 24.

5. James Reston, "Who Initiates Armed Action Still Senate Pact Problem," *NYT*, 26 March 1949, p. 4, and "148-Year-Old Issue Is Raised on President's Pact Powers," *NYT*, 3 May 1949, p. 6.

6. "Fiscal Pool Urged upon Democracies," *NYT*, 12 January 1948, p. 29; Harold C. Urey, "Alexander Hamilton, How Would He Apply His Ideas Today?" *VSD* 27, 14 (1 May 1961): 431–33.

7. *FED*, no. 70, pp. 472, 476; James Chace, *Acheson: The Secretary of State Who Created the American World* (New York: Simon and Schuster, 1998), p. 276; John Lewis Gaddis, *The United States and the End of the Cold War: Implications, Reconsiderations, Provocations* (New York: Oxford University Press, 1992), pp. 54–55; Hans J. Morgenthau, *In Defense of the National Interest: A Critical Examination of American Foreign Policy* (New York: Alfred A. Knopf, 1951), pp. 13–16; Les Ledbetter, "Hans J. Morgenthau Is Dead at 76," *NYT*, 20 July 1980, pp. 1, 34.

8. Felix Gilbert, *To the Farewell Address: Ideas of Early American Foreign Policy* (Princeton: Princeton University Press, 1961), pp. 111, 136; Peter B. Flint, "Felix Gilbert, Influential Author, Historian and Teacher, Dies at 85," *NYT*, 16 February 1991, p. 14. Another admirer of Hamilton's foreign policy prowess was Samuel Flagg Bemis, who described Hamilton as "that great American statesman" and viewed him as the father of the "American idea of limitation of armaments." Bemis wrote in the wake of the Washington Naval Disarmament Conference of 1921, "The student of American history must recognize that the germ of that idea sprang from the brain of Alexander Hamilton." Bemis also credited Hamilton for the Jay Treaty of 1794 with Great Britain, "which was really Hamilton's treaty" and one that "saved American nationality." See his "Alexander Hamilton and the Limitation of Armaments," in *American For-*

eign Policy and the Blessings of Liberty, and Other Essays, ed. Samuel Flagg Bemis (New Haven: Yale University Press, 1962), pp. 196–208, and idem, *A Diplomatic History of the United States* (New York: Henry Holt, 1936), p. 103.

9. Arthur H. Vandenberg, "Alexander Hamilton," *Life,* 7 July 1947, p. 65.

10. Duane Tanabaum, *The Bricker Amendment Controversy: A Test of Eisenhower's Political Leadership* (Ithaca, N.Y.: Cornell University Press, 1988), pp. ix–x, 221; R. Gordon Hoxie, "Presidential Leadership and American Foreign Policy: Some Reflections on the Taiwan Issue, with Particular Considerations on Alexander Hamilton, Dwight Eisenhower, and Jimmy Carter," *Presidential Studies Quarterly* 9, 2 (Spring 1979): 137–38; *Congressional Record,* Senate, Senator John Bricker, 4 March 1957, 85th Congress, 1st session, vol. 103, part 3, p. 2988.

11. "Hamilton Memorial Unveiled in Chicago," *NYT,* 7 July 1952, p. 35; Dumas Malone, "Was Washington the Greatest American?" *NYT Magazine,* 16 February 1958, p. 11; "Nixon Says Votes Will Rate Benson," *NYT,* 15 October 1956, p. 15; Robert D. Dean, "Masculinity as Ideology: John F. Kennedy and the Domestic Politics of Foreign Policy," *Diplomatic History* 22, 1 (Winter 1998): 44 n. 28; "Topics of the Times," *NYT,* 22 February 1953, sec. 4, p. 8. The Hamilton memorial in Chicago was erected in Lincoln Park after the city received a $1 million contribution from the heiress Kate Buckingham, who considered him "one of the least appreciated of the great Americans." The 130-square-foot memorial included a 70-foot pylon of black granite towering over a 13-foot statue of Hamilton. In 1993 the entire site was remodeled, downscaled, in order to fulfill Buckingham's original request for "a simple monument to the man — nothing else." That same year it was reported that the monument had become a gathering place for vagrants, drug users, drunks and graffiti artists. "Up Goes Hamilton," *Time,* 9 July 1951, p. 66, and Raymond R. Coffey, "Hamilton's Down, but He's Not Out," *Chicago Sun–Times,* 21 October 1993, p. 3.

12. Adlai E. Stevenson, *The Papers of Adlai E. Stevenson,* ed. Walter Johnson, 8 vols. (Boston: Little, Brown, 1972–1979), vol. 3, *Governor of Illinois, 1949–1953,* pp. 170, 272–73.

13. "Text of Stevenson's Address on His Party's New Role in Nation," *NYT,* 15 February 1953, p. 67; Johnson, ed., *The Papers of Adlai E. Stevenson,* vol. 4, *"Let's Talk Sense to the American People," 1952–1955,* pp. 144, 191, 299, 458, and vol. 7, *Continuing Education and the Unfinished Business of American Society, 1957–1961,* pp. 391, 454–56; Julian Boyd, *Number 7: Alexander Hamilton's Secret Attempts to Control American Foreign Policy* (Princeton: Princeton University Press, 1964). At the time *Number 7* was published, Boyd was the president of the American Historical Association. Though he stopped short of accusing Hamilton of treason, he did state that Hamilton committed "almost the gravest offense of which a cabinet officer can be guilty" and that his actions were "far indeed beyond the limits of honorable conduct in public office." See "Historian Assails Hamilton Action," *NYT,* 30 November 1964, p. 30, and "The Calculated Deceit," *Time,* 18 December 1964, p. 95. Reaction to Boyd's book was generally positive. Cecelia Kenyon writing in the *Nation* and Esmond Wright in the *Saturday Review* found it a persuasive account. See Kenyon, "Fatherly Sedition," *NAT* 200, 7 (15 February 1965): 172–76, and Wright, "A Code Name and a London Contact," *SR,* 28 November 1964, pp. 22–23. For a refutation of Boyd's argument, see Gilbert L. Lycan, *Alexander Hamilton and American Foreign Policy: A Design for Greatness* (Norman: University of Oklahoma Press, 1970), pp. 122–23. It should be noted

that Thomas Jefferson engaged in duplicitous behavior as a member of Washington's cabinet. In 1793, the secretary of state covertly assisted Andre Michaux, an agent of the French government. Operating under the cover of a scientific exploration, Michaux hoped to incite attacks against British and Spanish possessions in North America. By providing assistance to him, Jefferson defied his own government's policy designed to prevent such attacks. Jefferson persisted in concealing his role in the affair years after the fact. See Stephen F. Knott, *Secret and Sanctioned: Covert Operations and the American Presidency* (New York: Oxford University Press, 1996), p. 67.

14. Eric F. Goldman, "Books That Changed America," *SR,* 4 July 1953, pp. 8, 37–38.

15. "Philosophical Group Eulogizes Hamilton," *NYT,* 15 November 1957, p. 18; *Proceedings of the American Philosophical Society,* 102, 2 (April 1958); Louis M. Hacker, *Alexander Hamilton in the American Tradition* (New York: McGraw-Hill, 1957), pp. viii–x; J. H. Powell, "Two New Studies of Alexander Hamilton," *SR,* 19 January 1957, pp. 38–39. James Madison's biographer Irving Brant argued that the nation should have celebrated Hamilton's bicentennial in 1955 (see "Two Birthdays," *NYT Magazine,* 19 December 1954, p. 8). Some historians still adhere to the 1757 birth date. See for instance McDonald, *Alexander Hamilton,* p. 366 n. 8.

16. Mitchell, *Alexander Hamilton: Youth to Maturity, 1755–1788;* Joan Cook, "Broadus Mitchell, 95, Professor, Historian, and Hamilton Authority," *NYT,* 30 April 1988, p. 11; Broadus Mitchell, "Appraising Hamilton," *VQR* 33, 3 (summer 1957): 459; Keith Hutchison, "Refurbishing Hamilton," *NAT* 184, 19 (11 May 1957): 421, and "The Man Who Saved the Nation," *NAT* 184, 7 (16 February 1957): 142.

17. Miller, *Alexander Hamilton: Portrait in Paradox,* p. xii; Harold C. Syrett, "Maker and Shaper of a Nation," *NYT Book Review,* 22 November 1959, p. 67; Brown, *Charles Beard and the Constitution: A Critical Analysis of "An Economic Interpretation of the Constitution";* McDonald, *We the People.*

18. Richard Hofstadter, William Miller, Daniel Aaron, *The United States: The History of a Republic* (Englewood Cliffs, N.J.: Prentice-Hall, 1957), pp. 130, 147–48, 153–54; Louis Hartz, *The Liberal Tradition in America: An Interpretation of American Political Thought Since the Revolution* (New York: Harcourt, Brace, 1955), p. 111.

19. Michael Kammen, *Mystic Chords of Memory: The Transformation of Tradition in American Culture* (New York: Vintage Books, 1993), pp. 588–89; "Karl E. Mundt Dead at 74; Ex-South Dakota Senator," *NYT,* 17 August 1974, p. 26; Robert A. Devine, *Blowing on the Wind: The Nuclear Test Ban Debate, 1954–1960* (New York: Oxford University Press, 1978), p. 89; *Congressional Record,* Senate, Senator Karl Mundt, 4 March 1957, 85th Congress, 1st session, vol. 103, part 3, p. 2973; *Senate Documents,* 85th Congress, 2d session, vol. 1, miscellaneous 1, *Final Report of the Alexander Hamilton Bicentennial Commission,* 30 April 1958, p. ix.

20. "Country Will Honor 2 Famous Americans," *NYT,* 12 January 1955, p. 25; Goldman, "Books That Changed America," p. 37; "Historians Told Stalin Framed Soviet Policy When Near Death," *NYT,* 29 December 1955, p. 2; "Hamilton Day Jan. 11," *NYT,* 17 September 1956, p. 16; a copy of Eisenhower's bicentennial proclamation can be found in Alexander Hamilton, *The Basic Ideas of Alexander Hamilton,* ed. Richard B. Morris (New York: Washington Square Press, 1965), pp. vi–vii; U.S. Senate, *Final Report of the Alexander Hamilton Bicentennial Commission,* pp. 23–24.

21. U.S. Senate, *Final Report of the Alexander Hamilton Bicentennial Commission,* pp. 11–

12; "Ceremonies Hail Hamilton's Birth," *NYT*, 12 January 1957, p. 22; "Hamilton Is Hailed as Guide for Today," *NYT*, 11 January 1957, p. 17; *Congressional Record*, House, Extension of Remarks of Senator Karl Mundt, 30 January 1957, 85th Congress, 1st session, vol. 103, part 1, p. 1339; George M. Humphrey, *The Basic Papers of George M. Humphrey as Secretary of the Treasury, 1953–1957*, ed. Nathaniel R. Howard (Cleveland, Ohio: Western Reserve Historical Society, 1965), p. 632.

22. "Ceremonies Mark Hamilton's Birth," *NYT*, 5 August 1957, p. 22; "Topics of the Times," *NYT*, 11 January 1957, p. 22.

23. Thomas Lask, "Publishing: Finishing Alexander Hamilton," *NYT*, 8 June 1979, sec. 3, p. 26; "Columbia to Edit Hamilton Papers," *NYT*, 8 June 1955, p. 31; Jacob Ernest Cooke, "Historian by Happenstance: One Scholar's Odyssey," *WMQ*, 3d ser., vol. 52, no. 3 (July 1995): 467; U.S. Senate, *Final Report of the Alexander Hamilton Bicentennial Commission*, pp. 48–50. Columbia University Press also published Alexander Hamilton, *The Law Practice of Alexander Hamilton: Documents and Commentary*, ed. Julius Goebel Jr. and Joseph H. Smith, 5 vols. (New York: Columbia University Press, 1964–1981).

24. "Hamilton Papers to Be Published," *NYT*, 19 November 1961, p. 84; Clinton Rossiter, "Apprenticeship of a Master-Builder," *NYT Book Review*, 19 November 1961, p. 1; "An Unlucky Honest Man," *Time*, 22 December 1961, p. 54; Naomi Bliven, "Founding Fathers," *New Yorker*, 3 November 1962, p. 236.

25. Dumas Malone, "Tapping the Wisdom of the Founding Fathers," *NYT Magazine*, 27 May 1956, p. 39; John C. Livingston, "Alexander Hamilton and the American Tradition," *Midwest Journal of Political Science* 1, 3–4 (November 1957): 210; Chester J. Pach and Elmo Richardson, *The Presidency of Dwight D. Eisenhower* (Lawrence: University Press of Kansas, 1991), pp. 34–35.

26. Dumas Malone, "Reign of Witches," *NYT Book Review*, 5 August 1956, p. 3; letters to the editor, *NYT Book Review*, 9 September 1956, p. 30.

27. *Congressional Record*, House, extension of remarks by Representative Frederic R. Coudert Jr., 4 March 1957, 85th Congress, 1st session, vol. 103, part 3, p. 3071; Bower Aly, "Alexander Hamilton's Year," *Quarterly Journal of Speech* 43, 4 (December 1957): 427; U.S. Senate, *Final Report of the Alexander Hamilton Bicentennial Commission*, p. x. The Hamilton Papers Project at Columbia University was the first to trace the great beast quote back to the original source, *Memoir of Theophilus Parsons*. See "Communication," *APSR* 58, 1 (March 1964): 100, and William Ander Smith, "Henry Adams, Alexander Hamilton, and the American People as a 'Great Beast,'" p. 216.

28. Charles L. Black Jr., *The People and the Court: Judicial Review in a Democracy* (New York: Macmillan, 1960), pp. 75–76.

29. Arthur M. Schlesinger Jr., *A Thousand Days, John F. Kennedy in the White House* (Boston: Houghton Mifflin, 1965), p. 733; Henry Graff, "A Short Life of Liberty," *NYT Book Review*, 15 April 1962, p. 16; James MacGregor Burns, *Presidential Government: The Crucible of Leadership* (Boston: Houghton Mifflin, 1965), p. x.

30. John F. Kennedy, *Profiles in Courage* (New York: Harper and Row, 1956), pp. 25–26, 30; "Boarding Rule Outlined by Hamilton in 1790," *NYT*, 25 October 1962, p. 21; *PPP, John F. Kennedy, Containing the Public Messages, Speeches, and Statements of the President, January 1 to December 31, 1962* (Washington, D.C.: U.S. Government Printing Office, 1963), pp. 537–39, 618.

31. "A Historic Homestead Awaits a Shift of Position," *NYT*, 20 September 1998, sec. 14, p. 6; Alexander Burnham, "Hamilton's Home to Regain Glory," *NYT*, 6 May 1962, p. 136.

32. "Hamilton Grange Backed as U.S. Site," *NYT*, 12 May 1960, p. 28; "Historic Landmark," *NYT*, 22 December 1960, p. 22; "Javits and Lindsay See Hamilton Home," *NYT*, 7 December 1961, p. 39; Burnham, "Hamilton's Home to Regain Glory," p. 136.

33. "Mr. Hamilton's Ghost," *NYT*, 28 April 1960, p. 34; "Mr. Javits to the Rescue," *NYT*, 1 June 1960, p. 38; William M. Blair, "House Unit Votes Memorial in City," *NYT*, 15 March 1962, p. 37; *Congressional Record*, House, Representative John P. Saylor, 16 April 1962, 87th Congress, 2d session, vol. 108, part 5, p. 6679.

34. Anthony Lewis, "Senators Debate a Ban on Poll Tax," *NYT*, 15 March 1962, p. 71; *Congressional Record*, Senate, Senator Strom Thurmond, 22 March 1962, 87th Congress, 2d session, vol. 108, part 4, p. 4844; *Congressional Record*, Senate, Senator John Sparkman, 23 March 1962, 87th Congress, 2d session, vol. 108, part 4, p. 4925; *Congressional Record*, Senate, Senator Spessard Holland, 27 March 1962, 87th Congress, 2d session, vol. 108, part 4, p. 4845.

35. "Senators Halting Filibuster Blocking Poll Tax Action," *NYT*, 27 March 1962, pp. 1, 21; "Grange Bill Approved," *NYT*, 18 April 1962, p. 27; "Kennedy Makes Home of Hamilton a Shrine," *NYT*, 1 May 1962. As of the year 2000, Hamilton's home was still crammed between an apartment building and a church, despite the 1962 legislation requiring that it be moved to a more open location nearby and restored to its original design. According to the *New York Daily News*, the home was closed in 1992 because "it was falling down." Reopened to visitors in 1997, the house is scheduled to be moved and refurbished in time for its bicentennial in 2002, though many New Yorkers are skeptical this will happen. See "A Day to Remember," *New York Daily News*, 25 May 1998, p. 24. The top floor of the building was unopened to visitors due to structural concerns when I visited in April 2000, and the accessible portions of the home were sparsely furnished. Despite the presence of dedicated National Park Service personnel and the support of the Harlem community, the Grange remains a monument to the nation's neglect of Hamilton.

36. Arthur M. Schlesinger Jr., "The War Between Adams and Hamilton," *NR* 146 (1 January 1962): 16–17; Katherine Hamill, "Was Hamilton the First Keynesian?" *Fortune*, August 1957, pp. 128–29, 142, 146. Schlesinger had been critical of Hamilton in his Pulitzer Prize–winning *Age of Jackson* (1945). In the feud between the "house of Have and the house of Want" (a quote Schlesinger borrowed from his ancestor George Bancroft), Hamilton had represented the interests of the former. Hamilton, Schlesinger argued, "built his church" on the idea that society should be governed by an aristocracy of property. Late in his life Hamilton proposed a Christian Constitutional Society designed to reconcile "the lower classes to inequality" and to bind them to "absolute obedience to the laws." Writing in his memoir *A Life in the Twentieth Century: Innocent Beginnings, 1917–1950*, Schlesinger observed, "Looking back, I think I did Hamilton, Adams and Clay a good deal less than justice in *The Age of Jackson*" and added, "the Hamiltonians had a sounder conception of the role of government and a more constructive policy of economic development than the antistatist Jacksonians." See *The Age of Jackson*, epigraph and pp. 12, 16, and idem, *A Life in the Twentieth Century: Innocent Beginnings, 1917–1950* (Boston: Houghton, Mifflin, 2000), pp. 366–67.

37. Russell Kirk, *The Conservative Mind, from Burke to Santayana* (Chicago: Henry Regnery, 1953), pp. 64–70, 75.

38. Vincent Miller, "Perspective on the Founders," *National Review*, 12 February 1963, pp. 117–19 and "Whose Hamilton?" *National Review*, 19 May 1964, pp. 407–8; Clinton Rossiter, *Conservatism in America* (New York: Alfred A. Knopf, 1955), pp. 113, 120, 241; "A Prophet Revisited," *Time*, 20 March 1964, pp. 98–102. Rossiter's endnotes for *Alexander Hamilton and the Constitution* were a great source of information for this book.

39. Trevor Colbourn, "Before the Clash with Aaron Burr," *SR*, 21 April 1962, p. 27; James MacGregor Burns, *The Deadlock of Democracy: Four Party Politics in America* (Englewood Cliffs, N.J.: Prentice-Hall, 1963), pp. 10–11, 335. In 1965 Burns published *Presidential Government*, which opened with a discussion of the "Hamiltonian model" of presidential leadership. It included an odd passage: "In 1805 Aaron Burr, Jefferson's man in New York City whom Hamilton once had criticized for having no 'theory' or 'general principles,' blew out the brains of the Federalist party in the duel on the heights of Weehawken." Perhaps one must allow for some literary license, but this sentence appears to have three errors — the duel was in 1804, by which time Burr was not Jefferson's "man in New York City," and Hamilton wasn't shot in the head (see p. 27).

40. Richard N. Current, T. Harry Williams, Frank Freidel, *American History: A Survey* (New York: Alfred A. Knopf, 1961), p. 190.

41. Barry M. Goldwater, *The Conscience of a Conservative* (Shepherdsville, Ky.: Victor, 1960), p. 38; idem, "A Conservative's Creed," in *Mr. Conservative: Barry Goldwater*, Jack Bell (Garden City, N.Y.: Doubleday, 1962), p. 312; Frank R. Donovan, *The Americanism of Barry Goldwater* (New York: Macfadden-Bartell, 1964), pp. 16, 21; Barry M. Goldwater, *With No Apologies: The Personal and Political Memoirs of United States Senator Barry M. Goldwater* (New York: William Morrow, 1979), pp. 281–82; I. F. Stone, *In a Time of Torment* (New York: Random House, 1967), pp. 40–41.

42. Peterson, *The Jefferson Image in the American Mind;* Dumas Malone, *Jefferson and His Time*, 6 vols. (Boston: Little, Brown, 1948–1981); Merrill D. Peterson, review of *Alexander Hamilton and the Constitution,* by Clinton Rossiter, *WMQ*, 3d ser., vol. 22 (January 1965): 141–44, and review of *Alexander Hamilton in the American Tradition,* by Louis M. Hacker, *WMQ*, 3d ser., vol. 15 (January 1958): 117–120.

43. Levy, *Jefferson and Civil Liberties: The Darker Side*, p. xii. Levy observed that Jefferson "at one time or another supported loyalty oaths; countenanced internment camps for political suspects; drafted a bill of attainder; urged prosecutions for seditious libel; trampled on the Fourth Amendment; condoned military despotism; used the Army to enforce laws in time of peace; censored reading; chose professors for their political opinions" (p. 18). See also Robert W. Tucker and David C. Hendrickson, *Empire of Liberty: The Statecraft of Thomas Jefferson* (New York: Oxford University Press, 1990), pp. 7–8, 167–68, 306 n. 108 for an account of controversial actions undertaken by Jefferson and frequently ignored or minimized by his biographers. Tucker and Hendrickson note that the enforcement of Jefferson's embargo of 1807–1809 was "more draconian than anything attempted by British authorities throughout the years leading up to the American Revolution" (see p. 325 n. 45).

44. Rossiter, *Alexander Hamilton and the Constitution*, p. 331 n. 8; Dumas Malone, "Jefferson, Hamilton, and the Constitution," in *Theory and Practice in American Politics*, ed. William H. Nelson (Chicago: University of Chicago Press, 1964), pp. 13–23; Peterson, "Dumas Malone, an Appreciation," p. 248. James Thomas Flexner stated in his autobiography that Malone told him he was "leaving to younger scholars Jefferson's attitudes and behavior toward slavery, and that he was proud of writing as a Virginian" (*Maverick's Progress: An Autobiography* [New York: Fordham University Press, 1996], p. 407).

45. Sam J. Ervin Jr., "Alexander Hamilton's Phantom," *VSD* 22, 1 (15 October 1955): 23–26.

46. Adrienne Koch, "Hamilton and Power," *Yale Review* 47, 4 (June 1958): 537–51. Koch's essay was reprinted in a somewhat modified form in her *Power, Morals, and the Founding Fathers: Essays in the Interpretation of the American Enlightenment* (Ithaca, N.Y.: Cornell University Press, 1961), pp. 50–80.

47. Richard H. Kohn, *Eagle and Sword: The Federalists and the Creation of the Military Establishment in America, 1783–1802* (New York: Free Press, 1975), pp. xi, xii, 252–55, 272–73, 286, 303.

48. Douglass Adair, *Fame and the Founding Fathers: Essays by Douglass Adair*, ed. Trevor Colbourn (New York: W. W. Norton, 1974), pp. x, 16 n. 14, 281–85.

49. Ibid., pp. 152, 152 n. 17, 156–57.

50. Ibid., pp. 36, 49, 61 n. 87, 68.

51. Gerald Stourzh, *Alexander Hamilton and the Idea of Republican Government* (Stanford: Stanford University Press, 1970), pp. 2–3, 6–7, 128, 131, 164, 203–5, acknowledgments; Harvey Flaumenhaft, review of *Alexander Hamilton and the Idea of Republican Government*, by Gerald Stourzh, *APSR* 67, 2 (June 1973): 637–39.

52. Adrienne Koch, review of *Alexander Hamilton and the Idea of Republican Government*, by Gerald Stourzh, *WMQ*, 3d ser., vol. 28, no. 1 (January 1971): 661–64. For Stourzh's response to Koch's review, see letters to the editor, *WMQ*, 3d ser., vol. 29, no. 4 (October 1972): 669–72.

53. Arthur M. Schlesinger Jr., *The Imperial Presidency* (Boston: Houghton Mifflin, 1973), p. 161; Garry Wills, review of *The Imperial Presidency*, by Arthur M. Schlesinger Jr., *NYT Book Review*, 18 November 1973, p. 1.

54. Thomas F. Eagleton, *War and Presidential Power: A Chronicle of Congressional Surrender* (New York: Liveright, 1974), pp. 6, 25–26.

55. Neil Jumonville, *Henry Steele Commager: Mid-Century Liberalism and the History of the Present* (Chapel Hill: University of North Carolina Press, 1999), pp. 13, 22, 31–32, 35–37, 163, 180–83; Henry Steele Commager, *The Defeat of America: Presidential Power and the National Character* (New York: Simon and Schuster, 1974), pp. 61–63.

56. Jumonville, *Henry Steele Commager*, pp. 22, 34, 36, 62, 183; Allan Nevins, *The Evening Post: A Century of Journalism* (New York: Boni and Liveright, 1922), pp. 9–10, 29; Allan Nevins, *Allan Nevins on History*, ed. Ray Allen Billington (New York: Charles Scribner's Sons, 1975), pp. 10, 28, 45, 263–64, 383.

57. Howard Zinn, *A People's History of the United States* (New York: Harper and Row, 1980), pp. 76, 90, 94–101, 408.

58. James Miller, *"Democracy Is in the Streets": From Port Huron to the Siege of Chicago* (New York: Simon and Schuster, 1987), pp. 264–69; Staughton Lynd, *Class Conflict,*

Slavery, and the United States Constitution (Indianapolis: Bobbs-Merrill, 1967), pp. 9–11, 17, 21, 110–13. There is something of a convergence of opinion among the far right and the far left in America regarding Hamilton. In 1982, Willis A. Carto, the founder and leader of the Liberty Lobby, published *Profiles in Populism*, which stated that Hamilton "collaborated" with "powerful financial interests" and promoted policies designed to "accomplish [the middle class's] descent into poverty and servitude." The book also claimed that Hamilton's party wished to "establish a centralized autocracy." See *Profiles in Populism*, ed. Willis A. Carto (Old Greenwich, Conn.: Flag Press, 1982), pp. 11, 14. See also Lyman Tower Sargent, ed., *Extremism in America: A Reader* (New York: New York University Press, 1995), p. 17.

59. Joan Cook, "Sidney Lens Dies, Activist of the Left," *NYT*, 30 June 1986, sec. D, p. 23; Sidney Lens, *Radicalism in America* (New York: Thomas A. Crowell, 1969), pp. 50–51; Wolfgang Saxon, "F. Lundburg, 92, Author Who Wrote of the Rich," *NYT*, 3 March 1995, sec. B, p. 10; Ferdinand Lundberg, *The Rich and the Super-Rich: A Study in the Power of Money Today* (New York: Lyle Stuart, 1969), pp. 545, 638.

60. Ronald F. Stinnett, *Democrats, Dinners, and Dollars: A History of the Democratic Party, Its Dinners, Its Ritual* (Ames: Iowa State University Press, 1967), p. 4; Dick Gregory, *Dick Gregory's Political Primer*, ed. James R. McGraw (New York: Harper and Row, 1972), pp. 57–59; Thomas Lask, "Books of the Times," *NYT*, 4 July 1967, p. 17.

61. William H. Honan, "Quiz: Big Moments on Campus," *NYT*, 3 January 1999, sec. 4A, pp. 49, 51; Letters, *NYT*, 1 September 1968, sec. 4, p. 11; Deirdre Carmody, "A Radical Columbia Dropout Who Went On to Make It Big," *NYT*, 10 May 1975, p. 31. Hamilton's defense of President Myles Cooper of King's College in 1775 is accepted as fact by most historians but dismissed by some as myth.

62. "Hamilton Is Hailed as Guide for Today," *NYT*, 11 January 1957, p. 17; Donald W. White, *The American Century: The Rise and Decline of the United States as a World Power* (New Haven: Yale University Press, 1996), p. 357.

63. Irwin Unger and Debi Unger, eds., *The Times Were a Changin': The Sixties Reader* (New York: Three Rivers Press, 1998), p. 93. The Lycan quote can be found in Holmes Alexander, *To Covet Honor: A Biography of Alexander Hamilton* (Belmont, Mass.: Western Islands, 1977), p. 436.

64. Merrill D. Peterson, review of *The Papers of Thomas Jefferson*, vol. 17, ed. Julian Boyd, and *Number 7: Alexander Hamilton's Secret Attempts to Control American Foreign Policy, with Supporting Documents*, by Julian Boyd, *WMQ*, 3d ser., vol. 23, no. 1 (January 1966): 157; Thomas Jefferson, *The Papers of Thomas Jefferson*, ed. Julian Boyd (Princeton: Princeton University Press, 1971), vol. 18, *4 November 1790–24 January 1791*, pp. 611–88 (see especially pp. 682, 685, 687–88). Merrill Peterson abandoned his criticism of Boyd's wide-ranging editorial notes in his review of volume 18, which contained the lengthy account of the Hamilton-Reynolds scandal. "Boyd's historical essays are of great value, impressive in their documentation, astonishing in their range and insight" (Peterson, review of *The Papers of Thomas Jefferson*, vols. 18 and 19, ed. Julian Boyd, *WMQ*, 3d ser., vol. 32, no. 4 [October 1975]: 656–58). For a classic example of the tendency of Jefferson's admirers to view Hamilton as corrupt, see the review of volume 18 by Michelle Brant, which stated, "Hamilton, placing his faith in the monied interests, felt the speculator's rights of property had to be protected. Jefferson felt the government should not aid fraud" (review of *The Papers of Thomas Jefferson*, vol. 18, ed. Julian Boyd, *AHR* 79, 3 [June

1974]: 852–53).William Safire relied on Boyd's "scrupulously detailed case" as one source for his historical novel *Scandalmonger.* Safire's interpretation of the Reynolds affair was decidedly Jeffersonian. He dismissed as simplistic the claim that Maria Reynolds was a "blackmailing whore" and instead saw her as "the victim of Hamilton's need for a defense." Safire concluded that it was likely Hamilton's story of the affair was designed to conceal financial improprieties. Safire's novel also recounted James Callendar's alliance with Thomas Jefferson. Callendar, of course, later turned on his benefactor and revealed Jefferson's relationship with Sally Hemings. See *Scandalmonger, a Novel* (New York: Simon and Schuster, 2000), especially pp. 449, 474 n. 323.

65. *Congressional Record,* House, Congressman Peter Rodino, 4 March 1957, 85th Congress, 1st session, vol. 103, part 3, pp. 3035–36; Barbara C. Jordan, *Selected Speeches,* ed. Sandra Parham (Washington, D.C.: Howard University Press, 1999), p. 195; "The Fateful Vote to Impeach," *Time,* 5 August 1974, p. 15.

66. Philip Shabecoff, "Nixon Tax Report Raises New Issue," *NYT,* 5 April 1974, p. 19; U.S. Congress, House, *Impeachment of Richard M. Nixon, President of the United States, Report of the Committee on the Judiciary,* 92d Congress, 2d session, report. no. 93–1305, pp. 283–84; "Indictment of Burr Is Found in Trenton," *NYT,* 4 October 1973, p. 31.

67. Thomas Griffith, "The Proper Grounds for Impeachment," *Time,* 25 February 1974, p. 23; "Impeachment," *NYT,* 31 October 1973, p. 44; "Toward Impeachment," *NYT,* 20 February 1974, p. 36.

68. U.S. Congress, Senate, *The Final Report of the Select Committee on Presidential Campaign Activities,* 93d Congress, 2nd session, report no. 93–981, p. 1178 n. 7; Carl Rowan, "Legal and Moral Perspectives," in *Crisis in Confidence: The Impact of Watergate,* ed. Donald W. Harward (Boston: Little, Brown, 1974), pp. 35–37.

69. Stanley Cloud, "A Ghostly Conversation on the Meaning of Watergate," *Time,* 6 August 1973, pp. 14–15.

70. Christopher Lehmann-Haupt, "Back to the First Principals," *NYT,* 25 October 1973, p. 45; Saul Maloff, "A Fiction of History," *NR* 169 (10 November 1973): 23; Gore Vidal, *Burr: A Novel* (New York: Random House, 1973), pp. 142–44, 266–72. In a commentary written during the Watergate period, Vidal said that "the brilliant Alexander Hamilton was almost certainly corrupt during his years at the Treasury" and "was also a British secret agent." See "Political Melodramas," in his *United States, Essays, 1952–1992* (New York: Random House, 1993), p. 854.

71. Thomas Fleming, "The Duel That Changed Our History," *Reader's Digest,* August 1970, pp. 190–95; "Treasury Takes Down 'Aaron Burr' Plaque," *NYT,* 29 August 1972, p. 11; Phyllis Funke, "Al Carmines Opera to Debut," *NYT,* 21 April 1974, p. 118; Martin Waldron, "People," *NYT,* 18 July 1976, sec. 11, p. 2; Robert Hanley, "New Jersey Journal," *NYT,* 27 July 1980, sec. 11, p. 3.

72. Albin Krebs, "Notes on People," *NYT,* 12 January 1977, sec. C, p. 2; James R. Webb, "The Fateful Encounter," *American Heritage* 26 (August 1975): 45–52, 92–93; Merrill Lindsay, "Pistols Shed Light on Famed Duel," *Smithsonian* 7 (November 1976): 94–98; Albin Krebs and Robert McG. Thomas, "Birthday Marked for 'a Four-Letter Dirty Word,'" *NYT,* 7 February 1981, sec. 2, p. 30; James Barron, "Burrs Pay Homage to Their Vilified Ancestor," *NYT,* 15 September 1986, sec. B, p. 1.

73. Milton Friedman, "Alexander Hamilton on the Common Market," *Newsweek,* 4 June 1972, p. 92.

74. Leonard Silk, "Examining McGovern's New Populism," *NYT,* 10 May 1972, p. 65; *Rapid City Journal,* 4 July 1976, in *Editorials on File* (New York: Facts on File, 1976), 7: 858; Review of *Alexander Hamilton: A Concise Biography,* by Broadus Mitchell, *Economist* 260 (21 August 1976): 93.

75. Josh Getlin, "The Birth of the Headline Heard 'Round the World," *Los Angeles Times,* 28 July 1995, pt. E, p. 1; Letters to the Editor, *NYT,* 4 October 1975, p. 26, 2 November 1975, sec. 4, p. 14, and 9 November 1975, sec. 4, p. 14.

76. *Time,* Special 1776 Issue, 20 May 1975; Hugh Sidey, "Oh for Another Stargazing Gardener," *Time,* 26 April 1976, p. 19; *PPP, Gerald R. Ford, Containing the Public Messages, Speeches, and Statements of the President, 1976–1977, bk. 2, April 9 to July 9, 1976* (Washington, D.C.: U.S. Government Printing Office, 1979), pp. 1118–21; Fawn Brodie, *Thomas Jefferson: An Intimate History* (New York: W. W. Norton, 1974).

77. The quotes from Malone, Boyd, and Peterson on the Hemings story can be found in Virginius Dabney, "Facts and the Founding Fathers," *VSD* 41, 13 (15 April 1975): 389–90, and also in Peterson, *The Jefferson Image in the American Mind,* pp. 185–87.

78. Peoples Bicentennial Commission, *America's Birthday: A Planning and Activity Guide for Citizens' Participation During the Bicentennial Years* (New York: Simon and Schuster, 1974), pp. 13, 15, 77, 103, 137. A review in the *New York Times* described *America's Birthday* as a "readable, challenging and handsomely illustrated and designed book" from "the wonderful young folks who dumped symbolic tea (they didn't want to pollute the harbor with the real thing) in Boston a year ago." See Herbert Mitgang, "1976 and All That," *NYT,* 4 January 1975, p. 21.

79. Esmond Wright, "The Nation Takes Shape," in *The American Destiny: An Illustrated Bicentennial History of the United States,* ed. Henry Steele Commager, Marcus Cunliffe, Maldwyn A. Jones, and Edward Horton (Danbury, Conn.: Danbury Press, 1975), p. 40; Nathan Miller, *The Founding Finaglers* (New York: David McKay, 1976), pp. 93, 96.

80. *The Presidential Campaign of 1976* (Washington, D.C.: U.S. Government Printing Office, 1978), vol. 1, part 2, *Jimmy Carter,* pp. 804, 1103; Don Richardson, ed., *Conversations with Carter* (Boulder, Colo.: Lynne Rienner, 1998), p. 146.

81. James Thomas Flexner, *The Young Hamilton: A Biography* (Boston: Little, Brown, 1978), pp. 4–7, 26–27, 29, 335, 436–37, 442.

82. Flexner, *Maverick's Progress: An Autobiography,* p. 408.

83. The Schlesinger quote appears in an advertisement for *The Young Hamilton* in *AHR* 83, 3 (June 1978): 15(a); Peter S. Prescott, "Boy Wonder," *Newsweek,* 20 March 1978, pp. 85–88; Morton Borden, review of *The Young Hamilton: A Biography,* by James Thomas Flexner, *AHR* 84, 1 (February 1979): 252–53; "Books of the Times," *NYT,* 17 March 1978, sec. C, p. 27.

84. Justus D. Doenecke, "Forrest McDonald," in Wilson, ed., *Twentieth-Century American Historians,* pp. 258, 263–65; Forrest McDonald, *The Presidency of George Washington* (Lawrence: University Press of Kansas, 1974), pp. 46, 62, 65, and *The Presidency of Thomas Jefferson* (Lawrence: University Press of Kansas, 1976), pp. 162–166.

85. McDonald, *Alexander Hamilton,* pp. 3–4, 117–18, 212, 231, 235. McDonald's reviews of the *Hamilton Papers* can be found in *WMQ,* 3d ser., vol. 20, no. 2 (April 1963): 280–84; vol. 26, no. 1 (January 1969): 114–19; vol. 31, no. 4 (October 1974): 678–80; vol. 33, no. 4 (October 1976): 677–80; vol. 34, no. 4 (October 1977): 670–71; and vol. 37, no. 2 (April 1980): 330–33. It was these reviews that prompted the editor of the Hamilton

Papers, Harold C. Syrett, to comment that McDonald "while helpfully pointing out errors of fact and occasionally handing out some words of praise, took more whacks and wallops at those volumes than all other reviewers combined." See Syrett, review of *Alexander Hamilton: A Biography* by Forrest McDonald, *WMQ*, 3d ser., vol. 67, no. 4 (March 1981): 911.

86. Alexander C. Kern, review of *Alexander Hamilton: A Biography*, by Forrest McDonald, *Eighteenth-Century Studies* 16, 2 (winter 1982–1983): 202–4; David Herbert Donald, "The Gentleman and the Romantic," *NYT Book Review*, 23 September 1979, pp. 11, 30–31; Syrett, review of *Alexander Hamilton: A Biography*, pp. 912–13; David G. Santry, "The First Secretary of the U.S. Treasury," *Business Week*, 19 November 1979, pp. 9–13.

87. *PPP, Ronald Reagan, 1981, January 20 to December 31, 1981*, 15 vols. (Washington, D.C.: U.S. Government Printing Office, 1982–1991), p. 1. For a good overview of Reagan's blending of Hamiltonian and Jeffersonian elements, see Andrew E. Busch, "Ronald Reagan's Public Philosophy: Strands of Jefferson and Hamilton," in *Ronald Reagan's America*, ed. Eric J. Schmertz, Natalie Datlof, and Alexej Ugrinsky (Westport, Conn.: Greenwood Press, 1997), pp. 41–53.

88. The Boorstin quote can be found in Busch, "Ronald Reagan's Public Philosophy," p. 41.

8. AT CENTURY'S END

1. *PPP, Reagan, 1982*, Book 1, *January 1 to July 2, 1982*, p. 689, and *1982*, Book 2, *July 3 to December 31, 1982*, p. 1161, 1166. Hamilton's subsistence quote is one of his most frequently cited passages from *The Federalist*. See, for instance, an 1884 address by Mary B. Clay, president of the American Woman Suffrage Association, who recommended that women petition for property rights: "There never was a truer thought than that of Alexander Hamilton, when he said, 'He who controls my means of daily subsistence controls my whole moral being.'" See Susan B. Anthony and Ida Husted Harper, eds., *History of Woman Suffrage* (reprint, Salem, N.H.: Ayer, 1985), vol. 4, *1883–1900*, pp. 406–7.

2. *PPP, Reagan, 1986*, Book 2, *June 28 to December 31, 1986*, pp. 1268, 1270; *1987*, Book 2, *July 4 to December 31, 1987*, pp. 1230, 1294, 1296; *1988*, Book 1, *January 1 to July 1, 1988*, pp. 219–20.

3. Ibid., *1988–1989*, Book 2, *July 2, 1988 to January 19, 1989*, p. 1183; Ronald W. Reagan, Introduction, *Restoring the Presidency: Reconsidering the Twenty-second Amendment* (Washington, D.C.: National Legal Center for the Public Interest, 1990), pp. 1–13.

4. John M. Berry, "The Debt: Can It Be Managed?" *WP*, 3 February 1985, sec. G, p. 1; Letters, *NYT*, 16 April 1984, p. 20; David Lawsky, "History Lessons: Would Federalists Like Their Fans?" *NYT*, 12 February 1995, sec. 4, p. 3. For a lively discussion of a potentially boring topic, see John Steele Gordon, *Hamilton's Blessing: The Extraordinary Life and Times of Our National Debt* (New York: Walker, 1997).

5. Jack Egan, "The Man on the 10-spot Turns 200," *USNWR*, 18 September 1989, p. 57; Dennis M. Earle and Morris Mendelson, "A Comprehensive National Financial Policy Is Needed," *American Banker*, 17 March 1989, p. 10. A campaign to replace "the man on the 10-spot" with the visage of Ronald Reagan was launched in 2001 by Grover Norquist, a conservative activist. Norquist was a leader of the successful effort to re-

name Washington National Airport after the fortieth president. Setting his sights on the ten dollar bill, Norquist observed, "Hamilton was a great American, but it's time to move on." See Philip Shenon, "Celebrating the Birthday and Legacy of Reagan," *NYT*, 7 February 2001, p. A-14.

6. Fred Barbash, "Delegates Deliver a Senate with a Silver Spoon in Its Mouth," *WP*, 22 June 1987, p. A-9; *PAH*, vol. 4, *January 1787–May 1788*, p. 192. Forrest McDonald disagreed with the conventional view that Hamilton had little impact on the Constitutional Convention. He argued that Hamilton's June 18th speech, where he remarked on the tension between the few and the many, raised the tone of the proceedings and "repolarized the debates," pulling the convention in the direction of granting more power to the national government. See *Alexander Hamilton*, p. 105.

7. Charles L. Mee Jr., "The Prudential Presents September 17, 1787," advertisement, *Newsweek*, 21 September 1987, p. 10; idem, "The Prudential Presents Only in America: Playing Favorites," advertisement, *Newsweek*, 14 September 1987, p. 6; idem, *The Genius of the People* (New York: Harper and Row, 1987), pp. 78–79.

8. Benjamin Barber and Patrick Watson, *The Struggle for Democracy* (Boston: Little, Brown, 1988), pp. 36–37; Commission on the Bicentennial of the U.S. Constitution, *A Musical Skit for Children on the Constitution Convention* (Washington, D.C.: Commission on the Bicentennial of the U.S. Constitution, January 1987), pp. 2, 5–6.

9. James Reston, "Miracle at Philadelphia," *NYT*, 20 July 1986, sec. 4, p. 23; Ezra Bowen, "The Word from the Framers," *Time*, 6 July 1987, pp. 78–80; Hugh Sidey, "Fragmentation of Powers," *Time*, 6 July 1987, p. 37; Noble E. Cunningham, review of *The Papers of Alexander Hamilton*, vol. 27, ed. Harold C. Syrett and Patricia Syrett, *Journal of Southern History* 54, 4 (November 1988): 648–49.

10. Commission on the Bicentennial of the U.S. Constitution, *We the People: The Commission on the United States Constitution, 1985–1992, Final Report* (Washington, D.C.: Commission on the Bicentennial of the U.S. Constitution, 1992), pp. 34–35; "Erika Kane They Know, but Alexander Hamilton?" *Los Angeles Times*, 19 October 1986, p. 34; Roper Center at the University of Connecticut, Public Opinion Online, <www.ropercenter.uconn.edu> accession no. 0086421, question no. 024.

11. Edmund S. Muskie, "The Chains of Liberty: Congress, President, and American Security," *VSD* 54, 1 (15 October 1987): 4; *PPP, Reagan, 1988*, Book 1, p. 99; U.S. Congress, *Report of the Congressional Committees Investigating the Iran-Contra Affair, with Supplemental, Minority, and Additional Views*, H. Rept. no. 100-433 and S. Rept. No. 100-216, 100th Congress, 1st session, 1987. See the minority report, chaps. 2 and 3.

12. Wolfgang Saxon, "The New York Post Has a Long History," *NYT*, 20 November 1976, p. 29; Steven Cuozzo, *It's Alive: How America's Oldest Newspaper Cheated Death and Why It Matters* (New York: Times Books, 1996), pp. 3, 21–22.

13. Ron Rosenbaum, "Link Founding Father to Sleaze King," *Harper's*, January 1983, pp. 19–24; Mark Jurkowitz, "True-Blue Take on Yellow Journalism," *Boston Globe*, 13 September 1996, sec. D, p. 14; Philip H. Dougherty, "New York Post Sets Big Drive," *NYT*, 1 April 1988, sec. D, p. 5; Cuozzo, *It's Alive*, pp. 3, 281–88.

14. Rosenbaum, "Link Founding Father to Sleaze King," pp. 19–24.

15. J. Lee Schneidman and Conalee Levine-Schneidman, "Suicide or Murder? The Burr-Hamilton Duel," *Journal of Psychohistory* 8, 2 (fall 1980): 159–181.

16. Jacob E. Cooke, *Alexander Hamilton* (New York: Charles Scribner's Sons, 1982), pp. vi, 182–83, 241–42.

17. Forrest McDonald, review of *Alexander Hamilton*, by Jacob E. Cooke, *AHR* 87, 5 (December 1982): 145–59; Cooke, *Alexander Hamilton*, pp. 200–203; see also pp. 269 n. 19, 270 n. 21. Francisco de Miranda (1750–1816) was a Venezuelan who sought to enlist British and American support for the liberation of Spanish colonies in Latin America; see *PAH*, vol. 21, *April 1797–July 1798*, p. 1.

18. Cooke, *Alexander Hamilton*, pp. 112–113.

19. Ibid., pp. 107, 115–16.

20. Martin Diamond, *As Far as Republican Principles Will Admit: Essays by Martin Diamond*, ed. William A. Schambra (Washington, D.C.: AEI Press, 1992), p. 3; Martin Diamond, "The Federalist," in *History of Political Philosophy*, ed. Leo Strauss and Joseph Cropsey (Chicago: University of Chicago Press, 1972), pp. 638–39.

21. Herbert J. Storing, *Toward a More Perfect Union: Writings of Herbert J. Storing*, ed. Joseph M. Bessette (Washington, D.C.: AEI Press, 1995), pp. 25–26, 373, 376, 411.

22. Michael P. Zuckert, "Refinding the Founding: Martin Diamond, Leo Strauss, and the American Regime," in *Leo Strauss, the Straussians, and the American Regime*, ed. Kenneth L. Deutsch and John A. Murley (Lanham, Md.: Rowman and Littlefield, 1999), p. 235; Diamond, *As Far as Republican Principles Will Admit*, pp. 81, 190, 228–30, 232, 237; Martin Diamond, Winston Mills Fisk, and Herbert Garfinkel, *The Democratic Republic: An Introduction to American National Government* (Chicago: Rand McNally, 1970), dedication page.

23. Morton J. Frisch, *Alexander Hamilton and the Political Order: An Interpretation of His Political Thought and Practice* (Lanham, Md.: University Press of America, 1991), pp. 32, 118; Alexander Hamilton, *Selected Writings and Speeches of Alexander Hamilton*, ed. Morton J. Frisch (Washington, D.C.: American Enterprise Institute for Public Policy Research, 1985), p. 7.

24. Walter Berns, "On Hamilton and Popular Government," *Public Interest* 109 (fall 1992): 109–13.

25. Harvey Flaumenhaft, *The Effective Republic: Administration and Constitution in the Thought of Alexander Hamilton* (Durham, N.C.: Duke University Press, 1992), pp. 3, 10, 65, 69–70, 264–65.

26. Karl-Friedrich Walling, *Republican Empire: Alexander Hamilton on War and Free Government* (Lawrence: University Press of Kansas, 1999), pp. 3–5, 8–10, 17, 283–84, 288–89, 319 n. 38.

27. McNamara, *Political Economy and Statesmanship*, p. 150.

28. Thomas L. Friedman, "For Clinton Inauguration: A Plain and Fancy Affair," *NYT*, 3 December 1992, p. 20; White House, Office of the Press Secretary, "Remarks by the President at the Thomas Jefferson Movie Screening, 11 February 1997," <www.whitehouse.gov>; "Bill Clinton's Muse," *USNWR*, 1 February 1993, cover; *PPP, William J. Clinton, 1993*, Book 1, *January 20 to July 31, 1993* (Washington, D.C.: U.S. Government Printing Office, 1994), pp. 422–23.

29. White House, Office of the Press Secretary, "Remarks by the President and the Vice President at Electronic Commerce Event, 30 November 1998," <www. whitehouse.gov>.

30. William Kristol and David Brooks, "What Ails Conservatism," *WSJ*, 15 September 1997, p. 22.

31. Robert Novak, "Jefferson, Hamilton Still Shaping GOP's Direction," *Chicago Sun-Times*, 25 September 1997, p. 35; "Newt's Universe," *Time*, 25 December 1995–1 January 1996, pp. 86–87; Richard K. Armey, *The Freedom Revolution: The New Republican House Majority Leader Tells Why Big Government Failed, Why Freedom Works, and How We Will Rebuild America* (Washington, D.C.: Regnery, 1995), pp. 10–11.

32. Michael Lind, ed. *Hamilton's Republic: Readings in the American Democratic Nationalist Tradition* (New York: Free Press, 1997); letters to the editor, *WSJ*, 22 September 1997, p. 23.

33. Francis X. Clines, "Tapes by Tripp Are Distributed by House Panel," *NYT*, 3 October 1998, p. 1; Bob Davis, "He Had an Affair, Hid It, Got Caught and Still Kept His Job," *WSJ*, 19 November 1998, pp. 1, 12; "This Isn't Watergate," *St. Louis Post-Dispatch*, 7 October 1998, p. B6; NBC News Transcripts, *Today*, 6 October 1998; Jack Hitt, "America's First Lecher," *Gentlemen's Quarterly*, November 1998, p. 347; "Foundering Father," *Harper's*, November 1998, p. 51. While accusations abound that Hamilton was something of an unrestrained womanizer, rumors have also circulated suggesting that he was homosexual. In a 1992 television interview, a member of the predominantly gay Alexander Hamilton American Legion Post in San Francisco stated that "Hamilton himself . . . wrote love letters to that wonderful artillery officer during the revolutionary war, which is why we are so proud of him." The post included a number of former soldiers discharged as a result of their sexual orientation. The speaker was probably referring to Hamilton's affectionate letters to his friend and wartime colleague John Laurens. See Don Knapp, "Gay Vets in San Francisco Find Strength at V.A. Post," *CNN*, 20 November 1992, transcript no. 226-2.

34. Davis, "He Had an Affair, Hid It, Got Caught and Still Kept His Job," p. 12; letters, *NYT*, 9 October 1998, p. 28; David Frum, "Smearing Alexander Hamilton," *Weekly Standard*, 19 October 1998, pp. 14–15; Maury Maverick, "Most of All, Presidential Scandal Demeans Country," *San Antonio Express-News*, 11 October 1998, p. 3G.

35. CNN, *Inside Politics*, 9 October 1998, transcript no. 98100900v15; National Public Radio, *All Things Considered*, "How Reference to The Federalist Papers During Senate Trial Has Sparked Sales of the Documents," transcript, 22 January 1999; Francis X. Clines, "On the Eve of the Impeachment Trial, an Uneasy Quietude Slips over the Capitol," *NYT*, 14 January 1999, p. 17; Jennifer Harper, "Both Impeachment Sides Cite Federalist Papers," *Washington Times*, 24 January 1999, p. 6; R. W. Apple Jr., "House, in a Partisan 258–176 Vote, Approves a Broad, Open-Ended Impeachment Inquiry," *NYT*, 9 October 1998, p. 1; Steve Dunleavy, "Let Bubba and Newt Take Their Best Shot," *New York Post*, 11 October 1998, p. 4.

36. David Grann, "On the Hill: Moral Minority," *NR* 219 (26 October 1998): 10–11; Douglas Turner, "Our Founders Never Envisioned Leaders Embracing Ideology of Continuous Political Struggle," *Buffalo News*, 22 February 1999, p. 2B; Michael Rust, "Rediscovering Aaron Burr," *Washington Times*, 29 July 1998, p. 21; Martin Dyckman, "Incumbents in Hiding," *St. Petersburg Times*, 6 October 1994, p. 19; A. Dalton W. Dunning, "Class Warfare: Arrogance of Power Brokers," *Ottawa Citizen*, 27 August 1991, p. 10; Terry Morley, "The Real Loser in Election," *Vancouver Sun*, 17 October 1991, p. 21; Paul Greenberg, "Budget: Profiles in Cowardice," *Seattle Post Intelligencer*, 9 October 1990, p. 9.

37. Gerald Parshall, "The Feuding Fathers," *USNWR*, 1 February 1993, p. 55; Gordon S. Wood, "Impartiality in America," *NR* 221 (6 December 1999): 56.

38. Arthur Miller, *The Last Yankee, with a New Essay About Theatre Language and Broken Glass* (Garden City, N.Y.: Fireside Theatre, 1994): see especially pp. 18–19, 40.
39. Arnold A. Rogow, *A Fatal Friendship: Alexander Hamilton and Aaron Burr* (New York: Hill and Wang, 1998), p. 135; C-Span, *Booknotes*, Arnold Rogow, transcript, 13 September 1998, <www.booknotes.org>.
40. Thomas Fleming, *Duel: Alexander Hamilton, Aaron Burr and the Future of America* (New York: Basic Books, 1999), p. 304; National Public Radio, *All Things Considered*, "Author Roger G. Kennedy on Aaron Burr and Historical Political Imagery," transcript, 3 December 1999; Roger G. Kennedy, *Burr, Hamilton, and Jefferson: A Study in Character* (New York: Oxford University Press, 2000), pp. 42–43, 76–77, 138.
41. Roper Center at the University of Connecticut, Public Opinion Online, <www.ropercenter.uconn.edu> accession no. 0311401, question no. 007. Four percent of the respondents answered "don't know." The polling data did not explain the missing 1 percent.
42. Susan Milligan, "Jefferson's Secret Family: Foundation Backs Slave Ties," *Boston Globe*, 27 January 2000, p. 1; Joseph J. Ellis, *American Sphinx: The Character of Thomas Jefferson* (New York: Alfred A. Knopf, 1997); Robert Middlekauff, review of *American Sphinx*, by Joseph Ellis, *WMQ*, 3rd ser., vol. 55, no. 3 (July 1998): 435–37. Examples of balanced works on Jefferson published by the University Press of Virginia, Charlottesville, include Peter S. Onuf, ed. *Jeffersonian Legacies* (1993); Annette Gordon-Reed, *Thomas Jefferson and Sally Hemings: An American Controversy* (1998); Jan Ellen Lewis and Peter S. Onuf, eds. *Sally Hemings and Thomas Jefferson: History, Memory, and Civic Culture* (1999). The press also published a collection of thoughtful and balanced essays on the Federalists, Doron Ben-Atar and Barbara B. Oberg, eds., *Federalists Reconsidered* (1998).
43. Katarzyna Wandycz, "Lech Walesa, Meet Alexander Hamilton," *Forbes*, 26 November 1990, p. 116; Peter Nulty, "1995 National Business Hall of Fame Laureates," *Fortune*, 3 April 1995, pp. 108, 112–13.
44. Richard Brookhiser, "A Founding Father's Return to Grace," *USNWR*, 10 November 1997, pp. 71–72; Michael Lind, "Restore Hamilton to His Pedestal," *NYT*, 3 July 1998, p. 17; "A War of Myth and Memory," *Economist*, 6 December 1997, pp. 95–96; Michael Rust, "Hamilton's Ups and Downs," *Insight on the News*, 17 May 1999, p. 45.
45. Peterson, *The Jefferson Image in the American Mind*, p. 347.
46. Jefferson's comment was made in response to his placement of busts of Hamilton and himself facing each other in the entrance hall at Monticello; <www.monticello.org/jefferson/entrance/home.html>.

9. GETTING RIGHT WITH HAMILTON

1. Dumas Malone, *Jefferson and His Time*, Vol. 2, *Jefferson and the Rights of Man* (Boston: Little, Brown, 1951), p. 286; *PAH*, 25: 544–45.
2. *PAH*, 25: 544–45.
3. Malone, *Jefferson and His Time*, vol. 2, *Jefferson and the Rights of Man*, p. 287; Thomas P. Govan, "Alexander Hamilton and Julius Caesar: A Note on the Use of Historical Evidence," *WMQ*, 3d ser., vol. 32, no. 3 (July 1975): 475–80; *PAH*, 4: 218, 1: 122, and 19: 47. One piece of evidence often cited as proof of Hamilton's Caesarism was his alleged authorship of two essays in 1787 under the pseudonym Caesar. In 1960

Jacob Cooke made a compelling case that Hamilton was probably not the author of these essays; see his "Alexander Hamilton's Authorship of the 'Caesar' Letters," *WMQ*, 3rd ser., vol. 17, no. 1 (January 1960): 78–85.

4. Thomas P. Govan, "The Rich, the Well-Born, and Alexander Hamilton," *MVHR* 36, 4 (March 1950): 675–80. One of the more egregious examples of the distortion of Hamilton's rich and well-born comment can be found in Howard Zinn's *A People's History of the United States*. Quoting from the Convention notes on Hamilton's remarks, Zinn's calculated placement of ellipsis suggests that Hamilton was concerned exclusively with protecting the interests of the wealthy. In fact, he feared a monopoly of power by either the rich or the poor. See *A People's History of the United States, 1492–Present, Twentieth Anniversary Edition* (New York: Harper Collins Publishers, 1999), pp. 95–96.

5. Cooke, *Alexander Hamilton*, pp. 61–62; *PAH*, 5: 41.

6. Miller, *Alexander Hamilton: Portrait in Paradox*, p. 316.

7. The Jefferson quotes can be found in John Steele Gordon, "The Founding Wizard," *American Heritage* 41, 8 (July/August 1990): 52, 56; Cooke, *Alexander Hamilton*, p. 254 n. 13. See also *PAH*, 10: 253, 270. Syrett and Cooke noted in *The Papers of Alexander Hamilton*, "Advocacy of child labor and the industrial employment of women was, of course, common in the eighteenth century in Europe and America" (p. 253 n. 158).

8. See Cooke, *Alexander Hamilton*, pp. 146–53, 260 n. 24, McDonald, *Alexander Hamilton*, pp. 296–303, and *PAH*, 17: 159–61. Jacob Cooke's essay in *Pennsylvania History*, "The Whiskey Insurrection: A Re-evaluation," effectively refutes the many legends surrounding the event. Writing in the early 1960s, Cooke observed the "curious dualism" among historians who "in the name of democracy . . . condone in the past what in the name of law and order they condemn in the present. . . . Can one consistently praise the whiskey rebels and condemn Governor Ross Barnett? Can one attack Washington and Hamilton for using force to put down resistance to the laws and praise President Eisenhower and Kennedy" for the same thing? See *Pennsylvania History* 30 (1963): 316–46.

9. Cooke, *Alexander Hamilton*, pp. 190–93, 269 n. 19, 270 n. 28, and chap. 17; the Morison quote is cited on p. 201. The Jefferson dictator quote can be found in Lipscomb, ed., *The Writings of Thomas Jefferson*, 12: 183.

10. McDonald, *Alexander Hamilton*, pp. 348–49; 446 n. 42: *PAH*, 24: 464–67. See also, Pancake, *Thomas Jefferson and Alexander Hamilton*, p. 272, and Lucius Wilmerding Jr., *The Electoral College* (New Brunswick, N.J.: Rutgers University Press, 1958), pp. 19–20, 22, 60–61.

11. *PAH*, 25: 275.

12. George Washington, *The Writings of George Washington from the Original Manuscript Sources, 1745–1799*, ed. John C. Fitzpatrick, 39 vols. (Washington, D.C.: U.S. Government Printing Office, 1931–1944), 36: 460–61.

13. Jacob E. Cooke, "The Reports of Alexander Hamilton," in Sellers, ed., *Alexander Hamilton: A Profile*, pp. 71–73, and McDonald, *Alexander Hamilton*, pp. 181–87; "Final Version of the Second Report on the Further Provision Necessary for Establishing Public Credit (Report on a National Bank)," *PAH*, 7: 309.

14. "Alexander Hamilton's Final Version of the Report on the Subject of Manufactures," *PAH*, 10: 230, 256.

15. Thomas Jefferson, *Writings, Notes on the State of Virginia*, pp. 124, 291; Lipscomb, ed., *The Writings of Thomas Jefferson*, 14: 391–92.

16. McDonald, *Alexander Hamilton*, p. 49.

17. *FED*, no. 22, pp. 143–44, and no. 78, pp. 522–23, 525.

18. *FED*, no. 78, pp. 526–27, and pp. 529–30.

19. *Marbury v. Madison* (1803) in *Constitutional Interpretation*, ed. Craig R. Ducat and Harold W. Chase (St. Paul, Minn.: West Publishing Company, 1988), p. 24; Hobson, ed., *The Papers of John Marshall* 7: 229, 230 n. 14, and 8: 257.

20. *FED*, no. 24, pp. 156–57, and no. 25, pp. 161–62.

21. *PAH*, 23: 596, and Stephen E. Ambrose, *Duty, Honor, Country: A History of West Point* (Baltimore: Johns Hopkins University Press, 1966), pp. 11–14, 19.

22. Donald R. Hickey, *The War of 1812* (Urbana and Chicago: University of Illinois Press, 1989), p. 8; *FED*, no. 11, p. 68, and no. 24, p. 157; Harold Sprout and Margaret Sprout, *The Rise of American Naval Power, 1776–1918* (Princeton: Princeton University Press, 1939), p. 37; Fitzpatrick, ed., *The Writings of George Washington from the Original Manuscript Sources, 1745–1799*, 35: 314.

23. Hickey, *The War of 1812*, pp. 6, 8–9.

24. *FED*, no. 77, p. 520; no. 70, p. 471; and no. 74, p. 500.

25. Robert Scigliano, "The War Powers Resolution and the War Powers," in *The Presidency in the Constitutional Order*, ed. Joseph M. Bessette and Jeffrey Tulis (Baton Rouge: Louisiana State University Press, 1981), pp. 127–28; *FED*, no. 70, p. 472.

26. *FED*, no. 23, p. 147, and no. 25, p. 163.

ODD DESTINY

1. Peterson, *The Jefferson Image in the American Mind*, p. 223; Brookhiser, *Alexander Hamilton: American*, p. 4.

2. The Adams quote can be found in Lyman H. Butterfield, Wendell D. Garrett, and Marjorie E. Sprague, eds., *Adams Family Correspondence*, 6 vols. (Cambridge, Mass.: Belknap Press of Harvard University, 1963–1993), 3:342.

3. *FED*, no. 71, p. 482.

4. Ibid., 482–83; no. 68, p. 461; no. 70, p. 472; and no. 17, p. 105. Hamilton's argument in *Federalist* no. 68, defending the electoral college, was cited frequently in the aftermath of the disputed presidential election of 2000. Critics of the electoral college viewed it as an antiquated mechanism and a vestige of Hamiltonian elitism. Columnist Eileen McNamara of the *Boston Globe* observed, "Electors were to be drawn from the educated elite who, Alexander Hamilton wrote, would 'possess the information and the discernment requisite' to the task of choosing a president. We've come a long way since 1787. News no longer travels by horseback. Education is no longer limited to white men of means. The franchise has been extended to women and people of color. It's time the Constitution caught up." Craig Crawford of the online political journal *Hotline* claimed that the founders wanted "an Electoral College of wisemen, so to speak, who would make judgments and not turn it over to what Alexander Hamilton called the public beast." See Eileen McNamara, "Let's Vote Out Anachronism," *Boston Globe*, 8 November 2000, p. B1, and Craig Crawford, interview on *The Early Show*, Burrelle's Information Services, CBS News transcript, 8 November 2000.

5. Robin Toner, "The Right to Click," *NYT Book Review*, 27 February 2000, p. 7.

6. Hugh Heclo, "Hyperdemocracy," *Wilson Quarterly* 23, 1 (winter 1999): 62–71.

BOOKS

Aaron, Daniel. *Men of Good Hope: A Story of American Progressives.* New York: Oxford University Press, 1951.

Acheson, Dean. *Among Friends: Personal Letters of Dean Acheson,* Edited by David S. McLellan and David C. Acheson. New York: Dodd, Mead, 1980.

Adair, Douglass. *Fame and the Founding Fathers: Essays by Douglass Adair.* Edited by Trevor Colbourn. New York: W. W. Norton, 1974.

Adams, Charles Francis. *Diary of Charles Francis Adams.* Edited by Marc Friedlaender and L. H. Butterfield. 8 vols. Cambridge: Belknap Press of Harvard University Press, 1974.

Adams, Henry. *History of the United States of America During the First Administration of Thomas Jefferson.* Vol. 1. 2 vols. New York: Charles Scribner's Sons, 1889.

———. *John Randolph.* Greenwich, Conn.: Fawcett Publications, 1961.

———. *Letters of Henry Adams (1858–1891).* Edited by Worthington Chauncey Ford. Boston: Houghton Mifflin, 1930.

———. *The Letters of Henry Adams.* Vol. 2, *1868–1885.* Edited by J. C. Levenson, Ernest Samuels, Charles Vandersee, Viola Hopkins Winner. 6 vols. Cambridge: Belknap Press of Harvard University Press, 1982.

———. *The Life of Albert Gallatin.* Philadelphia: J. B. Lippincott, 1880.

Adams, James Truslow. *The Epic of America.* Garden City, N.Y.: Blue Ribbon Books, 1941.

———. *The March of Democracy: A History of the United States.* Vol. 1, *The Rise of the Union.* New York: Charles Scribner's Sons, 1965.

Adams, John. *Diary and Autobiography of John Adams.* Edited by Lyman H. Butterfield. Vol. 3, part 1, *Diary, 1782–1804, Autobiography, Part One to October 1776.* Cambridge, Mass.: Belknap Press, 1961.

Adams, John Quincy. *The Diary of John Quincy Adams, 1794–1845, American Diplomacy, and Political, Social, and Intellectual Life, from Washington to Polk.* Edited by Allan Nevins. New York: Charles Scribner's Sons, 1951.

———. *The Writings of John Quincy Adams.* Edited by Worthington Chauncey Ford. 7 vols. New York: Greenwood Press, 1968.

Adams, Larry L. *Walter Lippmann.* Boston: Twayne, 1977.

Agar, Herbert. *The People's Choice: From Washington to Harding, a Study in Democracy.* Boston: Houghton Mifflin, 1933.

Agar, Herbert, and Allen Tate, eds. *Who Owns America? A New Declaration of Independence.* Boston: Houghton Mifflin, 1936.

Alexander, Holmes. *To Covet Honor: A Biography of Alexander Hamilton.* Belmont: Western Islands, 1977.

Ambrose, Stephen E. *Duty, Honor, Country: A History of West Point.* Baltimore: The Johns Hopkins University Press, 1966.

Ames, Fisher. *Works of Fisher Ames, Compiled by a Number of his Friends.* Boston: T. B. Watt, 1809.

Ames, Seth. *Works of Fisher Ames.* Edited by William B. Allen. Indianapolis: Liberty Classics, 1983.

Anthony, Susan B., and Ida Husted Harper, eds. *History of Woman Suffrage.* Volume 4, *1883–1900.* Salem, N.H.: reprint, Ayer, 1985.

Arliss, George. *My Ten Years in the Studios.* Boston: Little, Brown, 1940.

———. *Up the Years from Bloomsbury: An Autobiography.* Boston: Little, Brown, 1928.

Armey, Richard K. *The Freedom Revolution: The New Republican House Majority Leader Tells Why Big Government Failed, Why Freedom Works, and How We Will Rebuild America.* Washington, D.C.: Regnery, 1995.

Arvin, Newton. *Whitman.* New York: Macmillan, 1938.

Ashworth, John. *"Agrarians" and "Aristocrats": Party Political Ideology in the United States, 1837–1846.* Cambridge: Cambridge University Press, 1987.

Atherton, Gertrude. *Adventures of a Novelist.* New York: Blue Ribbon Books, 1932.

———. *The Conqueror, Being the True and Romantic Story of Alexander Hamilton.* New York: Macmillan, 1914.

Axson, Stockton. *"Brother Woodrow," A Memoir of Woodrow Wilson.* Edited by Arthur S. Link. Princeton: Princeton University Press, 1993.

Bagehot, Walter. *The Collected Works of Walter Bagehot.* Edited by Norman St. John-Stevas. 15 vols. London: Economist, 1968.

Bailey, Fred Arthur. *William Edward Dodd: The South's Yeoman Scholar.* Charlottesville: University Press of Virginia, 1997.

Bain, Robert, Joseph M. Flora, and Louis D. Rubin Jr., eds. *Southern Writers: A Biographical Dictionary.* Baton Rouge: Louisiana State University Press, 1979.

Bancroft, George. *History of the Formation of the Constitution of the United States of America.* Vol. 2. 2 vols. New York: D. Appleton, 1903.

———. *History of the United States of America, From the Discovery of the American Continent.* Vol. 4. 6 vols. New York: D. Appleton, 1888.

Barber, Benjamin, and Patrick Watson. *The Struggle for Democracy.* Boston: Little, Brown, 1988.

Barkley, Alben W. *That Reminds Me.* Garden City, N.Y.: Doubleday, 1954.

Bartlett, Irving H. *John C. Calhoun: A Biography.* New York: W. W. Norton, 1993.

Beale, Howard K. *Theodore Roosevelt and the Rise of America to World Power.* Baltimore: Johns Hopkins University Press, 1956.

Beard, Charles A. *An Economic Interpretation of the Constitution of the United States.* New York: Macmillan, 1967.

———. *The American Party Battle.* New York: Book League of America, 1929.

Beard, Charles A., and Mary R. Beard. *The Rise of American Civilization.* Vol. 3, *America in Midpassage.* New York: Macmillan, 1941.

Beard, Charles A., with the collaboration of G. H. E. Smith. *The Open Door at Home: A Trial Philosophy of National Interest.* New York: Macmillan, 1935.

Bell, Jack. *Mr. Conservative: Barry Goldwater.* Garden City, N.Y.: Doubleday, 1962.

Bemis, Samuel Flagg. *A Diplomatic History of the United States.* New York: Henry Holt, 1936.

———. ed. *American Foreign Policy and the Blessings of Liberty, and Other Essays.* New Haven: Yale University Press, 1962.

Ben-Atar, Doron, and Barbara B. Oberg, eds. *Federalists Reconsidered*. Charlottesville: University Press of Virginia, 1998.

Benet, Rosemary, and Stephen Vincent Benet. *A Book of Americans*. New York: Farrar and Rinehart, 1933.

Benet, Stephen Vincent. *America*. New York: Farrar and Rinehart, 1944.

Benson, Allan L. *Our Dishonest Constitution*. New York: B. W. Huebsch, 1914.

Benson, Lee. *The Concept of Jacksonian Democracy: New York as a Test Case*. Princeton: Princeton University Press, 1961.

Benton, Thomas Hart. *Thirty Years' View; or, A History of the Working of the American Government for Thirty Years, from 1820 to 1850*. New York: Greenwood Press, 1968.

Berle, Adolph A. *Navigating the Rapids, 1918–1971: From the Papers of Adolf A. Berle*. Edited by Beatrice Bishop Berle and Travis Beal Jacobs. New York: Harcourt Brace Jovanovich, 1973.

Bernhard, Winfred E. A. *Fisher Ames: Federalist and Statesman, 1758–1808*. Chapel Hill: University of North Carolina Press, 1965.

Bessette, Joseph M., and Jeffrey Tulis, eds. *The Presidency in the Constitutional Order*. Baton Rouge: Louisiana State University Press, 1981.

Beveridge, Albert J. *The Life of John Marshall*. 3 vols. Boston: Houghton Mifflin, 1916–1919.

Biddle, Francis. *The World's Best Hope: A Discussion of the Role of the United States in the Modern World*. Chicago: University of Chicago Press, 1949.

Bishop, Joseph Bucklin. *Theodore Roosevelt and His Time, Shown in His Own Letters*. Vol. 2. 2 vols. New York: Charles Scribner's Sons, 1926.

Black, Charles L. Jr., *The People and the Court: Judicial Review in a Democracy*. New York: Macmillan, 1960.

Blaine, James G. *Twenty Years of Congress from Lincoln to Garfield, with a Review of the Events Which led to the Political Revolution of 1860*. Vol. 1. Norwich, Conn.: Henry Bill, 1884.

Boggs, Lindy. *Washington Through a Purple Veil: Memoirs of a Southern Woman*. New York: Harcourt Brace, 1994.

Boorstin, Daniel J. *The Americans: The National Experience*. New York: Random House, 1965.

———, ed. *An American Primer*. Chicago: University of Chicago Press, 1966.

Borah, William E. *American Problems: A Selection of Speeches and Prophecies by William E. Borah*. Edited by Horace Green. New York: Duffield, 1924.

Bowden, Mary Weatherspoon. *Washington Irving*. Boston: Twayne, 1981.

Bowers, Claude. *Jefferson and Hamilton: The Struggle for Democracy in America*. Boston: Houghton Mifflin, 1925.

———. *Jefferson in Power: The Death Struggle of the Federalists*. Boston: Houghton Mifflin, 1936.

———. *My Life: The Memoirs of Claude Bowers*. New York: Simon and Schuster, 1962.

———. *The Founders of the Republic*. Chicago: American Library Association, 1927.

———. *The Tragic Era: The Revolution After Lincoln*. Cambridge Mass.: Houghton Mifflin, 1929.

Bowers, Claude, Earl Browder, and Francis Franklin. *The Heritage of Jefferson*. New York: International Publishers, 1944.

Boyd, Julian. *Number 7: Alexander Hamilton's Secret Attempts to Control American Foreign Policy.* Princeton: Princeton University Press, 1964.

Braeman, John. *Albert J. Beveridge, American Nationalist.* Chicago: University of Chicago Press, 1971.

Bragdon, Henry Wilkinson. *Woodrow Wilson: The Academic Years.* Cambridge: Belknap Press of Harvard University Press, 1967.

Brandeis, Louis D. *The Curse of Bigness: Miscellaneous Papers of Louis D. Brandeis.* Edited by Osmond K. Fraenkel. Port Washington, N.Y.: Kennikat Press, 1965.

Brands, H. W. *T.R.: The Last Romantic.* New York: Basic Books, 1997.

———. *The Reckless Decade: America in the 1890s.* New York: St. Martin's Press, 1995.

Brant, Irving. *James Madison, Secretary of State, 1800–1809.* Indianapolis: Bobbs Merrill, 1953.

Brasher, Thomas L. *Whitman as Editor of the Brooklyn Daily Eagle.* Detroit: Wayne State University Press, 1970.

Brodie, Fawn. *Thomas Jefferson: An Intimate History.* New York: W. W. Norton, 1974.

Brookhiser, Richard. *Alexander Hamilton: American.* New York: Free Press, 1999.

Brooks, Van Wyck. *Makers and Finders: A History of the Writer in America 1800–1915.* Vol. 5, *The Confident Years: 1885–1915.* New York: E. P. Dutton, 1952.

———. *Opinions of Oliver Allston.* New York: E. P. Dutton, 1941.

———. *The Times of Melville and Whitman.* New York: E. P. Dutton, 1947.

———. *The World of Washington Irving.* New York: E. P. Dutton, 1950.

Broussard, James H. *The Southern Federalists, 1800–1816.* Baton Rouge: Louisiana State University Press, 1978.

Browder, Earl. *The People's Front.* New York: International Publishers, 1938.

Brown, Robert E. *Charles Beard and the Constitution: A Critical Analysis of "An Economic Interpretation of the Constitution."* Princeton: Princeton University Press, 1956.

Bryan, William Jennings. *The Real Bryan, Being Extracts from the Speeches and Writings of "A Well-Rounded Man."* Edited by Richard L. Metcalfe. Des Moines, Iowa: Personal Help Publishing, 1908.

Bryce, James. *The American Commonwealth.* 2 vols. New York: Macmillan, 1911.

Burns, James MacGregor. *Presidential Government: The Crucible of Leadership.* Boston: Houghton Mifflin, 1965.

———. *The Deadlock of Democracy: Four Party Politics in America.* Englewood Cliffs, N.J.: Prentice-Hall, 1963.

Butler, Benjamin F. *Butler's Book: A Review of His Legal, Political, and Military Career.* Boston: A. M. Thayer, 1892.

Butler, Nicholas Murray. *Across the Busy Years: Recollections and Reflections.* 2 vols. New York: Charles Scribner's Sons, 1939–1940.

Butt, Archibald. *Taft and Roosevelt: The Intimate Letters of Archie Butt, Military Aide.* Garden City, N.Y.: Doubleday, Doran, 1930.

Butterfield, Lyman H., Wendell D. Garrett, and Marjorie E. Sprague, eds. *Adams Family Correspondence.* 6 vols. Cambridge, Mass.: Belknap Press of Harvard University, 1963–1993.

Calhoun, John C. *The Papers of John C. Calhoun.* Edited by William E. Hemphill, Robert L. Meriwether, and Clyde N. Wilson. 25 vols. Columbia: University of South Carolina Press, 1959–.

———. *Union and Liberty: The Political Philosophy of John C. Calhoun.* Edited by Ross M. Lence. Indianapolis: Liberty Fund, 1992.

Cappon, Lester J., ed. *The Adams–Jefferson Letters: The Complete Correspondence Between Thomas Jefferson and Abigail and John Adams.* 2 vols. Chapel Hill: University of North Carolina Press, 1959.

Carto, Willis A., ed. *Profiles in Populism.* Old Greenwich, Conn.: Flag Press, 1982.

Chace, James. *Acheson: The Secretary of State Who Created the American World.* New York: Simon and Schuster, 1998.

Chace, William M. *The Political Identities of Ezra Pound and T. S. Eliot.* Stanford: Stanford University Press, 1973.

Chinard, Gilbert. *Thomas Jefferson: The Apostle of Americanism.* Boston: Little, Brown, 1929.

Chitwood, Oliver Perry, and Frank Lawrence Owsley. *A Short History of the American People.* Vol. 1, *1492–1865.* New York: D. Van Nostrand, 1945.

Choate, Joseph Hodges. *Arguments and Addresses of Joseph Hodges Choate.* Edited by Frederick C. Hicks. St. Paul, Minn.: West, 1926.

Choate, Rufus. *Addresses and Orations of Rufus Choate.* Boston: Little, Brown, 1891.

Clarfield, Gerald H. *Timothy Pickering and the American Republic.* Pittsburgh: University of Pittsburgh Press, 1980.

Clay, Henry. *The Papers of Henry Clay.* Edited by James F. Hopkins and Robert Seager II. 11 vols. Lexington: University Press of Kentucky, 1959–1992.

Clemens, Jeremiah. *The Rivals: A Tale of the Times of Aaron Burr, and Alexander Hamilton.* Philadelphia: J. B. Lippincott, 1860.

Clements, Kendrick A. *The Presidency of Woodrow Wilson.* Lawrence: University Press of Kansas, 1992.

Cole, Donald B. *Martin Van Buren and the American Political System.* Princeton: Princeton University Press, 1984.

———. *The Presidency of Andrew Jackson.* Lawrence: University Press of Kansas, 1993.

Coleman, William. *A Collection of the Facts and Documents Relative to the Death of Major General Alexander Hamilton; With Comments: Together with the various Orations, Sermons, and Eulogies that Have Been Published or Written on His Life and Character.* Austin, Tex.: Shoal Creek Publishers, 1972.

Commager, Henry Steele. *The Defeat of America: Presidential Power and the National Character.* New York: Simon and Schuster, 1974.

Commager, Henry Steele, Marcus Cunliffe, Maldwyn A. Jones, and Edward Horton. *The American Destiny: An Illustrated Bicentennial History of the United States.* Danbury Conn.: Danbury Press, 1975.

Conkin, Paul K. *The Southern Agrarians.* Knoxville: University of Tennessee Press, 1988.

Cook, Theodore P. *The Life and Public Services of Hon. Samuel J. Tilden, Democratic Nominee for President of the United States.* New York: D. Appleton, 1876.

Cooke, Jacob E. *Alexander Hamilton.* New York: Charles Scribner's Sons, 1982.

Coolidge, Calvin. *The Autobiography of Calvin Coolidge.* New York: Cosmopolitan Book Corporation, 1929.

———. *The Price of Freedom: Speeches and Addresses.* New York: Charles Scribner's Sons, 1924.

Cooper, James Fenimore. *Gleanings in Europe, Switzerland.* Albany: State University of New York Press, 1980.

————. *The Letters and Journals of James Fenimore Cooper.* Edited by James Franklin Beard. 6 vols. Cambridge: Harvard University Press, 1960.

Couch, Nena. *Sidney Kingsley: Five Prize-winning Plays.* Columbus: Ohio State University Press, 1995.

Coughlin, Charles E. *A Series of Lectures on Social Justice.* Royal Oak, Mich.: The Radio League of the Little Flower, 1935.

Cox, James M. *Journey Through My Years.* New York: Simon and Schuster, 1946.

Cox, Samuel S. *Three Decades of Federal Legislation, 1855 to 1885.* Providence, R.I.: J. A. & R. A. Reid, 1885.

Croly, Herbert. *Progressive Democracy.* New York: Macmillan, 1915.

————. *The Promise of American Life.* Cambridge: Belknap Press of Harvard University Press, 1965.

Cunningham, Noble E. Jr., *The Presidency of James Monroe.* Lawrence: University Press of Kansas, 1996.

Cuozzo, Steven. *It's Alive: How America's Oldest Newspaper Cheated Death and Why It Matters.* New York: Times Books, 1996.

Current, Richard N., T. Harry Williams, and Frank Freidel. *American History: A Survey.* New York: Alfred A. Knopf, 1961.

Curti, Merle. *Probing Our Past.* New York: Harper and Brothers, 1955.

————. *The Growth of American Thought.* New York: Harper and Brothers, 1943.

Curtis, George Ticknor. *History of the Origin, Formation, and Adoption of the Constitution of the United States; with Notices of Its Principal Framers.* Vol. 2. 2 vols. New York: Harper and Brothers, 1860.

Dallek, Robert. *Democrat and Diplomat: The Life of William E. Dodd.* New York: Oxford University Press, 1968.

Dana, Richard Henry Jr. *The Journal of Richard Henry Dana, Jr.* Edited by Robert F. Lucid. 3 vols. Cambridge: Belknap Press of Harvard University Press, 1968.

Daniels, Jonathan. *Three Presidents and Their Books: The Reading of Jefferson, Lincoln, F. D. Roosevelt.* Urbana: University of Illinois Press, 1955.

Davis, Jefferson. *Jefferson Davis, Constitutionalist, His Letters, Papers and Speeches,* Vol. 2. Edited by Dunbar Rowland. 10 vols. Jackson: Mississippi Department of Archives and History, 1923.

————. *The Papers of Jefferson Davis.* Edited by Haskell M. Monroe Jr., and James T. McIntosh. 7 vols. Baton Rouge: Louisiana State University Press, 1971–.

————. *The Rise and Fall of the Confederate Government.* Vol. 1. New York: Thomas Yoseloff, 1958.

Davis, John H. *The Guggenheims: An American Epic.* New York: William Morrow, 1978.

Dawes, Charles G. *Notes as Vice-President, 1928–1929.* Boston: Little, Brown, 1935.

Debs, Eugene V. *Letters of Eugene V. Debs.* Edited by Robert J. Constantine. 3 vols. Urbana and Chicago: University of Illinois Press, 1990.

Depew, Chauncey M. *Addresses and Literary Contributions on the Threshold of Eighty-two.* N.P., 1916(?).

Desmond, Alice Curtis. *Alexander Hamilton's Wife: A Romance of the Hudson.* New York: Dodd, Mead, 1953.

Deutsch, Kenneth L., and John A. Murley. *Leo Strauss, the Straussians, and the American Regime.* Lanham, Md.: Rowman and Littlefield, 1999.

Devine, Robert A. *Blowing on the Wind: The Nuclear Test Ban Debate, 1954–1960.* New York: Oxford University Press, 1978.

Diamond, Martin. *As Far as Republican Principles Will Admit: Essays by Martin Diamond.* Edited by William A. Schambra. Washington, D.C.: AEI Press, 1992.

Diamond, Martin, Winston Mills Fisk, and Herbert Garfinkel. *The Democratic Republic: An Introduction to American National Government.* Chicago: Rand McNally, 1970.

Dodd, William E. *Statesmen of the Old South, or From Radicalism to Conservative Revolt.* New York: Macmillan, 1929.

Dodge, Melvin Gilbert, ed. *Alexander Hamilton, Thirty-one Orations Delivered at Hamilton College from 1864 to 1895 upon the Prize Foundation Established by Franklin Harvey Head, A.M.* New York: G. P. Putnam's Sons, 1896.

Donovan, Frank R. *The Americanism of Barry Goldwater.* New York: Macfadden-Bartell, 1964.

Dos Passos, John. *The Ground We Stand On: Some Examples from the History of a Political Creed.* New York; Harcourt, Brace, 1941.

———. *The Head and the Heart of Thomas Jefferson.* Garden City, N.Y.: Doubleday, 1954.

———. *The Men Who Made the Nation.* Garden City, N.Y.: Doubleday, 1957.

Douglas, William O. *An Almanac of Liberty.* Garden City, N.Y.: Doubleday, 1954.

———. *The Right of the People.* Garden City, N.Y.: Doubleday, 1958.

Douglass, Frederick. *The Frederick Douglass Papers.* Vol. 3, *1855–1863,* series 1. Edited by John W. Blassingame. New Haven: Yale University Press, 1985.

DuBois, W. E. B. *Writings by W. E. B. Dubois in Periodicals Edited by Others.* Vol. 1, *1891–1909.* Edited by Herbert Aptheker. New York: Kraus-Thomson Organization, 1982.

———. *Writings in Periodicals Edited by W. E. B. DuBois: Selections from The Horizon.* Edited by Herbert Aptheker. White Plains, N.Y.: Kraus-Thomson Organization, 1985.

Ducat, Craig R., and Harold W. Chase, eds. *Constitutional Interpretation.* St. Paul, Minn.: West, 1988.

Eagleton, Thomas F. *War and Presidential Power: A Chronicle of Congressional Surrender.* New York: Liveright, 1974.

Editorials on File. Rapid City (S.D.) Journal. 4 July 1976. Vol. 7. New York: Facts on File 1976.

Elliott, Emory. *Revolutionary Writers: Literature and Authority in the New Republic, 1725–1810.* New York: Oxford University Press, 1982.

Ellis, Joseph J. *American Sphinx: The Character of Thomas Jefferson.* New York: Alfred A. Knopf, 1997.

———. *Passionate Sage: The Character and Legacy of John Adams.* New York: W. W. Norton, 1993.

Emerson, Ralph Waldo. *The Journals and Miscellaneous Notebooks of Ralph Waldo Emerson.* Edited by William H. Gilman et al. 16 vols. Cambridge: The Belknap Press of Harvard University Press, 1960–1982.

———. *The Letters of Ralph Waldo Emerson.* Vol. 2. Edited by Ralph L. Rusk. 6 vols. New York: Columbia University Press, 1939.

Emery, Noemie. *Alexander Hamilton: An Intimate Portrait.* New York: G. P. Putnam's Sons, 1982.

Ernst, Robert. *Rufus King: American Federalist.* Chapel Hill: University of North Carolina Press, 1968.

Evarts, William Maxwell. *Arguments and Speeches of William Maxwell Evarts.* 3 vols. Edited by Sherman Evarts. New York: Macmillan, 1919.

Everett, Edward. *Orations and Speeches on Various Occasions by Edward Everett.* 4 vols. Boston: Charles C. Little and James Brown, 1850–1868.

Farley, James A. *Behind the Ballots: The Personal History of a Politician.* New York: Harcourt, Brace, 1938.

Farrand, Max, ed. *The Records of the Federal Convention of 1787.* 4 vols. New Haven: Yale University Press, 1966.

Faulkner, Harold Underwood. *American Political and Social History.* New York: Appleton-Century-Crofts, 1952.

Fehrenbacher, Don E. *The Dred Scott Case: Its Significance in American Law and Politics.* New York: Oxford University Press, 1978.

Fischer, David Hackett. *The Revolution of American Conservatism: The Federalist Party in the Era of Jeffersonian Democracy.* New York: Harper and Row, 1965.

Fiske, John. *Essays Historical and Literary.* Vol. 1. 2 vols. New York: Macmillan, 1903.

———. *The Critical Period in American History, 1783–1789.* Boston: Houghton Mifflin, 1902.

Flaumenhaft, Harvey. *The Effective Republic: Administration and Constitution in the Thought of Alexander Hamilton.* Durham, N.C.: Duke University Press, 1992.

Fleming, Thomas. *Duel: Alexander Hamilton, Aaron Burr and the Future of America.* New York: Basic Books, 1999.

Flexner, James Thomas. *Maverick's Progress: An Autobiography.* New York: Fordham University Press, 1996.

———. *The Young Hamilton: A Biography.* Boston: Little, Brown, 1978.

Forcey, Charles. *The Crossroads of Liberalism: Croly, Weyl, Lippmann, and the Progressive Era, 1900–1925.* New York: Oxford University Press, 1961.

Ford, Paul Leicester. *Bibliotheca Hamiltoniana: A List of Books Written by, or Relating to Alexander Hamilton.* New York: Knickerbocker Press, 1886.

Ford, Worthington Chauncey, ed. *A Cycle of Adams Letters, 1861–1865.* Boston: Houghton Mifflin, 1920.

Frankfurter, Felix. *Of Law and Men: Papers and Addresses of Felix Frankfurter, 1939–1956.* Edited by Philip Elman. New York: Harcourt, Brace, 1956.

Freidel, Frank. *Francis Lieber, Nineteenth-Century Liberal.* Baton Rouge: Louisiana State University Press, 1947.

———. *Franklin D. Roosevelt: The Apprenticeship.* Boston: Little, Brown, 1952.

———. *Franklin D. Roosevelt: The Ordeal.* Boston: Little, Brown, 1954.

Frisch, Morton J. *Alexander Hamilton and the Political Order: An Interpretation of His Political Thought and Practice.* Lanham, Md.: University Press of America, 1991.

Fruchtman, Jack Jr. *Thomas Paine: Apostle of Freedom.* New York: Four Walls Eight Windows, 1994.

Fusfeld, Daniel R. *The Economic Thought of Franklin D. Roosevelt and the Origins of the New Deal.* New York: Columbia University Press, 1956.

Gaddis, John Lewis. *The United States and the End of the Cold War: Implications, Reconsiderations, Provocations.* New York: Oxford University Press, 1992.

Gaines, Francis Pendleton. *Southern Oratory: A Study in Idealism.* Huntsville: University of Alabama Press, 1946.

Gale, Robert L. *A Nathaniel Hawthorne Encyclopedia.* New York: Greenwood Press, 1991.

Gallatin, Albert. *The Writings of Albert Gallatin.* Edited by Henry Adams. 3 vols. Philadelphia: J. B. Lippincott, 1879.

Garfield, James. *The Diary of James A. Garfield.* Vol. 4, *1878–1881.* Edited by Harry James Brown and Frederick D. Williams. Lansing: Michigan State University Press, 1981.

———. *The Wild Life of the Army: Civil War Letters of James A. Garfield.* Edited by Frederick D. Williams. Lansing: Michigan State University Press, 1964.

———. *The Works of James Abram Garfield.* Edited by Burke A. Hinsdale. Boston: James R. Osgood, 1882.

Garraty, John A. *Henry Cabot Lodge: A Biography.* New York: Alfred A. Knopf, 1953.

Garrison, William Lloyd. *The Letters of William Lloyd Garrison.* Edited by Walter M. Merrill and Louis Ruchames. 6 vols. Cambridge: Belknap Press of Harvard University Press, 1971–1981.

Gatell, Frank Otto. *The Jacksonians and the Money Power, 1829–1840.* Chicago: Rand McNally, 1967.

———, ed. *Essays on Jacksonian America.* New York: Holt, Rinehart and Winston, 1970.

Gilbert, Felix. *To the Farewell Address: Ideas of Early American Foreign Policy.* Princeton: Princeton University Press, 1961.

Glad, Paul W. *The Trumpet Soundeth: William Jennings Bryan and his Democracy, 1896–1912.* Lincoln: University of Nebraska Press, 1960.

Goebel, Dorothy Burne. *William Henry Harrison: A Political Biography.* Indianapolis: Historical Bureau of the Indiana Library and Historical Department, 1926.

Goldwater, Barry M. *The Conscience of a Conservative.* Shepherdsville, Ky.: Victor Publishing Company, 1960.

———. *With No Apologies: The Personal and Political Memoirs of United States Senator Barry M. Goldwater.* New York: William Morrow, 1979.

Gordon, John Steele. *Hamilton's Blessing: The Extraordinary Life and Times of Our National Debt.* New York: Walker, 1997.

Gordon-Reed, Annette. *Thomas Jefferson and Sally Hemings: An American Controversy.* Charlottesville: University Press of Virginia, 1998.

Govan, Thomas Payne. *Nicholas Biddle, Nationalist and Public Banker, 1786–1844.* Chicago: University of Chicago Press, 1959.

Gregory, Dick. *Dick Gregory's Political Primer.* Edited by James R. McGraw. New York: Harper and Row, 1972.

Guelzo, Allen C. *Abraham Lincoln: Redeemer President.* Grand Rapids, Mich.: Wm. B. Eerdmans, 1999.

Gwinn, William Rea. *Uncle Joe Cannon: Archfoe of Insurgency, A History of the Rise and Fall of Cannonism.* New York: Bookman Associates, 1957.

Hacker, Louis M. *Alexander Hamilton in the American Tradition.* New York: McGraw-Hill, 1957.

Hall, Margaret Esther, ed. *Alexander Hamilton Reader: A Compilation of Materials by and Commenting on Hamilton.* New York: Oceana, 1957.

Hamilton, Alexander. *Hamiltonian Principles: Extracts from the Writings of Alexander Hamilton.* Edited by James Truslow Adams. Boston: Little, Brown, 1928.

———. *Papers on Public Credit, Commerce and Finance by Alexander Hamilton.* Edited by Samuel McKee Jr. New York: Columbia University Press, 1934.

————. *Selected Writings and Speeches of Alexander Hamilton.* Edited by Morton J. Frisch. Washington, D.C.: American Enterprise Institute for Public Policy Research, 1985.

————. *The Basic Ideas of Alexander Hamilton.* Edited by Richard B. Morris. New York: Washington Square Press, 1965.

————. *The Law Practice of Alexander Hamilton: Documents and Commentary.* Edited by Julius Goebel Jr., and Joseph H. Smith. 5 vols. New York: Columbia University Press, 1964–1981.

————. *The Papers of Alexander Hamilton.* Edited by Harold C. Syrett. 27 vols. New York: Columbia University Press, 1961–1987.

————. *The Works of Alexander Hamilton.* Edited by Henry Cabot Lodge. 12 vols. New York: G. P. Putnam's Sons, 1904.

————. *The Works of Alexander Hamilton Comprising His Correspondence, and His Political and Official Writings, Exclusive of The Federalist, Civil and Military.* Edited by John C. Hamilton. New York: John F. Trow, Printer, 1850–1851.

Hamilton, Alexander, James Madison, and John Jay. *The Federalist.* Edited by Jacob E. Cooke. Middletown, Conn.: Wesleyan University Press, 1961.

Hamilton, Allan McLane. *The Intimate Life of Alexander Hamilton.* New York: Charles Scribner's Sons, 1910.

Hamilton, John C. *The Life of Alexander Hamilton.* Vol. 1. New York: Halsted and Voorhies, 1834.

Hamlin, Mary P., and George Arliss. *Hamilton: A Play in Four Acts.* Boston: Walter H. Baker, 1918.

Handlin, Lillian. *George Bancroft: The Intellectual as Democrat.* New York: Harper and Row, 1984.

Harrison, Benjamin. *This Country of Ours.* New York: Charles Scribner's Sons, 1897.

Hart, Albert Bushnell, and Herbert Ronald Ferleger, eds. *Theodore Roosevelt Cyclopedia.* New York City: Roosevelt Memorial Association, 1941.

Hartz, Louis. *The Liberal Tradition in America: An Interpretation of American Political Thought Since the Revolution.* New York: Harcourt, Brace, 1955.

Harward, Donald W., ed. *Crisis in Confidence: The Impact of Watergate.* Boston: Little, Brown, 1974.

Hayes, Rutherford B. *Diary and Letters of Rutherford Birchard Hayes, Nineteenth President of the United States.* Vol. 1, *1834–1860.* Edited by Charles Richard Williams. 5 vols. Columbus: Ohio State Archaeological Society, 1922–1926.

Hecht, Marie B. *John Quincy Adams: A Personal History of an Independent Man.* New York: Macmillan, 1972.

————. *Odd Destiny: The Life of Alexander Hamilton.* New York: Macmillan, 1982.

Hendrick, Burton J. *Statesmen of the Lost Cause: Jefferson Davis and His Cabinet.* Boston: Little, Brown, 1944.

Hickey, Donald R. *The War of 1812.* Urbana and Chicago: University of Illinois Press, 1989.

Hildreth, Richard. *The History of the United States of America.* Vol. 5. New York: Harper and Brothers, 1851.

Hoar, George F. *Autobiography of Seventy Years.* 2 vols. New York: Charles Scribner's Sons, 1903.

Hofstadter, Richard. *The Progressive Historians: Turner, Beard, Parrington.* New York: Alfred A. Knopf, 1968.

Hofstadter, Richard, William Miller, and Daniel Aaron. *The United States: The History of a Republic.* Englewood Cliffs, N.J.: Prentice-Hall, 1957.

Hone, Philip. *The Diary of Philip Hone, 1828–1851.* Vol. 1. Edited by Allan Nevins. New York: Kraus Reprint Company, 1960.

Hovey, Richard B. *John Jay Chapman: An American Mind.* New York: Columbia University Press, 1959.

Humphrey, George M. *The Basic Papers of George M. Humphrey as Secretary of the Treasury, 1953–1957.* Edited by Nathaniel R. Howard. Cleveland, Ohio: Western Reserve Historical Society, 1965.

Irving, Washington. *Life of George Washington.* Part 2. New York: Peter Fenelon Collier, 1897.

———. *Washington Irving, Letters.* Edited by Ralph M. Aderman, Herbert Kleinfield, Jenifer S. Banks. 4 vols. Boston: Twayne, 1978–.

Jackson, Andrew. *The Papers of Andrew Jackson.* Edited by Harold D. Moser and Sharon Macpherson. Vol. 2, *1804–1813.* Knoxville: University of Tennessee Press, 1984.

Jaffe, Steven. *Who Were the Founding Fathers? Two Hundred Years of Reinventing American History.* New York: Henry Holt, 1996.

James, Marquis. *Andrew Jackson: The Border Captain.* Indianapolis: Bobbs-Merrill, 1933.

Jameson, John Franklin. *John Franklin Jameson and the Development of Humanistic Scholarship in America.* Vol. 1, *Selected Essays.* Edited by Morey Rothberg and Jacqueline Goggin. Athens: University of Georgia Press, 1993.

Jefferson, Thomas. *The Papers of Thomas Jefferson.* Edited by Julian Boyd, Charles T. Cullen, and John Catanzariti. 28 vols. Princeton: Princeton University Press, 1950–.

———. *The Writings of Thomas Jefferson.* Edited by Andrew A. Lipscomb. 10 vols. Washington, D.C.: Thomas Jefferson Memorial Association, 1903.

———. *Thomas Jefferson, Writings.* Edited by Merrill Peterson. New York: Library of America, 1984.

———. *Writings, Notes on the State of Virginia.* New York: Library of America, 1984.

Jessup, Philip C. *Elihu Root.* Vol. 2, *1905–1937.* New York: Dodd, Mead, 1938.

Johnson, Andrew. *The Papers of Andrew Johnson.* Vol. 2, *1852–1857.* Edited by Leroy P. Graf and Ralph W. Haskins. Knoxville: University of Tennessee Press, 1970.

Johnson, Gerald W. *American Heroes and Hero-Worship.* New York: Harper and Brothers, 1943.

Jordan, Barbara C. *Selected Speeches.* Edited by Sandra Parham. Washington, D.C.: Howard University Press, 1999.

Jumonville, Neil. *Henry Steele Commager: Mid-Century Liberalism and the History of the Present.* Chapel Hill: University of North Carolina Press, 1999.

Kammen, Michael. *A Season of Youth: The American Revolution and the Historical Imagination.* New York: Alfred A. Knopf, 1978.

———. *Mystic Chords of Memory: The Transformation of Tradition in American Culture.* New York: Vintage Books, 1993.

Kaplan, Justin. *Lincoln Steffens: A Biography.* New York: Simon and Schuster, 1974.

Kazin, Michael. *The Populist Persuasion: An American History.* New York: Basic Books, 1995.

Keane, John. *Tom Paine: A Political Life.* Boston: Little, Brown, 1995.

Kennedy, John F. *Profiles in Courage.* New York: Harper and Row, 1956.

Kennedy, Roger G. *Burr, Hamilton, and Jefferson: A Study in Character.* New York: Oxford University Press, 2000.

Kent, James. *Memoirs and Letters of James Kent, LL.D.* Edited by William Kent. Boston: Little, Brown, 1898.

Kingsley, Sidney. *The Patriots: A Play in a Prologue and Three Acts.* New York: Random House, 1943.

Kirk, Russell. *The Conservative Mind, from Burke to Santayana.* Chicago: Henry Regnery, 1953.

Koch, Adrienne. *Power, Morals, and the Founding Fathers: Essays in the Interpretation of the American Enlightenment.* Ithaca, N.Y.: Cornell University Press, 1961.

Kohn, Richard H. *Eagle and Sword: The Federalists and the Creation of the Military Establishment in America, 1783–1802.* New York: Free Press, 1975.

Knott, Stephen F. *Secret and Sanctioned: Covert Operations and the American Presidency.* New York: Oxford University Press, 1996.

Kraus, Michael. *A History of American History.* New York: Farrar and Rinehart, 1937.

Kunhardt, Philip B. Jr., Philip B. Kunhardt III, and Peter W. Kunhardt. *The American President.* New York: Riverhead Books, 1999.

Kurth, Peter. *American Cassandra: The Life of Dorothy Thompson.* Boston: Little, Brown, 1990.

La Follette, Robert M. *La Follette's Autobiography: A Personal Narrative of Political Experiences.* Madison, Wis.: Robert M. La Follette, 1913.

Leggett, William. *Democratick Editorials, Essays in Political Economy by William Leggett.* Edited by Lawrence H. White. Indianapolis: Liberty Press, 1984.

Leider, Emily Wortis. *California's Daughter: Gertrude Atherton and Her Times.* Stanford: Stanford University Press, 1991.

Lemke, William. *You and Your Money.* Philadelphia: Dorrance, 1938.

Lens, Sidney. *Radicalism in America.* New York: Thomas A. Crowell, 1969.

Lester, C. Edwards. *Life and Public Services of Charles Sumner.* New York: United States Publishing Company, 1874.

Levin, Phyllis Lee. *Abigail Adams: A Biography.* New York: St. Martin's Press, 1987.

Levine, Lawrence W. *Defender of the Faith, William Jennings Bryan: The Last Decade, 1915–1925.* Cambridge: Harvard University Press, 1987.

Levy, Leonard W. *Jefferson and Civil Liberties: The Darker Side.* Chicago: Ivan R. Dee, 1989.

Lewis, Jan Ellen, and Peter S. Onuf, eds. *Sally Hemings and Thomas Jefferson: History, Memory, and Civic Culture.* Charlottesville: University Press of Virginia, 1999.

Lincoln, Abraham. *Abraham Lincoln, Speeches and Writings, 1859–1865.* Edited by Don E. Fehrenbacher. New York: Library of America, 1989.

———. *The Collected Works of Abraham Lincoln.* Edited by Roy P. Basler. 9 vols. New Brunswick, N.J.: Rutgers University Press, 1953–1955.

Lind, Michael, ed. *Hamilton's Republic: Readings in the American Democratic Nationalist Tradition.* New York: Free Press, 1997.

Lippmann, Walter. *A Preface to Politics.* Ann Arbor: University of Michigan Press, 1962.

———. *Men of Destiny.* New York: Macmillan, 1927.

———. *Public Opinion.* New York: Macmillan, 1936.

Lodge, Henry Cabot. *Alexander Hamilton.* Boston: Houghton, Mifflin, 1898.

————, ed. *Selections from the Correspondence of Theodore Roosevelt and Henry Cabot Lodge.* Vol. 1, *1884–1918.* 2 vols. New York: Charles Scribner's Sons, 1925.

Logan, Rayford W., and Michael R. Winston, eds. *Dictionary of American Negro Biography.* New York: W. W. Norton, 1982.

Logue, Cal M., and Howard Dorgan, eds. *The Oratory of Southern Demagogues.* Baton Rouge: Louisiana State University Press, 1981.

Lomask, Milton. *Aaron Burr: The Years from Princeton to Vice President, 1756–1805.* New York: Farrar Straus Giroux, 1979.

Lundberg, Ferdinand. *The Rich and the Super-Rich: A Study in the Power of Money Today.* New York: Lyle Stuart, 1969.

Lycan, Gilbert L. *Alexander Hamilton and American Foreign Policy: A Design for Greatness.* Norman: University of Oklahoma Press, 1970.

Lynd, Staughton. *Class Conflict, Slavery, and the United States Constitution.* Indianapolis: Bobbs-Merrill, 1967.

MacKay, Kenneth Campbell. *The Progressive Movement of 1924.* New York: Columbia University Press, 1947.

Madison, James. *The Writings of James Madison.* Edited by Gaillard Hunt. 9 vols. New York: G. P. Putnam's Sons, 1908.

Malone, Dumas. *Jefferson and His Time.* 6 vols. Boston: Little, Brown, 1948–1981.

Malone, Dumas, and Allen Johnson, eds. *Dictionary of American Biography.* 20 vols. New York: Charles Scribner's Sons, 1928–1936.

Mappen, Marc. *Jerseyana: The Underside of New Jersey History.* New Brunswick, N.J.: Rutgers University Press, 1992.

Marshall, John. *An Autobiographical Sketch by John Marshall, Written at the Request of Joseph Story and Now Printed for the First Time from the Original Manuscript Preserved at the William L. Clements Library, Together with a Letter from Chief Justice Marshall to Justice Story Relating Thereto.* Edited by John Stokes Adams. Ann Arbor: University of Michigan Press, 1937.

————. *The Papers of John Marshall.* Edited by Charles F. Hobson. 10 vols. Chapel Hill: University of North Carolina Press, 1974–.

Martin, Edward Sandford. *The Life of Joseph Hodges Choate, As Gathered Chiefly from His Letters.* New York: Charles Scribner's Sons, 1920.

Masters, Edgar Lee. *Lincoln the Man.* New York: Dodd, Mead, 1931.

Matthiessen, F. O. *American Renaissance: Art and Expression in the Age of Emerson and Whitman.* New York: Oxford University Press, 1968.

Mayo, Bernard. *Henry Clay: Spokesman of the New West.* Boston: Houghton Mifflin, 1937.

McCaughey, Robert A. *Josiah Quincy, 1772–1864: The Last Federalist.* Cambridge: Harvard University Press, 1974.

McClellan, James. *Joseph Story and the American Constitution: A Study in Political and Legal Thought.* Norman: University of Oklahoma Press, 1971.

McCoy, Donald R. *Landon of Kansas.* Lincoln: University of Nebraska Press, 1966.

McDonald, Forrest. *Alexander Hamilton: A Biography.* New York: W. W. Norton, 1982.

————. *The Presidency of George Washington.* Lawrence: University Press of Kansas, 1974.

————. *The Presidency of Thomas Jefferson.* Lawrence: University Press of Kansas, 1976.

————. *We the People: The Economic Origins of the Constitution*. Chicago: University of Chicago Press, 1958.

McGuinness, Colleen, ed. *American Leaders, 1789–1994*. Washington, D.C.: Congressional Quarterly, 1994.

McKenna, Marian C. *Borah*. Ann Arbor: University of Michigan Press, 1961.

McMaster, John Bach. *A History of the People of the United States, from the Revolution to the Civil War*. Vol. 1, *1784–1790*. New York: D. Appleton, 1914.

McNamara, Peter. *Political Economy and Statesmanship: Smith, Hamilton, and the Foundation of the Commercial Republic*. DeKalb: Northern Illinois University Press, 1998.

Mee, Charles L. *The Genius of the People*. New York: Harper and Row, 1987.

Meigs, William M. *The Life of Thomas Hart Benton*. Philadelphia: J. B. Lippincott, 1904.

Meyers, Marvin. *The Jacksonian Persuasion: Politics and Belief*. Stanford: Stanford University Press, 1957.

Miers, Earl Schenck, ed. *Lincoln Day by Day: A Chronology, 1809–1865*. Washington, D.C.: Lincoln Sesquicentennial Commission, 1960.

Miller, Arthur. *The Last Yankee, with a New Essay About Theatre Language and Broken Glass*. Garden City, N.Y.: Fireside Theatre, 1994.

Miller, James. *"Democracy Is in the Streets": From Port Huron to the Siege of Chicago*. New York: Simon and Schuster, 1987.

Miller, John C. *Alexander Hamilton: Portrait in Paradox*. New York: Harper and Brothers, 1959.

Miller, Nathan. *The Founding Finaglers*. New York: David McKay, 1976.

————. *Theodore Roosevelt: A Life*. New York: William Morrow, 1992.

Millspaugh, Arthur C. *Democracy, Efficiency, Stability: An Appraisal of American Government*. Washington, D.C.: Brookings Institution, 1942.

Minor, Henry A. *The Story of the Democratic Party*. New York: Macmillan, 1928.

Mitchell, Broadus. *Alexander Hamilton: The National Adventure, 1788–1804*. New York: Macmillan, 1962.

————. *Alexander Hamilton: Youth to Maturity, 1755–1788*. New York: Macmillan, 1957.

————. *Heritage from Hamilton*. New York: Columbia University Press, 1957.

Mitgang, Herbert, ed. *Lincoln: As They Saw Him*. New York: Rinehart, 1956.

Moley, Raymond. *Twenty-seven Masters of Politics, in a Personal Perspective*. New York: Funk and Wagnalls, 1949.

Morgenthau, Hans J. *In Defense of the National Interest: A Critical Examination of American Foreign Policy*. New York: Alfred A. Knopf, 1951.

Morison, Elting E. *Turmoil and Tradition: A Study of the Life and Times of Henry L. Stimson*. Boston: Houghton Mifflin, 1960.

Morison, Samuel Eliot. *Harrison Gray Otis, 1765–1848: The Urbane Federalist*. Boston: Houghton Mifflin, 1969.

Morris, Gouverneur. *The Diary and Letters of Gouverneur Morris, Minister of the United States to France, Member of the Constitutional Convention, etc.* Edited by Anne Cary Morris. 2 vols. New York: Charles Scribner's Sons, 1888.

Morse, Anson Daniel. *Parties and Party Leaders*. Boston: Marshall Jones, 1923.

Morse, John T. *The Life of Alexander Hamilton*. 2 vols. Boston: Little, Brown, 1876.

Mott, Frank Luther. *American Journalism, A History: 1690–1960*. New York: Macmillan, 1962.

Muldoon, Sylvan J. *Alexander Hamilton's Pioneer Son: The Life and Times of Colonel William Stephen Hamilton, 1797–1850.* Harrisburg, Penn.: Aurand Press, 1930.

Murray, Robert K. *The Harding Era: Warren G. Harding and His Administration.* Minneapolis: University of Minnesota Press, 1969.

Neal, Steve. *Dark Horse: A Biography of Wendell Willkie.* Garden City, N.Y.: Doubleday, 1984.

Nelson, William H., ed. *Theory and Practice in American Politics.* Chicago: University of Chicago Press, 1964.

Nevins, Allan. *Allan Nevins on History.* Edited by Ray Allen Billington. New York: Charles Scribner's Sons, 1975.

———. *Grover Cleveland: A Study in Courage.* New York: Dodd, Mead, 1932.

———. *The Evening Post: A Century of Journalism.* New York: Boni and Liveright, 1922.

Newman, Roger K. *Hugo Black: A Biography.* New York: Pantheon Books, 1994.

Nichols, Jeanette P., and Roy F. Nichols. *The Republic of the United States: A History.* 2 vols. New York: D. Appleton-Century, 1942.

Nichols, Roy Franklin. *Franklin Pierce: Young Hickory of the Granite Hills.* Philadelphia: University of Pennsylvania Press, 1931.

Niven, John. *John C. Calhoun and the Price of Union: A Biography.* Baton Rouge: Louisiana State University Press, 1988.

Nolan, Charles J. *Aaron Burr and the American Literary Imagination.* Westport, Conn.: Greenwood Press, 1980.

Oates, Stephen B. *With Malice Toward None: The Life of Abraham Lincoln.* New York: Harper and Row, 1977.

O'Brien, Michael. *The Idea of the American South, 1920–1941.* Baltimore: Johns Hopkins University Press, 1979.

O'Connor, Harvey. *Mellon's Millions: The Biography of a Fortune.* New York: John Day, 1933.

Oliver, Frederick Scott. *Alexander Hamilton: An Essay on American Union.* New York: G. P. Putnam's Sons, 1923.

Onuf, Peter S., ed. *Jeffersonian Legacies.* Charlottesville: University Press of Virginia, 1993.

Osborn, George Coleman. *John Sharp Williams, Planter-Statesman of the Deep South.* Gloucester, Mass.: Peter Smith, 1964.

Pach, Chester J., and Elmo Richardson. *The Presidency of Dwight D. Eisenhower.* Lawrence: University Press of Kansas, 1991.

Padover, Saul K. *The Genius of America: Men Whose Ideas Shaped Our Civilization.* New York: McGraw-Hill, 1960.

Paine, Thomas. *Life and Writings of Thomas Paine.* Edited by Daniel Edwin Wheeler. 10 vols. New York: Vincent Parke, 1908.

Paludan, Phillip S. *A Covenant with Death: The Constitution, Law, and Equality in the Civil War Era.* Urbana: University of Illinois Press, 1975.

Pancake, John S. *Thomas Jefferson and Alexander Hamilton.* Woodbury, N.Y.: Barron's Educational Series, 1974.

Parker, Edward G. *Reminiscences of Rufus Choate, the Great American Advocate.* New York: Mason Brothers, 1860.

Parker, George F. *Recollections of Grover Cleveland.* New York: Century, 1909.

Parrington, Vernon L. *Main Currents in American Thought: An Interpretation of American Literature from the Beginnings to 1920.* 3 vols. New York: Harcourt, Brace, 1927–1930.

Parsons, Theophilus Jr., *Memoir of Theophilus Parsons, Chief Justice of the Supreme Judicial Court of Massachusetts; with Notices of Some of His Contemporaries. By His Son, Theophilus Parsons, Jr.* New York: Da Capo Press, 1970.

Peoples Bicentennial Commission. *America's Birthday: A Planning and Activity Guide for Citizens' Participation During the Bicentennial Years.* New York: Simon and Schuster, 1974.

Peterson, Merrill D. *The Great Triumvirate: Webster, Clay, and Calhoun.* New York: Oxford University Press, 1987.

———. *The Jefferson Image in the American Mind.* New York: Oxford University Press, 1960.

———. *Lincoln in American Memory.* New York: Oxford University Press, 1994.

———, ed. *Thomas Jefferson, Writings.* New York: Library of America, 1984.

Phillips, Ulrich Bonnel. *The Course of the South to Secession: An Interpretation by Ulrich Bonnel Phillips.* Edited by E. Merton Coulter. Gloucester, Mass.: Peter Smith, 1958.

———. *The Economic and Political Essays of the Ante-Bellum South.* New York: Burt Franklin, 1970.

Pickens, William. *The New Negro, His Political, Civil and Mental Status and Related Essays.* New York: Negro Universities Press, 1969.

Pilkington, Walter. *Hamilton College, 1812/1962.* Clinton, N.Y.: Hamilton College, 1962.

Polk, James K. *Polk: The Diary of a President, 1845–1849.* Edited by Allan Nevins. Longmans, Green, 1952.

———. *The Diary of James K. Polk During His Presidency, 1845–1849.* Edited by Milo M. Quaife. 4 vols. Chicago: A. C. McClurg, 1910.

Pound, Ezra. *"Dear Uncle George": The Correspondence Between Ezra Pound and Congressman Tinkham of Massachusetts.* Edited by Philip J. Burns. Orono: National Poetry Foundation, University of Maine, 1996.

———. *"I Cease Not to Yowl": Ezra Pound's Letters to Olivia Rossetti Agresti.* Edited by Demetres P. Tryphonopoulos and Leon Surette. Urbana and Chicago: University of Illinois Press, 1998.

———. *Impact: Essays on Ignorance and the Decline of American Civilization.* Edited by Noel Stock. Chicago: Henry Regnery, 1960.

———. *The Cantos of Ezra Pound.* New York: New Directions Books, 1948.

Pringle, Henry F. *Theodore Roosevelt: A Biography.* New York: Harcourt, Brace, 1931.

Putnam, Carleton. *Theodore Roosevelt.* Vol. 1, *The Formative Years, 1858–1886.* New York: Charles Scribner's Sons, 1958.

Rable, George C. *The Confederate Republic: A Revolution Against Politics.* Chapel Hill: University of North Carolina Press, 1994.

Randall, J. G. *Lincoln: The Liberal Statesman.* New York: Dodd, Mead, 1947.

———. *Lincoln the President: Springfield to Gettysburg.* New York: Dodd, Mead, 1945.

Redman, Tim. *Ezra Pound and Italian Fascism.* Cambridge: Cambridge University Press, 1991.

Reid, Whitelaw. *One Welshman: A Glance at a Great Career.* London: Macmillan, Limited, 1912.

Remini, Robert V. *Andrew Jackson and the Bank War: A Study in the Growth of Presidential Power.* New York: W. W. Norton, 1967.

————. *Andrew Jackson and the Course of American Democracy, 1833–1845*. New York: Harper and Row, 1984.

————. *Andrew Jackson and the Course of American Empire, 1767–1821*. New York: Harper and Row, 1977.

————. *Andrew Jackson and the Course of American Freedom, 1822–1832*. New York: Harper and Row, 1981.

————. *Daniel Webster: The Man and His Time*. New York: W. W. Norton, 1997.

Restoring the Presidency: Reconsidering the Twenty-second Amendment. Washington, D.C.: National Legal Center for the Public Interest, 1990.

Richardson, Don, ed. *Conversations with Carter*. Boulder, Colo.: Lynne Rienner, 1998.

Riethmuller, Christopher. *Alexander Hamilton and His Contemporaries, or The Rise of the American Commonwealth*. London: Bell and Daldy, 1864.

Riker, William H. *The Art of Political Manipulation*. New Haven: Yale University Press, 1986.

Ripley, Peter C. *The Black Abolitionist Papers*. Vol. 3, *The United States, 1830–1846*. Chapel Hill: University of North Carolina Press, 1991.

Robinson, William A. *Thomas B. Reed, Parliamentarian*. New York: Dodd, Mead, 1930.

Rogow, Arnold A. *A Fatal Friendship: Alexander Hamilton and Aaron Burr*. New York: Hill and Wang, 1998.

Roosevelt, Franklin D. *The Roosevelt Reader, Selected Speeches, Messages, Press Conferences, and Letters of Franklin D. Roosevelt*. Edited by Basil Rauch. New York: Rinehart, 1957.

————. *The Public Papers and Addresses of Franklin D. Roosevelt*. Edited by Samuel I. Rosenman. 13 vols. New York: Random House, 1938–1950.

Roosevelt, Theodore. *Gouverneur Morris*. Boston: Houghton, Mifflin, 1898.

————. *New York*. New York: Charles Scribner's Sons, 1924.

————. *The Letters of Theodore Roosevelt*. Edited by Elting E. Morison. 8 vols. Cambridge: Harvard University Press, 1951–1954.

————. *The New Nationalism*. New York: Outlook, 1910.

————. *Thomas Hart Benton*. Boston: Houghton, Mifflin, 1886.

Rossiter, Clinton. *Alexander Hamilton and the Constitution*. New York: Harcourt, Brace, and World, 1964.

————. *Conservatism in America*. New York: Alfred A. Knopf, 1955.

Rubin, Joseph Jay. *The Historic Whitman*. University Park: Pennsylvania State University Press, 1973.

Ruffin, Edmund. *The Diary of Edmund Ruffin*. Vol. 2, *The Years of Hope, April, 1861–June, 1863*. Edited by William Kauffman Scarborough. Baton Rouge: Louisiana State University Press, 1976.

Rush, Benjamin. *The Autobiography of Benjamin Rush: His "Travels Through Life" Together with his Commonplace Book for 1789–1813*. Edited by George W. Corner. Princeton: Princeton University Press, 1948.

Russell, Francis. *The Shadow of Blooming Grove: Warren G. Harding in His Times*. New York: McGraw-Hill, 1968.

Rutland, Robert Allen. *The Presidency of James Madison*. Lawrence: University Press of Kansas, 1990.

Safire, William. *Scandalmonger, a Novel.* New York: Simon and Schuster, 2000.

Saltonstall, Leverett. *The Papers of Leverett Saltonstall, 1816–1845.* Vol. 2, *1831–June 1840.* Edited by Robert E. Moody. Boston: Massachusetts Historical Society, 1981.

Samuels, Ernest. *Henry Adams: The Middle Years.* Cambridge: Belknap Press of Harvard University Press, 1958.

Sandburg, Carl. *The People, Yes.* New York: Harcourt, Brace, 1936.

Sargent, Lyman Tower, ed. *Extremism in America: A Reader.* New York: New York University Press, 1995.

Schaffer, Alan. *Vito Marcantonio, Radical in Congress.* Syracuse, N.Y.: Syracuse University Press, 1966.

Schapsmeier, Edward L., and Frederick H. Schapsmeier. *Walter Lippmann, Philosopher-Journalist.* Washington, D.C.: Public Affairs Press, 1969.

Schlesinger, Arthur M. Jr. *A Life in the Twentieth Century: Innocent Beginnings, 1917–1950.* Boston: Houghton Mifflin, 2000.

———. *A Thousand Days: John F. Kennedy in the White House.* Boston: Houghton Mifflin, 1965.

———. *The Age of Jackson.* New York: Book Find Club, 1945.

———. *The Age of Roosevelt: The Crisis of the Old Order, 1919–1933.* Boston: Houghton Mifflin, 1957.

———. *The Age of Roosevelt: The Politics of Upheaval.* Boston: Houghton Mifflin, 1960.

———. *The Imperial Presidency.* Boston: Houghton Mifflin, 1973.

Schmertz, Eric J., Natalie Datlof, and Alexej Ugrinsky. *Ronald Reagan's America.* Westport, Conn.: Greenwood Press, 1997.

Schmucker, Samuel M. *The Life and Times of Alexander Hamilton.* Philadelphia: J. W. Bradley, 1857.

Schouler, James. *Alexander Hamilton.* Boston: Small, Maynard, 1901.

———. *History of the United States of America, Under the Constitution.* Vol. 1, *1783–1801.* New York: Dodd, Mead, 1894.

Schuckers, J. W. *The Life and Public Services of Salmon Portland Chase.* New York: D. Appleton, 1874.

Schurz, Carl. *Speeches, Correspondence and Political Papers of Carl Schurz.* Vol. 4, *July 20, 1880–September 15, 1888.* Edited by Frederic Bancroft. New York: G. P. Putnam's Sons, 1913.

Sellers, Charles Grier Jr. *James K. Polk, Jacksonian, 1795–1843.* Princeton: Princeton University Press, 1957.

———, ed. *Andrew Jackson: A Profile.* New York: Hill and Wang, 1971.

Seward, William H. *An Autobiography, from 1801 to 1834; Memoir of His Life, and Selections from His Letters, 1831–1846.* Edited by Frederick W. Seward. New York: Derby and Miller, 1891.

Shea, George. *The Life and Epoch of Alexander Hamilton: A Historical Study.* Boston: Houghton, Osgood, 1879.

Shuffelton, Frank. *Thomas Jefferson: A Comprehensive, Annotated Bibliography of Writings About Him (1826–1980).* New York: Garland, 1983.

Sinclair, Andrew. *The Available Man: The Life Behind the Masks of Warren Gamaliel Harding.* New York: Macmillan, 1965.

Skeen, C. Edward. *John Armstrong, Jr., 1758–1843: A Biography.* Syracuse, N.Y.: Syracuse University Press, 1981.

Smertenko, Johan J. *Alexander Hamilton.* New York: Greenburg, 1932.

Smith, Chard Powers. *Hamilton: A Poetic Drama in Three Acts.* New York: Coward-McCann, 1930.

Smith, J. Allen. *The Growth and Decadence of Constitutional Government.* New York: Henry Holt, 1930.

Sprout, Harold, and Margaret Sprout. *The Rise of American Naval Power, 1776–1918.* Princeton: Princeton University Press, 1939.

Steffens, Lincoln. *The Autobiography of Lincoln Steffens.* New York: Harcourt, Brace, 1931.

Stephens, Alexander. *A Constitutional View of the Late War Between the States; Its Causes, Character, Conduct and Results.* Philadelphia: National Publishing Company, 1870.

Stevenson, Adlai. *The Papers of Adlai E. Stevenson.* Edited by Walter Johnson. 8 vols. Boston: Little, Brown, 1972–1979.

Stewart, Donald H. *The Opposition Press of the Federalist Period.* Albany: State University of New York Press, 1969.

Stinnett, Ronald F. *Democrats, Dinners, and Dollars: A History of the Democratic Party, Its Dinners, Its Ritual.* Ames: Iowa State University Press, 1967.

Stock, Noel. *Poet in Exile: Ezra Pound.* New York: Barnes and Noble, 1964.

Stone, I. F. *In a Time of Torment.* New York: Random House, 1967.

Storing, Herbert. *Toward a More Perfect Union: Writings of Herbert J. Storing.* Edited by Joseph M. Bessette. Washington, D.C.: AEI Press, 1995.

Stourzh, Gerald. *Alexander Hamilton and the Idea of Republican Government.* Stanford: Stanford University Press, 1970.

Strauss, Leo, and Joseph Cropsey. *History of Political Philosophy.* 2d ed. Chicago: University of Chicago Press, 1973.

Strong, George Templeton. *The Diary of George Templeton Strong: Young Man in New York, 1835–1849.* Edited by Allan Nevins and Milton Halsey Thomas. New York: Macmillan, 1952.

Stryker, Melancthon Woolsey. *Hamilton, Lincoln, and Other Addresses.* Utica, N.Y.: William T. Smith, 1896.

Sumner, William Graham. *Alexander Hamilton.* New York: Dodd, Mead, 1890.

———. *Andrew Jackson.* Boston: Houghton Mifflin, 1899.

Swanson, Marvin C., ed. *Charles A. Beard: An Observance of the Centennial of His Birth.* Greencastle, Ind.: Depauw University, 1976.

Swisher, Carl Brent. *Roger B. Taney.* Hamden, Conn.: Archon Books, 1961.

Taft, William Howard. *Our Chief Magistrate and His Powers.* New York: Columbia University Press, 1938.

Tanabaum, Duane. *The Bricker Amendment Controversy: A Test of Eisenhower's Political Leadership.* Ithaca, N.Y.: Cornell University Press, 1988.

Thistlethwaite, Frank. *The Great Experiment: An Introduction to the History of the American People.* Cambridge: Cambridge University Press, 1955.

Tompkins, C. David. *Senator Arthur H. Vandenberg: The Evolution of a Modern Republican, 1884–1945.* Lansing: Michigan State University Press, 1970.

Traubel, Horace. *With Walt Whitman in Camden (November 1, 1888–January 20, 1889).* New York: Rowman and Littlefield, 1961.

Truman, Harry S. *Memoirs by Harry S. Truman.* Vol. 2, *Years of Trial and Hope.* Garden City, N.Y.: Doubleday, 1956.

————. *Off the Record: The Private Papers of Harry S. Truman.* Edited by Robert H. Ferrell. New York: Harper and Row, 1980.

————. *The Autobiography of Harry S. Truman.* Edited by Robert H. Ferrell. Boulder: Colorado Associated University Press, 1980.

————. *Where the Buck Stops: The Personal and Private Writings of Harry S. Truman.* Edited by Margaret Truman. New York: Warner Books, 1989.

Tucker, Robert W., and David C. Hendrickson. *Empire of Liberty: The Statecraft of Thomas Jefferson.* New York: Oxford University Press, 1990.

Tugwell, Rexford Guy, and Joseph Dorfman. *Early American Policy, Six Columbia Contributors.* New York: Columbia University Press, 1960.

Turner, Arlin. *Hawthorne as Editor: Selections from His Writings in the American Magazine of Useful and Entertaining Knowledge.* Baton Rouge: Louisiana State University Press, 1941.

Twelve Southerners. *I'll Take My Stand: The South and the Agrarian Tradition.* New York: Peter Smith, 1951.

Unger, Irwin, and Debi Unger, eds. *The Times Were a Changin': The Sixties Reader.* New York: Three Rivers Press, 1998.

Van Buren, Martin. *Inquiry into the Origin and Course of Political Parties in the United States.* New York: Augustus M. Kelly, 1967.

————. *The Autobiography of Martin Van Buren.* Washington, D.C.: U.S. Government Printing Office, 1920.

Van Deusen, Glyndon G. *The Life of Henry Clay.* Boston: Little, Brown, 1937.

Vandenberg, Arthur H. *If Hamilton Were Here Today: American Fundamentals Applied to Modern Problems.* New York: G. P. Putnam's Sons, 1923.

————. *The Greatest American: Alexander Hamilton, An Historical Analysis of His Life and Works Together with a Symposium of Opinions by Distinguished Americans.* New York: G. P. Putnam's Sons, 1921.

Vidal, Gore. *Burr: A Novel.* New York: Random House, 1973.

————. *United States, Essays, 1952–1992.* New York: Random House, 1993.

Von Abele, Rudolph. *Alexander H. Stephens: A Biography.* New York: Alfred A. Knopf, 1946.

Von Holst, Hermann. *The Constitutional and Political History of the United States.* Vol. 1, *1750–1833, State Sovereignty and Slavery.* Chicago: Callaghan, 1877.

Wallace, Henry A. *Whose Constitution: An Inquiry into the General Welfare.* New York: Reynal and Hitchcock, 1936.

Walling, Karl-Friedrich. *Republican Empire: Alexander Hamilton on War and Free Government.* Lawrence: University Press of Kansas, 1999.

Walters, Raymond Jr. *Albert Gallatin: Jeffersonian Financier and Diplomat.* New York: Macmillan, 1957.

Ward, Geoffrey C. *Before the Trumpet, Young Franklin Roosevelt.* New York: Harper and Row, 1985.

Warshow, Robert Irving. *Alexander Hamilton: First American Business Man.* New York: Greenberg, 1931.

Washington, Booker T. *Black-Belt Diamonds: Gems from the Speeches, Addresses, and Talks to Students of Booker T. Washington.* Edited by Victoria Earle Matthews. New York: Fortune and Scott, 1898.

————. *The Booker T. Washington Papers.* Vol. 4, *1895–1898.* Edited by Louis R. Harlan. Urbana: University of Illinois Press, 1975.

Washington, George. *The Writings of George Washington from the Original Manuscript Sources, 1745–1799.* Edited by John C. Fitzpatrick. 39 vols. Washington, D.C.: U.S. Government Printing Office, 1931–1944.

Watson, Thomas E. *The Life and Times of Thomas Jefferson.* New York: D. Appleton, 1903.

Webster, Daniel. *The Papers of Daniel Webster, Correspondence.* Vol. 1, *1798–1824.* Edited by Charles M. Wiltse. Hanover, N.H.: University Press of New England, 1974.

————. *The Papers of Daniel Webster, Correspondence.* Vol. 2, *1825–1829.* Edited by Charles M. Wiltse and Harold D. Moser. Hanover, N.H.: University Press of New England, 1976.

————. *The Papers of Daniel Webster, Legal Papers.* Vol. 1, *The New Hampshire Practice.* Edited by Alfred S. Konefsky and Andrew J. King. Hanover, N.H.: University Press of New England, 1982.

————. *The Works of Daniel Webster.* Edited by Edward Everett. 6 vols. Boston: Charles C. Little and James Brown, 1851.

Weisberger, Bernard A. *The American Newspaperman.* Chicago: University of Chicago Press, 1961.

Weyl, Walter E. *The New Democracy: An Essay on Certain Political and Economic Tendencies in the United States.* New York: Macmillan, 1912.

White, Donald W. *The American Century: The Rise and Decline of the United States as a World Power.* New Haven: Yale University Press, 1996.

White, Leonard. *The Federalists: A Study in Administrative History, 1789–1801.* New York: Macmillan, 1948.

White, William Allen. *A Puritan in Babylon: The Story of Calvin Coolidge.* New York: Macmillan, 1938.

Whitman, Thomas Jefferson. *Dear Brother Walt: The Letters of Thomas Jefferson Whitman.* Edited by Dennis Berthold and Kenneth M. Price. Kent, Ohio: Kent State University Press, 1984.

Whitman, Walt. *The Gathering of the Forces: Editorials, Essays, Literary and Dramatic Reviews and Other Material Written by Walt Whitman as Editor of the Brooklyn Daily Eagle in 1846 and 1847.* 2 vols. Edited by Cleveland Rogers and John Black. New York: G. P. Putnam's Sons, 1920.

————. *Walt Whitman: The Correspondence.* Vol. 4, *1886–1889.* Edited by Edwin Haviland Miller. New York: New York University Press, 1969.

Who Was Who in America. Vol. 1, *1897–1942.* Chicago: A. N. Marquis, 1960.

Who Was Who in America. Vol. 2, *1943–1950.* Chicago: A. N. Marquis, 1950.

Widenor, William C. *Henry Cabot Lodge and the Search for an American Foreign Policy.* Berkeley: University of California Press, 1980.

Wilhelm, J. J. *Ezra Pound, The Tragic Years: 1925–1972.* University Park: Pennsylvania State University Press, 1994.

Will, George F. *Restoration: Congress, Term Limits, and the Recovery of Deliberative Democracy.* New York: Free Press, 1992.

Williams, Herbert Lee. *The Newspaperman's President, Harry S. Truman.* Chicago: Nelson-Hall, 1984.

Williams, John Sharp. *Thomas Jefferson: His Permanent Influence on American Institutions.* New York: AMS Press, 1967.

Williams, Stanley T. *The Life of Washington Irving.* Vol. 1. New York: Oxford University Press, 1935.
Williams, William Carlos. *In The American Grain.* Norfolk, Conn.: New Directions, 1939.
————. *Paterson.* New York: New Directions, 1992.
————. *The Autobiography of William Carlos Williams.* New York: Random House, 1951.
Wilmerding, Lucius Jr. *The Electoral College.* New Brunswick, NJ: Rutgers University Press, 1958.
Wilson, Clyde N., ed. *American Historians, 1607–1865.* Detroit: Gale Research, 1984.
————, ed. *American Historians, 1866–1912.* Detroit: Gale Research, 1986.
————, ed. *Twentieth-Century American Historians.* Detroit: Gale Research, 1983.
Wilson, James Grant, and John Fiske, eds. *Appletons' Cyclopaedia of American Biography.* 7 vols. New York: D. Appleton, 1888–1918.
Wilson, Major L. *The Presidency of Martin Van Buren.* Lawrence: University Press of Kansas, 1984.
Wilson, Woodrow. *The Papers of Woodrow Wilson.* Edited by Arthur S. Link. 69 vols. Princeton: Princeton University Press, 1966–1993.
Wiltse, Charles Maurice. *The Jeffersonian Tradition in American Democracy.* Chapel Hill: University of North Carolina Press, 1935.
Wish, Harvey. *The American Historian: A Social-Intellectual History of the Writing of the American Past.* New York: Oxford University Press, 1960.
Wood, Fernando. *An Address on the Genius, Public Life, and Opinions of Alexander Hamilton, Delivered at Richmond, Va., May 9, 1856, by the Request of the Ladies of the Central Mount Vernon Association, and in Aid of the Purchase of Mount Vernon.* New York: Evander Childs, Steam Book and Job Printer, 1856.
Woodward, C. Vann. *Tom Watson: Agrarian Rebel.* New York: Macmillan, 1938.
Woodward, W. E. *A New American History.* New York: Farrar and Rinehart, 1936.
————. *George Washington: The Image and the Man.* New York: Boni and Liveright, 1926.
————. *The Gift of Life: An Autobiography.* New York: E. P. Dutton, 1947.
Zahniser, Martin R. *Charles Cotesworth Pinckney: Founding Father.* Chapel Hill: University of North Carolina Press, 1967.
Zinn, Howard. *A People's History of the United States.* New York: Harper and Row, 1980.
————. *A People's History of the United States, 1492–Present, Twentieth Anniversary Edition.* New York: Harper Collins Publishers, 1999.

ARTICLES

"A Prophet Revisited." *Time,* 20 March 1964.
"A War of Myth and Memory." *Economist,* 6 December 1997.
"Albert Gallatin." *Fortune,* November 1942.
"An Unlucky Honest Man." *Time,* 22 December 1961.
"As Hamilton Went to a Cabinet Meeting." *Literary Digest,* 21 May 1921.
"Bill Clinton's Muse." *U.S. News and World Report,* 1 February 1993.
"Communication." *American Political Science Review,* March 1964.
"Early American Bigwigs on the Screen." *Literary Digest,* 3 October 1931.
"Foundering Father." *Harper's,* November 1998.
"Hamilton Explains." *Nation,* 20 March 1929.

"Newt's Universe." *Time,* 25 December 1995–1 January 1996.
"The Calculated Deceit." *Time,* 18 December 1964.
"The Fateful Vote to Impeach." *Time,* 5 August 1974.
"The Great Jefferson Joke." *New Republic,* 9 June 1926.
"The Reluctant Democrat." *Fortune,* 28 December 1943.
"Up Goes Hamilton." *Time,* 9 July 1951.

Aaron, Daniel. "The Mid-American Scholar." *New Republic* 211 (5 September 1994).
Adams, Brooks. "The Platform of the New Party." *North American Review* 119 (July 1874).
Adams, Charles Francis. "The Madison Papers." *North American Review* 53 (July 1841).
Adams, James Truslow. "Jefferson and Hamilton To-Day: The Dichotomy in American Thought." *Atlantic Monthly* 141 (April 1928).
Aly, Bower. "Alexander Hamilton's Year." *Quarterly Journal of Speech* 43, 4 (December 1957).
Apple, R. W. Jr. "House, in a Partisan 258–176 Vote, Approves a Broad, Open-Ended Impeachment Inquiry." *New York Times,* 9 October 1998.
Atherton, Gertrude. "The Hunt for Hamilton's Mother." *North American Review* 175 (August 1902).
———. Review of *Alexander Hamilton: An Essay on American Union,* by Frederick Scott Oliver. *North American Review* 183 (7 September 1906).
Bancroft, George, and Stephen Salisbury. "Report of the Council." *Proceedings of the American Antiquarian Society,* new series, 3 (October 1883–April 1885).
Barbash, Fred. "Delegates Deliver a Senate with a Silver Spoon in Its Mouth." *Washington Post,* 22 June 1987.
Barron, James. "Burrs Pay Homage to Their Vilified Ancestor." *New York Times,* 15 September 1986.
Beard, Charles A. "Government by Technologists." *New Republic,* 18 June 1930.
———. "Jefferson and the New Freedom." *New Republic,* 14 November 1914.
———. "Making the Fascist State." *New Republic,* 23 January 1929.
———. "Reconstructing State Government." *New Republic,* part two, 21 August 1915.
———. Review of *The Spirit of American Government,* by J. Allen Smith. *Political Science Quarterly* 23, 1 (March 1908).
———. "We, the People." *Life,* 17 January 1944.
Bemis, Samuel Flagg. "Alexander Hamilton and the Limitation of Armaments." In *American Foreign Policy and the Blessings of Liberty, and Other Essays.* Edited by Samuel Flagg Bemis. New Haven: Yale University Press, 1962.
———. Review of *Jefferson and Hamilton: The Struggle for Democracy in America,* by Claude Bowers. *American Historical Review* 31, 3 (April 1926).
Bergmann, Frederick L. "Symposium Marks the Birth of Charles A. Beard." In *Charles A. Beard: An Observance of the Centennial of His Birth.* Edited by Marvin C. Swanson. Greencastle, Ind.: DePauw University Press, 1976.
Berns, Walter. "On Hamilton and Popular Government." *Public Interest* 109 (fall 1992).
Berry, John M. "The Debt: Can It Be Managed?" *Washington Post,* 3 February 1985.
Blair, William M. "House Unit Votes Memorial in City." *New York Times,* 15 March 1962.
Blake, David Haven. "Exile and the Republic: Thomas McGrath and the Legacy of

Jefferson's America." *Prospects: An Annual Journal of American Cultural Studies* 23 (1998).

Bliven, Naomi. "Founding Fathers." *New Yorker,* 3 November 1962.

Blumenthal, Ralph. "Early Files Depict a Grim but Familiar City." *New York Times,* 29 March 1974.

Borah, William E. "Jefferson and Hamilton." *New Republic,* 23 December 1925.

Bordelon, Michael. "Claude G. Bowers." In *Twentieth-Century American Historians.* Edited by Clyde N. Wilson. Detroit: Gale Research Company, 1983.

Borden, Morton. Review of *The Young Hamilton: A Biography,* by James Thomas Flexner. *American Historical Review* 84, 1 (1 February 1979).

Bowen, Ezra. "The Word from the Framers." *Time,* 6 July 1987.

Bowers, Claude. "Jefferson and Civil Liberties." *Atlantic Monthly,* January 1953.

―――. "Lincoln the Man." *Saturday Review of Literature,* 21 February 1931.

―――. "Washington at Last?" *Nation,* 27 October 1926.

Braeman, John. "Charles A. Beard: Historian and Progressive." In *Charles A. Beard: An Observance of the Centennial of His Birth.* Edited by Marvin C. Swanson. Greencastle, Ind.: Depauw University Press, 1976.

―――. "Richard Hildreth (1807–1865)." In *American Historians, 1607–1865.* Edited by Clyde N. Wilson. Detroit: Gale Research Company, 1984.

Brant, Irving. "Two Birthdays." *New York Times Magazine,* 19 December 1954.

Brant, Michelle. Review of *The Papers of Thomas Jefferson.* Vol. 18. Edited by Julian Boyd. *American Historical Review* 79, 3 (June 1974).

Brookhiser, Richard. "A Founding Father's Return to Grace." *U.S. News and World Report,* 10 November 1997.

Browder, Earl. "Jefferson and the People's Revolution." In *The Heritage of Jefferson,* by Claude G. Bowers, Earl Browder, Francis Franklin. New York: International Publishers, 1944.

Bryan, William Jennings. "Jeffersonian Principles." *North American Review* 168 (June 1899).

Burnham, Alexander. "Hamilton's Home to Regain Glory." *New York Times,* 6 May 1962.

Busch, Andrew E. "Ronald Reagan's Public Philosophy: Strands of Jefferson and Hamilton." In *Ronald Reagan's America.* Edited by Eric J. Schmertz, Natalie Datlof, and Alexej Ugrinsky. Westport, Conn.: Greenwood Press, 1997.

Byrnes, James F. "The Supreme Court Must Be Curbed." *U.S. News and World Report,* 18 May 1956.

Caldwell, Christopher. "The Poet as Con Artist." *Weekly Standard,* 15 March 1999.

Carmody, Deirdre. "A Radical Columbia Dropout Who Went on to Make It Big." *New York Times,* 10 May 1975.

Clines, Francis X. "On the Eve of the Impeachment Trial, an Uneasy Quietude Slips over the Capitol." *New York Times,* 14 January 1999.

―――. "Tapes by Tripp Are Distributed by House Panel." *New York Times,* 3 October 1998.

Cloud, Stanley. "A Ghostly Conversation on the Meaning of Watergate." *Time,* 6 August 1973.

Coffey, Raymond R. "Hamilton's Down, but He's Not Out." *Chicago Sun-Times,* 21 October 1993.

Colbourn, Trevor. "Before the Clash with Aaron Burr." *Saturday Review*, 21 April 1962.

Conroy, Sarah Booth. "That Treasure, the Treasury." *Washington Post*, 4 March 1988.

Cook, Joan. "Broadus Mitchell, 95, Professor, Historian, and Hamilton Authority." *New York Times*, 30 April 1988.

———. "Sidney Lens Dies, Activist of the Left." *New York Times*, 30 June 1986.

Cooke, J. W. "Theodore Roosevelt (1858–1919)." In *American Historians, 1866–1912*. Edited by Clyde N. Wilson. Detroit: Gale Research Company, 1986.

Cooke, Jacob E. "Alexander Hamilton's Authorship of the 'Caesar' Letters." *William and Mary Quarterly*, 3d series, 17, 1 (January 1960).

———. "Historian by Happenstance: One Scholar's Odyssey." *William and Mary Quarterly*, 3d series, 52, 3 (July 1995).

———. "The Whiskey Insurrection: A Re-evaluation." *Pennsylvania History* 30 (1963).

Cousins, Norman. "Jefferson and Hamilton." *Saturday Review*, 17 April 1943.

Cunningham, Noble E. Review of *The Papers of Alexander Hamilton*. Vol. 27. Edited by Harold C. Syrett and Patricia Syrett. *Journal of Southern History* 54, 4 (November 1988).

Dabney, Virginius. "Facts and the Founding Fathers." *Vital Speeches of the Day* 41, 13 and 15 (15 April 1975).

Daniels, Jonathan. "Franklin Delano Roosevelt and Books." In *Three Presidents and Their Books: The Reading of Jefferson, Lincoln, F. D. Roosevelt*. Edited by Jonathan Daniels. Urbana: University of Illinois Press, 1955.

Davis, Bob. "He Had an Affair, Hid It, Got Caught and Still Kept His Job." *Wall Street Journal*, 19 November 1998.

Dawes, N. H., and F. T. Nichols. "Revaluing George Bancroft." *New England Quarterly* 6 (June 1933).

Dean, Howard E. "J. Allen Smith: Jeffersonian Critic of the Federalist State." *American Political Science Review* 50, 4 (December 1956).

Dean, Robert D. "Masculinity as Ideology: John F. Kennedy and the Domestic Politics of Foreign Policy." *Diplomatic History* 22, 1 (winter 1998).

Diamond, Martin. "The Federalist." In *History of Political Philosophy*. Edited by Leo Strauss and Joseph Cropsey. Chicago: University of Chicago Press, 1972.

Diggins, John P. "Flirtation with Fascism: American Pragmatic Liberals and Mussolini's Italy." *American Historical Review* 71 (October 1965).

Dodd, William E. "Washington Meets New Ordeal." *New York Times*, 21 November 1926.

Doenecke, Justus D. "Forrest McDonald." In *Twentieth-Century American Historians*. Edited by Clyde N. Wilson. Detroit: Gale Research Company, 1983.

Donald, David Herbert. "The Gentleman and the Romantic." *New York Times Book Review*, 23 September 1979.

Donnan, Elizabeth, and Leo F. Stock, eds. "Senator Beveridge, J. Franklin Jameson, and John Marshall." *Mississippi Valley Historical Review* 35, 3 (December 1948).

Dougherty, Philip H. "New York Post Sets Big Drive." *New York Times*, 1 April 1988.

Dunleavy, Steve. "Let Bubba and Newt Take Their Best Shot." *New York Post*, 11 October 1998.

Dunning, A. Dalton W. "Class Warfare: Arrogance of Power Brokers." *Ottawa Citizen*, 27 August 1991.

Dyckman, Martin. "Incumbents in Hiding." *St. Petersburg Times*, 6 October 1994.

Earle, Dennis M., and Morris Mendelson. "A Comprehensive National Financial Policy Is Needed." *American Banker,* 17 March 1989.

Egan, Jack. "The Man on the 10-Spot Turns 200." *U.S. News and World Report,* 18 September 1989.

Elkins, Stanley, and Eric McKitrick. "The Founding Fathers: Young Men of the Revolution." *Political Science Quarterly* 76, 2 (June 1961).

Ervin, Sam J. Jr. "Alexander Hamilton's Phantom." *Vital Speeches of the Day* 22, 1 (15 October 1955).

Flaumenhaft, Harvey. Review of *Alexander Hamilton and the Idea of Republican Government,* by Gerald Stourzh. *American Political Science Review* 67, 2 (June 1973).

Fleming, Thomas. "The Duel That Changed Our History." *Reader's Digest,* August 1970.

Flint, Peter B. "Felix Gilbert, Influential Author, Historian and Teacher, Dies at 85." *New York Times,* 16 February 1991.

Friedman, Milton. "Alexander Hamilton on the Common Market." *Newsweek,* 4 June 1972.

Friedman, Thomas L. "For Clinton Inauguration: A Plain and Fancy Affair." *New York Times,* 3 December 1992.

Frum, David. "Smearing Alexander Hamilton." *Weekly Standard,* 19 October 1998.

Funke, Phyllis. "Al Carmine's Opera to Debut." *New York Times,* 21 April 1974.

Getlin, Josh. "The Birth of the Headline Heard 'Round the World." *Los Angeles Times,* 28 July 1995.

Godbold, E. Stanly Jr. "John Bach McMaster (1852–1932)." In *American Historians, 1866– 1912.* Edited by Clyde N. Wilson. Detroit: Gale Research Company, 1986.

Goldman, Eric F. "Books That Changed America." *Saturday Review,* 4 July 1953.

———. "The Origin of Beard's Economic Interpretation of the Constitution." *Journal of the History of Ideas* 13, 2 (April 1952).

Goldwater, Barry. "A Conservative's Creed." In *Mr. Conservative: Barry Goldwater,* by Jack Bell. Garden City, N.Y.: Doubleday, 1962.

Gordon, John Steele. "The Founding Wizard." *American Heritage,* July/August 1990.

Govan, Thomas P. "Alexander Hamilton and Julius Caesar: A Note on the Use of Historical Evidence." *William and Mary Quarterly,* 3d series, 32, 3 (July 1975).

———. "The Rich, the Well-Born, and Alexander Hamilton." *Mississippi Valley Historical Review* 36, 4 (March 1950).

Graff, Henry. "A Short Life of Liberty." *New York Times Book Review,* 15 April 1962.

Grann, David. "On the Hill: Moral Minority." *New Republic,* 26 October 1998.

Gravlee, G. Jack. "Tom Watson: Disciple of 'Jeffersonian Democracy.'" In *The Oratory of Southern Demagogues.* Edited by Cal M. Logue and Howard Dorgan. Baton Rouge: Louisiana State University Press, 1981.

Greenberg, Paul. "Budget: Profiles in Cowardice." *Seattle Post Intelligencer,* 9 October 1990.

———. "Toward Impeachment." *New York Times,* 20 February 1974.

Griffith, Thomas. "Impeachment." *New York Times,* 31 October 1973.

———. "The Proper Grounds for Impeachment." *Time,* 25 February 1974.

Hamill, Katherine. "Was Hamilton the First Keynesian?" *Fortune,* August 1957.

Hamilton, Allan McLane. "The Peril of an Insane Administration." *New York Times,* 12 May 1912.

Hammond, Bray. "Jackson, Biddle, and the Bank of the United States." In *Essays on Jack-*

sonian America. Edited by Frank Otto Gatell. New York: Holt, Rinehart and Winston, 1970.

Hanley, Robert. "New Jersey Journal." *New York Times*, 27 July 1980.

Harper, Jennifer. "Both Impeachment Sides Cite Federalist Papers." *Washington Times*, 24 January 1999.

Hazewell, C. C. "Alexander Hamilton." *Atlantic Monthly*, November 1865.

Heclo, Hugh. "Hyperdemocracy." *Wilson Quarterly* 23, 1 (winter 1999).

Hitt, Jack. "America's First Lecher." *Gentlemen's Quarterly*, November 1998.

Holcombe, Arthur N. Review of *Jefferson and Hamilton: The Struggle for Democracy in America*, by Claude Bowers. *American Political Science Review* 20, 1 (February 1926).

Honan, William H. "Quiz: Big Moments on Campus." *New York Times*, 3 January 1999.

Hoxie, R. Gordon. "Presidential Leadership and American Foreign Policy: Some Reflections on the Taiwan Issue, with Particular Considerations on Alexander Hamilton, Dwight Eisenhower, and Jimmy Carter." *Presidential Studies Quarterly* 9, 2 (spring 1979).

Hunt, Gaillard. "The History of the Department of State." *American Journal of International Law* 6, 4 (October 1912).

Hutchison, Keith. "Refurbishing Hamilton." *Nation*, 11 May 1957.

————. "The Man Who Saved the Nation." *Nation*, 16 February 1957.

Jurkowitz, Mark. "True-Blue Take on Yellow Journalism." *Boston Globe*, 13 September 1996.

Kenyon, Cecelia. "Fatherly Sedition." *Nation*, 15 February 1965.

Kern, Alexander C. Review of *Alexander Hamilton: A Biography*, by Forrest McDonald. *Eighteenth-Century Studies* 16, 2 (winter 1982–1983).

Koch, Adrienne. "Hamilton and Power." *Yale Review* 47, 4 (June 1958).

————. Review of *Alexander Hamilton and the Idea of Republican Government*, by Gerald Stourzh. *William and Mary Quarterly*, 3d series, 28, 1 (January 1971).

Krebs, Albin. "Notes on People." *New York Times*, 12 January 1977.

Krebs, Albin, and Robert McG. Thomas. "Birthday Marked for 'A Four-Letter Dirty Word.'" *New York Times*, 7 February 1981.

Kristol, William, and David Brooks. "What Ails Conservatism?" *Wall Street Journal*, 15 September 1997.

Krock, Arthur. "In Washington: Some Contrasts of Jackson and Roosevelt Noted." *New York Times*, 14 January 1936.

Lask, Thomas. "Books of the Times." *New York Times*, 4 July 1967.

————. "Publishing: Finishing Alexander Hamilton." *New York Times*, 8 June 1979.

Lawsky, David. "History Lessons: Would Federalists Like Their Fans?" *New York Times*, 12 February 1995.

Ledbetter, Les. "Hans J. Morgenthau Is Dead at 76." *New York Times*, 20 July 1980.

Lehmann-Haupt, Christopher. "Back to the First Principals." *New York Times*, 25 October 1973.

Lewis, Anthony. "Senators Debate a Ban on Poll Tax." *New York Times*, 15 March 1962.

Lincove, David Alan. "John T. Morse, Jr. (1840–1937)." In *American Historians, 1866–1912*. Edited by Clyde N. Wilson. Detroit: Gale Research Company, 1986.

Lind, Michael. "Restore Hamilton to His Pedestal." *New York Times*, 3 July 1998.

Lindsay, Merrill. "Pistols Shed Light on Famed Duel." *Smithsonian*, November 1976.

Lippmann, Walter. "Integrated America." *New Republic,* 19 February 1916.

———. "Is Harding a Republican?" *New Republic,* 21 July 1920.

———. "Mr. Beard on Property and Politics." *New Republic,* 2 August 1922.

———. "Notes for a Biography." *New Republic,* 16 July 1930.

———. "The Greatness of Andrew Mellon." *New Republic,* 16 August 1924.

Livingston, John C. "Alexander Hamilton and the American Tradition." *Midwest Journal of Political Science* 1, 3–4 (November 1957).

Lodge, Henry Cabot. "The Life of Alexander Hamilton." *North American Review* 123 (July 1876).

Lowell, Robert. "Paterson II." *Nation,* 19 June 1948.

Maloff, Saul. "A Fiction of History." *New Republic,* 10 November 1973.

Malone, Dumas. "Jefferson and the New Deal." *Scribner's Magazine* (June 1933).

———. "Jefferson, Hamilton, and the Constitution." In *Theory and Practice in American Politics.* Edited by William H. Nelson. Chicago: University of Chicago Press, 1964.

———. "Mr. Jefferson to Mr. Roosevelt, an Imaginary Letter." *Virginia Quarterly Review* 19, 2 (spring 1943).

———. "Reign of Witches." *New York Times Book Review,* 5 August 1956.

———. "Tapping the Wisdom of the Founding Fathers." *New York Times Magazine,* 27 May 1956.

———. "The Jefferson Faith." *Saturday Review,* 17 April 1943.

———. "Was Washington the Greatest American?" *New York Times Magazine,* 16 February 1958.

———. "While American History Was Marching On." *New York Times Book Review,* 10 February 1957.

Maverick, Maury. "Most of All, Presidential Scandal Demeans Country." *San Antonio Express-News,* 11 October 1998.

McDonald, Forrest. Review of *Alexander Hamilton,* by Jacob E. Cooke. *American Historical Review* 87, 5 (December 1982).

———. Reviews of *The Papers of Alexander Hamilton.* Edited by Harold C. Syrett. *William and Mary Quarterly,* 3d series, 20, 2 (April 1963); 26, 1 (January 1969); 31, 4 (October 1974); 33, 4 (October 1976); 34, 4 (October 1977); 37, 2 (April 1980).

McNamara, Eileen. "Let's Vote out Anachronism." *Boston Globe,* 8 November 2000.

Mee, Charles L. Jr. "The Prudential Presents Only in America: Playing Favorites." Advertisement, *Newsweek,* 14 September 1987.

———. "The Prudential Presents September 17, 1787." Advertisement, *Newsweek,* 21 September 1987.

Middlekauff, Robert. Review of *American Sphinx,* by Joseph Ellis. *William and Mary Quarterly,* 3d series, 55, 3 (July 1998).

Miller, Vincent. "Perspective on the Founders." *National Review,* 12 February 1963.

———. "Whose Hamilton?" *National Review,* 19 May 1964.

Milligan, Susan. "Jefferson's Secret Family: Foundation Backs Slave Ties." *Boston Globe,* 27 January 2000.

Mitchell, Broadus. "Appraising Hamilton." *Virginia Quarterly Review* 33, 3 (summer 1957).

Mitgang, Herbert. "1976 and All That." *New York Times,* 4 January 1975.

Mixon, Wayne. "William E. Dodd." In *Twentieth-Century American Historians.* Edited by Clyde N. Wilson. Detroit: Gale Research Company, 1983.

Moley, Raymond. "The Wisdom of a Ghost." *Newsweek*, 21 November 1938.

Morley, Terry, "The Real Loser in Election." *Vancouver Sun*, 17 October 1991.

Morse, Anson Daniel. "Alexander Hamilton." *Political Science Quarterly* 5 (1890).

Muskie, Edmund S. "The Chains of Liberty: Congress, President, and American Security." *Vital Speeches of the Day* 54, 1 (15 October 1987).

Nichols, Lewis. "The Play." *New York Times*, 30 January 1943.

Novak, Robert. "Jefferson, Hamilton Still Shaping GOP's Direction." *Chicago Sun-Times*, 25 September 1997.

Nulty, Peter. "1995 National Business Hall of Fame Laureates." *Fortune*, 3 April 1995.

Owsley, Frank Lawrence. "Scottsboro: The Third Crusade, the Sequel to Abolition and Reconstruction." *American Review* 1 (June 1933).

———. "The Foundations of Democracy." In *Who Owns America? A New Declaration of Independence*. Edited by Herbert Agar and Allen Tate. Boston: Houghton Mifflin, 1936.

———. "The Irrepressible Conflict." In *I'll Take My Stand: The South in the Agrarian Tradition*, by Twelve Southerners. New York: Peter Smith: 1951.

Parshall, Gerald. "The Feuding Fathers." *U.S. News and World Report*, 1 February 1993.

Parsons, Lynn Hudson. "Continuing Crusade: Four Generations of the Adams Family View Alexander Hamilton." *New England Quarterly* 37 (March 1964).

Pearson, Sidney A. Jr. "Herbert Croly and Liberal Democracy." *Society* 35 (July/August 1998).

Peterson, Merrill D. "Dumas Malone: An Appreciation." *William and Mary Quarterly*, 3d series, 45, 2 (April 1988).

———. Review of *Alexander Hamilton and the Constitution*, by Clinton Rossiter. *William and Mary Quarterly*, 3d series, 22 (January 1964).

———. Review of *Alexander Hamilton in the American Tradition*, by Louis M. Hacker. *William and Mary Quarterly*, 3d series, 15 (January 1958).

———. Review of *The Papers of Thomas Jefferson*, vol. 17, edited by Julian Boyd, and *Number 7: Alexander Hamilton's Secret Attempts to Control American Foreign Policy, with Supporting Documents*, by Julian Boyd. *William and Mary Quarterly*, 3d series, 23, 1 (January 1966).

———. Review of *The Papers of Thomas Jefferson*, vols. 18 and 19, edited by Julian Boyd *William and Mary Quarterly*, 3d series, 32, 4 (October 1975).

Pound, Ezra. "America and the Second World War." In *Impact: Essays on Ignorance and the Decline of American Civilization*. Edited by Noel Stock. Chicago: Henry Regnery, 1960.

———. "An Introduction to the Economic Nature of the United States." In *Impact: Essays on Ignorance and the Decline of American Civilization*. Edited by Noel Stock. Chicago: Henry Regnery, 1960.

———. "W. E. Woodward, Historian." In *Impact: Essays on Ignorance and the Decline of American Civilization*. Edited by Noel Stock. Chicago: Henry Regnery, 1960.

Powell, J. H. "Two New Studies of Alexander Hamilton." *Saturday Review*, 19 January 1957.

Prescott, Peter S. "Boy Wonder." *Newsweek*, 20 March 1978.

Proceedings of the American Philosophical Society. 102, no. 2. (April 1958).

Quinlan, Michael. "Jousting Grows over State Lawmaker's Offer to Duel Ideological Foe." *(Louisville, Ky.) Courier-Journal*, 11 November 1998.

Ransom, John Crowe. "Reconstructed but Unregenerate." In *I'll Take My Stand: The South and the Agrarian Tradition*, by Twelve Southerners. New York: Peter Smith, 1951.

Reagan, Ronald W. "Introduction." In *Restoring the Presidency: Reconsidering the Twenty-second Amendment*. Washington, D.C.: National Legal Center for the Public Interest, 1990.

Reston, James. "148-Year-Old Issue Is Raised on President's Pact Powers." *New York Times*, 3 May 1949.

———. "Miracle at Philadelphia." *New York Times*, 20 July 1986.

———. "Who Initiates Armed Action Still Senate Pact Problem." *New York Times*, 26 March 1949.

Review of *Alexander Hamilton: A Concise Biography*, by Broadus Mitchell. *Economist*, 21 August 1976.

Rosenbaum, Ron. "Link Founding Father to Sleaze King." *Harper's*, January 1983.

Rossiter, Clinton. "Apprenticeship of a Master-Builder." *New York Times Book Review*, 19 November 1961.

Rowan, Carl. "Legal and Moral Perspectives." In *Crisis in Confidence: The Impact of Watergate*. Edited by Donald W. Harward. Boston: Little, Brown, 1974.

Rust, Michael. "Hamilton's Ups and Downs." *Insight on the News*, 17 May 1999.

———. "Rediscovering Aaron Burr." *Washington Times*, 29 July 1998.

Santry, David G. "The First Secretary of the U.S. Treasury." *Business Week*, 19 November 1979.

Saxon, Wolfgang. "F. Lundburg, 92, Author Who Wrote of the Rich." *New York Times*, 3 March 1995.

———. "The New York Post Has a Long History." *New York Times*, 20 November 1976.

Schachner, Nathan. "Alexander Hamilton Viewed by His Friends: The Narratives of Robert Troup and Hercules Mulligan." *William and Mary Quarterly*, 3d series, 4 (April 1947).

Schlesinger, Arthur M. Jr. "An Impressive Mandate and the Meaning of Jacksonianism." In *Andrew Jackson: A Profile*. Edited by Charles Sellers. New York: Hill and Wang, 1971.

———. "The Problem of Richard Hildreth." *New England Quarterly* 13, 2 (June 1940).

———. "The War Between Adams and Hamilton." *New Republic*, 1 January 1962.

Schneidman, J. Lee, and Conalee Levine-Schneidman. "Suicide or Murder? The Burr-Hamilton Duel." *Journal of Psychohistory* 8, 2 (fall 1980).

Schultz, Stanley K. "The Morality of Politics: The Muckrakers' Vision of Democracy." *Journal of American History* 52, 3 (December 1965).

Scigliano, Robert. "The War Powers Resolution and the War Powers." In *The Presidency in the Constitutional Order*. Edited by Joseph M. Bessette and Jeffrey Tulis. Baton Rouge: Louisiana State University Press, 1981.

Shabecoff, Philip. "Nixon Tax Report Raises New Issue." *New York Times*, 5 April 1974.

Shenon, Philip. "Celebrating the Birthday and Legacy of Reagan." *New York Times*, 7 February 2001.

Sidey, Hugh. "Fragmentation of Powers." *Time*, 6 July 1987.

———. "Oh for Another Stargazing Gardener." *Time*, 26 April 1976.

———. "We're Still Jefferson's Children." *Time*, 13 July 1987.

Silk, Leonard. "Examining McGovern's New Populism." *New York Times*, 10 May 1972.

Smith, William Ander. "Henry Adams, Alexander Hamilton, and the American People as a 'Great Beast.'" *New England Quarterly* 48 (June 1975).

Stone, I. F. "Patroon Schuyler's Son-in-Law." *Nation*, 11 November 1939.

Stourzh, Gerald. "Letters to the Editor." *William and Mary Quarterly,* 3d series, 29, 4 (October 1972).

Swope, Christopher. "Fighting Words and Unintended Consequences." *Governing Magazine,* February 1999.

Syrett, Harold C. "Maker and Shaper of a Nation." *New York Times Book Review,* 22 November 1959.

———. Review of *Alexander Hamilton: A Biography,* by Forrest McDonald. *William and Mary Quarterly,* 3d series, 67, 4 (March 1981).

Tate, Allen. "Life in the Old South." *New Republic,* 10 July 1929.

———. "Notes on Liberty and Property." *American Review* 6 (March 1936).

———. "Where Are the People?" *American Review* 2 (December 1933).

Toner, Robin. "The Right to Click." *New York Times Book Review,* 27 February 2000.

Tuckerman, Henry T. Review of *The Life and Times of Alexander Hamilton,* by Samuel Schmucker. *North American Review* 86 (April 1858).

Tugwell, Rexford Guy, and Joseph Dorfman. "Alexander Hamilton: Nation-Maker." *Columbia University Quarterly* 29 (December 1937) and 30 (March 1938).

Turner, Douglas. "Our Founders Never Envisioned Leaders Embracing Ideology of Continuous Political Struggle." *Buffalo News,* 22 February 1999.

Tyler, Lyon Gardiner. "William and Mary College as Expressing in its Origin, and in its Subsequent Influences, the American Principle of Democracy." *William and Mary Quarterly,* 2d series, 15, 3 (July 1935).

Urey, Harold C. "Alexander Hamilton: How Would He Apply His Ideas Today?" *Vital Speeches of the Day* 27, 14 (1 May 1961).

Vandenberg, Arthur H. "Alexander Hamilton." *Life,* 7 July 1947.

Vidal, Gore. "Political Melodramas." In *United States, Essays, 1952–1992,* by Gore Vidal. New York: Random House, 1993.

Waldron, Martin. "People." *New York Times,* 18 July 1976.

Wallace, William A. "The Mission of the Democratic Party." *North American Review* 132 (January 1881).

Wandycz, Katarzyna. "Lech Walesa, Meet Alexander Hamilton." *Forbes,* 26 November 1990.

Ward, John William. "Andrew Jackson: The Majority Is to Govern." In *An American Primer.* Edited by Daniel J. Boorstin. Chicago: University of Chicago Press, 1966.

Webb, James R. "The Fateful Encounter." *American Heritage,* August 1975.

White, William Allen. "White Sees Party Ready for Rebirth." *New York Times,* 8 June 1936.

Widenor, William C. "Henry Cabot Lodge (1850–1924)." In *American Historians, 1866–1912.* Edited by Clyde N. Wilson. Detroit: Gale Research Company, 1986.

Wills, Garry. Review of *The Imperial Presidency,* by Arthur M. Schlesinger Jr. *New York Times Book Review,* 18 November 1973.

Wood, Gordon S. "Impartiality in America." *New Republic,* 6 December 1999.

———. "The Ghosts of Monticello." In *Sally Hemings and Thomas Jefferson: History, Memory, and Civic Culture.* Edited by Jan Ellen Lewis and Peter S. Onuf. Charlottesville: University Press of Virginia, 1999.

Wood, Kirk. "George Bancroft (1800–1891)." In *American Historians, 1607–1865.* Edited by Clyde N. Wilson. Detroit: Gale Research Company, 1984.

Wright, Esmond. "A Code Name and a London Contact." *Saturday Review,* 28 November 1964.

———. "The Nation Takes Shape." In *The American Destiny: An Illustrated Bicentennial History of the United States*. Edited by Henry Steele Commager, Marcus Cunliffe, Maldwyn A. Jones, and Edward Horton. Danbury, Conn.: The Danbury Press, 1975.

Zuckert, Michael P. "Refinding the Founding: Martin Diamond, Leo Strauss, and the American Regime." In *Leo Strauss, the Straussians, and the American Regime*. Edited by Kenneth L. Deutsch and John A. Murley. Lanham, Md.: Rowman and Littlefield, 1999.

GOVERNMENT DOCUMENTS

Abraham Lincoln. Exhibition at the Library of Congress in Honor of the 150th Anniversary of His Birth. Washington, D.C.: Library of Congress, 1959.

Annual Report of the American Historical Association for the Year 1918. Washington, D.C.: U.S. Government Printing Office, 1920.

Commission on the Bicentennial of the United States Constitution. *A Musical Skit for Children on the Constitution Convention*. Washington, D.C.: Commission on the Bicentennial of the U.S. Constitution, January 1987.

———. *We the People: The Commission on the United States Constitution, 1985–1992, Final Report*. Washington, D.C.: Commission on the Bicentennial of the U.S. Constitution, 1992.

Congressional Digest. Vol. 19, no. 10, October 1940.

Congressional Record, House, Congressman Peter Rodino, 4 March 1957, 85th Congress, 1st session, vol. 103, part 3, pp. 3035–36.

———. Extension of Remarks by Representative Frederic R. Coudert Jr., 4 March 1957, 85th Congress, 1st session, vol. 103, part 3, p. 3071.

———. Extension of Remarks of Senator Karl Mundt, 30 January 1957, 85th Congress, 1st session, vol. 103, part 1, p. 1339.

———. Representative John P. Saylor, 16 April 1962, 87th Congress, 2d session, vol. 108, part 5, p. 6679.

———, Senate. Senator John Bricker, 4 March 1957, 85th Congress, 1st session, vol. 103, part 3, p. 2988.

———. Senate, Senator John Sparkman, 23 March 1962, 87th Congress, 2d session, vol. 108, part 4, p. 4925.

———. Senator Karl Mundt, 4 March 1957, 85th Congress, 1st session, vol. 103, part 3, p. 2973.

———. Senator Spessard Holland, 27 March 1962, 87th Congress, 2d session, vol. 108, part 4, p. 4845.

———. Senator Strom Thurmond, 22 March 1962, 87th Congress, 2d session, vol. 108, part 4, p. 4844.

Hamilton Grange National Memorial, New York. National Park Service, U.S. Department of the Interior. Washington, D.C.: U.S. Government Printing Office, 1992.

McCulloch v. Maryland, 4 Wheat. (17 U.S.) 316 (1819).

Public Papers of the Presidents. William J. Clinton, 1993, Book 1, January 20 to July 31, 1993. Washington, D.C.: U.S. Government Printing Office, 1994.

———. *Gerald R. Ford, Containing the Public Messages, Speeches, and Statements of the President, 1976–1977, Book 2, April 9 to July 9, 1976*. Washington, D.C.: U.S. Government Printing Office, 1979.

———. *John F. Kennedy, Containing the Public Messages, Speeches, and Statements of the President, January 1 to December 31, 1962*. Washington, D.C.: U.S. Government Printing Office, 1963.

————. *Ronald Reagan.* 15 vols. Washington, D.C.: U.S. Government Printing Office, 1982–1991.

————. *Harry S. Truman, Containing the Public Messages, Speeches, and Statements of the President, January 1 to December 31, 1948.* Washington, D.C.: U.S. Government Printing Office, 1964.

Richardson, James D., ed. *A Compilation of the Messages and Papers of the Presidents, 1789–1897.* Washington, D.C.: U.S. Government Printing Office, 1896.

The Presidential Campaign of 1976. Vol. 1, Part 2, *Jimmy Carter.* Washington, D.C.: U.S. Government Printing Office, 1978.

U.S. Congress. House. *Impeachment of Richard M. Nixon, President of the United States, Report of the Committee on the Judiciary,* 92d Congress, 2d session, report. no. 93-1305, pp. 283–84.

————. Senate. *Final Report of the Alexander Hamilton Bicentennial Commission,* 85th Congress, 2d session, vol. 1, micellaneous 1. 30 April 1958.

————. *Final Report of the Select Committee on Presidential Campaign Activities.* 93rd Congress, 2d session, report no. 93-981, p. 1178 n. 7.

U.S. Congress, *Report of the Congressional Committees Investigating the Iran-Contra Affair, with Supplemental, Minority, and Additional Views.* H. Rept. no. 100-433 and S. Rept. No. 100-216, 100th Congress, 1st session, 1987.

U.S. George Washington Bicentennial Commission. *Special News Releases Relating to the Life and Times of George Washington.* Vol. 1. Washington, D.C.: U.S. Government Printing Office, 1932.

TRANSCRIPTS, WEBSITES, AND INTERVIEWS
Biographical data. <www.infoplease.com>
Cable News Network. 20 November 1992, transcript no. 226-2.
Cable News Network. *Inside Politics.* 9 October 1998, transcript no. 98100900v15.
CBS News Transcripts. *The Early Show.* 8 November 2000, Burrelle's Information Services.
C-Span. *Booknotes.* Arnold Rogow, transcript. 13 September 1998. <www.booknotes.org>
E-mail correspondence with Frank K. Lorenz, curator of Special Collections, Hamilton College, Clinton, New York, 13–14 January 2000.
Monticello information. <www.monticello.org/jefferson/entrance/home.html>
NBC News Transcripts. *Today.* "Alan Dershowitz and Barbara Olson Debate Strength of Case for Impeachment of President Clinton." 6 October 1998.
NPR. *All Things Considered.* "Author Roger G. Kennedy on Aaron Burr and Historical Political Imagery." Transcript, 3 December 1999.
————. "How Reference to *The Federalist Papers* During Senate Trial Has Sparked Sales of the Documents." Transcript, 22 January 1999.
Roper Center, University of Connecticut, Public Opinion Online. <www.ropercenter. uconn.edu> accession no. 0086421, question no. 024, and accession no. 0311401, question no. 007.
White House, Office of the Press Secretary. "Remarks by the President at the Thomas Jefferson Movie Screening, 11 February 1997," and "Remarks by the President and the Vice President at Electronic Commerce Event, 30 November 1998." <www.whitehouse. gov>

INDEX